Systematic Approaches to Argument by Analogy

Argumentation Library

VOLUME 25

For further volumes:
http://www.springer.com/series/5642

Henrique Jales Ribeiro
Editor

Systematic Approaches to Argument by Analogy

Springer

Editor
Henrique Jales Ribeiro
Philosophy, Communication
and Information
University of Coimbra
Coimbra
Portugal

ISSN 1566-7650
ISBN 978-3-319-06333-1 ISBN 978-3-319-06334-8 (eBook)
DOI 10.1007/978-3-319-06334-8
Springer Cham Heidelberg New York Dordrecht London

Library of Congress Control Number: 2014939428

Printed on acid-free paper

Springer is part of Springer Science+Business Media (www.springer.com)

Contents

Contributors

Lilian Bermejo-Luque Department of Philosophy I, University of Granada, Granada, Spain

Damiano Canale Department of Legal Studies, Bocconi University, Milano, Italy

Giovanni Damele Institute for Philosophy of Language, New University of Lisbon, Lisbon, Portugal

Marianne Doury French National Center for Scientific Research (CNRS), Paris, France; University of Paris 3 (New Sorbonne), Paris, France

Frans H. van Eemeren Department of Speech Communication, Argumentation Theory and Rhetoric, University of Amsterdam, Amsterdam, The Netherlands

Christian J. Feldbacher Duesseldorf Center for Logic and Philosophy of Science, University of Duesseldorf, Duesseldorf, Germany

Eugen Fischer School of Philosophy, University of East Anglia, Norwich, UK

Nino Guallart Department of Philosophy, Logic and Philosophy of Science, University of Sevilla, Sevilla, Spain

Bart Garssen Department of Speech Communication, Argumentation Theory and Rhetoric, University of Amsterdam, Amsterdam, The Netherlands

André Juthe Department of Speech Communication, Argumentation Theory and Rhetoric, University of Amsterdam, Amsterdam, The Netherlands

Fabrizio Macagno Institute for Philosophy of Language, New University of Lisbon, Lisbon, Portugal

Paula Olmos Department of Logic, History and Philosophy of Science, National Distance Education University (UNED), Madrid, Spain

Rosalice Pinto Research Centre for Linguistics, New University of Lisbon, Lisbon, Portugal

Henrique Jales Ribeiro Department of Philosophy, Communication and Information, Faculty of Letters, University of Coimbra, Coimbra, Portugal

Giovanni Tuzet Department of Legal Studies, Bocconi University, Milano, Italy

Jan Albert van Laar Faculty of Philosophy, University of Groningen, Groningen, The Netherlands

Douglas N. Walton Centre for Research in Reasoning, Argumentation and Rhetoric, University of Windsor, Windsor, ON, Canada

About the Authors

Lilian Bermejo-Luque is research fellow at the Department of Philosophy I of the University of Granada (Spain). Her areas of expertise are argumentation theory and theories of rationality. She has published several articles in well-known journals in those fields, such as *Informal Logic* or *Argumentation*, and in edited volumes such as *Arguing on the Toulmin model* (2006) or *Understanding argumentation* (2008). She is the author of the monograph *Giving reasons: A linguistic-pragmatic approach to argumentation theory* (2011). She is member of the editorial board of several academic journals and member of the AILACT board of directors.

Damiano Canale is full professor of legal philosophy and head of the Department of Legal Studies at Bocconi University, Milan. He is a member of the editorial board of *Law and Philosophy*, the *Journal of Argumentation in Context*, and *Ars Interpretandi*. His research interests cover language philosophy, legal argumentation, and history of legal and political concepts. His publications include the books *La costituzione delle differenze. Giusnaturalismo e codificazione del diritto civile nella Prussia del '700* (2000) and *Forme del limite nell'interpretazione giudiziale* (2003). He is co-editor of *A history of the philosophy of law in the civil law world, 1600–1900* (2009), *The rules of inference. Inferentialism in law and philosophy* (2009) and *The planning theory of law: A critical reading* (2013). His papers on legal theory and legal argumentation have been published in *Ratio Juris; Informal Logic; and Argumentation.*

Giovanni Damele is post-doctoral fellow at the Institute for Philosophy of Language of the New University of Lisbon. His main fields of academic interest include philosophy of law, philosophy of politics, argumentation theory and rhetoric. He is particularly focused on legal argumentation and, generally speaking, on the persuasive and strategic dimension of practical argumentation.

Marianne Doury is tenured researcher at the "Laboratoire Communication et Politique" (Paris, CNRS) and associate researcher at Cediscor-Syled (University of Paris 3–New Sorbonne). She is a member of the editorial board of the journal *Argumentation et Analyse du Discours*, and of the book series *Argumentation in Context* (AIC); and a referee for the journals *Communication, Mots—Les Langages du Politique; Langage et Société; Argumentation.* Marianne Doury's key publications include: *Le débat immobile* (1997), *Les émotions dans les interactions* (editor with C. Plantin and V. Traverso, 2000), *L'argumentation aujourd'hui: Positions théoriques en confrontation* (editor with S. Moirand, 2004). She teaches argumentation at Paris 3 University.

Frans H. van Eemeren is Emeritus Professor of Speech Communication, Argumentation Theory and Rhetoric. He is a Distinguished Scholar of the American National Communication Association and Doctor Honoris Causa of the University of Lugano. His book publications include: *Speech acts in argumentative discussions* (1984); *Argumentation, communication, and fallacies* (1992), *Reconstructing argumentative discourse* (1993), *Fundamentals of argumentation theory* (1996), *A systematic theory of argumentation* (2004), *Argumentative indicators in discourse* (2007), *Fallacies and judgments of reasonableness* (2009), and *Strategic manoeuvring in argumentative discourse* (2010). Professor van Eemeren is President of ISSA, editor of the journal *Argumentation*, the Journal *of Argumentation in Context*, and the accompanying book series.

Christian J. Feldbacherc is enrolled in the Ph.D programme of the University of Innsbruck. His thesis addresses analogies in scientific explanations. He is research fellow at the DCLPS (Duesseldorf Center for Logic and Philosophy of Science) and lecturer at the University of Duesseldorf. His main area of research is analogies as well as strategy-selection by meta-induction and social opinion pooling. His area of interest is mainly social epistemology, ethics, and general philosophy of science. Recent publications: "Meta-induction and the wisdom of crowds" (*Analyse & Kritik*, 2012) and "Knowledge by narratives: On the methodology of Stump's defence" (*EJPR*, 2012).

Eugen Fischer (BPhil, DPhil Oxford, PD Munich) is a senior lecturer of Philosophy at the University of East Anglia. He has been a Heisenberg Research Reader (DFG) and Fellow at the Netherlands Institute of Advanced Study and the Collegium of Budapest. One focus of his research is how analogies, metaphors, and "philosophical pictures" shape philosophical thought. He authored *Philosophical delusion and its therapy* (2011) and *Linguistic creativity* (2000), and co-edited *Philosophical insights: Essays in metaphilosophy* (in press) and *Wittgenstein at work—Method in the 'Philosophical Investigations'* (2004).

Nino Guallart Forés is B.A. in Philosophy (Universidad de Zaragoza, 2010), Master in Logic and Philosophy of Science (Universidad de Salamanca, 2012). He is currently working on his Ph.D under the supervision of Dr. Ángel Nepomuceno (Universidad de Sevilla). His thesis aims to explore different types of lambda calculi, mainly intuitionistic type theory. Along with logic, other relevant lines of research are argumentation and philosophy of science, especially philosophy of biology and questions related to statistics, induction and verification.

Bart Garssen is lecturer at the Department of Speech Communication, Argumentation Theory and Rhetoric, at Amsterdam University. His research interests include argument schemes, fallacies and political argumentation. He is editor of the Journal of Argumentation in Context (Benjamins) and book review editor of *Argumentation* (Springer). His main publications are: *Fallacies and judgments of reasonableness: Empirical research concerning the pragma-dialectical discussion rules* (2009), *"In varietate concordia*—United in diversity: European parliamentary debate as an argumentative activity type" (2010), and "The disguised 'abusive ad hominem' empirically investigated: Strategic maneuvering with direct personal attacks" (2012).

André Juthe is a Ph.D student in Argumentation Theory at the University of Amsterdam, the Netherlands. His thesis focuses on arguments by analogy. He has published the articles "Arguments by analogy" (2005) and "Refutation by parallel argument" (2009) in the journal *Argumentation: An International Journal on Reasoning*. He received his undergraduate degrees (Ma; Ba; Ma) from the University of Uppsala, in Sweden.

Jan Albert van Laar is working at the Faculty of Philosophy, University of Groningen (the Netherlands). He defended his Ph.D dissertation on *The dialectic of ambiguity* in 2003, and has worked ever since on the philosophy of argument, publishing in journals such as *Argumentation; Informal Logic; Synthesis and Argument & Computation*. Some of his current interests are: argument and emotion; norms for argumentative criticism; and political deliberation.

Fabrizio Macagno (Ph.D in Linguistics, UCSC, Milan, 2003) works as a researcher and senior lecturer at the New University of Lisbon. His current research is focused on the persuasive use of emotional language and on the dialectical dimension of discourse implicitness. He is author of several papers on definition, informal fallacies, argumentation schemes and dialogue theory, published in major international peer-reviewed journals. His most relevant publications include *Argumentation schemes* (2008) and *Emotive language in argumentation* (in press).

Paula Olmos has conducted research in Philosophy and Classical Studies in several Spanish academic centres (UC3M, UNED). Her research lines include different aspects of the History of Logic, Argumentation and Rhetoric as well as the contemporary Theory of Argumentation, in which she takes a rhetorical stance. She has published papers on these issues in journals like *Informal Logic; Theoria; Renaissance Studies; Argumentation* or *Studies in History and Philosophy of Science*. She is the author of a monographic volume on Spanish sixteen-century philosopher Pedro Simón Abril (2010), editor of the collection of essays *Greek science in the long run* (2012) and co-editor of the collective volume *Compendio de lógica, argumentación y retórica* (2011, 2012).

Rosalice Pinto is a researcher of the Centre for Linguistics at the New University of Lisbon. Her main interests are argumentation, rhetoric, texts in professional contexts, Portuguese for specific purposes. She has a Ph.D in linguistics from Lisbon New University, in Portugal, and a post-doctoral degree in "Social Media" from the University of Geneva and Lisbon New University. She has published papers in peer review and prominent international papers in Portugal and abroad.

Henrique Jales Ribeiro is associate professor at Coimbra University's Faculty of Letters (Portugal), Department of Philosophy, Communication and Information. He is the principal investigator of the research group "Teaching logic & argumentation" of the Portuguese Foundation for Science and Technology (FCT). His core areas of research are logic, argumentation theory and philosophy didactics. His publications include: *Rhetoric and argumentation in the beginning of the XXIst Century* (2009); *Inside arguments: Logic and the study of argumentation* (2012); and *Aristotle and argumentation theory* (2013).

Giovanni Tuzet is assistant professor of philosophy of law, at Bocconi University (Italy). He studied law and philosophy in Turin and Paris and wrote his Ph.D thesis on Peirce's theory of inference. His publications include several papers on legal theory, legal reasoning, and legal argumentation, and the books *La prima inferenza. L'abduzione di C.S. Peirce fra scienza e diritto* (2006), *Dover decidere. Diritto, incertezza e ragionamento* (2010), *La pratica dei valori. Nodi fra conoscenza e azione* (2012) and *Filosofia della prova giuridica* (2013). He co-edited *The rules of inference: Inferentialism in law and philosophy* (2009) and *The planning theory of law: A critical reading* (2013).

Douglas N. Walton is a Canadian academic, well known for his many widely published books and papers on argumentation. He is at present Distinguished Research Fellow of the Centre for Research in Reasoning, Argumentation and Rhetoric at the University of Windsor, Canada. His theories are increasingly finding applications in education, computer science, especially artificial intelligence, and evidential reasoning in law.

Chapter 1
Introduction

Henrique Jales Ribeiro

1.1 The Status of Analogy in the History of Rhetoric and Argumentation

The study of the argument by analogy has produced in the past decades vast and profuse literature, which in view of its scale may not be quoted, nor mentioned in this introduction. However, it is far from evident, not so much what such argument consists of, but particularly how it may be analysed and represented. In this regard, there are actually deep divides and disagreements between theorists and contemporary researchers, as the reader will surely find out on his own throughout this book. One example of argument by analogy may be analysed, represented and classified in several very distinctive ways, i.e. as if we were addressing different examples and not necessarily the same. One researcher in his interpretation may even introduce more than one analysis and representation of a single example of that type of argument, and claim that they are all equally legitimate and pertinent. This fact should not disturb the reader, nor the researcher of argumentation theory. Which does not mean—quite on the contrary—that the study of argument by analogy has not made significant and undeniable progress in the past decades; rather it signifies that the argumentation theories which lie at the root of such study are not in tune. The issue, if any, is essentially about these theories. The variety and plurality of evaluations of argument by analogy must, therefore, be envisaged as a sign of wealth and not of poverty or lack of resources. Similar circumstances (and this is an analogy) arise in such prestigious and (apparently) uncontroversial scientific fields as that of quantum physics, without affecting their credibility; so this is no reason for scepticism or lack of confidence.

Anyhow, the situation we have just mentioned essentially characterises contemporary argumentation theories, and not those that, since Aristotle and the classical era (Greek and Latin), were delivered regarding argument by analogy. It was

H. J. Ribeiro (✉)
Department of Philosophy, Communication and Information, Faculty of Letters, University of Coimbra, Coimbra, Portugal
e-mail: jalesribeiro@gmail.com

H. J. Ribeiro (ed.), *Systematic Approaches to Argument by Analogy*,
Argumentation Library 25, DOI 10.1007/978-3-319-06334-8_1,

not until the twentieth century and, in particular, Perelman and Olbrechts-Tyteca's (1969) pioneering research that this argument was granted due relevance in the context of a new conception of rationality and argumentation in general. (Note, in this respect, that even Toulmin (1958) apparently does not present a conception of analogy or analogical reasoning in general, although one may argue, in the same way as one of the papers in this volume, that this author's argumentation model may be extended to the particular case of that reasoning.) Before the research we have alluded to, the problem was that analogy is an apparently strange, puzzling and complex thought process, when compared to other processes which, at least implicitly, were envisaged and elected since Aristotle as the canons of rationality (of logic and philosophical rationality, in particular), as is the case of deduction and induction—but which in spite it all, as today we understand, are connected with it, in one way or the other, when analysed closely. In Perelman and Olbrechts-Tyteca (1969, p. 393) it is noted significantly in this regard that:

> Analogy is an unstable means of argument. For the person, who rejects the conclusions, will tend to assert that "there is not even an analogy", and will minimize the value of the statement by reducing it to a vague comparison or merely verbal resemblance. On the other hand, the person invoking an analogy will almost invariably endeavour to assert that it is more than just a simple analogy. The analogy is thus stuck between two disavowals—disavowal by its opponents and disavowal by its supporters.

The truth is that, like Perelman (1989) exemplifies, analogy is not merely an aid of our reasoning in general, and of philosophical reasoning in particular, but it structures both intrinsically in a much more prominent and meaningful fashion than deduction or induction. In other words, analogy comes first. According to the author, philosophy history in its entirety could be reinterpreted from this perspective, including traditional authors (like Plato) who, apparently, contested the importance of rhetoric and argumentation, and supported the conception of a pure and orthodox rationality. Even when apparently only deduction and induction are in question, there is analogical macro-reasoning underlying, which ultimately informs and explains the relevant intelligibility. It would thus be interesting to reread Aristotle's predication theory in the view of analogical reasoning (as actually some of the authors in this collection do).

The strange and complex nature of analogy arises from its own nature, or is intrinsically inherent to it. In analogy, two entities or state of affairs are compared, as they have a property or predicate in common. In structural terms, the link between all of the terms involved entails shifting from the entities compared to that property, or from the latter to the entities it refers to. This, as mentioned before, may be analysed nowadays in different ways. What is, however, characteristic of analogies in general, what explains their importance and impact, is that this relation is essentially fuzzy, in the sense that it is not always conceptually clear, nor explicit, as is otherwise the case of typically deductive and/or inductive reasoning. The propositions which make up analogies are not mere statements. In fact, in most cases, they presuppose and involve ambiguous and diffuse cognitive proposals submitted to whom they are addressed, i.e. rhetorical guidelines (implicit by definition) about the way the link may be interpreted or conceptualised. On the other hand, not all analogy has necessarily an argumentative scope, i.e. analogies are not always used to sustain a claim in a context in which a topic is disputed between two or more interlocutors. In all, as Perelman and Olbrechts-Tyteca highlight in the aforementioned text, they may be disputed since they merely establish a comparison, and do not support a thesis, or such thesis does not meet the goals of argumentative discourse in general (particularly those with which both deduction and induction were identified).

All of this explains, in our view, the ungrateful destiny of argument by analogy in philosophy history and, especially, in the history of rhetoric and argumentation until very close to the twentieth century. In brief, although for obvious reasons analogy has not been definitely excluded from the field of rationality, its epistemological relevance, when compared to other kinds of reasoning, was largely underestimated or even ignored (at least from a philosophical perspective). (As we have suggested, this was even the case of philosophers, like Plato, in whose theories analogy plays a fundamental part.) To put argumentation at the top of the agenda of contemporary philosophy, as Perelman and Olbrechts-Tyteca (1969) did, inevitably entailed putting at the top too the study of that reasoning. One could say that we had to wait for a change in our rationality paradigm or in our standards in respect thereof, which arose precisely in the mid twentieth century with Perelman, Toulmin and others, in which the "reasonable" gained supremacy at all levels over the "rational" (not only on the theoretical plane, but also social, cultural and political), for special attention to be accorded to argument by analogy. Given its diffuse and complex nature in conceptual, rhetorical and argumentative terms, argument by analogy apparently has much more to do with the former (the reasonable) than with the latter (the rational). In this respect, contemporary research into analogy, of which this volume is a modest yet meaningful collection, is not lagging behind in historical terms; it was conducted, one might say, in the right and appropriate time; in other words, the time when it was possible to accord to it due importance in the context of in depth restructuring and revaluation of argumentation problems in general.

The aforementioned restructuring and revaluation feature three fundamental aspects, from Perelman and Olbrechts-Tyteca (1969) and Toulmin (1958), which are essential for understanding the texts collected herein: multidisciplinarity, or even interdisciplinarity of argumentation theory in general; the contemporary distinction between descriptive vs. normative approaches to argumentation; and the introduction of the capital and revolutionary notion of *argumentation schemes*, which is partly intended with the first two aspects.

Beginning with the first, argumentation theory is not one more among other fields of human knowledge, since its object is precisely these fields overall, in the sense that in all of them, one way or the other, one argues, and such theory deals with the issue of understanding how this happens in each of them; in other words, it appears as a theory of the argument in all of its forms (van Eemeren et al. 1996). This is what the authors do in the present publication regarding argument by analogy: analogy in everyday discourse, in science, in law theory, in medicine, in literature, etc. To the extent that there are concepts which are shared by different multidisciplinary approaches to argumentation, argumentation theory normally appears as an interdisciplinary undertaking, therefore enjoying a privileged status in relation to all other fields of knowledge. One could say to some extent that this theory, partly playing the part that logic and philosophy held traditionally until the mid twentieth century, unfolds today as a new paradigm of rationality (Ribeiro 2012, p. 1 ff.). It is a truly historical and revolutionary achievement since Aristotle, which is largely owed to Perelman and Toulmin, as mentioned before.

Such achievement was more or less concurrent with the resurgence of the normative approaches to argumentation, with the advent of the dialectical schools in the last quarter of the twentieth century (pragma-dialectics and formal dialectic). These approaches clearly characterise Aristotle's treatise *Topics*; and they were never disregarded by philosophers and argumentation theorists throughout the history of rhetoric. However, it was in the twentieth century, with the aforementioned schools, that they progressed the most. The distinction between normative and descriptive approaches to argumentation and, in particular, to the argument by analogy, is paramount for understanding the viewpoint of most of the authors in this volume. As far as this argument is concerned, for some authors this is basically a question of characterising and describing closely the use thereof, specially in everyday discourse; and with that description one is supposed to meet the essential goals of argumentation theory. From the outset it is obvious that there may be multiple and different descriptive approaches to argumentation. The problem with these approaches is that, apparently, there are no criteria allowing us to decide satisfactorily which is the best or the most pertinent one. Instead, from a normative perspective argumentation is seen in dialogical and dialectical terms as the outcome of rules or conventions which govern discourse between two opposite parties on a specific subject being discussed. It is in this context that argumentation by analogy is studied. It does not exclude description, which occurs basically when argumentative discourse, for example everyday discourse, is reconstructed in the light of the rules mentioned before. The question is whether that reconstruction is capable of suitably translating all linguistic, semantic and pragmatic features of argumentative discourse, in all of its different contexts.

Finally, perhaps the most spectacular and meritorious achievement of the aforementioned restructuring and revaluation of the problems of argumentation has been the emergence of the notion of *argumentation schemes*, to which Perelman and Olbrechts-Tyteca (1969), Hastings (1963), Kienpointner (2012), van Eemeren and Grootendorst (1992) and, perhaps more decisively, Walton (1996, 2012), and Walton et al. (2008) contributed. This notion illustrates brilliantly the idea, which we have already mentioned, that contemporary argumentation theory consists essentially of a theory of the argument in all of its different shapes, in particular in that of the argument by analogy, as is the case of Walton's contribution and that of other authors to this book. And it is overall accepted both by the descriptive and the normative conceptions, although it plays a more relevant part in the latter, as is visible in this book. Its connections with formal logic (in particular, the idea of inference schemes, as the *modus ponens* and other) are visible from the beginning. According to Walton et al. (2008, p. 11), "Argumentation schemes are the form of arguments (structures of inferences) that enable one to identify and evaluate common types of argumentation in everyday discourse." Each scheme, particularly from a dialogical and dialectical perspective, is accompanied by a set of critical issues that are used to assess the argument in question in a particular case, or "in relation to a context of dialogue in which the argument occurred." (Walton et al. 2008, pp. 11–12) In the particular case of the argument by analogy, the notion of argumentation scheme fosters a much more refined analysis than that which is provided, in principle, by a purely descriptive approach to argumentation. The problem—that we have highlighted, but which the reader will note on his own—is that, apparently and until now, this notion—in spite of all of its merits—has not been sufficiently worked out so that, through it, all features of the use of argumentative discourse in context may be captured and explained, as is the case of the argument by analogy. It is a work in progress, from which a lot can still be expected.

1.2 Overview of the Author's Contributions

The present book is divided into two parts: in the first (Part 1: Theoretical Approaches to Argument by Analogy), we have sorted the inputs of the authors who address the argument by analogy mostly from a theoretical standpoint, although they do not ignore, quite on the contrary, its practical uses and/or applications in context. In the second part (Part 2: Applied Approaches to Argument by Analogy), we have organised inputs which focus essentially on that argument applied to different areas and contexts, such as politics, linguistics, literature, law theory, etc. These uses sometimes produce important, or even fundamental, theoretical effects. Therefore, once more, the two parts are not different in absolute or strict terms. Nonetheless, we thought it useful and relevant to establish such divide.

1.2.1 Part I: Theoretical Approaches to Argument by Analogy

In Chapter 2, "Argumentation Schemes for Argument from Analogy", Douglas Walton, following previous research, introduces two schemes of argument by analogy and describes the requirements and the critical issues which can be used to assess the implementation of each of them. The disturbing fact that there are two and not just a single scheme is something the author understands quite well, considering, as he underscores, there is broad disagreement on how to interpret that argument (which the reader finds out for himself in this book). The author first introduces and closely analyses the first scheme, providing both a general diagram of it, and a representation made in the light of Carneades's argumentation system, according to which each argument is considered an argument pro or against a given claim. Next he applies this representation to a known analogical example (the violinist, Thomson 1971), highlighting the difficulty, only with the help of that scheme, of analysing and defining the notion of similarity. The second scheme is drawn from classical textbooks on logic, the best known example being Copi and Cohen (1994). Unlike the former, it addresses argument by analogy as an inductive form of analogy, which does not require any reference to similarity. Some of the more recent versions of this scheme (Hurley 2003; Guarini 2004) are closely analysed. In such versions argument by analogy is regarded as a defeasible form of argument in which some factors sustain the argument, while others do not; and the issue raised by Walton is that to assess the strength of the argument one must weigh the pros against the cons, and it is not clear how to do it. In this regard, the author analyses the methods of assessing argument by analogy in standard case-based reasoning (CBR), in particular that in which it is shaped, dialectically speaking, as a series of movements in a formal dialogue. Anyhow, we cannot suitably capture, not without difficulties, neither in the first nor in the second scheme, at least apparently, the peculiar nature of the sequence of reasoning of which the argument is composed. This is what Walton shows immediately afterwards, specially in relation to the first, on one more example (the Silkwood case: Lief et al. 1998). Therefore, the author turns to the script theory coming from artificial intelligence, which he developed himself in some of his work (Walton 2012). The greatest advantage and strength of that theory is that it allows us to represent that reasoning as a sequence of actions similar to the ones studied in action theory; like stories or narratives, which, although not schemes of arguments themselves, are tightly linked to them, in particular to the scheme of practical reasoning. The author outlines that advantage and strength using a diagram—and the script theory—of the two arguments by analogy presented before. In conclusion, Walton upholds that the answer to the issues with each scheme resides in combining them; in the case of the first, it entails using a script-based model to the benefit of both.

In Chapter 3, "Argumentation by Analogy in Stereotypical Argumentative Patterns", Frans van Eemeren and Bart Garssen study the role of analogy in argumentative discourse from the perspective of pragma-dialectics. These authors first emphasise that, for over 30 years, this prestigious school of argumentation theory developed systematically their conceptions based on the ideal and rather abstract model of critical discussion (van Eemeren and Grootendorst 1984, 2004) to start addressing concrete, institutionalised and conventional circumstances of argumentative discourse in its variety of domains (legal, political, scientific, medical, academic, etc.). As they note, the nuclear pragma-dialectical concept of 'strategic manoeuvring' and the analogical use of argumentation, in particular, are not part of a critical discussion idealised, normatively, but they do arise in the multiple and varied communication practices conducted in different kinds of domains which have been mentioned. The institutional preconditions of argumentative discourse and the relevant and related critical reactions, from type to type, are essential to understand the "argumentative pattern" in question. In general terms, that pattern features a constellation of strategic argumentative positions supporting a certain standpoint, in the scope of a difference of opinion, which uses a given scheme of arguments or, as is more often the case, a combination of several of these. In this context, the authors resume the types of pragma-dialectics argument schemes and the definition, in particular, of the argument by analogy (van Eemeren and Grootendorst 1992), by highlighting and clarifying the place which the argument occupies there. An essential point in the aforementioned approach is that, depending on the institutional context and/or the kind of communicational activity, analogical argumentation may appear linked to other types of argumentation within a given argumentative pattern. Another point is that the appraisal of the use of each of these analogy types involves submitting them to special test or critical contestation procedures, which are specified and analysed. Next, after Garssen (2009), the distinction between two fundamental variants of argument by analogy—descriptive and normative—is presented and developed closely, and its place and meaning is researched in the general scope of contemporary analogy theories. The status of the so-called "figurative analogy" and its connections with normative analogy, in particular, is discussed; the thesis is that this alleged type of analogical argumentation may be reduced and compared to what in pragma-dialectics is considered argumentation based on a causal connection or symptomatic argumentation. The authors conclude by addressing the peculiar nature of analogical argumentation when it appears embedded in argumentative patterns. This is perhaps the form in which argumentation is most often used, and other contemporary theories in general do not always highlight it appropriately.

In Chapter 4, "The Uses of Analogies" (evoking the title of the renowned book by Toulmin 1958), Lilian Bermejo-Luque begins by separating quantitative from qualitative analogies. This is a general separation, and targets the field of argument by analogy as a whole, thus responding, on the other hand, to the challenges of contemporary theories about such argument. In the former, this is actually a set of properties which share the analogues among themselves, whereas in the latter it is the question of knowing to what extent they may be compared in a relatively sound and/or significant manner. Considering their essentially fuzzy content, analogies have according to the author a cognitive exploratory use, which allows us to perceive substantial news regarding the areas which they concern; these are tools which function as "cognitive proposals". This is where their explanatory capacity, either figurative or classificatory, and their great rhetorical power come from. Some analogies may, however, be used for communication and argumentation, as vehicles not only to compare the analogues, but to persuade those to whom they are addressed and to defend/justify any claim. In the aftermath of her own research (Bermejo-Luque 2012), the author proposes to adopt Toulmin's (1958) argument model to study the analogical use of argumentation in general and, in particular, to clarify the distinction between the explanatory use, on the one hand, and the argumentative use, on the other. Furthermore, she introduces criteria, which she analyses closely to assess one or the other. In this regard, the essential point is that when an analogy is used mostly for explanatory purposes, it cannot be assessed according to its propositional contents (it is not exactly "true" or "false"), because the formulation thereof involves particularly cognitive propositions, and not fact judgements. In contrast, when used for argumentative purposes, it may be interpreted as an assertion and it is its power of justification which is essentially at stake, although it still preserves the same ambiguity, which characterises the exploratory nature (as a cognitive proposal) of the whole analogy in general. This also explains its charming nature. In effect, as we began to say, who argues using analogy does not need to commit itself expressly with the alleged similarity between analogues. What makes a good analogy from the perspective of rhetoric may be entirely different from that which makes it good from an epistemological perspective; which largely explains, we add, the disturbing nature of reasoning by analogy, when compared to other kinds of arguments. From this fundamental perspective, Lilian Bermejo Luque rereads and reinterprets the standard/initial distinction between quantitative and qualitative analogies, and projects it in other contemporary theories about argument by analogy, which is the case of Govier's (1989) and Walton's (2012). To conclude, the author established a separation between analogies and classifications, not without clarifying the important links between both.

In Chapter 5, "Analogy and Redefinition", Fabrizio Macagno defines analogy as reasoning which is based on the abstraction of a general property drawn from two comparable entities or state of affairs. Analogical reasoning thus involves two different procedures: the relation between the two terms of comparison and the general property that they have in common; and the relation between this common general property and the entities which are subsumed under it, in which a predicate or a classification is involved. In the first part of the paper, the author focuses particularly on the first type of relation. The essential virtue of analogy and abstraction of a general property consists precisely of identifying when and how the compared entities can be similar and, at the same time, different. Such property can be considered a pragmatic and functional *genre*, this is to say essentially contextual and different from the definitional genre *per se*, which mirrors an essential feature of the two terms of comparison which it applies to. The comparison may be explicit or implicit; but in both cases the analogy redefines contingently the concepts which are used, in such a way that the two terms or entities are characterised through it, by semantic aspects which, as the author underlines, do not describe "what something absolutely is", but only "what it is in context", according to the communicational and pragmatic objectives of the analogy. Therefore, analogy may be considered a strategy for redefining a concept in a contextual and contingent manner. The analogical *genre* is a new abstract category, i.e. did not exist before, which is created *ad hoc* to sustain the reasonableness of awarding a common predicate to both terms of comparison. However, analogical reasoning can also be used as a tool to generate an ambiguous category; the issue being precisely that of identifying the *genre* in question. The author illustrates how each of these situations may occur. Analogies, on the other hand, may be structured differently, in the sense that the "identity of relations" involved, case by case, may be established according to different propositional forms and communication goals. In particular, different argumentative relations can be the basis of the more or less pertinent connection between the analogical *genre* and the predicate awarded to it. Once more the author exemplifies the way this can happen. He further focuses, in the second part of his paper, particularly on the relation between the analogical *genre* and the terms or entities subsumed thereunder and which provide the basis for the comparison. The author highlights the essentially defeasible nature of that relation: *genre* by definition is semantically more general than species, in the sense that it may be essentially their predicate, but not vice-versa. Macagno analyses and illustrates closely this kind of connections. Concluding, he focuses on the use of analogy in the legal and/or statutory context and, in particular, on the well-known distinction between "*analogy iuris*" and "*analogy legis*".

He finds that this distinction mirrors the difference between two fundamental uses of analogical reasoning, which he studied before: in the former case, that through which a concept is redefined; in the latter, that in which a new property is introduced.

In Chapter 6, "Arguments from Parallel Reasoning", Jan Albert van Laar studies dialogical and dialectical conceptions (those which are traditionally identified with the Krabbe and Walton's schools of dialogical logic, and van Eemeren and Grootendorts's pragma-dialectics) applied to a certain kind of argument by analogy: argument from parallel reasoning. Arguments like those are considered both case-based and defeasible arguments. In abstract, the former are arguments which can be assessed without having to resort to a universal and substantially different principle to the argumentation scheme involved; the latter leave open the possibility of an opposing party challenging the conclusion of the argument in question, even after the relevant premises have been granted. The author first addresses the argumentation scheme underlying those arguments in general, proving that they are a sort of meta-dialogical arguments from analogy. The definitions of Woods and Hudak (1989) on this matter are retrieved and analysed closely, and this scheme is discerned and discussed from the perspective of the dialogical and dialectical conceptions mentioned before. In particular, when the argument involved is defeasible, the role of one of its fundamental premises—which van Laar calls "connection premises"—is analysed and highlighted. The opponent's obligations and responsibilities in a critical discussion are addressed closely within this theoretical framework: through his counter-considerations, he decides which type of propositions he grants the proponent, which premises and argumentative connections he will criticise and, more generally, he informs the proponent about the sort of argumentation he finds convincing. Namely, the opponent may ask the proponent to use an argument from parallel reasoning, or, when this is used by the former, challenge and contest the connection between the premises and the relevant conclusion. It is what the author calls 'the burden of criticism', by analysing, expanding and applying, in the aftermath of his own prior research, the rules for a critical discussion of van Eemeren and Grootendorst (2004) to the particular case of the opponent and, more particularly, to the counter-considerations concerning an argument from parallel reasoning. Van Laar examines carefully the dialogical circumstances in which the opponent may require from the proponent such an argument, suggesting that it deserves a special status in any classification drawn of argument schemes. And specifies the conditions, giving examples, according to which an argument from parallel reasoning may be critically tested (challenging the premises or the link between such premises and the conclusion). Finally, taking Mill's (1979) argument by analogy as the case-study, regarding the existence of other minds (which is identified as an argument from parallel reasoning), the author illustrates how the dialogical approach to argumentation is confined not only to the situations in which there are two interlocutors, and how it allows us to reconstruct suitably those arguments in which an author is at the same time the proponent and opponent.

In Chapter 7, "A Systematic Review of Classifications of Arguments by Analogy", André Juthe highlights the crucial role that these classifications play in contemporary argumentation theory, and introduces his own classification. Argumentation by analogy can vary, and the assessment thereof depends on which category or sub-category each belongs to. However, as the author first notes, the problem with contemporary classifications is that their authors use different words to classify what is essentially the same kind of analogical argument; and generally they choose different parameters to classify that argument. On the other hand, within the same classification different parameters may be used to interpret the same arguments. For example, arguments which were sub-divided according to their function may be sub-divided if we consider different logical forms. In this context, Juthe's objective is twofold: by studying and analysing contemporary classifications of the argument by analogy, a meta-classification or classification of those classifications is delivered, and their parameters may be used to interpret that argument, i.e. to sub-divide into the relevant sub-types. The author suggests at least nine parameters to classify argument by analogy, which are in turn divided into as many sub-types, which are: (1) epistemological status of the analogue, (2) argument's function or purpose, (3) logical form, (4) domain constraint, (5) nature of inference, (6) amount of sources, (7) matters of comparison, (8) miscellaneous, (9) critical issues. The present research focuses particularly on the first four. The sub-division based on the epistemic status of the analogue is related to the issue of finding out how this is known and whether it does or does not have empirical content; for example, if the premises of the analogue are known empirically, or whether it is an a priori case or a hypothetically invented one. The author delivers a meta-classification with the list of authors involved; and Govier (1989, 2010) and Doury's (2009) theories on the subject are commented. The sub-division according to analogy function or purpose classifies arguments according to their function in discourse. The author shows that the parameter is very broad, and can result in several sub-types, which sometimes appear with different terminology in different classifications; and that, on the other hand, several of the arguments or sub-types established by the previous parameter may also be classified by it. Once again, he introduces a list of meta-classified authors. Brown (1989) and Guarini's (2004) theories in particular are analysed. The third parameter (logical form) draws a distinction between the sub-types on the basis of the intrinsic logical structure of the underlying argumentation schemes. Of the list of authors covered by this parameter, the author focuses particularly on the theories of Prade and Richard (2009, 2010), Wreen (2007) and Brewer (1996). Finally, the fourth parameter meta-classifies the arguments, and assays whether they belong to the same dominion, or not; it is the case of the separation between figurative and literal comparison. Of the list of authors mentioned before, Weitzenfeld's (1984) theory is commented and discussed in some detail. The author ends where he began, underscoring both the originality, and the complex and problematic nature of his own research.

In Chapter 8, "Messing Up the Mind? Analogical Reasoning with Metaphors", Eugen Fischer studies the formation process of metaphorical concepts and analogical reasoning in general in the light of philosophy of the mind and cognitive psychology. In his paper, he uses a structure-mapping theory, drawn from those fields, to explain how simple analogical reasoning generates conceptual metaphors that facilitate more complex analogical reasoning, which is generally unintentional. The purpose is to show how, in the framework of this process, fallacies can arise, in particular that which shape introspective conceptions of the mind that dominated philosophical discourse from early modernity to the present day, as is the case of Descartes's. In the beginning of his study, the author analyses the fundamental steps involved in analogical reasoning from the perspective of cognitive psychology and which are mostly unconscious and unintentional. First, a source-model is identified, and knowledge about it is retrieved from memory; then model and target are aligned and elements of the source-model are mapped onto elements of the target domain; finally, actual inferences are made. Exemplifying, analogical reasoning forges conceptual metaphors by building up from "basic mapping" like: "S see x (source domain)→ S knows x (target domain)". Such metaphors can motivate the metaphorical extension of terms from their source (seeing) to their target domains (knowledge): if "X is easily visible", "X is easily knowable"; or if "X is a lion", and x is strong, courageous, etc., "Aquiles is a lion", and strong, courageous, etc. The author's theory is, thus, that extending metaphorically the relational terms to their stereotypical implications can motivate the basic mapping of conceptual metaphors. All cognitive processes involved are not necessarily conscious, but, as the author carefully explains, are automatic, in the sense that they are effortless, non-intentional, and autonomous. They duplicate or reproduce inferences governed by rules, which made cognitivist psychologists discuss "automatic analogical inferences". In this context, Fischer introduces the concept of "semantic memory", which is generally designed as a network which duplicates as information-storage and inference-facilitator. Such a network consists of nodes representing concepts and links between them that can automatically pass on activation from stimuli, verbal and other. The author examines in particular how analogical reasoning interacts with partial-matching effects in memory-based processing. Finally, based on a computational model of "information-based processing", he shows that this interaction leads to predictable fallacies, as happened, for example, with the known philosophical representation of the mind, like a space which is founded on the analogical reasoning alluded to before between "seeing/looking at" and "knowing". One mapping, in analogical inference, of a conceptual metaphor may be defective, when it takes us to conclusions that lack determinate meaning or content, in other words, when it projects a rich relational structure from a metaphor's source domain onto a target domain, which in fact does not contain any elements standing in the projected relations.

1.2.2 Part 2: Applied Approaches to Argument by Analogy

In Chapter 9, "How to Make Figures Talk: Comparative Argument in TV Election Night Specials", Marianne Doury looks into the connection between the special category of comparative arguments—those which are based on comparisons, which have a quantitative dimension, of elements drawn from the same domain—and the comments made on two special television shows on the results of the French presidential elections held in April 2012. Theoretically, its purpose is to describe form and clarify the function of that kind of arguments, and of the critical discourse which it may raise; generally speaking, it is to add—following previous research (Doury 2009)—to a systematic classification of arguments by analogy. Pointing at research conducted in pragma-dialectics, the comments we refer to are assessed as "presentational devices", i.e., strategic manoeuvres when presenting arguments which are intended to conduct them in a specific direction in order to achieve rhetorical advantages: for example, announcing a candidate's rank (1st, 2nd, etc.) rather than indicating the percentage of votes; or using argumentative operators ("only", "less than", "close to", etc.) when announcing the results. However, it is particularly the study of argumentative sequences that seeks to justify these results and includes the "presentational devices", on which the author focuses in the first part of her paper: comparing the results achieved by different candidates in the same elections; the results achieved by a political party in consecutive presidential elections; the results achieved by leaders in different countries facing similar economic crises; and the result forecasts in polls and the actual outcomes. In all of these cases, comparative argumentation—by both candidates and their opponents—is strategically oriented, in rhetorical terms, for certain type of conclusions, according to the interests of stakeholders. In a first formal assessment of the arguments in question, the author suggests their reconstruction in the light of theory of argument schemes which is characteristic of contemporary argumentation studies, pragma-dialectics in particular, concluding, however, that that reconstruction does not suitably capture the specificity of those arguments: they entail a comparison not exactly between the *similarity* of its elements, but more appropriately between the relevant *difference*. She thus suggests we return—within the framework of what she calls "a reconstruction *a fortiori*"—to Ducrot's (1973) concept of argumentative scale to help us understand that specificity. Which she does pertinently, first by outlining some of the challenges faced when applying that concept. The reconstruction "*a fortiori*" of these comparative arguments from the perspective of that concept may be understood only by resorting to a polyphonic interpretation of the relevant elements, without translating, in formal terms, all relations between them. However, as the author finally notes, based on the findings of the present research, this conclusion is only apparently disappointing.

In Chapter 10, "Analogical Argumentation in Textes Genres: Empirical Studies", Rosalice Pinto studies analogical argumentation from the perspective of linguistics and, more specifically, of persuasive genre, which is the case of the political billboards and advertisements of commercial and non-commercial activities. The purpose is to show how the construction of analogical argumentation varies according to the type of text which is discussed and, in particular, to characterise how it is constructed when the genre is persuasive. First, the author introduces several linguistic theories about text genres, and defines what is meant by genre when it has a persuasive function, and by empirical text. The author elects as her theoretical framework argumentation studies conducted by francophone text linguistics, particularly in the works of Ducrot and Anscombre (1983), Adam (1999) and Bronckart (1999). She upholds that the empirical text has two inherent features: on the one hand, contextual, which concern the constraints that influence the textual materialisation and, on the other hand, linguistic *per se*, which concern macro and micro text organisation. This kind of texts is regarded as a psycho-social-plurisemiotic object; when its purpose is to persuade, it presents what Pinto calls "plurimodal materialisation acting as argumentative strategies". The word "argumentation", in this context, corresponds to the way plurimodal aspects in general (linguistic elements, implicit or explicit, typography, image, colours) interact in a persuasive text. The latter, in general, but in line with Bronckart's social-discursive interactionism, are regarded as global communicative units. In the second part of the paper, the author analyses the three subtypes of texts mentioned: a political poster used in an electoral campaign in Portugal; a commercial ad of a Portuguese airline; and an ad from a non-profit making association, also in Portugal. Analogical argumentation, in each of these cases, is reconstructed attentively. One particularity of that argumentation is that it does not appear explicitly materialised in the current language, as is the case when we argue in daily life; it must thus be inferred from the way textual, verbal or non-verbal and explicit or inexplicit components or units relate to each other. For example, as for non-verbal components, the configuration of the image of the candidate for Prime Minister of Portugal on the political poster, conveys a message and a powerful rhetorical and argumentative meaning. On the other hand, this textual unit is closely connected with other, verbal and non-verbal, units, as is the case of the wording on the poster, or the relevant colours and other typographic elements. The argument at issue (assumptions and conclusion or conclusions) must thus be reconstructed overall, from the connection between all of these explicit and implicit components; which does not mean, for that reason, that it is less powerful or effective than any other explicitly presented in current language.

In Chapter 11, "Classical Fables as Arguments: Narration and Analogy", Paula Olmos undertakes to find out to what extent the classical fables (ancient Greece particularly) may or may not be considered narrative—and, more specifically, analogical—arguments. In the first part of the paper, the author begins to analyse and discuss whether the narratives, in the light of contemporary argumentation theories, may involve or not several kinds of arguments, and whether, more generally speaking, they may constitute arguments. The implementation and development, by some of these theories, of the script theory (like Walton's in 2012), conducive to an understanding of argumentation as a story, narrative, is an important step in this direction. Since in fables there is the assumption that a comparison is made between imaginary and the fantasised world and the real world, and that one can draw consequences from such comparison about how a human being may perceive the latter, they may be considered analogies about different story-schemes. According to the author, however, in an interpretation thereof—like Walton's (see above)—the analogy seems to be inappropriately compared to the concept of similarity (which raises issues for understanding the use of argumentation in fables) and there is nothing linking narrative and analogy directly in a narrow sense, nor even putting them side by side. (From this perspective, a theory like Perelman and Olbrechts-Tyteca's (1969) is still in her view quite topical.) On the other hand, some specialised research into narrative-based arguments, in particular where fiction is concerned, is faced with the same kind of constraints and/or the same consequences. In the second part of her paper, Olmos analyses the place and the part that fables and parables play in classical argumentation theory, in particular in Aristotle and Aeluis Theon. In the former, she shows that, in spite of his relevant approach in the treaty of *Rhetoric*, the philosopher does not seem too concerned about the realistic or unrealistic features of fables and parables, addressing them as equals in terms of arguments; which still contrasts with the important part that education and teaching based on fables played in classical Greek rhetoric, particularly from a literary perspective. And, in this respect, she studies Theon's conceptions, which focus particularly on the epistemic status of fables, very close to our contemporaneous concerns. Next, the author highlights the enormous variety of types of fables in the classical tradition, in argumentative and rhetorical terms (not all of which have a moral lesson, not all fantasise only about inter-animal relations and involve human characteristics too, etc.), and illustrates that variety by studying fables about bears. To conclude, regarding argument by analogy, when applied to fables, she suggests that we need a more sophisticated concept of that argument like something that is essentially different, in Perelman's words, from arguments by similarity, example and comparison.

In Chapter 12, "Analogies in Scientific Explanations: Concept Formation by Analogies in Cultural Evolutionary Theory", Christian J. Feldbacher studies the process of formation alluded to, based on the analogy between the theory of genes and the theory of memes. The author's starting point, historically speaking, is the conception of Dawkins (1976), according to whom the elementary units of research into natural evolution are not populations, nor mere organisms; they are reproducers like genes; similarly, there should be reproducers of cultural evolution, which are exactly memes; and the fundamental parameters of a theory of the evolution of species like Darwin's may be fruitfully extended to the theory of genes and, more generally, to the theory of memes. Just as the theory of genes allows us to explain diversity in nature, the theory of memes will allow us to explain diversity in culture. More generally, cultural evolution theorists aspire to seeing their research programme into that diversity and cultural phenomena achieve similar success as that enjoyed by natural evolution theorists by explaining the diversity of species. However, as Feldbacher highlights, the meaning of "memes" is far from being clear. The following is thus the territory of analogy and the subsequent concept formation: considering the ambiguity of the concept, there has been an attempt to develop the relevant theory from the perspective of the theory of genes and the implementation, in particular, of the aforementioned parameters (reproduction, variation and selection); it is the "genes-memes" analogy. According to the author, one may argue whether that implementation has been successful until now; and to illustrate exactly this, he presents a wide variety of definitions of the concept of "meme" and the relevant conceptualisation in specialised literature. Memes have been designed as entities that can be mimicked, information contents, "brain software" or what has been called "neuronemes", etc. Criticism directed at the programme of cultural evolution theorists range from the idea that culture may not be divided into discrete units, as memes should in the light of the genes-memes analogy, to the idea that similarities between the two fields are too general to be fruitful. Anyhow, the entity 'meme' has many basic properties (i.e., that which can be reproduced and is appropriately variable), which we can come to an agreement about and which are introduced through analogy; which means that the notion thereof is not problematic, or only partially. As the author illustrates, it is possible to formalise the genes-memes analogy, which entails formalising the interdependence of the mentioned parameters. To conclude, he explains how the diversity of meanings linked to the concept of meme is part of the current theoretical framework of the cultural evolution.

In Chapter 13, "Analogy and Interpretation in Legal Argumentation", Damiano Canale and Giovanni Tuzet study the ties between analogical reasoning and extensive interpretation in forensic argumentation. In most legal systems this reasoning is forbidden (unless where used in favour of the defendant), whereas the aforementioned interpretation is not. The problem, which authors analyse closely, is that it is very hard to separate the analogy of extensive interpretation in forensic practice, since both justify extending regulation to a case that is not explicitly provided for by law. This is why it is suggested that the division between one and the other is an issue of strategic manoeuvre in argumentation. Canale and Tuzet first address the traditional outlook on this matter, distinguishing "restrictive interpretation" from "extensive interpretation", and the latter from analogical reasoning. His theory is that extensive interpretation is not itself an argumentative tool: it departs from the assumption that the meaning intended by the legislator with one or other legal regulation needs to be explained, which justifies abandoning a literal interpretation thereof. In contrast, with analogical reasoning a gap in the law is filled by arguing analogically from a source to a target case: where there is significant similarity between the two, the rule which governs the former is extended to the latter; the gap is filled by the judge who creates a second rule which extends beyond the former. The authors analyse both the common features of analogy and extensive interpretation, and that which distinguish them. Focusing on the former: both address cases which are not explicitly governed by the legal provisions; on the other hand, both produce to a certain extent the same practical results. Regarding some of the latter: analogical reasoning presupposes a given interpretation of the relevant legal provisions, which is precisely what is at stake in extensive interpretation. On the other hand, that reasoning creates a rule which fills in a gap, while said interpretation extends the content of the reading of the relevant legal provisions. This theoretical framework is applied to the study of the case of electromagnetic wave emissions by the Vatican's radio, which was judged by the Italian Supreme Court of Cassation in 2008. In that case there was clearly a gap in the law which favoured the use of analogical reasoning; but as we said the use of analogy was forbidden by criminal law. Argumentation between the parties involved (prosecution and defense) and the Court's decision are discussed in detail by the authors, in the attempt to find out whether this is extensive interpretation or a veiled, or hidden, use of analogy. Regarding the findings of fact in question, they show that both readings are possible, although the prosecution and the Court evoked having made an extensive interpretation thereof. Underlying this issue is the vague nature of the regulatory legal provisions in question, and the greater or lesser semantic tolerance which it raises, addressed from the perspective of extensive interpretation or, alternatively, of analogy. Canale and Tuzet conclude that, although both "semantic games" are similar and are conducive to the same result, in the sense that they justify the extension of the scope of the regulation to a case which is not directly governed by it, the epistemological status of one is essentially different from the other.

In Chapter 14, "*Analogia Legis* and *Analogia Iuris:* An Overview from a Rhetorical Perspective", Giovanni Damele studies the difference between two types of analogy which Damiano Canale and Giovanni Tuzet addressed, partly, in the paper immediately preceding. He argues that such distinction is neither essential, nor substantive, in the sense that, from a rhetorical perspective, both types of analogy include an argument whose persuasive strength depends on the justification of the degree of similarity between the compared terms or cases; consequently, the individual use of each of these types in a given context of legal argumentation must be perceived, as Canale and Tuzet had upheld, as a strategic manoeuvre or a rhetorical device; so, any distinction is marginal and essentially rhetorical. Damele's paper is original insofar as it highlights precisely that, in the light of an analysis and interpretation of the more relevant contemporary theories about the topic. The author first discusses the distinction between analogy and extensive interpretation, suggesting that it concerns, fundamentally, the prohibition in most Western legal frameworks of the use of analogy in criminal law, or its limitations in the fields of civil law. Both the differences, and the similarities, between types of argumentation involved are analysed closely. In this context, a distinction is drawn—on the basis of the research conducted into the subject—between three fundamental types of use of analogical argument in legal terms: descriptive, normative and characteristically rhetorical. The essential point concerning the difference between *analogy legis* and *analogy iuris*, according to Damele, has to do with the way the interpreter fills a gap: according to a rule or a given statute (in the first case) or a general principle inspired by the legal system and, consequently, by the same statutes (in the second). In both cases, the rationale of analogical argumentation is, ultimately, more abstract than the statute itself. What is at issue with such argumentation is, therefore, not merely interpreting or reinterpreting statutes or legal provisions, but redesigning and extending their meaning. All of which means and/or implies, as is first mentioned regarding the author's fundamental thesis, that the analogical argument, when used in legal contexts, is essentially a "rhetorical device". It is what the author shows about Posner's (2006) conceptions of this subject. Towards the end of his paper, Damele analyses and closely specifies this rhetorical nature of the analogical argument. He shows that it has to do with the fact that, with such argument, one seeks essentially a persuasive justification. Therefore, the argument depends on its context. However, the psychological aspects and other similar aspects of the process of discovery of that argument, by the judges, are not pertinent. It is from this perspective that the known distinction between context of discovery and context of justification must be understood, when it is applied to the way such argument is used. Finally, the author analyses closely G. Tarello's (1980) interpretation of the difference between *analogy legis* and *analogy iuris*. He concludes that it neatly illustrates his own thesis of the fundamentally rhetorical nature—generally speaking—of analogical argumentation in legal terms.

In Chapter 15, "Analogical Reasoning in Clinical Practice", Nino Guallart studies the part which reasoning plays in the diagnostic phase of clinical practice and clarifies its main characteristics. Doctors must interpret patients' symptoms in the light of their professional experience in varying degrees, or greater or lesser theoretical knowledge of medicine; and analogy, when combined with other methods like induction and causality, is one of the most important tools to this end. The author first analyses the main features of the clinical reasoning in general, and the epistemological requirements in particular; then it introduces a set of definitions of some of the fundamental concepts concerning the diagnostic process, of which analogy forms an essential part. When doctors make analogies in clinical terms, they not only establish similarities between the symptoms that the patient refers to then and on previous occasions, but they are also capable of guessing symptoms which are not visible and will show later, thus inferring correlations between them; and can, therefore, establish probable causes thereof on the basis of a diagnosis. This means that analogical reasoning—and not other methods, like the deductive or statistical—plays a central role in each of the stages of clinical diagnosis: gathering information through anamnesis and physical examination; more or less in depth interpretation of symptoms; formulation of provisional hypotheses about possible diseases; hypothesis assessment and confirmation/rejection. In this context, highlighting the relevance of reasoning, the author reinterprets the process of clinical diagnosis in the light of the known hypothetical-deductive model of explanation used in physical-natural sciences: in his view it is not a set of separate stages, distinct from each other, as in their interpretation younger and more inexperienced doctors might imagine. On the contrary, the more experienced a doctor is, the more he will resort to analogies; instead of using that model, experienced and competent doctors resort systematically to analogies between current and previous cases. They are capable of recognising immediately complex symptom patterns which are, in principle, connected, rapidly relating them to the corresponding diseases, and focusing on a small set of realistically probable causes, in place of beginning to formulate a huge amount of hypotheses, as is the case of inexperienced doctors. Actually, the more complex a disease is, the more pronounced doctors' use of analogical reasoning will be. Therefore, analogy is a dynamic and creative reality, which must not be confused with an induction from a particular case: the latter compares the current case with a general theoretical model of a disease; whereas in the former the same case is compared to previous patients in the light of the theoretical knowledge and the experience accumulated through clinical practice; which enables more subtle and complex comparisons.

Finally, in Chapter 16, "The Role of Analogy in Philosophical Discourse", Henrique Jales Ribeiro first questions whether philosophy is or is not argumentative discourse, i.e. whether it can be or not understood according to those conditions which make argumentation in daily life possible. This is an essential issue for analysing the characteristics of the use of analogies in philosophy and, where possible, for typifying them. The author suggests that, in a first analysis, the conditions alluded to do not apply to philosophical discourse. In contrast with daily argumentation, philosophical concepts ("subject", "object", "experience", etc.) are generally metatheoretical concepts, i.e. they do not report directly to the real world like empirical concepts themselves, but they do seek to encompass the latter. On the other hand, these concepts vary significantly from one philosopher to another (or from one system to another) throughout the history of philosophy. There are certainly matters which philosophers do not agree on, such as daily argumentation, but it is not possible to assess the answers to such questions in a clear and coherent manner, nor ultimately decide which would be the best or the most appropriate of them all. In other words, the assessment of philosophical arguments, where existing, apparently raises the same kind of issues of hermeneutics as raised by the interpretation of any work of art. In this context, Ribeiro suggests that, to understand philosophical discourse, we must still turn to the known distinction between argumentation and explanation, namely the definitions which Copi and Cohen (1994) first introduced. In that discourse one does not necessarily argue, but generally explains, in other words one describes and analyses, without debating problematic issues and delivering the grounds to sustain the theses in question. This means that philosophical analogies are used particularly to explain, and not to argue. But when that happens, we do not have the tools—for the reasons mentioned before—to analyse it suitably and appropriately. (As far as philosophy is concerned, the author has in mind a similar approach to that which M. Finocchiaro (2005) adopted to the scientific discourse in Galileo Galilei.) In both cases, however, the analogies are real shows, i.e. recreations of the conceptual imagery of the philosophers themselves, which as mentioned have no direct bearing on the world of everyday experience. The author upholds that analogical reasoning, from Plato to the present day, is the perfect means to deliver philosophical discourse, which includes both the typical metaphysical shows of each philosophy, those which are inspired by the need to apply the relevant conceptions to other fields (like science or art), and shows which entail the comparison between those conceptions and other philosophers' conceptions. One set of examples is analysed and commented on in some detail.

References

Adam, J.-M. 1999. *Linguistique textuelle: Des genres de discours aux textes*. Paris: Nathan.

Bermejo-Luque, L. 2012. A unitary schema for arguments by analogy. *Informal Logic* 32 (1): 1–24.

Brewer, S. 1996. Exemplary reasoning: Semantics, pragmatics, and the rational force of legal argument by analogy. *Harvard Law Review* 109 (5): 923–1028.

Bronckart, J.-P. 1999. *Atividade de linguagem, textos e discursos. Por um interacionismo sociodiscursivo*. São Paulo: EDUC.

Brown, W. R. 1989. Two traditions of analogy. *Informal Logic* XI (3): 161–172.

Copi, I. M., and C. Cohen. 1994. *Introduction to logic*. 9th ed. New York: Macmillan Publishing Company (First published 1953 and 1961 by Macmillan Publishing Company).

Dawkins, R. 1976. *The selfish gene*. Oxford: Oxford University Press.

Doury, M. 2009. Argument schemes typologies in practice: The case of comparative arguments. In *Pondering on problems of argumentation: Twenty essays on theoretical issues,* eds. F. H. van Eemeren and B. Garssen, 141–155. Dordrecht: Springer.

Ducrot, O. 1973. *La preuve et le dire*. Paris: Mame.

Ducrot, O., and J.-C. Anscombre. 1983. *L'argumentation dans la langue*. Liège: Mardaga.

van Eemeren, F. H., and R. Grootendorst. 1984. *Speech acts in argumentative discussions. A theoretical model for the analysis of discussions directed towards solving conflicts of opinion*. Berlin/Dordrecht/Cinnaminson: De Gruyter/Foris.

van Eemeren, F. H., and R. Grootendorst. 1992. *Argumentation, communication, and fallacies: A pragma-dialectical perspective*. Hillsdale: Lawrence Erlbaum.
van Eemeren, Frans H., and R. Grootendorst. 2004. *A systematic theory of argumentation*. Cambridge: Cambridge University Press.
van Eemeren, F. H., R. Grootendorts, F. Snoeck Henkemans, et al. 1996. *Fundamentals of argumentation theory: A handbook of historical backgrounds and contemporary developments*. Mahwah: Lawrence Erlbaum Associates.
Finocchiaro, M. 2005. *Arguments about arguments: Systematic, critical and historical essays in logical theory*. New York: Cambridge University Press.
Garssen, B. 2009. Comparing the incomparable. Figurative analogies in a dialectical testing procedure. In *Pondering on problems of argumentation: Twenty essays on theoretical issues,* eds. F. H. van Eemeren and B. Garssen, 133–140. Dordrecht: Springer.
Govier, T. 1989. Analogies and missing premises. *Informal Logic* 11 (3): 141–152.
Govier, T. 2010. *A practical study of arguments*. 7th ed. Belmont: Wadsworth Cengage Learning.
Guarini, M. 2004. A defense of non-deductive reconstructions of analogical arguments. *Informal Logic* 24:153–168.
Hastings, A. C. 1963. *A reformulation of the modes of reasoning in argumentation*. PhD diss., Northwestern University, Evanston, IL.
Hurley, P. J. 2003. *A concise introduction to logic*. Belmont: Wadsworth.
Kienpointner, M. 2012. When figurative analogies fail: Fallacious uses of arguments from analogy. In *Topical themes in argumentation theory: Twenty exploratory studies,* eds. F. H. van Eemeren and Bart Garssen, 111–126. Dordrecht: Springer.
Lief, M. S., M. Caldwell, and B. Bryce. 1998. *Ladies and Gentlemen of the jury: Greatest closing arguments in modern law*. New York: Scribner.
Mill, J. S. 1979. An examination of William Hamilton's philosophy and of the principal philosophical questions discussed in his writings. In *The collected works of John Stuart Mill,* ed. J. M. Robson, vol. IX. Toronto: University of Toronto Press; London: Routledge/Kegan Paul (Originally published 1889).
Perelman, C. 1989. *Rhétoriques*. Bruxelles: Éditions de l'Université Libre de Bruxelles.
Perelman, C., and L. Olbrechts-Tyteca. 1969. *The new rhetoric: A treatise on argumentation* (trans: Wilkinson, J., and Weaver, P.). Notre Dame: University of Notre Dame Press. French edition: Perelman, C., and L. Olbrechts-Tyteca. 1958. *La nouvelle rhétorique: Traité de l'argumentation*. Paris: Presses Universitaires de France.
Posner, R. A. 2006. Book review. Reasoning by analogy. *Cornell Law Review* 91:761–774.
Prade, H., and G. Richard. 2009. Analogy, paralogy and reverse analogy: Postulates and inferences. In *KI 2009, LNAI 5803,* eds. B. Mertsching, M. Hund, and Z. Aziz, 306–314. Berlin: Springer.
Prade, H., and G. Richard. 2010. Analogical proportions: Another logical view. In *Research and development in intelligent systems XXVI,* ed. M. Bramer, et al., 306–314. London: Springer.
Ribeiro, H. J. 2012. Introduction: The birth of argumentation theory in the XXIst century. In *Inside arguments: Logic and the study of argumentation,* ed. H. Ribeiro, 1–21. New Castle upon Tyne: Cambridge Scholars Publishing.
Tarello, G. 1980. *L'interpretazione della legge*. Milano: Giuffré.
Thomson, J. 1971. A defense of abortion. *Philosophy and Public Affairs* 1 (1): 47–66.
Toulmin, S. 1958. *The uses of argument*. Cambridge: Cambridge University Press.
Walton, D. 1996. *Argumentation schemes from presumptive reasoning*. Mahwah: Erlbaum.
Walton, D. 2012. Story similarity in arguments from analogy. *Informal Logic* 32:190–221.
Walton, D., C. Reed, and F. Macagno. 2008. *Argumentation schemes*. Cambridge: Cambridge University Press.
Weitzenfeld, J. S. 1984. Valid reasoning by analogy. *Philosophy of Science* 51:137–149.
Woods, J., and B. Hudak. 1989. By parity of reasoning. *Informal Logic* XI (3): 125–139.
Wreen, M. J. 2007. A second form of argument from analogy. *Theoria* 73 (3): 221–239.

Part I
Theoretical Approaches to Argument by Analogy

Chapter 2
Argumentation Schemes for Argument from Analogy

Douglas N. Walton

There is such a huge literature on argument from analogy that during the early stages of my career I avoided work on the subject because so many scholars in so many fields had already written so much about it. When asked by a group of graduate students whether it would be a good idea to start a research project on argument from analogy some time ago, I cautioned them against it, or at least warned them about the dangers inherent in such a project, simply because of this huge existing literature they would have to go through. The fields that comprise this literature include not only argumentation studies, but also logic, cognitive science, ethics, law, literature, philosophy of science, computer science and the social sciences generally (Guarini et al. 2009). However, it is an important type of argument for us in the field of argumentation studies to deal with, if only because it is such a common and pervasive form of argument almost everywhere, but also because many logic textbooks have emphasized how it is an important informal fallacy by citing examples of improper uses of argument from analogy (Kienpointner 2012). So recently I too, yielding to necessity, have taken up writing on argument from analogy.

After surveying the literature on argument from analogy in some recent work, I came to the conclusion that there are two different types of argument from analogy, each represented by its own argumentation scheme (Walton 2010; Walton 2012). This was very puzzling at first, because normally we would just like to have one scheme representing such a basic and distinctive type of argument. But it appears that there is wide disagreement on precisely what form the argument from analogy should be represented by, and below I will try to explain why in the end the hypothesis that argument from analogy has two separate schemes is not such a bad one and how this double scheme approach can be justified.

The first section of the paper uses some standard argument diagrams to explain how the first scheme represents argument from analogy as proceeding from a source case to a target case. The second section shows how this scheme applies to a famous

D. N. Walton (✉)
Centre for Research in Reasoning, Argumentation and Rhetoric,
University of Windsor,
Windsor, ON, Canada
e-mail: waltoncrrar@gmail.com

H. J. Ribeiro (ed.), *Systematic Approaches to Argument by Analogy*,
Argumentation Library 25, DOI 10.1007/978-3-319-06334-8_2,

case of argument from analogy in philosophy. The third section introduces the second argumentation scheme, based on comparing factors in two cases. The fourth section shows how factors are weighed in systems of case-based reasoning. The fifth section presents a famous case of argument from analogy in legal rhetoric. The sixth section models a notion of similarity using script-based technology from artificial intelligence. The last section provides conclusions on how to evaluate argument from analogy.

2.1 The First Scheme

The following scheme (Walton et al. 2008, p. 315) represents what is probably the most widely accepted version of the scheme for argument from analogy advocated in the logic textbooks and other relevant sources. C_1 and C_2 represent two cases.

Similarity Premise: Generally, case C_1 is similar to case C_2.
Base Premise: A is true (false) in case C_1.
Conclusion: A is true (false) in case C_2.

This scheme requires that in order for something to qualify as an argument from analogy it must have one premise asserting that there is a similarity between two cases. A second requirement is that a proposition A must hold in the first case, or must be a conclusion that can be drawn in the first case. The conclusion drawn by the argument from analogy is that that A also holds in the second case. This version of the scheme for argument from analogy is the one used in the textbook (Walton 2006, p. 96).

The above version of the scheme conveys the basic idea behind it very well, but its ease of applicability to real cases can be improved (as will be shown below) by modifying it slightly. In the sequel, we will use this modified version.

Base Premise: A situation is described in C_1.
Derived Premise: A is plausibly drawn as an acceptable conclusion in case C_1.
Similarity Premise: Generally, case C_1 is similar to case C_2.
Conclusion: A is plausibly drawn as an acceptable conclusion in case C_2.

It doesn't matter too critically which scheme you use. Using either one is better than using none at all. Whether a conclusion is plausibly drawn from a case depends on the audience to whom the argument was supposedly directed. The modified version brings out better how the derived premise is drawn as a conclusion by the audience from the source case. This modification makes the base premise slightly more complex and wordy, but as the reader will shortly see, it fits cases in a more natural way. Let us henceforth call this modified scheme the basic scheme for argument from analogy.

It is part of every argumentation scheme that it must have a matching set of critical questions that can be used to probe into weak parts of the argument of the type represented by the scheme The following set of critical questions according to the account given (Walton et al. 2008, p. 315) matches the basic scheme for argument from analogy.

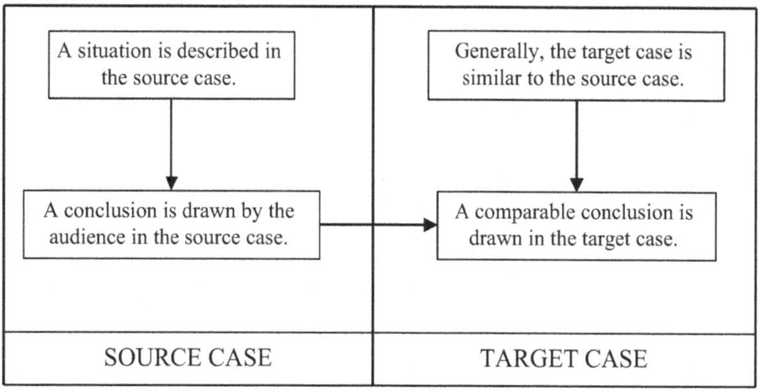

Fig. 2.1 The transition from the source case to the target case

CQ_1: Are there respects in which C_1 and C_2 are different that would tend to undermine the eforce of the similarity cited?
CQ_2: Is A the right conclusion to be drawn in C_1?
CQ_3: Is there some other case C_3 that is also similar to C_1, but in which some conclusion other than A should be drawn?

The first critical question relates to differences between the two cases that could detract from the strength of the argument from analogy, but respects in which two cases are similar could also be used to support the argument from analogy. The second critical question rather nicely paves the way to indicating why the reformulated version of the scheme is an improvement. A third critical question is associated with a familiar type of counterargument called the argument from counter-analogy. The function of this critical question is to suggest doubt that could lead possibly to a plausible counterargument that could be used to attack the original argument.

It will also help us to use the standard terminology in the literature on argument from analogy to talk about the structure of argument from analogy.

In the argumentation scheme above, the original case C_1 used to set up the argument from analogy is called the source case. The case C_2 to which the situation in the first case is compared is called the target case. How argument works as a transfer of data from one case through an argument to another case is graphically shown in Fig. 2.1.

In Fig. 2.2 we see the characteristic movement from one case to another that is the basic mechanism of argument from analogy. But the structure of the argument as a sequence of reasoning where the basic scheme links the premises to the conclusion has not been revealed yet.

Fig. 2.2 shows how argument from analogy, and also argument from counter-analogy poised to attack an argument from analogy that was originally set forth, can be visually represented using an argument diagram. In this diagram the propositions composing the premises and conclusion are shown in text boxes, and the inferential link leading from a premise or a set of premises to a conclusion is drawn by an arrow leading to the conclusion on a set of lines leading to the premises. In the intersection

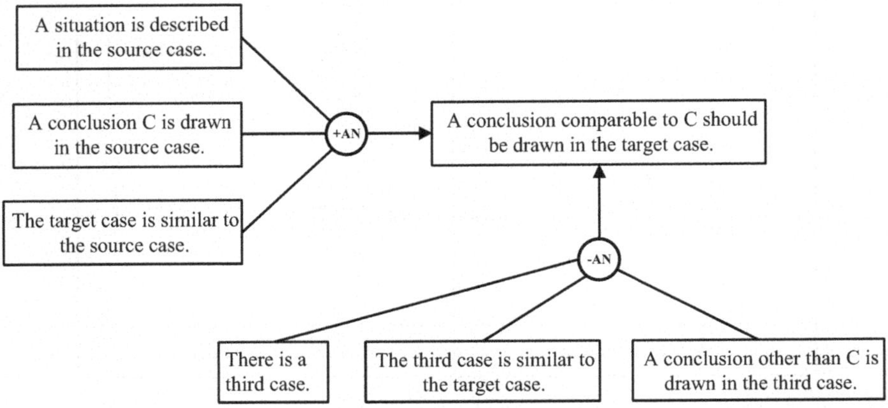

Fig. 2.2 Argument from analogy with argument from counteranalogy

of these lines there is a node representing the argument itself, which is shown on the diagram containing annotation representing the name of the argumentation scheme.

The diagram has been drawn in the style of an argument map drawn with the Carneades Argumentation System, where every argument is represented as a pro or con argument. A pro argument has a plus sign in its argument node while a con argument has a minus sign in its argument node. Accordingly, in Fig. 2.2, the argument from analogy at the top is represented as a pro argument supporting conclusion on the right. The argument at the bottom is represented as a con argument that attacks the conclusion of the prior argument.

It is often said in argumentation studies that there are three basic ways an argument can be attacked. You can attack one or more of the premises, you can attack the conclusion, or you can attack the inferential link between the premises and conclusion. In this instance the argument from counteranalogy is used to argue that the conclusion of the prior argument from analogy is not acceptable. The type of attack represented in Fig. 2.2 is of the second type where the attack is against the conclusion of the prior argument.

2.2 The Violinist Example

Possibly the most famous use of argument from analogy argument from analogy in twentieth-century philosophy was the violinist example of Thomson (1971, pp. 48–49), quoted below.

> You wake up in the morning and find yourself back to back in bed with an unconscious violinist. A famous unconscious violinist. He has been found to have a fatal kidney ailment, and the Society of Music Lovers has canvassed all the available medical records and found that you alone have the right blood type to help. They have therefore kidnapped you, and last night the violinist's circulatory system was plugged into yours, so that your kidneys

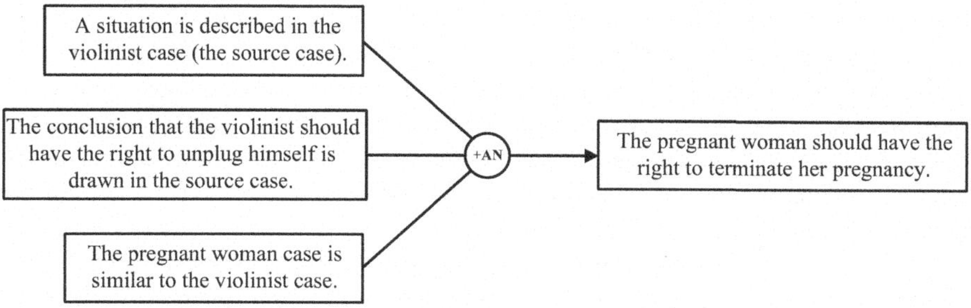

Fig. 2.3 Argument from analogy in the violinist case

> can be used to extract poisons from his blood as well as your own. The director of the hospital now tells you, "Look, we're sorry the Society of Music Lovers did this to you—we would never have permitted it if we had known. But still, they did it, and the violinist now is plugged into you. To unplug you would be to kill him. But never mind, it's only for nine months. By then he will have recovered from his ailment, and can safely be unplugged from you."

This argument was deployed by Thomson to support the thesis that a woman should have the right to terminate her pregnancy, by arguing that the person in the example should have the right to unhook the violinist. The basis of the argument is that the situation of the violinist is similar to the situation of a pregnant woman. The conclusion that will plausibly be drawn by anyone presented with the situation of the violinist, as Thomson rightly supposed, is that the person in the example should have the right to unplug himself from the violinist, even though the violinist will die as a result. But since this source case is similar to the target case of a woman who is pregnant, the conclusion suggested in the target case is that a pregnant woman may terminate her pregnancy, even though the fetus will die as a result.

How the refined version of the basic scheme for argument from analogy applies to the violinist argument can be shown visually in Fig. 2.3.

There are many ways to support or attack this argument. Some might want to extend it further by claiming that it justifies abortion. However, this particular issue has been so widely and hotly disputed that it also turns on how the term "abortion" is defined. The pro-choice side defines it as removal of the fetus whereas the pro-life side defines it as the killing of a person. So there are all kinds of controversial counterargument moves surrounding this case, but this paper is not the place to comment on these. Nevertheless, the case can be used to illustrate how some types of arguments from analogy work, precisely because it is a powerful and clever argument, and probably the best-known use of argument from analogy in recent philosophy.

There are many ways to support or attack Thomson's argument in the huge literature it provoked, but that is not our subject here. All we need to observe is that CQ_2 is possibly the critical question that an audience who is not so enthusiastically pro-choice or pro-life would be most naturally inclined to raise. In the source case the violinist and the person to whom he was attached are presumed to be unrelated, while in the abortion case the woman and the fetus are arguably related. There is also another aspect of the argument to be careful about. Because it is true in the source case that the person in the example was kidnapped and so did nothing himself to cause the violinist to be attached to him, the argument from analogy is only applicable to cases where the woman had no choice about becoming pregnant, for example, cases of rape. This narrowing of the range of the argument detracts considerably for the weight of its support for the conclusion that abortion should be generally acceptable if a woman chooses it.

From a point of view of argumentation theory, the most interesting aspect of the example is how the notion of similarity in the similarity premise can be defined or analyzed. I have previously put forward a theory that provides an answer to this question, but before introducing it, let's go on to consider another very different but equally interesting kind of example.

2.3 The Second Scheme

The second scheme proposed to model analogical argument is the dominant one in the logic textbooks. It is advocated in the two most widely used logic textbooks. It treats the argument from analogy as an inductive form of argument that requires no reference to similarity. In this respect, it can be sharply contrasted with the first scheme.

Copi and Cohen (1990, p. 358) offer the example of a conjecture on whether the planets Saturn, Jupiter, Mars, Venus and Mercury, might have living creatures on them. This example is an old one that has been superseded by the advance of science, but it is at least clear enough to be used to try to grasp how Copi and Cohen's form of analogical argument is supposed to fit some more or less realistic case. The premises are the observations of similarities between these planets and earth. All these planets revolve around the sun, collect light from the sun, revolve around their axis, have a succession of day and night, and so forth. They all share all these characteristics with planet Earth. There are also certain respects in which they differ from Earth. Some of them revolve around their axis in a manner like Earth, while others do not. Some have moons, while others do not. According to the example, the conclusion drawn from these similarities, despite the differences, is that it is reasonable to think that these planets may, like Earth, exhibit the habitation of various orders of living creatures.

To represent the structure of argument from analogy in this example Copi and Cohen (1990, p. 360) offer the following form they call analogical argument.

Entities *a*, *b*, *c*, *d* all have the attributes *P* and *Q*.
a, *b*, *c* all have the attribute *R*.
Therefore *d* probably has the attribute *R*.

Copi and Cohen (1990, p. 357) state that arguments of this form are inductive, not deductive. They (pp. 363–365) offer six criteria for appraising analogical arguments. Four are worth mentioning here: the number of entities compared, the number of respects in which the things compared are said to be analogous, the number of disanalogies or points of differences between the entities compared and the entity in the conclusion, and whether the analogies are relevant.

Let's try to see how their form of argument fits their planets example. Start with the conclusion. Earth fits in for the variable *d*, and *R* means having habitation of living creatures, since the conclusion is the statement that Earth exhibits the habitation of various orders of living creatures. But that is not the conclusion. As noted above, the conclusion is the statement that it is reasonable to think that these other planets may, like Earth, exhibit the habitation of various orders of living creatures. How the form fits the example is unclear.

Hurley (2003, p. 469) offers the following structure to represent the form of argument from analogy.

> Entity *A* has attributes *a*, *b*, *c* and *z*.
> Entity *B* has attributes *a*, *b*, *c*.
> Therefore, entity *B* probably has *z* also.

This format of this structure for argument from analogy is different from the one offered by Copi and Cohen (1990), but the motivating idea behind it seems to be pretty much the same. Hurley (2003) also classifies argument from analogy as an inductive form of argument. Also in a manner quite similar to Copi and Cohen's approach, Hurley (2003, pp. 469–470) offers six criteria for appraising analogical arguments: (1) relevance of the similarities, (2) number of similarities, (3) nature and degree of disanalogy, (4) number of primary analogues, (5) diversity among the primary analogues, and (6) specificity of the conclusion.

Hurley (2003) illustrates these criteria using with a leading example. In this example a woman called Lucy is deciding on which new car to buy. She decides in favor of the Chevrolet because she wants good gas mileage and she has observed that her friend Tom has a new Chevrolet and it gets good gas mileage. But some other similarities might be irrelevant. Both cars have a padded steering wheel, vinyl upholstery, tinted windows and white paint. Additional similarities which would support the argument from analogy might include such things as the weight of the car, whether it has an aerodynamic body, and the kinds of tires that are on it. Differences between the two cars might be that Tom's car has overdrive but Lucy's does not, or that Lucy's car is equipped with a turbocharger and Tom's is not. The number of analogues might include additional cases known to Lucy. Three of her friends drive cars similar to Tom's and all three get good gas mileage. The factor of diversity among the cases cited is illustrated by the example of Lucy's four friends who all do their driving on level streets in a cautious manner that minimizes fuel consumption. The sixth criterion of specificity of the conclusion is less easy to explain, but what Hurley is telling us is that we have to pay attention to the way the conclusion is stated because a more specific conclusion will be harder to prove and easier to falsify than one that is less specific.

How Hurley's (2003) proposed form of the argument from analogy fits his example is clearer. The conclusion is the presumably the statement that if Lucy buys a Chevrolet, this car will get good gas mileage According to Hurley (2003, p. 470), Lucy's conclusion is that her car will get good gas mileage, but technically it is not her car until she buys it. The argument is also an instance of goal-directed decision-making on what to do under conditions of uncertainty. The argument supporting this conclusion is that Tom's Chevrolet (assumed to share many attributes with the one Lucy will buy), has the attribute of good gas mileage. The variable *B* represents the car Lucy is considering buying, and the variable *z* represents the attribute of getting good gas mileage. The example can then be expanded to take other Chevrolet owners in to account. If they get good mileage this evidence supports the argument from analogy. If there are some Chevrolets that do not get good gas mileage, this evidence undermines (weakens) the argument from analogy.

For purposes of ease of applicability to cases, I would say that Hurley's version is an improvement on Copi and Cohen's (1990). But the main thing we need take from these observations is that the two leading logic textbooks both present a fundamentally similar account of the form of the argument from analogy. Both have this same sort of underlying structure as arguments, which can be formulated succinctly as a rule of inference. To grasp the rule of inference begin with the instance of it in Hurley's example. If Lucy's car shares a set of properties with other Chevrolets, and the other Chevrolets also exhibit some new property not included in the original set, then Lucy's car is likely to have this new property as well. The general rule of inference can now be formulated as follows: if one designated entity shares a set of properties with other entities, and the other entities also exhibit some new property not included in the original set, the designated entity is likely, on a balance of considerations, to have this new property as well.

The most important thing to notice about this way of representing the logical form of argument from analogy is that it makes no reference to the notion of similarity. The textbook accounts make argument from analogy seem highly objective. It looks like it represents a type of argument that can be evaluated in a scientific and objective manner using inductive reasoning to count up the properties shared by a set of entities to provide positive evidence supporting the argument from analogy and subtract the negative evidence of entities that fail to share common properties. There is no need for students to ask embarrassing questions about similarity.

2.4 Weighing Factors Using the Second Scheme

Now we turn to the second scheme for argument from analogy. The problem with this scheme, as set forth in the standard textbook treatments, is that it is unclear in many respects how it fits real examples, and hence trying to apply schemes offered in the textbooks was somewhat confusing. Luckily this scheme has been formulated in a simpler way that is more useful. Guarini (2004, p. 161) offered a scheme for argument from analogy that he calls the core scheme, where *a* and *b* are individual objects.

Premise 1: *a* has features $f_1, f_2, \ldots, f_n$.
Premise 2: *b* has features $f_1, f_2, \ldots, f_n$.
Conclusion: *a* and *b* should be treated or classified in the same way with respect to $f_1, f_2, \ldots, f_n$.

It would seem plausible that the features $f_1, f_2, \ldots, f_n$ can be treated as representing the factors that were discussed above in relating case-based reasoning to the second scheme. The Chevrolet case we looked at from Hurley showed how the second scheme is applied to cases by identifying pro and contra factors, factors in which the two cases at issue are similar or different. In the discussion above we already identified the rule underlying this scheme. The rule basically states that the argument from analogy is supported by factors both cases share, but at the same time the argument from analogy is undermined by factors that both cases fail to share. This rule is fine as far as it goes, but the problem is that it is not just counting up of the factors that make the argument from analogy weaker or stronger. In addition some level of importance or weight has to be attached to each factor. In case-based reasoning, the more a factor is "on point" (relevant), the greater weight it carries. Any factor that is irrelevant carries no weight.

The methods of evaluating an argument from analogy in standard case-based reasoning (CBR) uses respects in which two cases are similar or different called dimensions and factors. The HYPO system (Ashley 2006) uses dimensions. A dimension is a relevant aspect of the case that can take a range of values that move along the scale with values that support one side on a disputed issue at one end and the opposed party at the other end. CATO is a simpler CBR system (Aleven 1997) that uses factors.

Factors in Hurley's (2003) case of Lucy buying the car would include the following: the model of car, the size of the motor, having overdrive, having a turbocharger, the weight of the car, what kinds of tires are on the car, having a padded steering wheel, having tinted windows, and paint color. Some factors are relevant while others are not. Factors can also be seen as arguments favoring one side or the other in relation to the issue being disputed. Having more relevant factors in common between the source case and the target case supports the argument from analogy. Having more relevant factors not in common between the source case and the target case detracts from the argument from analogy.

Factors can also be seen as arguments favoring one side or the other in relation to the issue being disputed. On this approach, argument from analogy is seen as a defeasible form of argument in which pro factors represents similarities that support the argument while con factors represent dissimilarities undermine or detract from the argument. Typically in argument from analogy some factors support the argument, while other factors undermine it. Then to weigh the strength of the argument from analogy, we have to weigh the pro factors against the con factors. To do this numerically we have to attach a positive or negative number to each factor providing a measure of how relevant that factor is one way or the other. If we could use numbers of this sort to calculate the strength of an argument from analogy, the argument could rightly be classified as inductive, as they advocate. But if this numerical approach does not seem promising, there is also another approach. On this approach, argument from analogy can be seen as dialectical.

Typically, in this kind of format, we have an argument from analogy that supports a claim A made by one side, and then on the other side an opposed argument from analogy that supports claim not-A. To comparatively weigh up the strength of the one argument as compared to the strength of the opposed argument, we have to bring in factors that identify the respects in which one case is similar to the other, and have some device for estimating how similar one is to the other by attaching weights to similarity. But there is always the problem of how misleading it might be to attach numbers to the weight of importance each factor should have in a given case. There may be a way we can use argumentation methods to solve this problem however. We can get a clue how it should work by looking at CBR.

HYPO evaluates arguments from analogy in a three-step method called three-ply argumentation (Ashley 1988, p. 206), which can also be modeled as a series of moves in a formal dialogue. At the first move, the proponent puts forward an argument from analogy by finding a comparable past case in which the outcome closely matches that of the proponent's thesis because the two cases share one or more factors. At the second move, the respondent can reply to the original argument from analogy in one of the following ways, corresponding to critical questions matching the scheme for argument from analogy. She can reply by finding a counter-analogy, a past case that matches the current case but which has the opposite outcome. Another reply is to "distinguish" the case (as this move often called) by pointing to factors present in the new case that are absent in the previous one. At the third move, the proponent can reply in one of several ways. These might include distinguishing counterexamples, pointing out additional factors, or citing other cases showing that the respondent's attack does not really rebut his argument from analogy. The three-ply argumentation could be used to effectively set up the pre and post conditions for a formal dialogue model of a critical discussion in which one type of move is the bringing forth of an argument from analogy by citing factors common to the source case and the target case, and another type of move allows an appropriate critical response of the kinds outlined above.

2.5 The Silkwood Case

The next example is a use of argument from analogy by attorney Gerry Spence in the case of Silkwood v. Kerr-McGee Corporation. Karen Silkwood was a technician who had the job of grinding and polishing plutonium pins used to make fuel rods for nuclear reactors. She was active in union activities and had investigated health and safety issues at the plant. She had testified before an atomic energy commission that Kerr-McGee had violated safety regulations. Tests in 1974 showed that she that she had been exposed to dangerously high levels of plutonium radiation. High levels of radioactive contamination were found in her apartment. After she died from radiation poisoning, her father brought an action against Kerr-McGee in which the Corporation was held to be at fault for her death on the basis of strict liability. According to strict liability law, a person can be held accountable for the harmful consequences of some dangerous activity he was engaged in, without having to prove that he was aware of or intended the outcome, or even that he was negligent. The standard example is that if the zookeeper has a dangerous lion in a cage, if the lion escapes and causes harm to some person, the zookeeper is strictly liable for the harm that was caused.

Spence's closing argument in the case used the analogy of the escaping lion with great rhetorical effect on the jury. In his speech to the jury he emphasized and repeated this statement "If the lion got away, Kerr-McGee has to pay" (Lief et al. 1998, p. 129).

> Some guy brought an old lion on his ground, and he put it in a cage—and lions are dangerous—and through no negligence of his own through no fault of his own, the lion got away. Nobody knew how—like in this case, "nobody knew how". And, the lion went out and he ate up some people—and they sued the man. And they said, you know: "Pay. It was your lion, and he got away". And the man says: "But I did everything in my power—I had a good cage—had a lock on the door—I did everything that I could—I had security—I had trained people watching the lion—and it isn't my fault that he got away". Why should we punish him? They said: "We have to punish him—we have to punish you—you have to pay". You have to pay because it was your lion—unless the person who was hurt let the lion out himself.

In this instance Spence used the lion analogy during his closing argument, a part of the trial for summing up one's argument in a case. In his opening statement, Spence had also used the example of the escaping lion to illustrate to the jury how strict liability works, showing them how cases of this kind had originated in English common law. In his closing argument, he was using the same argument about the lion over again with great rhetorical effect. Spence's argument in this famous case has been said to be "as fine a closing argument as has ever been delivered in an American courtroom" (Lief et al. 1998, pp. 123–124).

Spence was using an analogy to compare what happened in the Silkwood case to what happened in the lion example that is described in simple and graphic terms. The lion example is the source case in the argument from analogy. Spence used the example to illustrate that strict liability law would hold the lion owner responsible for the harm that took place when the lion attacked some innocent person and injured her, even though the lion keeper had taken great care to have proper security, including trained people watching the animal. The target case is similar to the source case. The plutonium escaped from Silkwood's workplace, so to speak, and caused harm to her, and this sequence of events is similar to the ones in the lion case. Therefore all Spence had to prove is that Karen Silkwood was harmed by the plutonium. In his summary argument, Spence reminds the jury that this claim has been proved during the trial by the evidence brought forward, and that there is no need to repeat the facts that were used to prove it. All that needs to be proved, Spence maintains, in parallel with the lion case, is that the plutonium got away and that Karen Silkwood was damaged. This argument was a rhetorically powerful one. It persuaded the jury to find the Kerr-McGee Corporation liable for over ten million dollars.

In this case, the argument from analogy does all the work. The problem is to grasp how it does that. As a first attempt, we can visualize the argument as shown in Fig. 2.4.

To get a clue how Spence's argument in the Silkwood case could be represented using the scheme for argument from analogy, we need to recall how in section 1 the argument from analogy was described as a two-step argument from the base

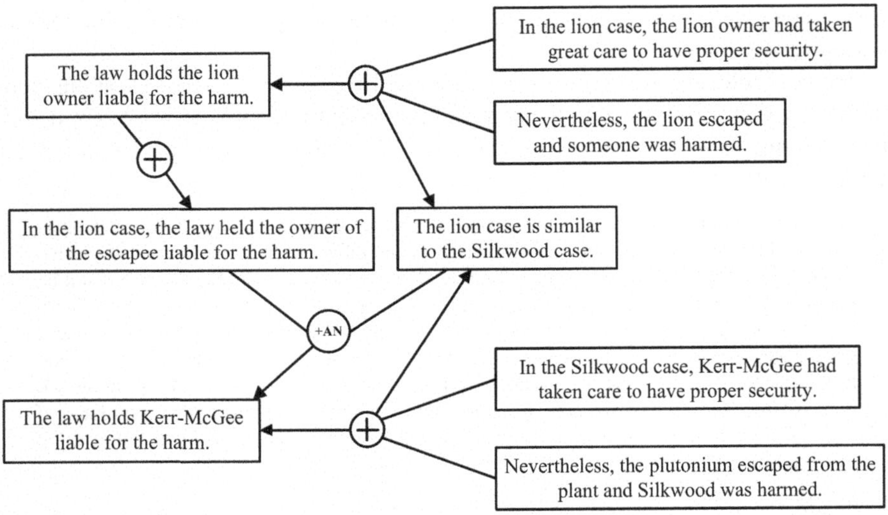

Fig. 2.4 How the source case supports the argument of the target case

premise to a derived premise, and from there to a conclusion. Using this scheme, argument from analogy represents a two-step type of argument. This two-step configuration is shown in Fig. 2.4. At the top the lion argument is shown, representing the source case. At the bottom the Silkwood case is shown, representing the target case. In the middle, an argument from analogy goes from a premise derived from the conclusion of the source case, along with the similarity premise, to the ultimate conclusion that the law holds Kerr-McGee liable. In the source case, as well as the target case, the argument is also at taken to support the similarity premise of the argument from analogy.

This structure is a rather complicated one, however, and not very helpful in giving us a clear and easily understandable analysis of how the argument from analogy works in transferring evidence from the source case to the target case. Hence we need to look for another method of modeling structure of the argument from analogy in the Silkwood case. It is a simple and powerful argument, and that is part of what accounts for its rhetorical success when used by Spence. But we still haven't been able to model the structure of that simple and powerful argument in a satisfactory way. So now we turn to an altogether different approach.

2.6 Scripts and Similarity

The first scheme is most markedly different from the second one in that it had a premise stating that one case is similar to another. The main problem with applying the first scheme to any realistic examples of arguments from analogy is to define the notion of similarity. There can be different kinds of similarity, but there is a way of defining one kind that can be shown to be important in building a method for evaluating arguments from analogy.

The notion of a script has been around for a while in artificial intelligence (Schank and Abelson 1977). According to the theory of scripts put forward here, a script is defined as a sequence of states where one state follows naturally from another so that a sequence of states can be chained together. The scripts we are concerned with in this paper are comparable to sequences of actions of the kind studied in the branch of philosophy called action theory. An example is the following sequence: Bob swings his golf club, he hits a golf ball, the golf ball flies through the air, the golf ball lands on the grass, the golf ball rolls towards the cup, the golf ball stops at a point six inches short of the cup. We can see from the example that each state in the sequence is represented as a proposition in which an agent carries out an action. All of us understand that in order for the sequence to be comprehensible the propositions fall naturally into a certain ordering so that it can be established by a participant in an argument using common knowledge what that ordering is. A script can be defined as a set of states and a set of so-called links. A script in this sense is (1) a finite sequence of states, S_1, S_2,…,S_n, and a set of links, L_1, L_2,.., L_n, joining each state to the one before and one after it, excluding only the first state L_1 and the last state, L_n, (2) such that it is clear to participants in an argument which is the first member of the sequence, which is the last member of the sequence, and for any member of the sequence between the first and the last member, which is the one before and the one after it. The ordering is not necessarily a temporal one, but it often is, and it is not necessarily a causal one but it often is. Links can be of different kinds, so that the sequence is not defined by any one kind of link. Rather the sequence is defined by the way it hangs together in common knowledge we all have about the way things can be normally expected to go in a kind of situation familiar to us from past experiences.

A sequence of this sort is often called a story or narrative. Pennington and Hastie (1992, 1993) studied many examples to show how juries in trials use story structures to organize and interpret evidence in a legal case at trial, enabling them to make sense of the evidence as a whole by organizing it into a mental representation. Stories are different from argumentation schemes, but they are often based on argumentation schemes, especially the scheme for practical reasoning. In practical reasoning an agent has a goal, and sees that carrying out an action would be a means to realize the goal. For this reason the agent concludes that it ought practically speaking to carry out the action. This kind of reasoning is very common in legal cases, for example in criminal cases where an action is presumed to have a goal.

Bex (2011) built a hybrid theory of reasoning with stories to reconstruct complex networks of evidence in criminal cases. His theory is called a hybrid system because it combines story-based explanations with arguments. One feature of it is that evidence in the form of arguments can support parts of an explanation that can be modeled with a script. Another aspect of Bex's theory that will be applied here is that something called a story scheme can be derived from the events in a script through a process of applying abstractions. By this means a script that links together

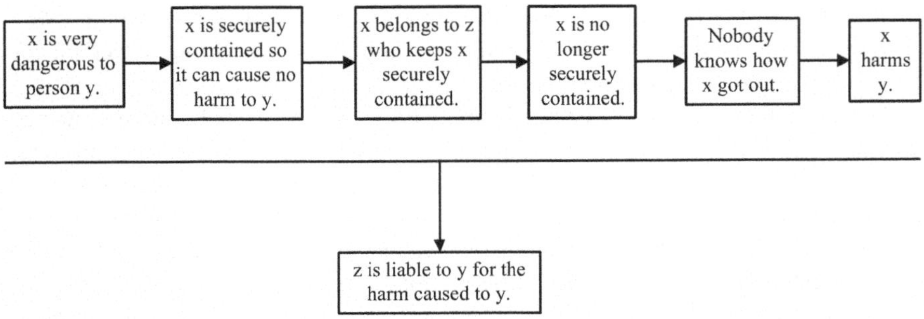

Fig.2.5 Story scheme for Spence's argument from analogy in the Silkwood case

a sequence of events or actions described in the story can also be represented at a more abstract level by means of a story scheme. Bex and Prakken (2010) have shown how stories can be investigated and evaluated in a formal dialogue game.

The device of the story scheme can be applied to Spence's argument from analogy in the Silkwood case to map the sequence in the source case to the sequence in the target case. If we put the lion in for x, the person who was injured in for y, and the lion owner in for z, we get the story of the lion that escaped and attacked the person who was harmed. But we can also fill in the variables as shown in Fig. 2.5, and then we get the Silkwood story. It is this abstract story scheme that shows how the target case is similar to the source case in the most significant respect. The script in the two cases can be seen to be similar by the audience (in this instance, the jury), and because of their common knowledge of the way things generally work, they are impressed by the analogy and draw the conclusion that Spence wants them to.

A notion of similarity that can be used to model many cases of argument from analogy can be modeled using this hybrid theory of scripts (Walton 2012). Gerry Spence's argument from analogy in his closing argument in the Silkwood case can be used as an illustration.

If we look along the middle row of Fig. 2.6, we see this story in the Silkwood case instantiated as an instance of the story scheme shown in Fig. 2.5. While the story scheme shown in Fig. 2.5 is an abstract sequence, the Silkwood story shown along the middle row of Fig. 2.6 represents the actual sequence of events representing the story in the case. To show how the similarity between the two cases is modeled, we could also make a figure of the similar story in the lion case: the lion is very dangerous, the lion was securely contained so it could cause no harm, the lion belong to the lion owner who kept it securely contained, the lion was no longer securely contained, nobody knows how the lion got out, a person was harmed by the lion after it escaped. What explains the similarity is that both the sequence of events in the lion case and in the Silkwood case is the abstract story scheme shown in Fig. 2.5.

It could be stressed that what is especially interesting here is that the matching of the two stories shows that the similarity between the two cases holds not just because each state in the one case matches a comparable state in the other case. Over

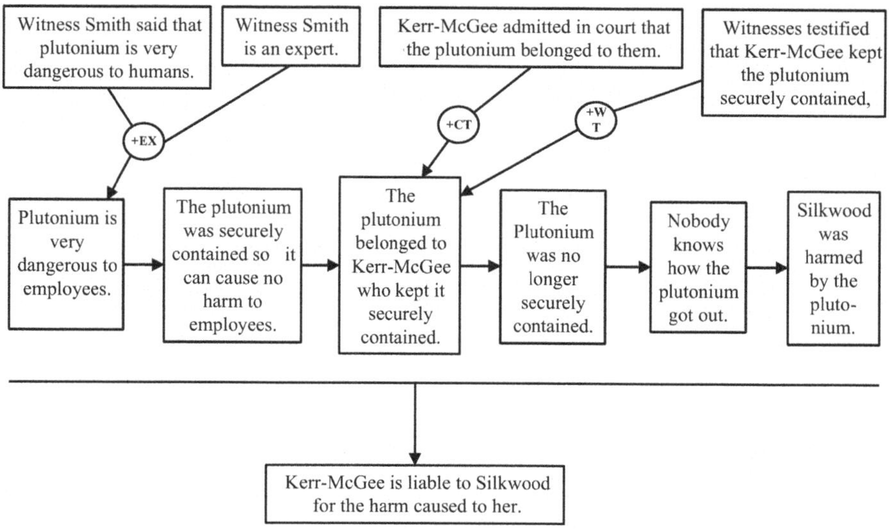

Fig. 2.6 The Silkwood case modeled as a story with evidential backing

and above this matching of single states, the matching of two stories represents the kind of similarity that supports an argument from analogy because it is the same story scheme applicable to both cases that makes the one case similar to the other in the most important respect.

There are some other aspects shown in Fig. 2.6 that are also important to comment on. One is the conclusion drawn from the sequence of states shown in the middle row. This conclusion is the proposition that Kerr-McGee is liable to Silkwood for the harm caused to her. According to the theory advocated here, this conclusion is the one drawn from the sequence of states shown above it. Another important aspect of Fig. 2.6 is that four statements appear in text boxes along the top row of the diagram, displaying three arguments that are used as evidence to support some of the elements in the sequence of propositions in the middle row. In each case the name of the argumentation scheme is shown in the node of the argument. The argument on the left is a pro argument from expert opinion. The argument in the middle is a pro argument from commitment. The argument on the right is a pro argument from witness testimony.

Thus we can see that Fig. 2.6 displays the five characteristic elements of the theory of similarity put forward. The first one is that there is a sequence of propositions (a set of states and links joining them), that makes up the story in the target case, and is an instance of a story scheme. The second one is that there is a conclusion drawn from the story. The third one is that evidence in the form of arguments can be used to support the elements of the story, make it more plausible. The fourth one is that the story in the target case is an instance of an abstract story scheme. The fifth one is that the story in the source case fits the same story scheme.

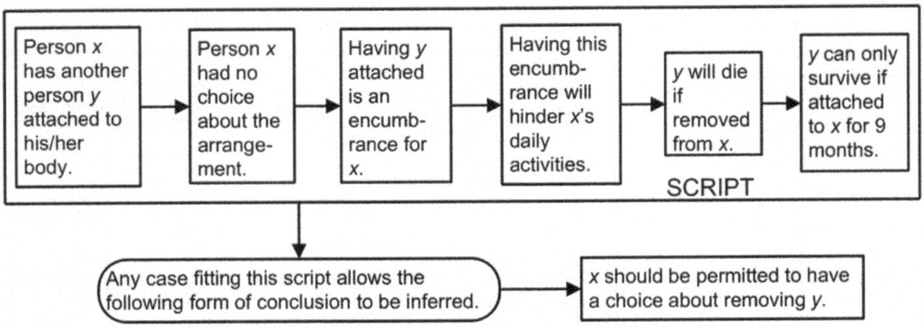

Fig. 2.7 The story scheme supporting the argument from analogy of the violinist case

2.7 Conclusions

The solution to the problem is to combine the two argumentation schemes for argument from analogy. The first scheme can be applied to a text to identify an argument from analogy and explain its initial impact. The second scheme allows for deeper analysis and evaluation of the argument by weighing the pro against the con factors.

The first scheme is simple enough. It simply says that if two cases are similar, and a particular conclusion can be drawn in the first case, then the same conclusion (or a comparable one) can be drawn in the second case. That conditional represents the rule of inference (the so-called warrant) behind the first scheme. The problem with the first scheme was to define the notion of similarity. Above a script-based model of how to represent similarity was presented and illustrated using the argument from analogy put forward by Gerry Spence in Silkwood case.

Now we can see how the same script-based theory of similarity can also be applied to the violinist case. Figure 2.7 shows how the abstract story script that displays the similarity between the case of the violinist and the case of the justification of abortion leads to the abstract conclusion that is applicable to both cases.

What the diagram in Fig. 2.7 shows in an abstract way is the similarity underlying the two cases that is the basis of the argument from analogy from the source case to the target case. The story scheme representing the similarity in an abstract manner supports the similarity premise of the basic argumentation scheme for argument from analogy.

As shown in Sect. 4, applying the second scheme requires a three-ply case-based dialogue system. How would such a formal dialogue model solve the problem of assigning weights to the factors in an argument from analogy without running afoul of the problem of assigning numerical weights to each factor that might be arbitrary? The solution advocated here is to do this in the normal way we are familiar with in formal dialogue models of argumentation. The claim that a factor is present in a given case, or is not present in a given case, or the claim that the factor is important in deciding the outcome of the case, or is not, can be evaluated by examining the details of the case, or the pair of cases at issue. Such a procedure can be used to see how the arguments in the case support or undermine these claims. The method that CBR uses to weigh factors is to place values on them representing the extent to which factor is "on point". To be on point essentially means that the factor is relevant in relation to the issue being disputed. What this observation reveals is that ultimately CBR depends on an analysis of the notion of relevance. But the best way to model relevance is to use a formal model of the critical discussion requiring that a conflict of opinions is identified at the opening stage. It is this initial conflict of opinions that determines whether a given argument is relevant or not, and it can also be used to determine whether a factor in an argument from analogy is on point or not.

This project can be carried out formally in a number of ways. One way would be to use a formal computational system such as the Carneades Argumentation System (CAS), a three-valued system in which premises and conclusions are assigned one of the following three values: (in) accepted, (out) rejected, or (neither in nor out) stated but not accepted (Gordon 2010). CAS has an opening stage, an argumentation stage and a closing stage (Gordon et al. 2007). Relevance of the kind discussed above can be modeled in CAS or comparable knowledge-based argumentation systems. Modeling the evaluation of arguments from analogy in this way has not yet been carried out in any formal dialectical model, but the research project of constructing such a model is within the reach of the current technology of formal dialogue systems. Such a project, at any rate, presents us with an alternative to the Bayesian proposal of treating argument from analogy as an inductive form of argument that can be evaluated using numerical probability values.

Acknowledgements The author would like to thank the Social Sciences and Humanities Research Council of Canada for support of this work by Insight Grant 435-2012-0104.

References

Aleven, V. 1997. Teaching case based argumentation through an example and models. PhD diss., University of Pittsburgh, Pittsburgh, Pennsylvania.

Ashley, K. 1988. Arguing by analogy in law: A case-based model. In *Analogical reasoning,* ed. D. H. Helman, 205–224. Dordrecht: Kluwer Academic Publishers.

Ashley, K. 2006. Case-based reasoning. In *Information technology and lawyers,* eds. A. R. Lodder and A. Oskamp, 23–60. Berlin: Springer.

Bex, F. 2011. *Arguments, stories and criminal evidence: A formal hybrid theory*. Dordrecht: Springer.

Bex, F., and H. Prakken. 2010. Investigating stories in a formal dialogue game. In *Computational models of argument: Proceedings of COMMA 2008,* eds. P. Besnard, S. Doutre and A. Hunter, 3–84. Amsterdam: IOS press.

Copi, I. M., and C. Cohen, C. 1990. *Introduction to logic*. 8th ed. New York: Macmillan. (First published 1953).

Gordon, T. F. 2010. An overview of the Carneades argumentation support system. In *Dialectics, dialogue and argumentation,* eds. C. Reed and C. W. Tindale, 145–156. London: College Publications.

Gordon, T. F., H. Prakken, and D. Walton 2007. The Carneades model of argument and burden of proof. *Artificial Intelligence* 171:875–896.
Guarini, M. 2004. A defense of non-deductive reconstructions of analogical arguments. *Informal Logic* 24:153–168.
Guarini, M., S. P. Smith, and A. Moldovan. 2009. Resources for research on analogy: A multi-disciplinary guide. *Informal Logic* 29 (2): 84–197.
Hurley, P. J. 2003. *A concise introduction to logic*. Belmont: Wadsworth.
Kienpointner, M. 2012. When figurative analogies fail: Fallacious uses of arguments from analogy. In *Topical themes in argumentation theory: Twenty exploratory studies,* eds. F. H. van Eemeren and B. Garssen, 111–126. Dordrecht: Springer.
Lief, M. S., M. Caldwell, and B. Bryce. 1998. *Ladies and gentlemen of the jury. Greatest closing arguments in modern law*. New York: Scribner.
Pennington, N., and R. Hastie, 1992. Explaining the evidence: Tests of the story model for juror decision-making. *Journal of Personality and Social Psychology* 62(2): 189–206.
Pennington, N., and R. Hastie. 1993. The story model for juror decision making. In *Inside the juror. The psychology of juror decision making,* ed. R. Hastie, 192–221. Cambridge: Cambridge University Press.
Schank, R. C., and R. P. Abelson. 1977. *Scripts, plans, goals and understanding*. Hillsdale: Erlbaum.
Thomson, J. 1971. A defense of abortion. *Philosophy and Public Affairs* 1 (1): 47–66.
Walton, D. 2006. *Fundamentals of critical argumentation*. Cambridge: Cambridge University Press.
Walton, D. 2010. Similarity, precedent and argument from analogy. *Artificial Intelligence and Law* 18 (3): 217–246.
Walton, D. 2012. Similarity in arguments from analogy. *Informal Logic* 32 (2): 190–218.
Walton, D., C. Reed, and F. Macagno. 2008. *Argumentation schemes*. Cambridge: Cambridge University Press.

Chapter 3
Argumentation by Analogy in Stereotypical Argumentative Patterns

Frans H. van Eemeren and Bart Garssen

3.1 From Ideal Model of Critical Discussion to Situated Argumentative Discourse

Over the past decades the pragma-dialectical theory of argumentation has been developed systematically from the abstract level of an ideal model of a critical discussion to the concrete reality of situated argumentative discourse. After van Eemeren and Grootendorst (1984, 2004) introduced the model of a critical discussion and the rules for conducting a critical discussion in the early 1980s, step by step more and more properties of actual argumentative discourse have been taken into account. The step that eventually immersed the pragma-dialectical theory fully in the nitty-gritty of real-life argumentative practice was taken in the late 1990s when van Eemeren and Houtlosser (2002) included accounting for the "strategic design" of argumentative discourse in the theorizing. The "extended" version of the pragma-dialectical theory was in 2010 expounded by van Eemeren in the monograph *Strategic Maneuvering in Argumentative Discourse.*

Strategic manoeuvring does not take part in an idealized critical discussion but in the multi-varied communicative practices that have developed in the various communicative domains. In the extended pragma-dialectical theory the institutionally motivated conventionalization of these communicative practices is therefore duly taken into account (van Eemeren 2010, pp. 129–162). Because these practices have been established in specific *communicative activity types*, which are characterized by the way in which they have been conventionalized, these communicative activity types constitute the institutional macro-context in which argumentative discourse is to be examined. The conventionalization of an activity type may be formalized, as is

F. H. van Eemeren (✉) · B. Garssen
Department of Speech Communication, Argumentation Theory and Rhetoric,
University of Amsterdam, Amsterdam, The Netherlands
e-mail: F.H.vanEemeren@uva.nl

B. Garssen
e-mail: B.J.Garssen@uva.nl

H. J. Ribeiro (ed.), *Systematic Approaches to Argument by Analogy,*
Argumentation Library 25, DOI 10.1007/978-3-319-06334-8_3,

generally the case in the legal domain, but the conventionalization may also be less formal or even informal, as is customary in the political and interpersonal domains.

The *institutional point* of a communicative activity type, which defines its rationale, reflects the institutional exigency in response to which an activity type has come into being and the conventionalization of the communicative activity type is instrumental in realizing the institutional point. The genres of communicative activity used to realize the institutional points of the various communicative activity types vary from "adjudication" and "deliberation" to "disputation" and "communion-seeking." In the strictly conventionalized communicative activity types of the legal domain, for instance, adjudication is used to maintain justice by getting to legal verdicts; in the less strictly conventionalized communicative activity types of the political domain deliberation is used to make the political system operate by debating policy decisions; in the inter-subjectively conventionalized communicative activity types of the academic domain disputation is used to bring about intellectual progress by testing scientific claims; and in the informally conventionalized communicative activity types of the interpersonal domain communion-seeking is used to confirm interpersonal relationships by creating a shared background of mutually accepted opinions. A great many communicative activity types are "hybrids", whose conventionalization combines the use of several genres of communicative activity. A political interview, for example, prototypically combines deliberation with dissemination of information to stimulate the development of well-informed views in the audience.

3.2 The Impact of Institutional Preconditions on Argumentative Discourse

The incorporation of the macro-contextual dimension of the communicative activity types in the theorizing has led pragma-dialecticians to research a great many argumentative practices in a variety of communicative domains. The primary aim of this research is to find out in what ways the possibilities for strategic manoeuvring are in these domains determined by extrinsic institutional constraints ensuing from the conventionalization of the communicative activity types concerned. These extrinsic constraints are imposed on the discourse by the way in which the conventionalization of the discourse has been made instrumental for realizing the institutional point of the communicative activity type and the institutional aims that go with it. Because the extrinsic constraints have an effect on the kind of argumentative moves that may be made in the communicative activity type, they constitute *institutional preconditions* for strategic manoeuvring in the argumentative practice concerned.

The communicative activity types that have come into being in the various communicative domains to comply with the exigencies of the institutional macro-context revolve around different kinds of differences of opinion. These differences of opinion vary from formally defined disputes in the legal domain and mixed disagreements in the political domain to dissent among peers in the academic domain and conflicts of opinion in the interpersonal domain. The standpoints at issue may vary from an evaluative standpoint in a juridical verdict or a prescriptive standpoint in a policy statement to a descriptive standpoint in a scientific claim or a hybrid standpoint combining descriptive, evaluative and prescriptive elements in a personal opinion. Due to the specific nature of what is at stake in the communicative activity types in a certain communicative domain, more often than not the 'initial situation' that is described in an *argumentative characterization* of the communicative activity types associated with that particular communicative domain will be characterized by the immanence of a *specific kind of difference of opinion* in which a *specific type of standpoint* is at issue.[1]

In combination with the specific starting points that are characteristic of a communicative activity type or cluster of communicative activity types, the specific characteristics of the initial situation will lead to specific kinds of argumentative exchanges in the empirical counterpart of the argumentation stage of a critical discussion and specific kinds of outcome. The kinds of argumentative exchanges that will develop, or are likely to develop, in the various kinds of communicative activity types are to some extent dependent on the exigencies of the institutional macro-context in which they take place. The kind of argumentative exchange that will develop in a legal activity type, for instance, will usually differ considerably from the kind of argumentative exchanges developing in a political, an academic or an interpersonal activity type. The differences are not only caused by the differences between the kind of difference of opinion to which they respond, the types of standpoints at issue, and the procedural and material starting points, but also by the specific requirements pertaining in a certain communicative domain to the way in which in a communicative activity type the exchange between argumentation and criticism is to take place and the kinds of outcome that are allowed to be reached.

Viewed against this background, in the communicative activity types associated with a particular communicative domain different types of argumentation will be instrumental in reaching the kind of outcome that is aimed for than in communicative activity types in a different domain. In an argumentative exchange taking place in a communicative activity type in the legal domain, for instance, the use of "analogy" argumentation may be a prototypical way to legitimize the legal verdict that is the outcome of the exchange; in an argumentative exchange in a communicative activity type in the political domain the use of "pragmatic" argumentation may be a prototypical way to defend a policy standpoint; in an argumentative exchange taking place in a communicative activity type in the academic domain the use of "causal" argumentation may be a prototypical way to establish the truth of a scientific claim; and in an exchange taking place in a communicative activity type in the interpersonal domain the use of "symptomatic" argumentation may be a prototypical way to justify a personal opinion. If these expectations are realistic, and a certain estimate applies indeed to the particular case concerned, in the communicative activity types associated with a specific communicative domain, in the empirical

[1] What is involved in characterizing a communicative activity type argumentatively is explained in van Eemeren (2010, pp. 146–151).

counterpart of the argumentation stage specific types of argumentation may be expected and, depending on the kind of argument scheme used in the main argumentation in support of the standpoint at issue and the critical questions pertaining to that particular scheme, specific kinds of critical reactions may be expected that need to be anticipated or responded to.[2]

Taking the institutional preconditions and the critical reactions that are pertinent in the case concerned into account in conducting the argumentative exchange will result in the creation of a specific *argumentative pattern* in the discourse.[3] Such an argumentative pattern is characterized by a constellation of argumentative moves in which in defense of a particular type of standpoint a particular argument scheme or combination of argument schemes is used in a particular kind of argumentation structure to deal with a particular kind of difference of opinion (van Eemeren 2013).[4] Although certain argumentative patterns that occur may well be incidental, argumentative patterns can be typical of the way in which argumentative discourse is generally conducted in a specific communicative activity type or cluster of communicative activity types.[5] The latter is in principle the case if the argumentative pattern concerned is immediately connected with the institutional preconditions for strategic manoeuvring pertaining to the communicative activity type that is examined. Such "stereotypical" argumentative patterns, whose occurrence can be explained by the institutional preconditions prevailing in the communicative activity types in which they occur, are currently of particular interest to pragma-dialectical researchers focusing on determining the context-dependency of argumentative discourse.[6]

---

[2] The critical questions that are relevant here need to be envisaged in the specification that is pertinent to the implementation of the argument scheme concerned in the specific macro-context of the communicative activity type in which the argumentation is put forward.

[3] The argumentative patterns that can be observed in argumentative discourse can be viewed as empirical analogues of the patterns of analytically relevant moves in a critical discussion that are on theoretical grounds distinguished in dialectical profiles. For the notion of dialectical profile see van Eemeren (2010, pp. 98–100).

[4] If an argument in defense of a standpoint is expected not to be accepted immediately, more arguments needs to be advanced, which leads to an argumentative pattern with a complex argumentation structure.

[5] The underlying assumption here is that in the argumentation stage protagonists may in principle be supposed to aim for making the strongest case in the macro-context concerned by trying to advance a combination of reasons that will satisfy the antagonist by leaving no critical doubts unanswered. In the process they may be expected to exploit the argument schemes they consider most effective in the situation at hand and to use all multiple, coordinative and subordinative argumentation that is necessary to respond to the critical reactions the antagonist may be expected to come up with.

[6] The stereotypical argumentative patterns pragma-dialecticians are interested in result from the use of certain modes of strategic manoeuvring instrumental in reaching the institutional point in accordance with the institutional preconditions of the communicative activity type and responding to the exigencies of the communicative domain.

Argumentative patterns that can be explained with the help of the institutional preconditions pertaining to the communicative activity types in which they occur can be considered stereotypical argumentative patterns. The term stereotypical is then used in the sense of characteristic: stereotypical argumentative patterns are patterns which are characteristic of a specific type of communicative activity. This means in this case that they are instrumental in realizing the institutional point of the activity type concerned. For this reason it is likely that they will occur regularly in this type of activity, but it does not necessarily mean that they occur frequently, let alone always. (If one considers the term stereotypical too closely connected with frequency of occurrence, it can be replaced by characteristic.) The frequency of occurrence of the argumentative patterns identified as stereotypical is to be determined in empirical follow-up research. In principle, no quantitative research is required to tell that certain patterns are stereotypical.

Pragma-dialectical research into strategic manoeuvring is currently aimed at detecting the regular patterns of standpoints, argument schemes and argumentation structures that are stereotypically activated in the various kinds of argumentative practices in the legal, political, medical, and academic domains to realize the institutional points of the communicative activity types concerned in agreement with their institutional conventionalization. The research concentrates on identifying and explaining the argumentative patterns coming about in specific communicative activity types or clusters of communicative activity types as a consequence of the institutional preconditions for strategic manoeuvring pertaining to these communicative activity types. We will make use of the qualitative method of analytic induction (see, for instance, Jackson, 1986). In disclosing through qualitative empirical research the argumentative patterns occurring in argumentative reality the researchers make use of the various theoretical instruments that have been made available in pragma-dialectics, including the typologies of standpoints, differences of opinions, argument schemes, and argumentation structures. The argumentative patterns as they manifest themselves in specific constellations of argumentative moves are described in terms of the categories that are distinguished in these typologies. Documenting the institutional diversification of argumentative practices systematically in this way not only provides insight in the proliferation of argumentative practices, but also paves the way for giving a more thorough theoretical account of the relationship between context-independency and context-dependency in argumentative discourse—which is the current focus of attention in the pragma-dialectical research program.

3.3 Argumentation by Analogy

Argumentation by analogy, also called *comparison argumentation,* is one of the three main categories that are distinguished in the pragma-dialectical typology of argument schemes. The other two are *causal argumentation* and *symptomatic argumentation.* The distinction between the three categories is that in each of them a different inferential principle is appealed to in order to bridge the gap between the reason advanced in support of the standpoint and the standpoint defended. In other words, each of the three categories of argument schemes motivates a specific kind of "transfer" of acceptability from the reason to the standpoint. Because of the different inferential principles that are involved, the use of the three categories of argument schemes calls for a different kind of evaluation in each case. When they are employed in argumentative discourse each of them instigates a different kind of dialectical testing procedure for the antagonist—or an outsider acting as an external judge—to establish whether the reason that has been advanced supports the standpoint in an adequate way. This difference between the dialectical routes that the various argument schemes initiate is in fact the rationale for distinguishing between them in pragma-dialectics.

The specific testing procedure instigated by the appeal to a particular inferential principle involves the use of certain critical questions that are systematically related to the inferential principle concerned. The general critical questions pertinent to a particular inferential principle apply to all specimens of argumentation belonging to argumentation of that type. In practice however each main type of argumentation comes in various subtypes, in which the relevant inferential principle is appealed to in a specific way. In each of these subtypes the general questions pertinent to the main type of argumentation will be implemented somewhat differently, depending on the specification of the inferential relationship concerned.

According to van Eemeren and Grootendorst (1992, p. 97), in analogy argumentation the argumentation is presented "as if there were a resemblance, an agreement, a likeness a parallel, a correspondence or some other kind of similarity between that which is stated in the argument and that which is stated in the standpoint." This type of argumentation can be generally characterized in the following way:

Y is true of X
because: Y is true of Z,
and: Z is comparable to X.

Argumentation by analogy is a type of argumentation that is widely used. With a few notable exceptions, such as the conduct of argumentative discourse in criminal lawsuits in the Netherlands, argumentation by analogy occurs in communicative activity types in virtually all communicative domains. In the political domain, for instance, its presence is striking in a great many speech events. Prototypical however is the use of argumentation by analogy in some of the communicative activity types in the legal domain where a verdict is pronounced. Its rationale in these cases is derived from the so-called *rule of justice*.

In communicative activity types in the legal domain in which a legal verdict is justified by making use of the communicative genre of adjudication an evaluative standpoint in the form of a legal judgment is made acceptable in view of the relevant juridical requirements while the institutional preconditions imposed on the justification process by the conventionalization of the communicative activity type concerned are duly taken into account. This means that in the process of justification the critical questions need to be responded to or anticipated that are pertinent to the kind of argumentation that is used—argumentation by analogy and other types of argumentation that may have been advanced. If the adequacy of the argumentation cannot be established by dealing in a satisfactory way with the relevant critical questions, the argumentation by analogy will not be effective and may even be fallacious—and the same applies to other types of argumentation.

Depending on—and therefore to some extent explained by—the institutional contextual demands prevailing in the communicative activity type concerned, the argumentative patterns that come into being when argumentation by analogy is used to justify a legal verdict may consist of a combination of analogy argumentation with other types of argumentation, such as authority argumentation or another subtype of symptomatic argumentation. As a consequence of such complications, in communicative practice the use of the argument scheme of analogy argumentation is often embedded in a specific pattern of argumentative moves. In explaining the occurrence of such an argumentative pattern, the institutional preconditions for strategic manoeuvring ensuing from the institutional point, conventionalization and extrinsic constraints of the communicative activity type concerned should be taken into account.

It is a distinctive feature of analogy argumentation that it can be instrumental in offering conclusive support of a standpoint only if the appropriateness of the comparison that is made is beyond doubt. If the appropriateness of the comparison is not obvious to some or to all of the addressees, its appropriateness needs to be motivated. When the latter happens, more or less automatically more complex argumentation, with a more complicated argumentation structure, will come into being as a result. Although the argumentation by analogy used in support of the standpoint is then one of its constituents, this complex argumentation is not argumentation by analogy *in toto*, let alone that the argumentative discourse as a whole can be described as analogy argumentation. As a consequence of such complications, in argumentative practice the use of the argument scheme of argumentation by analogy is—like the use of other argument schemes—more often than not embedded in a specific pattern of argumentative moves.

3.4 Descriptive Analogy

Two variants of analogy argumentation prominently represented in the various argumentative patterns in which analogy argumentation is embedded are "descriptive analogy" and "normative analogy" (Garssen 2009, p. 134). A typical characteristic of *descriptive* analogy argumentation is that both the standpoint that is defended and the reason that is advanced in its support are descriptive: in both propositions a certain state of affairs is expressed. The standpoint will in these cases invariably be a prediction (*Y will be the case*), a hypothetical prediction (*If X will be the case, then Y will be the case*), or a quasi-prediction predicting something about the past or the present instead of about the future (*At time t Y was to be expected*). This explains why the first kind of analogy argumentation is called "descriptive" analogy.

Situation referred to in the premise	Situation referred to in the standpoint
Relevant similarity 1	Relevant similarity 1
Relevant similarity 2	Relevant similarity 2
Similarity 3	[Similarity 3 extrapolated]

Fig. 3.1 Analogy argumentation as an extrapolation of properties

In descriptive analogy a comparison is made between the actual characteristics of one thing, person or situation and the actual characteristics of another thing, person or situation. This happens, for instance, in the following example:

(1) Camera surveillance in the centre of Amsterdam will be effective, because in London camera surveillance proved to be effective.

In this argumentation two things are compared which belong to the same class (London and Amsterdam are both cities). It is claimed that something will be the case in Amsterdam because it is already the case in London and Amsterdam is comparable to London.

It is assumed in this argumentation that there are a number of similarities directly relevant to safety between Amsterdam and London. Because of these similarities we have to take it that the property of London mentioned in the standpoint that camera surveillance is effective will also be shared by Amsterdam. In other words, the presence of the property that is discussed is "extrapolated" from the properties the two cities already share.

It is important to realize that these similarities are often not mentioned explicitly in the argumentation. In claiming that what is mentioned in the standpoint is similar to what is mentioned in the premise, the similarities are only assumed. However, as we shall see, the similarities often come into play in the evaluation of the analogy argumentation.

In this type of analogy argumentation the inferential principle of analogy is used in extrapolating a property from a list of commonalities. Because the two things, persons or situations compared have a series of properties in common, they are assumed to share also another property that is mentioned in the standpoint. In this sense this type of analogy argumentation, which others sometimes call *case by case reasoning*, involves an inductive process. Figure 3.1 provides a general characterization of this kind of analogy argumentation.[7]

The first step in the testing procedure for descriptive analogy argumentation is to ask whether the things, persons or situations compared in the argumentation are, in principle, comparable. If asked to do so, the protagonist is obliged to show that the things, persons or situations compared indeed belong to the same class. From then onwards the testing procedure can take different routes. Since the relevant similarities on which the extrapolation is based remain implicit, the antagonist may ask the protagonist to add to what has been said by mentioning the relevant similarities. The protagonist is then forced to provide additional argumentation in which one or more

[7] See Fearnside and Holther (1959, p. 23) for a similar representation of the internal organization of this variant of analogy argumentation.

relevant similarities are mentioned. The similarities to be mentioned are the properties that allow for the extrapolation step. Mentioning similarities can again lead to criticism from the antagonist because the similarities that are mentioned may not be recognized as actual similarities, or they may be seen as similarities which are not relevant to the issue at hand.

The antagonist can also criticize the argumentation by pointing at differences between the things, persons or situations that are compared. The protagonist is then forced to show either that these differences are not relevant or that the similarities outweigh the differences. In this way it is established in the testing procedure whether or not the intended extrapolation of characteristics is allowed. The more similarities there are, the more likely it is in principle that an extrapolation is successful.

It is important to emphasize that it is not enough to just point to similarities and differences: these similarities and differences should also be *relevant* to the standpoint that is defended by putting forward analogy argumentation. The question however of what exactly makes similarities relevant will generally be hard to answer. Crucial in this regard is the claim that is made in the standpoint that is defended. In our example the (descriptive) standpoint is that in Amsterdam camera surveillance will lead to more safety. Relevant factors in this case are all conditions necessary for upholding this causal claim. The commonality between Amsterdam and London that they are both capitals is not relevant here, since that is a fact that is not directly related to safety in the streets. Instead, in the case of this claim it may be an important fact that Amsterdam and London are both big cities.

These are the kind of issues that are pertinent to a continuation of the evaluation of argumentation that is part of the critical testing procedure for descriptive analogy argumentation. The question vital to the testing procedure for this type of analogy argumentation is whether the step of extrapolating properties is indeed acceptable to both parties.

3.5 Normative Analogy

In the second type of analogy argumentation, *normative* analogy, the principle of consistency plays a central role. In analogy argumentation of this kind it is claimed that a thing, situation, person, group or institution mentioned in the standpoint belongs to the same category as the person, group or institution mentioned in the reason that is advanced, and that this thing, situation, person, group or institution should be treated in the same way.

In analogy argumentation about people the principle of consistency is called "the rule of justice." According to the rule of justice, persons, groups of people and institutions which belong to the same category should be treated similarly. Just like in the descriptive variant of analogy argumentation, the arguer claims in this kind of analogy argumentation that what is mentioned in the standpoint is comparable to what is mentioned in the premise. This happens for instance in the following example:

(2) The employees in the administration department should get a salary raise because the sales persons in our firm also get a salary raise.

Normative analogy argumentation differs from descriptive analogy argumentation because in a normative analogy the use of the principle of consistency does not involve an extrapolation of characteristics. Here the central issue is whether the two things, groups, persons, etc. that are compared do really belong to the same category.

Another difference when compared with descriptive analogy argumentation is the fact that in normative analogy argumentation the standpoint is by definition normative in nature. Invariably, argumentation of this kind involves a call for consistent behaviour: the standpoint always contains a claim that for the sake of consistency a person, institution, thing, etc. should be treated in a certain way.[8]

Just like in the use of descriptive analogy argumentation, in using normative analogy argumentation it is presumed that there are similarities between what is mentioned in the standpoint that is defended and what is mentioned in the reason that is advanced. Again, these similarities are not mentioned in the premises that make up the analogy argumentation, but come up in the testing procedure. Although the critical questions that go with the two kinds of analogy argumentation are more or less identical, the dialectical testing procedure proceeds in the two cases in a different manner. A preliminarily step in testing normative analogy argumentation is, again, to establish whether what is mentioned in the standpoint that is defended is really comparable to what is mentioned in the reason that is advanced.[9] After this has been established, the antagonist can ask the protagonist to mention the similarities justifying the claim that the two persons, groups or institutions that are compared really belong to the same relevant category. In response, the protagonist is then forced to present additional argumentation. In case the antagonist points at differences showing that the two persons, groups or institutions compared do not belong to the same category, the protagonist's response has to make clear that the differences are not relevant or are outweighed by the similarities. Again, like in testing descriptive analogy argumentation, it has to be determined whether the similarities and differences playing a part in the argumentation are really relevant for the claim made in the standpoint.

Normative analogy argumentation shares some crucial characteristics with the form of reasoning that Govier (1987) calls *a priori* reasoning. In both cases some person, group or institution is prompted to act consistently: "You should do X, because in a similar situation you would also do X." According to Govier, it is an

[8] A special case of the normative analogy is the technique of refuting arguments that is called *parallel reasoning* (Juthe 2009). Parallel reasoning boils down to refuting in the case of two arguments which are structurally similar one of the arguments by showing that the other one is flawed.

[9] Even more basic is the question of whether there is in the discussion concerned intersubjective agreement about the use of the rule of justice. It is in principle possible that one of the parties refuses to agree with the use of this rule.

essential property of *a priori* reasoning that the example that is used in the comparison can be fictitious in the sense that the similar situation compared to does not necessarily exist.

An example of a comparison with a non-existing situation is the commonplace question pacifists are stereotypically faced with: "But you would use violence if your mother was attacked, wouldn't you?" The idea behind this example is that if it is admitted in the answer to the question that a person—imaginary or not—would be treated in a certain way, the answerer should admit that (real) persons belonging to the same category are to be treated in the same way.

Viewed from the perspective of a dialectical testing procedure, we are well-advised to distinguish clearly between the descriptive and the normative kinds of analogy argumentation. In both variants the inferential principle of comparison is appealed to, but the critical testing of the two kinds of argumentation differs. Although these two types of analogy argumentation may not necessarily be the only two variants, the frequency of their occurrence makes it worthwhile to pay special attention to them.

Another clarification that is needed to avoid misunderstandings in dealing with normative analogy argumentation concerns so-called *figurative* analogy, sometimes simply referred to as *analogy*. Although figurative analogy argumentation looks like normative analogy argumentation it is in fact quite a different means of persuasion. At first sight figurative analogy seems to have the same general argument scheme of analogy argumentation, but argumentation in which a figurative analogy is used should be treated differently (see Garssen 2009, pp. 137–139). The reason for this is that it is a distinctive feature of a figurative analogy that the elements that are being compared are situated on different levels of experience, stem from different "spheres," or are of a completely different kind. This is illustrated by the following example of a figurative analogy, mentioned by Hastings (1962), which President Truman put forward at the beginning of the Korea conflict in defense of his claim that the United States should strike immediately:

(3) The best time to meet the threat is in the beginning. It is easier to put out a fire in the beginning when it is small than after it has become a roaring blaze. (Hastings 1962, p. 114)

Fire and war belong to different classes of events, which makes it impossible to compare them directly. In this case however the similarities we have to look for are not so much between the concrete features of fire and war, but between the abstract relationship between what is said in the reason that is advanced and what is said in the standpoint that is defended. It is predicted that the war in Korea will become unmanageable if we do not act now and this is the reason why we should act now. Because, viewed literally, President Truman does not make a direct comparison between war and fire, the standard critical questions going with analogy argumentation (*Are there relevant similarities? Are there relevant differences?*) do not really apply. In fact, if we would require asking these questions in this form, no figurative analogy could stand the test. In the case of figurative analogy it would not be of much help either to amend the standard critical questions of analogy argumentation for application to figurative analogies.

Apparently figurative analogy does not involve a normal comparison but a comparison of the abstract relations within one situation and within another situation. Hence Hastings's characterization of the relationship as a "comparison of ratios." Perelman and Olbrechts-Tyteca (1969, p. 373) characterize the "resemblance of structures" that is at issue here as follows:

> *A* and *B* together, the terms to which the conclusion relates (…), we shall call the *theme*, and *C* and *D* together, the terms that serve to buttress the argument (…), we shall call the *phoros*.

This use of figurative analogy can be illustrated by means of a much-quoted argument put forward by President Lincoln in his reply to the National Union League on 9 June, 1864:

> (4) I have not permitted myself, gentleman, to conclude that I am the best man in the country: but I am reminded, in this connection, of a story of an old Dutch farmer who remarked to a companion once that "it was not best to swap horses while crossing a stream."

The figurative analogy in Lincoln's argument (I should not resign at this moment because one should not swap horses while crossing a stream) can be schematised as follows:

Standpoint: Theme (*A*—*B*): changing president—being in the midst of a war
Premise: Phoros (*C*—*D*): swapping horses—crossing a stream

What becomes clear in this schematization is that the two situations share only one similarity. In both cases the general rule "it is unwise to make important changes while being in a difficult situation" applies. Once this general rule is reconstructed it makes no sense to look for more similarities. This distinguishes the figurative analogy in a crucial way from both descriptive analogy and normative analogy, which always imply that there are a number of similarities.

Perelman and Olbrechts-Tyteca (1969, p. 374) stress the fact that the situation mentioned in the *phoros* (the premise or reason) is supposed to be better known than the situation mentioned in the *theme* (the standpoint): the *phoros* should clarify the structure of the theme. In other words, the general rule underlying the situations that are mentioned in the standpoint and the premise stands out in the *phoros*.

Figurative analogy argumentation is based on a *metaphorical* relation that serves as an indirect means of expressing a general rule which serves as a reason put forward in defense of the standpoint. After the reconstruction of the argument has taken place it becomes clear that in fact no analogy argumentation was used but another type of argumentation: argumentation based on a causal relation or symptomatic argumentation.

It is immediately clear that in idiomatic expressions of comparisons like "That is like throwing out the baby with the bathwater" no real argumentative comparison is made. In evaluating argumentation in which such an idiomatic expression is used it is ludicrous to ask the standard critical questions going with analogy argumentation, since the meaning of the proverb is something like "You should be careful not to lose the good parts of something when you get rid of the bad parts." Although the reconstruction of such idiomatic proverbs may be much easier, in principle less idiomatic figurative analogies can be reconstructed in the same kind of way.[10]

It is not so that it is inherent in figurative analogies that they are logically weak; they are weak in this respect only when they are treated as real analogy arguments. When properly reconstructed, what is presented as a figurative analogy can just as well prove to be compelling argumentation in a different way. When studying the use of analogy argumentation in argumentative patterns however, figurative analogy should be treated as something different from descriptive and normative analogy. In this essay we fully concentrate on argumentative patterns containing descriptive and normative analogy.

3.6 Analogy Argumentation Embedded in Argumentative Patterns

Let us now turn to the link between the occurrence of analogy argumentation and the argumentative patterns stereotypically displayed in argumentative discourse due to the institutional preconditions that need to be observed in specific communicative activity types. Generally speaking analogy argumentation typically occurs in argumentative patterns in two ways: it may be used to defend another type of argumentation and when it is used it may be defended itself by another type of argumentation. We will take a closer look at these two argumentative patterns involving analogy argumentation as they stereotypically occur in political argumentation, in particular in argumentation put forward in plenary debates in the European Parliament.

One way in which an argumentative pattern may come into being is when a specific reason which serves as a premise of an argument scheme that is used is defended in the discourse by means of argumentation that is based on another argument scheme. In this case the argumentative pattern consists of two arguments, the one defending the standpoint and the other defending the argument advanced in support of the standpoint. This means that the argumentative pattern displayed here is characterized by a combination of two different argument schemes that are by a subordinative argumentation structure connected with each other. In the case of analogy argumentation such an argumentative pattern occurs, for instance, in a stereotypical way in argumentative discourse in the political domain when a descriptive analogy argumentation is in a subordinative argumentation structure combined with *pragmatic argumentation* that is supported by it.

[10] The principles at work in reconstructing figurative analogies are very similar to Searle's principles of metaphorical interpretation (Searle 1979, pp. 103–112). According to Searle, the interpretation of a metaphorical statement such as "Sam is a pig" as "Sam is filthy, gluttonous and sloppy, etc." is possible because of Principle 2: "Things which are P are contingently R. (…) if the metaphor works, the property R should be a salient or well-known property of P things" (p. 107). It is a well-known and salient property of pigs (P) that they are filthy etc. (R). The same applies to the phoros used in a figurative analogy.

In pragmatic argumentation the causal claim is that the course of action proposed in the standpoint will lead to desirable (or undesirable) consequences. This causal claim is in practice often defended by descriptive analogy argumentation. In political argumentation the use of such analogy argumentation to support the causal claim in pragmatic argumentation is stereotypical. The causal claim made in the pragmatic argumentation that the United States should adopt a policy of gun control because this leads to a safer social environment can, for instance, be readily defended by way of descriptive analogy argumentation in which the situation in the United States is compared to the situation in Canada, where gun control does indeed lead to fewer casualties. This particular defense results in an argumentative pattern consisting of pragmatic argumentation defended by the use of analogy argumentation in a subordinative argument structure.[11]

An example of this pattern is provided by Catherine Grèze, rapporteur for the opinion of the Committee on Development, in a debate in the European Parliament held on 20 November, 2012. This debate is about the environmental impact of shale gas and shale oil extraction activities. Ms Grèze:

> (5) I am absolutely against the extraction of shale gas. These are matters that go way beyond our European borders with appalling effects on our water resources. Imagine yourselves what the consequences could be, and how devastating they could be, in developing countries where access to water is vital. But the extraction of shale gas is also about land grabbing and poor land quality; in other words, it brings into question food sovereignty in many countries. Therefore, ladies and gentlemen, despite the publicity, despite the brazen lobbying that has been carried out even at the very door of the hemicycle, I would urge you to shoulder your responsibilities. We need a binding legal framework for European businesses. (…) Allow me to ask in return whether you are aware that in a large number of developing countries there is no water?

After being interrupted by a series of questions from Members of the European Parliament, Grèze is forced to explain the relationship between shale gas and water:

> (6) On the issue of water, raised by my colleague, and the impact on water resources, it seems we have different sources of information. I saw an excellent film, Gasland, which is worth seeing, and which showed the truly dramatic consequences, no pun intended, on water resources and human and animal health in the United States, which as you know is a highly developed and technologically advanced country.

Grèze points in her pragmatic argumentation at the negative consequences of shale gas exploitation for water resources. She then defends the causal claim involved in

---

[11] An argumentative pattern resembling this one is the combination of pragmatic argumentation and argumentation by example. As we have shown in van Eemeren and Garssen (2010), in political discourse pragmatic argumentation is frequently encountered in combination with other types of argumentation, especially argumentation by example and analogy argumentation. In debates in the European Parliament about agricultural legislation, for instance, the Members of the European Parliament often resort to arguments by example to show that certain measures defended by pragmatic argumentation will in fact be disastrous. It depends on the nature of the causal claim whether analogy argumentation or argumentation by example is used to support it. General causal claims need to be defended by argumentation by example. Singular causal claims can be defended by analogy argumentation. Note that the causal claim is in this case a specific one: it only refers to the United States. If the causal claim had been general (Gun control generally leads to fewer casualties), argument from example instead of analogy argumentation would have been needed.

this argument by comparing exploiting shale gas in developing countries with the exploitation of shale gas in the United States. By her addition that the United States is a highly developed and technologically advanced country the analogy argumentation becomes *a fortiori*.

The second way in which a stereotypical argumentative pattern involving analogy argumentation may come into being is when descriptive or normative analogy argumentation is sustained by subordinative argumentation of another type. In defending the analogy argumentation, the arguer anticipates the critical questions that pertain to analogy argumentation. In the subordinative argumentation put forward in defense of analogy argumentation the arguer tries to show that the two things, persons or situations that are compared are indeed similar by pointing at the relevant similarities or by pointing out that the similarities outweigh the differences. This type of subordinative argumentation will in principle be symptomatic.

In cases in which the arguer makes use of normative analogy argumentation the stereotypical follow-up is in most communicative activity types that the arguer tries to show that the things, acts or people that are compared are indeed on the same line. This means in practice that the arguer needs to offer subordinative argumentation that refers to similar characteristics of the things, acts or people involved that make them alike in a certain respect. In this endeavour the arguer can, for instance, refer to the fact that the people compared are of the same age, come from the same country, had the same grades for an exam, etc. This stereotypical argumentative pattern generally involves subordinative argumentation that is symptomatic. If additional argumentation establishing the relevance of the similarities that are mentioned is advanced, then this results in an argumentative pattern involving complementary coordinative argumentation.

In conclusion of our contribution we refer to an example of a debate in the European Parliament which illustrates the use of normative analogy argumentation in such political discourse. In the example this kind of argumentation is in fact used a couple of times. The debate concerned, held on 13 March, 2012, was about the internet website set up in the Netherlands in 2012 by the Dutch Party for Freedom for complaints about workers from Eastern European countries. The Dutch citizens were encouraged to complain about problems caused by these workers, such as losing their jobs to them etc. A majority of the Members of the European Parliament judged the website to be discriminatory.

In a blue-card question Jacek Saryusz-Wolski, a Polish Member of the European Parliament representing the European People's Party, reacts to a statement by the Belgian liberal Member of the European Parliament Guy Verhofstadt, who had claimed to have nothing but contempt for this internet initiative:

> (7) Madam President, my question to Mr Verhofstadt is why does he refer only to the very important aspect of it, which is xenophobic racism, but does not refer to the data protection aspect? I recall how fiercely he attacked Prime Minister Orbán on one of the three legislative issues in this Chamber on data protection. What is happening in the Netherlands is a violation of the Data Protection Directive of 1995, just as much as it was invoked vis-à-vis the Hungarian Prime Minister. Could he please apply the same standard?

The use of the phrase "applying the same standard" in this quotation makes clear that Saryusz-Wolski uses normative analogy argumentation. In his comparison he refers to Hungary's controversial constitution, which came into force in January of the year 2012, when the debate was held. Saryusz-Wolski supports the comparison by advancing subordinative argumentation in which he explains that in both cases the DATA Protection Directive of 1995 was violated.

References

van Eemeren, F. H. 2010. *Strategic maneuvering in argumentative discourse: Extending the pragma-dialectical theory of argumentation*. Amsterdam: John Benjamins.

van Eemeren, F. H. 2013. Strategic maneuvering in argumentative discourse in political deliberation. *Journal of Argumentation in Context* 2 (1): 11–32.

van Eemeren, F. H., and B. Garssen. 2010. In varietate concordia—united in diversity. European-parliamentary debate as an argumentative activity type. *Controversia*. 7 (1): 19–37.

van Eemeren, F. H., and R. Grootendorst. 1984. *Speech acts in argumentative discussions: A theoretical model for the analysis of discussions directed towards solving conflicts of opinion*. Berlin: De Gruyter/Foris.

van Eemeren, F. H., and R. Grootendorst. 1992. *Argumentation, communication, and fallacies: A pragma-dialectical perspective*. Hillsdale: Lawrence Erlbaum.

van Eemeren, F. H., and R. Grootendorst. 2004. *A systematic theory of argumentation: The pragma-dialectical approach*. Cambridge: Cambridge University Press.

van Eemeren, F. H., and P. Houtlosser. 2002. Strategic maneuvering in argumentative discourse: Maintaining a delicate balance. In *Dialectic and rhetoric: The warp and woof of argumentation analysis*, ed. F. H. van Eemeren and P. Houtlosser, 131–159. Dordrecht: Kluwer Academic.

Fearnside, W. W., and W. B. Holther. 1959. *Fallacy: The counterfeit of argument*. Englewood Cliffs: Prentice Hall.

Garssen, B. 2009. Comparing the incomparable. Figurative analogies in a dialectical testing procedure. In *Pondering on problems of argumentation: Twenty essays on theoretical issues*, ed. F. H. van Eemeren and B. Garssen, 133–140. Dordrecht: Springer.

Govier, T. 1987. *Problems in argument analysis and evaluation*. Dordrecht: Foris.

Hastings, A. C. 1962. *A reformulation of the modes of reasoning in argumentation*. Unpublished PhD diss., Northwestern University, Evanston, IL.

Jackson, S. (1986). Building a case for claims about discourse structure. In D. G. Ellis & W. A. Donohane (Eds.). *Contemporary issues in language and discourse*. (pp. 129–147). Hillsdale: Erlbaum.

Juthe, A. 2009. Refutation by parallel argument. *Argumentation* 23 (2): 133–169.

Perelman, C., and L. Olbrechts-Tyteca. 1969. *The new rhetoric: A treatise on argumentation* (trans.: Wilkinson, J., & Weaver, P.). Notre Dame: University of Notre Dame Press. French edition: Perelman, C., and L. Olbrechts-Tyteca. 1958. *La nouvelle rhétorique: Traité de l'argumentation*. Paris: Presses Universitaires de France.

Searle, J. R. 1979. *Expression and meaning: Studies in the theory of speech acts*. Cambridge: Cambridge University Press.

Chapter 4
The Uses of Analogies

Lilian Bermejo-Luque

4.1 Introduction

One of the main goals of this paper is to provide a preliminary inventory of the different ways in which analogies can be used. To this end, I will firstly characterize two conceptions of analogy that seem to be at play in literature—namely, quantitative and qualitative conceptions. Then, I will distinguish between the communicative and the non-communicative uses of analogies, and explain the general features of the former in terms of the features of the latter. Within the communicative uses of analogies, I will distinguish between explanatory and justificatory uses and, within each of them, between classificatory and illustrative uses on the one hand, and between analogical reasons and analogical backings on the other—this is, I will argue, what we may call analogical inference.

In addition, I will briefly characterize the rhetorical power of analogies when used as communicative devices, whether they are argumentative or not, because, as I will try to show, such rhetorical power is something special that metaphors and analogies share and the source of the peculiarities that the use of analogies involves—including what Trudy Govier has called its "trick" and its "charm" (Govier 1989, p. 148).

The interest of this inventory has to do with the task of providing criteria for the assessment of analogies: after all, such criteria will depend on the functions that each analogy is meant to play. In particular, I will focus on the criteria for the assessment of analogies within argumentative discourse—but I will not directly deal with the assessment of argumentation containing analogies, which is something I have done somewhere else (Bermejo-Luque 2012).

L. Bermejo-Luque (✉)
Department of Philosophy I, University of Granada, Granada, Spain
e-mail: lilian.bermejoluque@gmail.com

H. J. Ribeiro (ed.), *Systematic Approaches to Argument by Analogy*,
Argumentation Library 25, DOI 10.1007/978-3-319-06334-8_4,

4.2 Qualitative and Quantitative Analogies

Before going on with our inventory of uses, it seems convenient to start from an overall characterization of analogies themselves.

Analogies are powerful cognitive tools: in thinking of unfamiliar objects as similar to familiar ones, we enable working hypotheses for dealing with novelties, paths to become familiar with new things and phenomena. But what does it mean to say that two things are "similar"? As it is well known, similarity is a concept difficult to define non-circularly (in fact, dictionaries usually bring you from "similarity" to "alikeness", "comparability" or "resemblance", and from these, to "similarity" again). I myself will not try a definition—at least, not in so many words.

Current literature on analogies—and especially, on analogical argumentation and reasoning—seems to be torn between two conceptions of similarity. On the one hand, there is a quantitative view, according to which two things are similar when they have enough relevant properties in common. For example, you are about to buy a new car, and your partner observes that the one you are considering now is like another one that you have already refused: it is about the same size, both engines are basically the same, the quality of the finish is on a par, similar shape, and so forth. On these conditions, we deem the comparison to be very sound: in other words, quantitative analogies are better or worse depending on the amount of relevant properties in common.

Of course, you probably don't care about the similarities between their plate numbers or the first names of the owners of the companies that manufacture each car. Remarkably, because anything has indefinitely many properties, in principle, the amount of properties that any two things have in common is as indefinitely big as the amount of properties that they don't. This is why we must always judge analogies by taking into account the context and purposes for which they have been put forward. Regarding quantitative analogies, such context and purposes determine the sets of properties that count for making the comparisons as well as the amount of properties in common that is enough for establishing the corresponding analogies: whether or not two things have enough relevant properties in common is a contextual matter in this double sense. Yet, it is also critical: not enough relevant properties in common would just render the analogy (more or less) unsound.

This quantitative conception of similarity is particularly at stake in law courts, when one of the parties' strategy is to show that the case under consideration is analogous to another one already judged.

However, we frequently establish similarities that do not fit this quantitative conception. On the one hand, we say things like "these colours are alike", "our kids are about the same size", "I feel as a child", etc. This sense of "similarity" does not pivot on a set of relevant properties in common, but rather on a particular quality and the idea of proximity of the things compared to something like a point in a scale of this quality (i.e., a colour spectrum, human size, vitality, etc.). This conception of similarity is qualitative in the following sense: it is not the amount of properties in common what makes the similarity claim more or less sound, but the proximity between the properties at stake within a given scale. Of course, "proximity" in this case is, again, contextual. For example, because we are talking about kids, and not about ants, a difference in millimetres happens to be irrelevant—the appropriate scale is, in this case, centimetres or inches. And when the properties at stake are not close enough to each other in the relevant scale, the similarity is dismissed.

Certainly, this is another way of establishing similarities; yet, I think we should regard claims establishing this kind of similarities as mere comparisons, rather than as analogies proper.

On the other hand, we also establish similarities between things actually having almost nothing in common when, at least, they share something very significant. Such comparisons—i.e., "a life without friends is like a garden without flowers", "character is like a tree and reputation is like a shadow", "love is like a butterfly", "love is like a rock", "love is like a bottle of gin"—also pivot on a qualitative conception of similarity, in the sense that it is not the amount of relevant properties in common that makes the comparison more or less sound, but rather how significant and close to each other are the only properties that both things share.

Noticeably, in formulating this type of similarity we pose a previous limit to the way in which it makes sense to compare the two things: we do not claim that this similarity is an empirical matter—as in the case of quantitative comparisons—but an *a priori* one, that is, a matter of inclusion in a category settled *eo ipso*—i.e., a "new" category for which the very analogy stands.

Let us then distinguish between quantitative analogies, i.e., analogies whose soundness is a matter of how many properties are shared by both analogs, and qualitative analogies, i.e., analogies whose soundness is a matter of how significant is the comparison between them, how solid is the establishment of a category consisting, at least, of both analogs. In contrast with mere comparisons —which, as we have seen, are also claims of similarity, but do not pivot on the idea of sharing relevant features—both quantitative and qualitative analogies may be dismissed by pointing out that there is some relevant feature that is not actually shared by both analogs. In the case of qualitative analogies, pointing at this feature would amount to point out that the alleged category is ill-founded.

4.3 Non-communicative Uses of Analogies

Taking into account these two conceptions of analogy, let us consider now the variety of uses that analogies can have, and whether quantitative or qualitative conceptions are more characteristic and adequate for any of these uses.

One of the most interesting things about the uses of analogies is their ability to make familiar new objects and phenomena: by thinking of a new cell phone as relevantly similar to an old one, we learn to use it easier and faster; by thinking of umbilical cord cells storage as relevantly similar to blood storage, we understand better the former phenomenon and the sanitary and legal questions associated with it, and we can also guide our expectations and decisions. This is why analogies have what we may call a cognitive-exploratory use, which is particularly widespread in those fields in which substantive novelties abound, like the new technologies, and the reflection on their ethical, legal and social implications.

Substantive novelties—that is, novelties that are far too different from anything else we knew before—cannot be completely apprehended by means of just one comparison. Yet, it is in dealing with these novelties that analogies show their potential as cognitive-exploratory tools. For, as such, they work as mere steps in our way to become familiar with something, not as definite judgments on it, and this is precisely what is needed in this trial-and-error kind of learning that is analogical mapping.

Analogical mapping is an extraordinarily useful and widespread cognitive process. Actually, cognitive psychologists even take it to be the basis of our learning abilities. In it, individuals make successive and, eventually, supplementary comparisons in order to apprehend the particular intricacies of the novelty they try to deal with.

Characteristically, this cognitive-exploratory use of analogies does not aim at finding the analog that better suits the novelty; rather, it pursues checking the extent to which the novelty and the analog are alike, and then leave the door open for finding new analogs able to capture other relevant properties of the novelty that do not perfectly fit former analogies. In this cognitive process, one single analogy is not meant to do all the work: after all, if such analogy were enough to fully characterize the new object, it would not be a proper analogy, but an identity judgment, which, from a cognitive point of view, is a very different kind of judgment.

The cognitive-exploratory use of analogies shows that analogies, just like metaphors, work as cognitive proposals or working hypotheses rather than as mere judgments of similarities. That is, at least in their cognitive uses, analogies cannot stand for a definite list of the features that two things are supposed to have in common. Rather, as working hypotheses, the content of analogies is essentially fuzzy, and this fuzziness is a necessary condition for their cognitive-exploratory usefulness: after all, if establishing an analogy between A and B where the same as establishing the set of relevant properties that A and B have in common, analogies would not be so useful as tools for investigating novelties and making them familiar to us, because we would have to know already that which is what we actually want to know—that is, the relevant properties of the novelty. As we are going to see, such indefinition in their content is idiosyncratic of analogies and metaphors in general, and explains not only their cognitive-exploratory potential but also their communicative-rhetorical power.

On the other hand, regarding their cognitive-exploratory functions, qualitative and quantitative analogies seem to be equally useful. For example, in handling a situation like a job interview, it may be useful both to think of such situation as having many features in common with some other already knonw, like, for example, meeting your parents-in-law for the first time. Yet, it may also be useful to think of that situation as something like mountain climbing: you'll probably wish to abandon in the middle of it, but you'll have to continue. In the former case, you may fathom information on further characteristics that the two situations probably share by considering those characteristics that they actually share: by comparing both situations you can get something like a map for the new one. In the latter case, you just face the new situation as qualitatively similar to this other and behave accordingly: by doing so you can get something like a compass.

4.4 Communicative Uses: Explanatory Analogies

Apart from these non-communicative cognitive-exploratory uses, analogies can also be used communicatively as powerful explanatory devices. For, by pointing out that A is like B, we usually make our explanations of A clearer and more vivid than by merely stating a list of A's attributes.

Noticeably, merely pointing out that A is like B is, in principle, quite a trivial, uninformative move: we can say of almost any pair of things that one of them is like the other. In turn, making fully explicit the sense in which A is like B makes the analogy redundant. These are the two extremes between which the interpretation of analogical statements struggles.

Fortunately, when we put forward an analogy, we do it within a certain context and with certain purposes. Such context and purposes point at the way or ways in which the things compared are said to resemble each other. For example, Waller (2001) cites Samuel Johnson's analogy between argument as an arrow shot from a crossbow and testimony as an arrow shot from a long bow. As he points out, it is only in the context of comparing the origins of the force of argumentation and testimony that we understand the sense in which arguments and crossbows, on the one hand, and testimony and long bows, on the other, are said to resemble each other: the force of the former does not depend on who "makes the shot", whereas the force of the latter is essentially dependent on who makes it (that would be a qualitative analogy, by the way).

Waller (2001, p. 200) calls this type of explanatory use of analogies *figurative*. Its explanatory function consists in making salient and more vivid the most relevant features of something by comparing it with something else.

Yet, there is another way in which analogies can be used as explanatory devices. For example, as Hofmann et al. (2006) have argued, when bioethicists discuss on whether umbilical cord blood should be understood by an analogy with waste, or rather by an analogy with natural resources, they are also discussing on whether umbilical cord blood should count as a type of left-overs or rather as a form of natural resource. In proposing these analogies, bioethicists do not only aim at explaining the salient features of umbilical cord blood, but also at classifying it one way or another—and, thereby, establishing some consequences for its management. This classificatory use of analogies is also very frequent, and, as we are going to see in Sect. 4.9, it involves some intricacies that have to be taken into account in order to avert certain illegitimate manoeuvres of persuasion.

At any rate, both qualitative and quantitative analogies seem to be adequate for explanatory purposes—whether figurative or classificatory. Yet, there is a slight difference between them. For example, in order to explain to lay people what a Beckman Coulter DNA sequencer is, it may work to say that it is like a bar code reader for living creatures. This is a qualitative analogy: it doesn't mean that bar code readers and Beckman Coulter DNA sequencers have many features in common, just a relevant one. In contrast, in order to explain this device to an expert, it may be better to say something like "it's like a PCR reader": for an expert, the former qualitative analogy would be insufficiently informative, whereas a quantitative analogy like this one, in which the point of the explanation is the amount of similarities between both technologies, will be more informative.

Obviously, for an analogy to work as an illustrative tool, the addressee has to be able to already understand well enough the source analog. This is why qualitative analogies will normally be more effective than quantitative ones when used for providing mere glances of the explanans for addressees who know very little about it or anything related.

4.5 Communicative Uses: Argumentative Analogies

Apart from these explanatory uses—i.e., figurative and classificatory—, analogies can also be used in communication as means to show further claims to be correct. This is the argumentative use of analogies. As Waller (2001) pointed out, it is very important to distinguish between explanatory and argumentative uses of analogies; otherwise, we might incur in mislead criticisms. This is so because in their explanatory uses, there is no other claim that analogies are meant to support, apart from the comparisons themselves. Particularly, such analogies will not amount to reasons for other claims. Consequently, if we think of an explanatory analogy as a consideration aimed at showing a claim to be correct, we may interpret the alleged argumentation as question begging. As Waller says, "if you are not independently convinced that testimony depends for its reliability on its source, while argument must stand or fall on its own merits, then Johnson's analogy offers nothing to persuade you." (Waller 2001, p. 200).

So, what is analogical argumentation? In order to provide a response, I take it to be convenient to adopt Toulmin's model of argument (Toulmin 1958). As I will try to show, Toulmin's model enables us to appreciate the difference between two types of argumentative uses of analogies—or, if you prefer, between two types of analogical argumentation.

In principle, analogical argumentation is argumentation in which an analogy is adduced in order to support a further claim. What we have in these cases is, paradigmatically, arguments of the form: "A is like B, therefore A is Z". In this type of argument, the analogy corresponds to the data in Toulmin's model, i.e., the evidence that is pointed out in support of a conclusion. For example, in "The political situation is like in the past elections; therefore, the party in office will win again", a quantitative analogy is used as a reason, whereas in "The news has dropped on the Peace Conference like a bomb; probably, there will be retaliatory actions", it is a qualitative analogy what makes the work.

However, arguments of the form "B is Z, therefore A is Z" may also be analogical in particular circumstances, namely, when the inference is drawn in virtue of an alleged similarity between A and B. In this case, the analogy would correspond to the backing in Toulmin's model, i.e., the fact that stands behind the warrant of the argument and justifies the step from reason to conclusion. In these cases, the context can make it clear that there is an analogy adduced as a reason for the inference-claim “if B is Z, then A is Z”. “Why?”—“Because A is like B”. For example, in saying something like “That strategy didn’t work last time; so it won’t work now”, we are reasoning or inferring analogically: we infer that a given strategy won’t work from the fact that it didn’t work earlier because we take both situations to be (quantitatively) alike. Also, in “don’t ask Jane to pay her bill; you wouldn’t ask such a thing to a goddess”, it is the alleged (qualitative) similarity of Jane with a goddess what justifies the inference from “you wouldn’t ask a goddess such a thing” to “don’t ask Jane to pay her bill”.

In sum, within the argumentative uses of analogies, we can distinguish between using analogies as data or premises, and using analogies as backings. And both quantitative and qualitative analogies can be used as data, and also as backings.

4.6 The Rhetorical Power of Analogies as Communicative Devices

As far as we use analogies with communicative purposes, that is, as part of processes where two subjects interact—i.e., a speaker that puts forward the analogy and an addressee that is put in the situation of either accepting or resisting the analogy thereof—both explanatory and argumentative uses of analogies involve rhetorical properties.

Actually, discursive analogies happen to be rhetorically powerful: as pointed out above, using analogies to explain the features of a certain object or phenomenon makes our explanations more vivid and efficient. And, regarding their argumentative role, given the fact that, by using analogies, we can show our claims to be correct, analogies are also valuable tools to make others to be persuaded of such claims. Yet, the rhetorical power of analogies goes further than this, both in their argumentative and their explanatory uses.

To begin with, it is important to keep in mind that, in principle, the persuasive effect of analogies is meant to be different when we use them with explanatory purposes than when we use them argumentatively. As we have seen, in their explanatory uses, analogies are not meant to induce a belief in anything other than the analogy itself. Explanatory analogies are persuasive in the sense of making more vivid the characteristics of that aspect of the target object or phenomenon that we try to illustrate by means of the comparison. As in the case of exploratory analogies, the fact that analogies do not exhaust the ways in which the analogs are supposed to be alike does not count as a problem, but as a virtue: by considering and pondering the possible resemblances between A and B, the addressee may find by herself new explanations of B’s properties and get further knowledge of B. Normally, the fact that she does it by herself is, in addition, pedagogically valuable.

Contrastingly, when we use analogies argumentatively, persuasion is the expected effect of supporting a claim whose content goes beyond the content of the analogy itself: in these cases, speakers do not aim at persuading their addressees of the adequacy of the analogy itself but at persuading them of the acceptability of a further claim that is meant to depend on the acceptability of the analogy.

When we succeed in explaining the features of a given object or phenomenon by means of an analogy, our addressees come to see this object or phenomenon as we suggest them to see it, in the direction or directions that our analogy points at. Why is this so? In a few words, because the rhetorical power of analogies is a correlate of their power as exploratory mechanisms, and this power depends on the fact that analogies have an open and fuzzy content, as we have seen. Because of that, in order to understand a proposed analogy, the addressee has to supply the sense in which the two analogs are said to be alike. In doing so, the addressee herself works out the alleged similarities between the two analogs.

For example, in conveying that time is like money (a qualitative analogy), we convey an idea of time being as money in some relevant sense; a sense that, on the other hand, needs not be made explicit. What we convey is not mere information, but rather a cognitive proposal of seeing time as money in a certain way, i.e., the way in which the comparison is relevant. As far as the addressee fully understands the analogy, i.e., the relevance of comparing time with money, she will be somehow thinking of time as money in this sense: after all, the point of a qualitative analogy is to create a category, so that being able to understand the analogy is, somehow, acknowledging it as acceptable. And yet, the speaker will not need to say what this category is.

In turn, in conveying that two cars are about the same (quantitative analogy), we convey the idea that the set of features that they have in common is the relevant one (after all, there are also many features that they probably don't share), so that in understanding why the speaker says that both cars are about the same, we are somehow pressed to accept as relevant a particular set of features. This is why understanding an analogy—whether qualitative or quantitative—is, at the end, tantamount to falling, at least a little, under its rhetorical spell.

This was, very roughly, the view of metaphors that Lakoff and Johnson (1980) developed in their well-known *Metaphors We Live By*. Black (1954) and Davidson (1978), among others, had already maintained similar views. On their perspective, it would be useless to try to find the truth-conditions of metaphorical propositions because "much of what we are caused to notice [in a metaphor] is not propositional in character" (Davidson 1978, p. 33). Certainly, there is a key difference between metaphors and analogies: literally, metaphorical sentences are always false (time is not money, two cars cannot be the same) whereas, literally, analogical sentences are always true (there is surely more than one aspect in which time is like money or a car is like another car). But as long as, literally, analogies are trivially true, current literature tends to cancel the distinction between metaphors and analogies, at least regarding the cognitive processes involved in interpreting them. On such account, the content of analogical statements is not merely propositional, which is the reason why accepting or refusing an analogy or a metaphor is accepting or refusing a cognitive proposal rather than merely agreeing or disagreeing with a claim.

Now, as we have seen, the persuasive effect that we pursue when we adduce an analogy as a reason for a target-claim is, in principle, different from the mere rhetorical power of analogies, in general: in these cases, speakers are supposed to try to persuade their addressees, not of the acceptability of the analogy itself, but of a further claim whose acceptability allegedly depends on the acceptability of the analogy. However, an analogy is an analogy, and it does not loose its spell just because we are using it argumentatively. Argumentation is a justificatory and a persuasive device at the same time, and argumentative analogies can be used not only for justifying, but also for persuading someone of our claims. Certainly, when we use an analogy for justifying a claim, we put at work its epistemic properties as a means to support this claim. Contrastingly, when we use an analogy for persuading someone of a further claim, we put at work its rhetorical properties as a means to induce beliefs and attitudes. No doubt, this distinction is merely conceptual: we normally use argumentative analogies with both purposes at the same time. However, it is important to keep both functions conceptually separate in order to be clear that what makes an analogy good as a justificatory device is not necessarily what makes it good as a persuasive device. When we use argumentative analogies for persuading, we have to take into account that proposing certain comparisons, despite their justificatory power, may be inadequate because they provoke incomprehension, rejection, distaste, etc., so as to finally making it more difficult to get the persuasion of our addressees. And, conversely: analogies that result inadequate from an epistemological point of view may happen to be powerful from a rhetorical perspective; for example, because they appeal to strong feelings, norms, practices, institutions, etc. that we do not dare to criticise, or because they summarize well-established views, or are commonplace, etc.

It is precisely this distance between the rhetorical quality and the epistemological quality of analogies what poses the main legitimacy problem of their use in argumentation. Specially, when we take into account that putting forward an analogy is already pressing our addressees to see things in a certain way, without actually saying which way this is. In other words, the legitimacy problem posed by the argumentative use of analogies is not only a matter of the fact that, in general, good argumentation is not the same as effective argumentation. It is also a matter of the particular spell of analogies: as we have seen, to a great extent, understanding an analogy, like understanding a metaphor, is all the same as accepting it in some sense, namely, as a cognitive proposal. When we understand the meaning of someone's claim that time is like money, we feel inclined to agree that we should not waste it; and when we understand in which sense two cars are said to be alike, we are somehow agreeing, at least in principle, on the set of relevant features for assessing cars.

Of course, we can always resist the analogy. Yet, this resistance cannot be a matter of appealing to the differences between time and money—which are evident—or between two cars that are not the same car. That is, it would make little sense to reply "No, time is not like money" or "But they are not the same": the proponent could just suggest that we are missing her point by saying "of course they are not". Rather, the opponent's move can only be a matter of appealing to the inconvenience or inadequacy of thinking of time as money, or thinking of two cars as about the same in this context or for these purposes.

The particular rhetorical spell of analogies is the reason why it is important to be in a position to determine their acceptability when used for argumentative purposes, and their real justificatory power. In Bermejo-Luque (2012), I suggested that, when used as reasons, analogical statements should be understood as non-literal statements. In the following sections, I will insert this discussion within the analysis of the criteria for assessing analogies in general.

4.7 Criteria for Assessing Analogies: Exploratory and Explanatory Uses

The distinction between a qualitative and a quantitative conception of similarity is, at the end, a distinction between two types of standards for setting analogies. My goal in this section is to provide criteria for assessing both qualitative and quantitative analogies when used for exploratory and explanatory purposes.

As we have seen, analogies, just like metaphors, cannot be assessed, in principle, as simple propositional contents, because their formulation involves cognitive proposals, rather than mere judgments of fact. Particularly, when we use analogies non-communicatively, for cognitive-exploratory purposes, our goal is to deep into the comprehension of a novelty by means of comparing it with something already known or, at least, more familiar to us. In Sect. 4.3, I pointed out that, in this type of uses, quantitative analogies work like a map, whereas qualitative analogies rather work like a compass. In either case, the point of an exploratory analogy is not to settle judgments of similarity, because these analogies are not a matter of pre-determining the relevant properties that both analogs share; rather, its point is to make such properties explicit by means of the analogy itself, working as an exploratory tool.

Consequently, exploratory analogies will be good if they happen to be fruitful, illuminating, powerful, and even elegant, in the sense of gathering in an efficient and simple way a big amount of cognitively relevant contents. The value of an analogy, when used for exploratory purposes, will then depend on its power to provide a gateway to the novelty we try to handle. Yet, this power should not jeopardize our comprehension of the novelty by becoming a cognitive bias: once we get further information we must be able to leave the analogy behind. The formulation of exploratory analogies must remain provisional, hypothetical. In this regard, qualitative analogies may pose more problems than quantitative ones: after all, qualitative analogies somehow create a category that might work as a framework, but also as a harness.

Likewise, when we put forward an analogy for explanatory purposes, we cannot interpret that statement as a plain assertion. As we have seen, the communicative value of such statements is not a matter of truth or plausibility, but of their acceptability as cognitive proposals. Even though it may be true that A is like B in a relevant respect (qualitative analogy) or regarding features a, b, c (quantitative analogy), the explanatory value of the analogy is rather a matter of its ability to prompt new cognitive inputs or orientation in the addressee.

On the other hand, as Waller warned us, in formulating an analogy with explanatory purposes, we do not aim at settling anything beyond the comparison itself. As we have seen, this is also the case with exploratory analogies. Actually, the sort of features that count as epistemic virtues for exploratory analogies, is also the sort of features that count as epistemic virtues for explanatory ones: ability to illuminate, fruitfulness, power, elegance, etc. And the same goes with its vices: analogies that pose a bias to our comprehension of new phenomena should be regarded as bad or defective explanatory strategies; and in this respect, like in the case of exploratory uses, qualitative analogies are, in principle, more risky/tricky than quantitative ones.

In sum, both the exploratory and the explanatory value of analogies have to do with their fertility and usefulness. Yet, when used for explaining, we will have to mind two requisites in addition: on the one hand, pointing out that A is like B as a means to explain A will not work if our addressees know little about B. On the other hand, if the similarities between both analogs, A and B, are obvious but of little significance or interest, pointing out that A is like B will not be an effective way of increasing our addressees' comprehension of A. This is why, despite being risky, formulating qualitative analogies between objects that, in fact, are far too different from each other may be a valuable explanatory strategy.

4.8 Criteria for Assessing Analogies: Argumentative Uses

As we have seen, in principle, analogies, like metaphors, do not have a definite propositional content: they do not count as plain assertions but rather as cognitive proposals. As argued above, this fact would explain their characteristic rhetorical charm.

No doubt, the way in which analogies bridge the gap between what is known and the novelties we investigate partially explains their justificatory and persuasive powers. That is, the explanatory value of an analogy may make its argumentative use more efficient. However, as we have seen, when used for explanatory purposes, the "truth" of the analogy is not one of its virtues. Actually, as we have seen, it does not make too much sense to talk about "truth" in these cases.

Contrastingly, when used in argumentation, analogies are good depending on their acceptability as bases for drawing the corresponding conclusions. To this end, it is not necessary that the source of the analogy is more familiar to our addressee than its target, nor it is necessary that the analogy is fruitful, significant or interesting. If the analogy used as a reason or backing has these features, it may make the argument more convincing; but if it hasn't them, its justificatory power would remain the same. What is necessary in this case is the possibility of settling the way in which both analogs are said to be alike, because this constitutes the basis of the justificatory power of the analogy. This means, among other things, that the analogy must be suitable for negation, and that it must make sense to take its content as a better or worse way of saying how the world is. In other words, in order to be able to play as reasons or backings, analogies have to be able to play as full-fledged assertions, and therefore, as having a definite propositional content. But how can we do this? Certainly, we have seen, in saying that A is like B, the speaker passes on the addressee the task of working out which are the ways in which A and B are alike. Moreover, in being offered an analogy as a reason or backing, the addressee cannot take it literally and just reply: "no, A is not like B", because, in principle, analogies are trivially true. So, how can we make sense of both intuitions, namely, that analogies in analogical argumentation must be interpreted as assertions while preserving the indefinition that explains their particular charm and rhetorical power? In my view, the way out of this quandary is considering that conceding an argumentative analogy is conceding that, regarding a certain aspect—not necessarily made explicit in the argument—, the two analogues can be considered the same or treated the same way. Yet, this is not to concede *eo ipso* how they should be considered or treated. Let me recall Thomson's (1971) well-known argument in defense of abortion in order to explain this. In "aborting when you become pregnant as a result of rape is like disconnecting yourself from a violinist when you've been involuntarily connected to him; therefore, it is legitimate to abort when you become pregnant as a result of rape", the content of the analogy, if used as a reason for "it should be allowed", would be "aborting in such and such circumstances is like disconnecting yourself in such and such circumstances regarding their legitimacy". A person thinking that abortion in these circumstances is legitimate and a person thinking that it is not may agree on this analogy if they think that both cases are the same regarding their legitimacy, and yet disagree on whether they both are legitimate or illegitimate. As a consequence, they will agree on the reason, but disagree on the conclusion.

By interpreting this way the meaning of analogies when used as reasons or backings we are able to preserve both the intuition that argumentative analogies are full-fledged assertions and also the idea that they are not mere nicknames for a set of similarities between the two analogs (quantitative analogies) or for the particular feature that the analogs are supposed to share (qualitative analogies).

On this view, the value of an analogy when used as a reason will be a matter of both, whether the proposed interpretation of the analogy as a literal claim makes it correct, and how much support does it provide to the conclusion.

To be true, the claim that A and B are the same regarding aspect C is something that may be assessed in turn. To this end, something like Walton's story scheme similarity (Walton 2012) may be very useful: after all, when the schema shows that both analogs are the same, it does it so regarding certain aspect, namely, the one depicted by the particular formalization carried out for showing the similarities. In other words, the schema, as construed by Walton, provides the theme rather than the plot itself.

To be true, Walton's proposal seems to be better suited for what we are calling quantitative analogies: actually, Walton's target is "legal arguments from analogy of the kind used in arguments from precedent in law" (Walton 2012, p. 190). However, the schema can also be used for testing qualitative similarities. As we have seen, qualitative analogies are those whose soundness is a matter of how significant is the comparison between them, of how solid is the establishment of a category consisting, at least, of both analogs. Thus, in order to use Walton's story scheme similarity, we will have to think of the schema as depicting the key features of the category that the analogy is meant to stand for—again, the theme rather than the plot. In case of pointing at a relevant feature that does not fit with one of the analogs, the schema will show that the alleged category is ill-founded.

Let me point out a final remark concerning the distinction between quantitative and qualitative analogies when used as argumentative devices. Govier (1989) has set a trend in distinguishing between inductive and *a priori* analogical arguments. In her account, the distinction has to do with the topic of the analogy and the sort of inferences that it enables: particularly, ethical and legal analogies would be *a priori,* because when used as reasons, they would be meant to establish the corresponding conclusions non-inductively. Contrastingly, in our account, this distinction would rather be a matter of whether the analogy is quantitative or qualitative. As pointed out in Sect. 4.2, the strength of a quantitative analogy is an empirical, probabilistic matter, whereas the strength of qualitative analogies is something that can be determined *a priori,* in the sense of being a matter of the soundness of the pre-settled category for which the very analogy stands for.

4.9 Analogies and Classifications

I would like to finish this brief inventory of uses of analogies and the corresponding criteria for assessing them by pointing at the need of distinguishing analogies from classifications. For, even though analogical and classificatory statements may be superficially identical, they actually have very different conditions of adequacy, and confusion between one and the other may give rise to illegitimate persuasive strategies.

In saying that A is like B, we may be saying either that A and B share, as a matter of fact, some relevant properties, or that A and B share all possible relevant properties. In the first case, we will be formulating a quantitative analogy; in the second case, we will be formulating either a qualitative analogy, or a classification.

According to our definition, qualitative analogies are those in which, by means of comparing two things, a new category is settled—like, for example, the category of things that are all-purpose valuable and can be gained or wasted, as time and money. Contrastingly, when we make a classification, what we do is to use a category already settled, and subsume A and B as belonging to it. Remarkably, both comparisons and qualitative analogies are *a priori* in this sense: given the characterization of the category as providing the set of relevant properties, and the properties of A and B, whether A and B share all the relevant properties is something true or false by definition.

Let me offer an example: if I compare human tissues with waste products, I may be either saying that human tissues and waste products share the relevant property of being something of no value, unpleasant, which can be freely disposed of (qualitative analogy), or I may be saying that human tissues are, like waste products, a type of rubbish (classification). As we have seen, qualitative analogies can be criticised because the alleged category it stands for is ill-founded: in this case, we may point out, for example, that anything that can be used has some value, and reply that, instead of making a category with human tissues and waste products, we should think of both as having something in common with something else, e.g., natural resources. Contrastingly, classifications pivot on categories already established, and they can only be criticised if some of the prescriptive features for being a member of the category do not apply in this case: in our example, we may point out that, contrary to mere rubbish, human tissues carry important information and are a valuable resource, so that their management requires specific regulations that makes them closer to hazardous waste, on the one hand, and to natural resources, on the other.

This difference has important rhetorical consequences: classifications pre-settle the issue by pre-determining the set of properties that are relevant in order to understand the novelty in a given context. When we convey that A is like B because they both are a type of C, we implicitly contend that the properties that define the category exhaust the relevant properties of A. Contrastingly, analogies leave the door open to the possibility of finding new relevant properties that make A different from B. For example, in the debate about how to manage human tissues, the analogy with waste products has a tentative character, open to scrutiny. On the contrary, classifying human tissues as waste products is a way of shifting the burden of proof to those who deny that what applies to the rest of the members of the category applies to this alleged member.

This is why, when used as reasons, it is always possible to concede the analogy and yet refuse the conclusion: as we have seen, even if A is like B in some respect and B is W, this does not necessarily mean that A will be W. On the contrary, if we concede the classification and the rest of the members of the category are W, it will be very difficult to say that this is mere coincidence, and not something essential to the category, so that A will also be W.

This is why we will have to be careful in distinguishing analogical from classificatory statements, as they involve very different commitments. Analogies in communication have an open character. Not only because their content is essentially fuzzy, as we have seen, but also because they leave the door open to refutation, and they invite to debate and inquiry in a way that is alien to classifications.

4.10 Conclusions

There is always a way of saying of any pair of things that they are alike, just as, if they are two things indeed and not just one, it is also always possible to say that they are not the same. This is why, as Govier warns us, analogies are particularly charming and tricky.

As we have seen, the use of analogies poses three main hazards. On the one hand, when used as exploratory devices, they may be so influential as to prejudice our comprehension of the novelty we try to apprehend. Paradoxically, in this respect, the more brilliant, useful and cogent the analogy, the more constrictive it may happen to be. On the other hand, when used for explanatory purposes, they may also bias our comprehension of the explananas—as we have seen, this is particularly the case when analogies are used for classificatory purposes. Finally, when used in argumentation, the need to re-interpret the indefinite content of analogies, together with the fact that, in arguing by analogy, speakers do not need to commit themselves with the alleged way in which the two analogs are suppsed to be alike, poses an extra load in those interpreting and assessing such argumentation. In addition, because classifications may look like analogies, there is also the problem of conceding too much by conceding that A is like B.

Remarkably, our brief inventory of uses of analogies has not included among its categories a persuasive use. This is so because, in my view, any communicative use of analogies does already involve a certain persuasive or rhetorical purpose. Certainly, that which makes good an analogy from a rhetorical point of view may be completely different from that which makes it good from an epistemological point of view. When an analogy is epistemically defective, its rhetorical power is illegitimate: after all, this means that the analogy is good at persuading us of something that is poorly justified. The main goal of this paper has been to provide criteria for assessing the epistemological value of both qualitative and quantitative analogies in their exploratory, explanatory and argumentative uses, as a means to resist their rhetorical charm when this is illegitimate.

Acknowledgments I wish to thank Javier Rodríguez Alcázar, Frank Zenker and David Hitchcock for helpful discussions on the topic of this paper. I am also indebted to the participants and audience of the Colloquium *The Role of Analogy in Argumentative Discourse,* held in Coimbra in May 2013, for a lively debate of some of the ideas presented here.

This work has been financed by a Ramón y Cajal Research Fellowship of the Spanish Ministry of Science and Innovation and by the research projects FFI2011-23125 and FFI2011-24414 of the Spanish Ministry of Science and Innovation.

References

Bermejo-Luque, L. 2012. A unitary schema for arguments by analogy. *Informal Logic* 32 (1): 1–24.
Black, M. 1954. Metaphor. *Proceedings of the Aristotelian Society* 55:273–294.
Davidson, D. 1978. What metaphors mean. *Critical Inquiry* 5:31–47.
Govier, T. 1989. Analogies and missing premises. *Informal Logic* 11 (3): 141–152.
Guarini, M. 2004. A defence of non-deductive reconstructions of analogical arguments. *Informal Logic* 24 (2): 153–168.
Hofmann, B., J. H. Solbakk, and S. Holm. 2006. Teaching old dogs new tricks: The role of analogies in bioethical analysis and argumentation concerning new technologies. *Theoretical Medicine & Bioethics* 27 (5): 397–413.
Lakoff, G., and M. Johnson. 1980. *Metaphors we live by*. Chicago: University of Chicago Press.
Thompson, J. J. 1971. In defense of abortion. *Philosophy and Public Affairs* 1 (1): 47–66.
Toulmin, S. 1958. *The uses of argument*. Cambridge: Cambridge University Press.
Waller, B. 2001. Classifying and analyzing analogies. *Informal Logic* 21 (3): 199–218.
Walton, D. 2012. Story similarity in arguments from analogy. *Informal Logic* 32 (2): 190–221.

Chapter 5
Analogy and Redefinition

Fabrizio Macagno

5.1 Introduction

The word "analogy", in Greek "according to ratio", originally meant rational correspondence. In the *Posterior Analytics*, Aristotle pointed out that this type of reasoning could be used for identifying a fundamental characteristic common to various entities, and for which no name exists. As Aristotle put it (*Posterior Analytics* 98a20-23):

> Again, another way is excerpting in virtue of analogy; for you cannot get one identical thing which pounce and spine and bone should be called; but there will be things that follow them too, as though there were some single nature of this sort.

Aristotle noticed that there is not a specific generic class (a genus in his system of predicables, or rather logic-semantic relations, see Macagno and Walton 2009a) that groups together the pounce (of a cuttlefish), the spine (of a fish), and the bone (of an animal). In this case there is no name referring to this category, which, however, represents an essential feature (or a generic ontological aspect) common to the three entities. These three different concepts share a substantial characteristic that indicates what they are; however, this generic feature has no name. Analogy, in this sense, reveals a genus (a generic, common and essential feature) that can be considered as an ontological and semantic property that does not have a conventional name (see Glucksberg and Keysar 1990, p. 8; Hesse 1965, p. 331).

The purpose of this paper is to investigate analogy from the point of view of its function as a mechanism for abstracting a new common property from different concepts and drawing inferences from it (Macagno and Walton 2009b). In this sense, the goal is to show how this process, which can be considered as semantic, can justify the ancient topic that Boethius expressed as "Regarding similar, the judgment is one and the same" (*De Topicis Differentiis* 1197B 27-28), and that

F. Macagno (✉)
Institute for Philosophy of Language,
New University of Lisbon, Lisbon, Portugal
e-mail: fabrizio.macagno@fcsh.unl.pt

H. J. Ribeiro (ed.), *Systematic Approaches to Argument by Analogy*,
Argumentation Library 25, DOI 10.1007/978-3-319-06334-8_5,

Table 5.1 Argumentation scheme 1: argument from analogy

Major premise	Generally, case C_1 is similar to case C_2
Minor premise	Proposition A is true (false) in case C_1
Conclusion	Proposition A is true (false) in case C_2

in the modern theory of argumentation schemes is represented as follows (Walton et al. 2008, p. 315; Table 5.1):

The aim is to investigate how and why a common property, which represents the similarity between C1 and C2, can be abstracted from two distinct concepts, and how and why this new generic category can support the inferential passage. A possible answer can be found by developing the Aristotelian idea of analogy as a semantic process, and combining it with the logic-semantic concept of genus.

5.2 Analogy and Functional Genus

The argumentation scheme from analogy is grounded on two components: a comparison between two different entities or facts, and a predicate attributed to the primary subject. However, the crucial problem is to understand what a comparison is, and what are the mechanisms underlying it. In particular, it is necessary to distinguish between two distinct reasoning processes: (1) the relation between the two terms of comparison and the property or the properties that they have in common; and (2) the relation between the generic common property and the entities that fall under it. The first crucial dimension of analogy that needs to be investigated is how comparison works, and how it can be used for classifying two different concepts under a common characteristic.

We can notice that the fundamental characteristic of comparison corresponds to the relationship between the similarity and the difference between the two entities or facts compared, in this case the primary subject and the analogue. The two terms of the comparison can be compared not only because they are similar in some respects, but because they are also different in others (Glucksberg and Keysar 1990, p. 7). The point is to identify when and how they can be similar and at the same time different. Two varieties of apples (such as the Golden Delicious and the Granny Smith) cannot be compared from the point of view of their generic essential properties (they are fruits, they come from Malus trees…), but only from the perspective of some characteristics that do not constitute their commonly accepted meaning or classification. For instance, the two varieties of apples can be compared by taking into consideration their flavor, shape, or sweetness. Likely, a steamboat can be considered as similar to an inn because these two entities are not lodging houses. Similarly, a fetus can be compared to a violinist plugged into a person's circulatory system because the two terms of the comparison cannot fall within the same category of "unborn young (of a human being)."

Analogy can be considered as grounded on a similarity that includes the two terms of the comparison under a common characteristic, which does not correspond to the definitional genus or a commonly accepted generic category. This common characteristic can be considered as the very purpose of the analogy or it is functional to the attribution of the predicate to the two entities or events. The common characteristic can be thought of as a "super-ordinate category" (Glucksberg and Keysar 1990, p. 8), in which the two terms of the primary subject and the analogue are included. This generic category does not correspond to the definitional or taxonomic genus of the analogue, but rather to a new property (Glucksberg and Keysar 1990, p. 9; Macagno and Walton 2009b) that is functional to the attribution of the predicate or to a classification.

This new category can be considered as a pragmatic or functional genus from a logic-semantic perspective. Aristotle described the genus as "what is predicated in what a thing is of a number of things exhibiting differences in kind" (*Topics* 102a 31-32). According to the Aristotelian account, this predicable is an ontological and logical relation that is connected with the essence, or rather fundamental characteristics, of a concept, such as the relation between "animate being" and "man." The need of classifying the category according to the traditional system of the predicables is grounded on the need of justifying the reasoning process underlying the passage from the attribution of a property A to a specific concept (C1) to the attribution of the same property to a more generic one (encompassing both C1 and C2). In the system of the predicables, this type of reasoning was justified by a fundamental principle expressed by Boethius in his *De Differentiis Topicis*. The attribution of the property A of the species P to the (functional) genus G is supported by the maxim connecting the species to the genus (Boethii *De Differentiis Topicis*, 1189A): "What is predicated of the parts (in this case essential part, the species) is predicated also of the whole (in this case essential whole, the genus)."

In case of analogy the crucial problem is the requirement of the "essentiality" of the genus. The idea of functional (or pragmatic) genus is self-contradictory if we conceive "essence" as something immutable and pre-existing the utterance. However, from a pragmatic perspective, the "sentence or word meaning", or rather what the "word, expression or sentence actually means" (Searle 1981, p. 77), can be different speaker's meaning, i.e. what the speaker wants to communicate through his speech act (Stern 2008, p. 263; Carston 2002). The use of a sentence in a speech act can create meaning that is different from the semantic one. In case of analogy, the comparison is functional to a communicative goal, which can be explicit (the attribution of a predicate) or implicit (a new classification). In both cases, analogy redefines contingently the concepts used, in the sense that for the purpose of the comparison the two terms are characterized by semantic features that are different from the definitional ones. The new property provides a new criterion that does not represent the most generic fundamental characteristic of the concept (constituting its "dictionary" meaning), but only a functional one. The abstract property, in this sense, has the function of making the equivalence between the two compared entities relevant for a communicative purpose. For this reason, the analogical genus does not refer to a characteristic of the terms of the comparison that describes "what a thing is absolutely", but simply "what a thing is contextually," for the specific communicative and pragmatic purpose of the analogy. On this perspective, the primary subject and the analogous are functionally and contingently redefined.

5.3 Abstraction and Relevance

In order to describe the process of abstraction on which analogy is based, we need to analyze two district reasoning passages: the mechanism of abstraction of the functional genus, and the different ways in which this genus is triggered and supported.

5.3.1 Abstracting the Functional Genus

The creation of a functional genus is an implicit mechanism in which an abstract and not pre-existing category is created ad hoc to support the reasonableness of the attribution of the predicate to both terms of comparison. For instance, we consider a famous legal analogy between innkeepers and steamboat operators (*Adams v. New Jersey Steamboat Co.*, 151 N.Y. 163, 1896):

Case 1
It was deemed to be a sound and necessary rule that this class of persons should be subjected to a high degree of responsibility in cases where an extraordinary confidence is necessarily reposed in them, and where great temptation to fraud and danger of plunder exists by reason of the peculiar relations of the parties. The relations that exist between a steamboat company and its passengers, who have procured staterooms for their comfort during the journey, differ in no essential respect from those that exist between the innkeeper and his guests. (…) A steamer carrying passengers upon the water, and furnishing them with rooms and entertainment, is, for all practical purposes, a floating inn, and hence the duties which the proprietors owe to the passengers in their charge ought to be the same.

This analogy is used to attribute the same predicate "to be liable for the guests' losses" to a category of individuals that cannot be considered as innkeepers, i.e. steamboat operators. This analogy creates a new functional genus, i.e. a category characterized by a specific property (or bundle of properties) that constitutes the reason for attributing the predicate to its hyponyms. In this case, the reasoning is explicit and provides the characteristics defining this new genus: "providers of accommodation to guests reposing in them extraordinary confidence."

Sometimes, however, the creation of a new functional genus can be used as an instrument for generating an ambiguous category. The crucial dimension of analogy is the relationship between the predicate and the property that grounds its predication. However, when this relation is not made explicit, it can be reconstructed in different fashions, leading to the abstraction of different properties and, therefore, of implicit categories. For instance, we consider the famous case used by Thomson in defense of abortion (Thomson 1971, pp. 48–49):

Case 2
You wake up in the morning and find yourself back to back in bed with an unconscious violinist. A famous unconscious violinist. He has been found to have a fatal kidney ailment, and the Society of Music Lovers has canvassed all the available medical records and found that you alone have the right blood type to help. They have therefore kidnapped you, and last night the violinist's circulatory system was plugged into yours, so that your kidneys can be used to extract poisons from his blood as well as your own. [If he is unplugged from you now, he will die; but] in nine months he will have recovered from his ailment, and can safely be unplugged from you.

In this case, the problem is to identify the functional genus, and more specifically the relevant property thereof, warranting the attribution of the predicate "to have no right to be left to use the other's body." Both a fetus and the violinist are beings, both are human according to some views, but certainly they are not both persons from a legal perspective. Moreover, is it possible to claim that the predicate can be attributed to the two beings because they are using the other's body without any consent of the host? Or that the host is not bound to the two beings by any responsibility or obligation? The problem in this case is to identify the reason why the predicate can be attributed to the functional genus, which specifies the characteristics that the latter needs to have.

5.3.2 Types of Analogy and the Functions of the Abstracted Genus

Analogies can have different structures in the sense that the "identity of relations" can be shaped according distinct propositional forms and communicative purposes. We can consider the following cases:

1. I am to dancing what Roseanne is to singing and Donald Duck to motivational speeches. I am as graceful as a refrigerator falling down a flight of stairs. (Leonard Pitts, "Curse of Rhythm Impairment" Miami Herald, Sep. 28, 2009)
2. If you want my final opinion on the mystery of life and all that, I can give it to you in a nutshell. The universe is like a safe to which there is a combination. But the combination is locked up in the safe. (De Vries 1965, p. 307)
3. Thus (e.g.) inasmuch as the relation of a doctor towards the possession of ability to produce health is like that of a trainer towards the possession of ability to produce vigour, and it is a property of a trainer to possess the ability to produce vigour, it will be a property of a doctor to possess the ability to produce health. (Aristotle, *Topics* 137a4-8).
4. Public officials ought not to be selected by lot. That is like using the lot to select athletes, instead of choosing those who are fit for the contest; or using the lot to select a steers-man from among a ship's crew, as if we ought to take the man on whom the lot falls, and not the man who knows most about it. (Aristotle, *Rhetoric* 1393b4-1393b8).

In (1), the dancing ability of the primary subject (the speaker) is compared with other cases of "complete inability" in performing specific activities. The analogues in this case illustrate a new genus that constitutes the purpose of the analogy, namely classifying the primary subject under a new category. This new category contains in itself a value judgment, which is the very purpose of the move. In (2), the analogy consists in an illustration of a genus from a single case that is created specifically in order to exemplify this abstract genus (Goodman 1968, pp. 52–66; Stern 2000, pp. 153–156). This new category can be represented by different predicates such as "to be a problem that makes no sense to try to solve." It constitutes the purpose of the analogy, i.e. the classification of the primary subject under a specific functional genus, which contains the judgment that is the conclusion of the analogical move. In both cases, the analogy works as the construction of a genus through illustration and exemplification. In (3) and (4), however, the mechanism is noticeably different.

In (3), the doctor is compared to a trainer from the point of view of a common property, i.e. possessing the ability of producing health and vigor. The doctor and the trainer are regarded from a specific perspective, namely the ability that characterizes them. The two entities are placed as species of the generic category of professions, and the attribution of the generic predicate to the category of the entities is grounded on the semantic relation of "property." In (4), the reasoning is different because only one functional category is abstracted from the comparison, the one under which the subject and the analogues fall. The different entities are regarded from the point of view of "being not selectable by lot." The characteristic that grounds this predication is "to be a duty requiring a specific ability or knowledge," because chance cannot reveal ability. In these two latter cases of analogy there is an unbalance between the attribution of the predicate to the analogues and to the primary subject. Whereas the predication is uncontroversial for the analogue, it can be problematic when attributed to the primary subject. For this reason, the creation of a functional genus under which analogues and primary subject fall and the attribution of the predicate to it constitute the core of the argumentative move. The force of this mechanism lies in the relationship between the predicate and the functional genus, which can based on a semantic property, or cause-effect, or values. For instance, while in (3) the relation is semantic (absence of the specific ability results in not being a specific professional, in (4) values or consequences combine with sign (lot does not reveal ability; one should choose the most skilled person in charge for an activity/unskilled persons cannot perform their activities properly). In this sense, the relevance of the functional genus to the property can be represented by a specific argumentative relation.

Different argumentative relations can establish the link of relevance between the predicate and the genus. Such relations constitute a fundamental dimension of the strength of an analogy. For instance, we consider the famous case quoted by Aristotle (*Prior Analytics* 68b38-69a19):

Case 3

If we want to show that the aggression of Athens against Thebes was evil, we must first know that aggressive war on neighbours is evil. Evidence of it is obtained from similar cases, e.g. the aggressive war of Thebes on Phocis. Assuming then that aggressive war on neighbours is evil, and that the attack of Athens on Thebes was aggressive war on neighbours, it follows that the attack of Athens on Thebes was evil.

Here the abstraction of the genus "aggressive war against neighbors" is functional to the attribution of "to be evil" because it can be supported by a possible implicit causal relation (wars against neighbors can be dangerous or lead to unfortunate aftermaths). The acceptability of this analogy depends on the degree of acceptability of this relation. For instance, the acceptability of this analogy would have been noticeably different if the genus had been simply "wars between Greek cities," which would be hardly acceptable as a cause of evil consequences.

The correlation between the strength of the relevance relation and the force of the analogical reasoning emerges clearly in cases in which the first one is based on values. For instance, we consider the following famous analogy (Aristotle, *Rhetoric* 1399b 1-5):

Case 4
And Theodectes in his Law said, "You make citizens of such mercenaries as Strabax and Charidemus, as a reward of their merits; will you not make exiles of such citizens as those who have done irreparable harm among the mercenaries?"

This analogy is grounded on the relevance relation between "social behavior of a person" and "implementation of punishment or rewards connected to the status of citizenship." This relation is value-based, as the quality of a person's behavior is considered to be a principle for attributing rewards or punishments. Moreover, in this case the strength of the analogy is grounded on an implicit threat of inconsistent commitment, as failure to punish the citizens that misbehaved in war would contradict the value that the agent advocated in his first decision.

5.4 The Logic of Genus-species

As mentioned above, reasoning from analogy is characterized by two steps: the abstraction of a functional property to which a predicate is or can be attributed, and the classification of the primary subject according to the new category or the predicate attributed to the category. In the subsections above the first reasoning passage has been described as a process of abstraction grounded on exemplification or reasons supporting the attribution of a predicate. The other passage, the one from the category to the primary subject, needs to be clarified. This relationship is clearly defeasible and, for this reason, it can be explained by using the ancient system of *loci* (Rigotti 2006; Rigotti and Greco Morasso 2010; Kienpointner 1986) and in particular the maxims concerning the genus.

The abstraction of a new ad hoc category results from a logic-semantic point of view in the creation of a functional genus, i.e. a relational predicate that is characterized by specific logical and semantic properties. The genus is semantically more generic than the species, in the sense that the genus can be predicated essentially of the species, but not vice-versa. For example, if "animate being" is the genus of "man," a man can be considered as an animal, but an animal is not a man based on the principle that "species partake of the genera, but not the genera of the species" (Aristotle, *Topics* 121a 12). Similarly, the functional genus abstracted from the analogous can be used for classifying the primary subject, as it is regarded as a species of the new superordinate category. For this reason, in case 1 above, the speaker is described as belonging to a species of individuals characterized by "complete inability in performing specific activities," as "of the objects of which the species is predicated, the genus ought to be predicated" (Aristotle, *Topics* 121a 26).

The other types of analogy, based on the attribution of a predicate to the functional genus, are governed by a different *locus*, described by Boethius as follows: "Whatever is present to the genus is present to the species" (De *Topicis Differentiis* 1188B 21-22), in the sense that "the essence of the genus and the accidents adhering to that essence are also part of the species" (note 67). As the genus is functional to the predication of the predicate, namely it is warranted by the genus, it is predicated also of the specific concepts falling under it. For instance, in case 4 above, public officials are presented as a species of the generic category of "duties requiring a specific ability or knowledge," which justifies the attribution of the predicate "not being selectable by lot." For this reason, the following reasoning is triggered (Table 5.2):

Table 5.2 Analogy as a genus-species relation

Maxim	Whatever is present to the genus is present to the species.
Assumption	Public officials are a species of "duties requiring a specific ability or knowledge," of which "to be not selectable by lot" is said.
Syllogism 1	Whatever is present to the genus is present to the species.
	"Duties requiring a specific ability or knowledge" is the genus of "public officials."
	Therefore, whatever is present to "duties requiring a specific ability or knowledge" is also present to "public officials."
Syllogism 2	Whatever is present to "duties requiring a specific ability or knowledge" is also present to "public officials."
	Duties requiring a specific ability or knowledge are not selectable by lot.
	Therefore public officials are not selectable by lot.

This mechanism can explain also the strategic role of analogy. The hearer can attack the aforementioned classification by either denying the belonging of the primary subject to the functional genus, or the attribution of the predicate to the genus. As mentioned above, the first passage is implicit, and the specific features of the genus can be ambiguous, making the defense of the functional genus easier for the speaker. Otherwise, the hearer can reject the relationship functional genus—predicate by denying that the predicate applies to one of the species. However, by providing extreme and almost irrefutable cases, the speaker increases the burden of denial.

5.5 Analogical Redefinitions and Analogical Definitions

As seen above, analogy is based on a semantic operation of abstracting a generic property that is contextually needed for the attribution of a predicate or a classification. This mechanism is contextual, as the process of abstraction does not involve the commonly shared (and defined) concepts, but rather a specific use thereof, a pragmatic and contextual function. The idea of analogy as a form of contextual definition or redefinition can be analyzed by taking into account the distinct definitional processes based on analogical reasoning. The starting point is the analysis of the reasoning mechanisms underlying legal analogy. In law, analogical reasoning is a fundamental interpretative technique. For this reason, the contextual analogical abstraction becomes relevant from a semantic and legal perspective, as it provides a redefinition or a definition that constitutes a new interpretation, i.e. a new contextual meaning of a concept.

In law, arguments from analogy extend the attribution of a legal predicate to entities that are different from the ones falling within the existing legal categories. As Tarello (1980) put it, if a rule attributes any normative qualification (such as a power, an obligation or a status) to an individual or a category of individuals, it can be concluded that there is a different rule in force (or a different rule exists, is valid) that attributes the same quality to another individual or category of individuals connected with the former class by a similarity or an analogy relation. Such a relation shall be relevant from the perspective of the applicable law, or the qualification to be attributed (Tarello 1980, p. 351). However, this pattern of reasoning can have two different variants. The cases compared can be instances of the same category governed by the legal qualification A, or two categories (P and Q) of which the second (Q) is not governed by A. In other words, there is a crucial difference between a similarity of two cases (a and b) that can belong to the same class P, and a similarity of two distinct categories (P and Q).

This difference of reasoning can be mirrored by the structure of two distinct schemes of legal analogy, the so-called *analogia legis*, or the application of a written law to a different, similar case (Colombo 2003, pp. 96–97; Cendon 2011, p. 236), and *analogia iuris*, or the application of an abstract and unexpressed principle of law from which the stated law is drawn (Guastini 2011, p. 281). In the first case analogy is used to apply the law to borderline or controversial cases, not by abstracting a new generic concept but rather by specifying the conditions defining an already existing legal category. If we analyze the *analogia iuris*, or rather if we interpret the mechanism underlying this process of reasoning from a purely argumentative perspective, we notice that this type of reasoning is used to construct an unwritten category (a principle of law). This reading of the two legal interpretative strategies is clearly not intended to explain what these two types of legal analogy are. On the contrary, such reasoning processes have been used only to draw a distinction that applies to ordinary reasoning, and for this reason they have been analyzed only focusing on their logical and semantic dimension, without considering their legal implications or foundations. This distinction is needed to point out a crucial difference between the use of analogy to redefine an already existing and defined concept, and it role in creating and defining new or implicit ones. In this sense, *analogia legis* and *analogia iuris* can be considered from a logical perspective as two distinct analogical processes, consisting respectively in the renegotiation of an existing meaning and the creation of a new (or undefined) concept.

5.6 Analogical Redefinitions and Analogia Legis

Analogia legis consists in the comparison between two cases, a clear case (governed by a legal provision) and a borderline case, to which it is not clear whether the legal predicate A applies or not. The analogy specifies, or rather redefines, the relevant category P under which the clear case falls, so that the borderline case can also be included in it. From a reasoning perspective, *analogia legis* can be conceived as a form of specification of the properties of the legal category P. Since the existing definition does not allow a classification of borderline cases, through analogy the relevant, unstated factors are pointed out. This type of reasoning can be represented as follows (Ashley 1991, p. 758; Table 5.3):

Table 5.3 Argumentation scheme 2: specific scheme from *analogia legis*

Premise 1 (rule)	If x is P, then x has the right/is A
Premise 2 (borderline)	It is not clear whether a (a borderline case) is P
Similarity premise	a is similar to b
Premise 3 (principle of classification)	b was classified as P because of the factors $f_1, f_2, \ldots, f_n$
Redefinition premise	If x has the factors $f_1, f_2, \ldots, f_n$, then x is P
Premise 4 (factors)	a has $f_1, f_2, \ldots, f_n$
Conclusion	Therefore, a is P

The predicate is specified (or rather redefined, see Sorensen 1991) by highlighting the factors that are considered as essential for the legal qualification to apply. In this sense, it points out the characteristics that support the attribution of the legal predicate A to the category P, based on shared legal values.

The argument from *analogia legis* can be illustrated in the civil law by the following case from the Italian Corte Costituzionale (Judgment no. 0280 of 2010). The article no. 180, 4th paragraph of the Legislative Decree no. 285 of 1992 allows public transport (vehicles for the transportation of persons) and vehicles for rental (without driver) to keep on board only the photocopy of the registration document, authenticated by the owner. The problem arose when a police officer stopped the driver of a vehicle owned by a company of waste management. The driver showed him the driving license and the photocopy of the registration documents, authenticated by the company, instead of the original copies. However, the purpose of the vehicle was not the transportation of people, but of objects. For this reason, the case did not fall clearly within the category provided for by the aforementioned law, even though it shared some similarities with it. The case was analyzed by the Italian Corte Costituzionale, which reasoned as follows:

Case 5
The law that allowed the drivers of vehicles for public transport of persons to carry the photocopy of the registration document instead of the original copy was based on the need of promptly and systematically retrieving the original documents for purpose of renewal, updating and periodical service, in order to avoid the risk of their loss and the consequent custody of the vehicle (…). These purposes concern also any other types of public services characterized by essentiality,—as specified in art. 1 of the law no. 146/1990—and involving the management of a fleet of vehicles.

Table 5.4 Reconstructing *analogia legis*

Premise 1 (rule)	If x is a "*driver of vehicles for public transport of persons*" (P), then x has the right to "*carry the photocopy of the registration document instead of the original copy*" (A).
Premise 2 (borderline)	It is not clear whether a "*driver of a waste management vehicle*" is P.
Similarity premise	A "*driver of a waste management vehicle*" is similar to a "*driver of a vehicle for public transport of persons.*"
Premise 3 (principle of classification)	A "*driver of a vehicle for public transport of persons*" was classified as P because of the "*essentiality of the service proivided*" (f_1) and the "*management of a fleet of vehicles*" (f_2).
Redefinition premise	If x has the factors f_1 and f_2, then x is P.
Premise 4 (factors)	A "*driver of a waste management vehicle*" has f_1 and f_2.
Conclusion	Therefore, a "*driver of a waste management vehicle*" is P.

In this case, the category of "vehicles for public transport of persons" was redefined by means of analogy. The court set out the relevant features that could support the attribution of the right, i.e. "being an essential public service" and "managing a fleet of vehicles." These two features justified a permission based on the legal value of avoiding risks that can cause the failure to provide essential services, and thereby affect the public good. The reasoning can be represented as follows (Table 5.4):

Analogia legis can be considered as a type of reasoning used for extending a category governed by a legal provision, which can be set out in a statutory provision or in a previous decision (case law). *Analogia legis* can be used to interpret a state or federal law, such as in the following case (*Dooley v. Parker-Hannifin Corp.*, 817 F. Supp. 245, at 248 1993):

Case 6

Under Rhode Island Law, the "sale" of a product may create a variety of warranties regarding that product. Thus, a warranty of merchantability is implied in a contract for the "sale" of goods if the "seller" is a merchant with respect to goods of that type. [...] Breach of those warranties exposes the "seller" to liability for personal injury that proximately results from the breach. [...] Responsibility for personal injury caused by a defective product also may be imposed on one who "sells" the product on the theory of strict liability in tort as set forth in Restatement (Second) of Torts § 402A (1965).

This provision of law covers the category of "sold products," but it does not provide any indication for leasing agreements. A seller of a defective product is liable for it, but it is unclear whether lessors are exposed to the same liability. The court reasoned by analogy, pointing out characteristics common to both sale and lease, i.e. the placing of "(...) products in the stream of commerce by means of transactions very similar to sales." The fact that in both cases a product is put on the market by means of a transaction justifies liability based on the legal value of protecting the customer and the public. However, the characteristic of "placing products in the stream of commerce" redefines the concept of "sale" used in the law. In this specific context, this category is extended by redefinition, so that borderline cases are included.

In case law, the mechanism is more complex because there is not an explicit provision of law setting out a category and attributing a legal predicate to it. Instead, at common law the judge both applies and defines the legal rules based on previously decided cases (Friesen 1996, pp. 12–13). In this system the mechanism of *analogia legis* works as a specification or an extension of a category that is implicit or not explicitly defined by law. Analogy is used to point out characteristics (or factors) that are essential or fundamental for the attribution of the relevant legal predicate, and in this fashion provides a definition of an otherwise undefined or insufficiently defined concept.

One of the most famous cases involving this use of analogy is *Popov v. Hayashi* (WL 31833731, Cal. Super. Ct. 2002). The plaintiff (Popov), a baseball fan, stopped with his glove the ball hit by a famous player, who set a new record with it. However, in order to reach for the ball, Popov lost his balance and was forced to the ground by the crowd, leaving the ball loose on the ground. The defendant (Hayashi) was involuntarily forced to the ground as well, and when he saw the loose ball, he picked it up, rose to his feet, and put it in his pocket. Popov, who intended to establish and maintain possession of the ball, could not prove that he secured it. The crucial concept in this case is the definition of "possession," which was fundamental for classifying Popov's act and, as a consequence, charging Hayashi with conversion. The problem was the absence of a clear and univocal definition of "possession" in the California case law. Since a specific definition could not be found in both the written law and the case law, the parties supported their own redefinitions by means of analogy. For instance, the plaintiff used the following argument (*Popov v. Hayashi,* WL 31833731, at 8, Cal. Super. Ct. 2002):

Case 7
The hunting and fishing cases recognize that a mortally wounded animal may run for a distance before falling. The hunter acquires possession upon the act of wounding the animal not the eventual capture. Similarly, whalers acquire possession by landing a harpoon, not by subduing the animal.

The plaintiff compared the possession of the ball with the possession of an animal or a whale in hunting and fishing. In such cases, the value supporting the classification is to protect the interests of the party that makes the biggest efforts to capture the animal, which lead causally to the capture or subduing thereof. For this reason, the criteria, or rather factors, essential for the protection of such a value were stated as follows: "The actor to be actively and ably engaged in efforts to establish complete control" (f1); "Such efforts must be significant and they must be reasonably calculated to result in unequivocal dominion and control at some point in the near future" (f2). For this reason, the plaintiff claimed that the calculated efforts made to establish complete control on the ball could warrant the classification of his relationship with the ball as possession.

However, the court noticed that a ball is not an animal, and the efforts to secure a ball are not the same as the ones made to capture a whale or a fox. For this reason, the crucial problem was to determine whether partial possession of an object could be considered as full possession. To this purpose, the court used a different analogy to establish the factors that could lead to a more viable specification (or redefinition) of "possession." The analogy used by the court was the following (*Popov v. Hayashi*, WL 31833731, at 7, Cal. Super. Ct. 2002):

Case 8
(…) five boys were walking home along a railroad track in the city of Elizabeth New Jersey. The youngest of the boys came upon an old sock that was tied shut and contained something heavy. He picked it up and swung it. The oldest boy took it away from him and beat the others with it. The sock passes from boy to boy. Each controlled it for a short time. At some point in the course of play, the sock broke open and out spilled $ 775 as well as some rags, cloths and ribbons.

The court noted that possession requires both physical control and the intent to reduce the property to one's possession. Control and intent must be concurrent. None of the boys intended to take possession until it became apparent that the sock contained money. Each boy had physical control of the sock at some point before that discovery was made.

The relevant properties supporting the determination of "possession" (and, as a consequence, of the rights associated thereto) were considered to be physical control and intent, which need to be concurrent. The value supporting the classification (and the attribution of the relevant legal predicates) was equality, i.e. the protection of the interest and rights of parties having the same claims on a piece of property. Since both parties had physical control and intent, they were found equally entitled to the ball.

5.7 Analogy as an Instrument for Introducing New Generic Categories

The analogical mechanism labeled above "*analogia legis*" is aimed at redefining an already existing concept, which is, however, not defined, or not sufficiently specified. Considering the idea of analogy described in the first sections, this type of reasoning encompasses another mechanism, which we can refer to as *analogia iuris*. This label is only intended to cover a specific logical dimension of analogy, which can be compared to the reasoning aspect of this instrument of legal interpretation (without any pretense to discuss the legal implications or characteristics thereof). From a purely argumentative perspective, we can describe *analogia iuris* as the application to a specific case of an implicit ratio or principle of a law governing a different case. For this reason, this analogical process consists in introducing a new category that includes both the primary subject and the target, which can be implicit or explicit. This argument can be represented as follows (Macagno and Walton 2009b, p. 173; Guastini 2011, pp. 280–281; Table 5.5):

Table 5.5 Argumentation scheme 3: specific scheme from *analogia iuris*

Premise 1 (target)	No law provides for the *x*'s that are *Q*
Premise 2 (property)	If *x* is *P*, then *x* has the right/is *A*
Similarity premise	*P* and *Q* belong to the same functional genus *G*
Species—Genus premise	If *x* is *G*, then *x* has the right/is *A*
Conclusion	If *x* is *Q*, then *x* has the right/is *A*

This pattern describes a reasoning structure that can be used for different purposes according to the legal system. In civil law, it can be considered as a reason provided for the use of a systematic interpretation. In lack of a source statement governing a specific case, the enforceable rule needs to be found within the legal system, by interpreting one of the provisions already in force. Analogy in this case provides the "surface reasoning structure" which actually draws its force from the authority of the completeness of the legal system. This mechanism represents the reasoning underlying the "construction of an unexpressed rule" (Guastini 2011, p. 278), which can be illustrated by the following case (Guastini 2011, p. 280):

Case 9
According to art. 2038 of the Italian Civil code, anyone who has unduly received some goods and has transferred them in good faith, ignoring the obligation to return them, shall return the consideration thereof and not the very goods or their value. The ratio of the law is the principle of protecting good faith. On this view, the law provides only for the restitution of the consideration and not more burdensome obligations in order to protect the good faith of the individual. The undue receipt together with the transferal subsequent thereof is similar to the purchase and sale of stolen goods when their illicit provenience is unknown. Therefore, art. 2038, 1st paragraph, shall be interpreted as applicable also to the case of purchase in good faith of stolen goods.

In this case, an unexpressed principle is abstracted from a law and applied to a case not possibly falling thereunder, so that the scope of an existent provision is broadened. The new category "transferal of goods obtained in good faith" is introduced, encompassing both the goods that have been purchased and the ones that have been simply received.

The creation of a new abstract functional genus by means of analogy is clear in opinion rendered by the court the aforementioned case *Popov v. Hayashi.* Using the analogy mentioned at case 8 above, the Court provided the criteria for defining the concept of "possession," establishing that according to this (re)definition both parties had both possessed the ball. However, the problem was to determine the legal title to the ball, considering that both parties possessed it equally, and that no precedent existed in California. The court reached a conclusion by drawing an analogy from a case that was noticeably different, as it did not involve possession at all (*Popov v. Hayashi,* WL 31833731, at 7, Cal. Super. Ct. 2002):

Case 10
Although there is no California case directly on point, *Arnold v. Producers Fruit Company* (1900) 128 Cal. 637 provides some insight. There, a number of different rune growers contracted with Producer's Fruit Company to dry and market their product. Producers did a bad job. They mixed fruit from many different growers together in a single bin and much of the fruit rotted because it was improperly treated. When one of the plaintiffs offered proof that the fruit in general was rotten, Producers objected on the theory that the plaintiff could not prove that the prunes he contributed to the mix were the same prunes that rotted. The court concluded that it did not matter. After the mixing was done, each grower had an undivided interest in the whole, in proportion to the amount of fruit each had originally contributed. The principle at work here is that where more than one party has a valid claim to a single piece of property, the court will recognize an undivided interest in the property in proportion to the strength of the claim.

Table 5.6 Reconstructing *analogia iuris*

Premise 1 (target)	No law provides for the *x*'s that "have partial possession in a ball" (*x* are *Q*).
Premise 2 (property)	If *x* "contributed to the mix of fruit" (*x* is *P*), then *x* "has an undivided interest in the whole" (*x* has the right/is *A*).
Similarity premise	*P* and *Q* belong to the same functional genus "to have a valid claim to a single piece of property" (*G*).
Species—Genus premise	If *x* is *G*, then *x* has the right/is *A*.
Conclusion	If *x* is *Q*, then *x* has the right/is *A*.

In this case, the analogy is between two distinct categories, "to have partial possession in a ball" (primary subject) and "to contribute to the mix of fruit" (analogous), to the latter of which the legal predicate "to have an undivided interest in the whole" is attributed. The two categories are placed under a common generic property, a genus that is functional to the attribution of the predicate, i.e. "to have a valid claim to a single piece of property." As a result of this abstraction, all parties having a valid claim to a single piece of property have also an undivided interest in it and, therefore, the parties that have partial possession of a piece of property have also an undivided interest in it. This argument can be reconstructed following the aforementioned more abstract pattern (Table 5.6):

Unlike the process labeled "*analogia legis*," this type of analogical reasoning is not used for redefining an already existing concept, but rather for introducing a new one. The new category of "having a valid claim to a single piece of property" was not an already existing legal category. On the contrary, it was introduced by means of analogical reasoning.

5.8 Conclusion

Analogy can be regarded as a reasoning process grounded on the abstraction of a generic property from two comparable entities or states of affairs. This generic property can be considered from a logic-semantic perspective as a functional genus, in the sense that it is a contextually essential characteristic of the two terms of the comparison, under which both of them fall both of them. A pragmatic and contingent essence of a concept can be justified by considering the analogical process as a mechanism of contextual redefinition grounded on relevance. This approach is based on two crucial dimensions, the analysis of relevance as an argumentative relation of justification, and the account of the process of selecting the relevant features of a concept as a mechanism of contextual redefinition. The common generic property is a property that is fundamental (i.e. relevant) for the attribution of the relevant predicate or the achievement of the communicative intention. This relevance relation can be accounted for as an argument that justifies the predication of the property based on different principles, such as cause-effect, values, consequences, etc. On this perspective, the force of an analogy depends on the acceptability of this argumentative relation. The second crucial dimension of analogy pointed out in this paper is the role of analogy as a re-definitional process. The functional genus abstracted from the terms of the comparison is not simply a focus on some characteristics instead of others, it cannot be considered as a category in the sense of a collection of concepts or individuals. The genus redefines implicitly and contextually its species, i.e. the concepts that in that specific analogy are placed under it. For the purpose of the analogy (and the communicative move) the two concepts have a specific contextual meaning established by the new functional genus. For this reason, analogy can be considered as a strategy for contextually and contingently redefining a concept.

The mechanism of analogy can be used for distinct purposes. The analogical processes that have been referred to as "*analogia legis*" and "*analogia iuris*" mirror at a more conceptual level a difference between two different uses of reasoning from analogy. The first one is a form of (implicit or explicit) redefinition of a concept, while the second one consists in the introduction of a new generic property, under which the two compared terms fall.

References

Aristotle 1991. *Posterior Analytics*. Translated by J. Barnes. In *The Works of Aristotle,* ed. J. Barnes. Princeton: Princeton University Press.

Aristotle 1991. *Prior Analytics*. Translated by A. J. Jenkinson. In *The Works of Aristotle,* ed. J. Barnes. Princeton: Princeton University Press.

Aristotle 1991. *Rhetoric*. Translated by W. Rhys Roberts. In *The Works of Aristotle,* ed. J. Barnes. Princeton: Princeton University Press.

Aristotle 1991. *Topics*. Translated by W. A. Pickard-Cambridge. In *The Works of Aristotle,* ed. J. Barnes. Princeton: Princeton University Press.

Ashley, K. 1991. Reasoning with cases and hypotheticals in HYPO. *International Journal of Man-Machine Studies* 34 (6): 753–796.

Boethius, A. M. S. 1978. Translated by E. Stump. *De topicis differentiis*. Ithaca: Cornell University Press.

Carston, R. 2002. *Thoughts and utterances*. Malden: Blackwell.Carston, R. 2002. *Thoughts and utterances*. Malden: Blackwell.

Cendon, P., ed. 2011. *Commentario al codice civile*. Milano: Giuffrè.

Colombo, G. M. 2003. *Sapiens aequitas: L'equitā nella riflessione canonistica tra i due codici*. Roma: Pontificia Università Gregoriana.

De Vries, P. 1965. *Let me count the ways*. Boston: Little Brown.

Friesen, J. 1996. When common law courts interpret civil codes. *Wisconsin International Law Journal* 15:1–27.

Glucksberg, S., and B. Keysar. 1990. Understanding metaphorical comparisons: Beyond similarity. *Psychological Review* 97 (1): 3–18.

Goodman, N. 1968. *Languages of art: An approach to a theory of symbols*. Indianapolis: Bobbs-Merrill.

Guastini, R. 2011. *Interpretare e argomentare*. Milano: Giuffrè.

Hesse, M. 1965. Aristotle's logic of analogy. *The Philosophical Quarterly* 15 (61): 328–340.

Kienpointner, M. 1986. Towards a typology of argument schemes. In *Argumentation across the lines of discipline: Proceedings of the conference on argumentation 1986,* eds. H. van Eemeren, R Grootendorst, J. A. Blair, and C. A. Willard, 275–297. Amsterdam: Amsterdam University Press.

Macagno, F., and D. Walton. 2009a. Reasoning from classification and definition. *Argumentation* 23:81–107.

Macagno, F., and D. Walton. 2009b. Argument from analogy in law, the classical tradition, and recent theories. *Philosophy and Rhetoric* 42 (2): 154–182.

Rigotti, E. 2006. Relevance of context-bound loci to topical potential in the argumentation stage. *Argumentation* 20:519–540.

Rigotti, E., and S. Greco-Morasso. 2010. Comparing the argumentum model of *Topics* to other contemporary approaches to argument schemes: The procedural and material components. *Argumentation* 24:489–512.

Searle, J. 1981. *Expression and meaning: Studies in the theory of speech acts*. Cambridge: Cambridge University Press.

Sorensen, R. 1991. Vagueness and the desiderata for definition. In *Definitions and definability: philosophical perspectives,* eds. J. Fetzer, D. Shatz, and N. Schlesinger, 71–109. Dordrecht: Kluwer.

Stern, J. 2000. *Metaphor in context*. Cambridge: MIT.

Stern, J. 2008. Metaphor, semantics and context. In *The Cambridge handbook of metaphor and thought,* ed. R. Gibbs, 262–279. Cambridge: Cambridge University Press.

Tarello, G. 1980. *L'interpretazione della legge*. Milano: Giuffrè.

Thomson, J. 1971. A defense of abortion. *Philosophy and Public Affairs* 1 (1): 47–66.

Walton, D., C. Reed, and F. Macagno. 2008. *Argumentation schemes*. Cambridge: Cambridge University Press.

Chapter 6
Arguments from Parallel Reasoning

Jan Albert van Laar

6.1 Introduction

Argumentation is a co-production by a proponent and an opponent who engage in a critical examination of their difference of opinion, aiming to resolve it on the merits of both sides, or so it is assumed in this paper on the dialectic of arguments from analogy. I shall investigate the consequences of the dialogical view for a particular type of argument from analogy, called *argument from parallel reasoning*, that has been discussed in some detail by Woods and Hudak (1989). I shall be concerned with the characterization of this type of argumentation, as well as with the norms for evaluating instances of such argumentation. Arguments from parallel reasoning are analyzed as both case-based and defeasible arguments. The first is taken to mean that an argument from parallel reasoning can be evaluated without an appeal to a substantial universal principle different from the underlying abstract argumentation scheme. The latter is taken to mean that a critical opponent has the possibility to challenge the argument's conclusion, even after having conceded each of the argument's premises, so that I also need to deal with the question of what use, if any, an argument from parallel reasoning has for a proponent.

Suppose, a proponent contends that we should allow camera surveillance with drones by the Amsterdam police, on account of these drones' cost-effectiveness. Suppose further, that the opponent addressed makes it clear that she acknowledges the drones' cost-effectiveness, as well as the relevance of this consideration, but that she remains, nevertheless, critical towards the proponent's thesis for worrying about intrusions on privacy. In such a case, the proponent may consider it to be expedient to put forward an argument such as: "I happen to know that (or: I would expect that) you consent to cameras on satellites on account of their cost-effectiveness, and despite privacy considerations. Well, reasoning from cost-effectiveness to cameras on drones, despite privacy considerations, is comparable to reasoning from cost-effectiveness to cameras on satellites, despite privacy considerations." The proponent

J. A. van Laar (✉)
Faculty of Philosophy, University of Groningen, Groningen, The Netherlands
e-mail: j.a.van.laar@rug.nl

H. J. Ribeiro (ed.), *Systematic Approaches to Argument by Analogy*,
Argumentation Library 25, DOI 10.1007/978-3-319-06334-8_6,

has drawn an analogy, albeit on analogy of a special kind where he compares two dialogical situations, to the effect that if the opponent has been willing, or—if it concerns a hypothetical case—*would* be willing to draw a conclusion in the one dialogical situation, she also should be prepared, on pain of inconsistency, to draw a similar conclusion in the dialogical situation at hand. First, I attempt to conceive of such an argument from parallel reasoning as an example of case-based reasoning, for the reason that it seems implausible and uncharitable to hold the proponent responsible for any universal principle linking, in this example, privacy considerations and cost-effectiveness considerations. The argument's proponent does not commit himself to *more* than there being some relevant similarity in these two dialogical situations. Second, I attempt to explain how such arguments from parallel reasoning can be seen as both being defeasible, in the sense of allowing the opponent the option to challenge the argument's conclusion, even after having conceded each of its regular premises, and yet providing the proponent with a device to bind the opponent to the argument's connection between premises and conclusion.

Before entering into the issue of how an argument from parallel reasoning is co-produced in critical dialogue (Sect. 4), I shall, first, elaborate on the argumentation scheme that underlies arguments from parallel reasoning (Sect. 2), and, second, deal with the importance of criticism as a driving force within dialogue (Sect. 3). Afterwards, I shall indicate the critical options for any opponent confronted with such an argument and show how such arguments are both case-based and defeasible yet binding (Sect. 5). Before concluding, I shall illustrate my findings with a famous, but a-typical example of an argument from parallel reasoning, put forward by John Stuart Mill, in favour of the existence of other minds (Sect. 6).

6.2 Argument from Parallel Reasoning

Arguments from parallel reasoning form a special kind of argument from analogy. What I understand by *analogy* is taken from Perelman and Olbrechts-Tyteca (1969), who, following Aristotle, characterize an analogy as a proposition of the form "A is to B as C is to D" (p. 372). In the numerous and extensive literatures on the topic (Guarini et al. 2009), many purposes are attributed to analogies, a prominent one among them to clarify something. This paper, however, shall be concerned only with argumentative uses of analogy.

Yet, not all arguments from analogy are on a par. I shall distinguish between a ground-dialogical and a metadialogical type of argumentation from analogy, and deal with argument from parallel reasoning as kind of metadialogical argument from analogy. I consider the following example to be a prototypical example of the ground dialogical kind of argument from analogy. "Elstar apples are sweet. Jonagold apples look like Elstar apples. Therefore, presumably, Jonagold apples are sweet." This example easily fits, what Walton refers to as, the *basic scheme for argument from analogy*: "Generally Case 1 is similar to Case 2. A is true in Case 1. Therefore, A is true in Case 2" (Walton 2012, p. 192).[1]

I consider the following to be a prototypical example of the metadialogical type: "You ought to define the term *drone* to me in our discussion about police surveillance, because you requested me to define *drone* in our earlier discussion on their military uses." Also the following argument schemes are metadialogical: "you should challenge (or alternatively: *withdraw commitment to*, or *concede*) proposition P, because you would be willing to challenge (withdraw commitment to, concede) Q, and P and Q are comparable." In each of these cases, some specific dialogue move is required from the interlocutor in the current dialogical situation on the basis of the interlocutor's acceptance of a comparable move in a comparable dialogical situation. An argument from parallel reasoning fits this pattern, but deals specifically with the dialogical move of accepting an argument's conclusion on account of the argument's premises. [2]

I consider the following to be a prototypical example of an argument from parallel reasoning: "We should allow the Amsterdam police force to use camera surveillance with drones on account of their cost-effectiveness, and despite privacy considerations, for we also allow cameras on satellites on account of their cost-effectiveness, and despite privacy considerations, and these cases are comparable."

My treatment of this special class of arguments from analogy connects with what Woods and Hudak have contended about arguments from analogy generally. What they characterize as argumentation from analogy, *tout cours*, I consider to be the characterization of a particularly interesting subclass of arguments from analogy.

According to these authors (Woods and Hudak 1989, p. 127):

> [a]rguments from analogy are arguments by parity of reasoning, so-called. They are arguments about arguments, *meta-arguments*. They argue that two or more target arguments stand or fall together and that they do so because they are relevantly at parity, that they possess similar deep structures by virtue of which they coincide in logical form. The target arguments of the meta-argument are thus *analogues* of each other.

I shall transpose their meta-argumentative view to a full-fledged dialogical setting, so as to embed these metadialogical arguments in a setting where an opponent is examining whether she can remain critical—in a consistent and tenable manner—vis-à-vis the proponent's standpoint.[3]

Three comments on Woods and Hudak's theory are in order. First, from the examples they give, it becomes clear that arguments from analogy cannot only

[1] The analogy appealed to in the second premise can be phrased as: "the way Elstar apples look is to their taste as the way Jonagold apples look is to their taste", and is special in so far as "taste" occurs both in the comparison case as well as in the target case.

[2] Govier distinguishes between *a priori* arguments from analogy, which start from a hypothetical comparison case, and inductive arguments from analogy, which start from an analogue that is non-hypothetical (Govier 1989, pp. 141–142). Metadialogical arguments from analogy can both be *a priori* as well as *inductive*, in this sense.

[3] My treatment connects with Juthe's ideas on "refutation by parallel argument" (Juthe 2009), but where his main interest is with meta-argumentative criticism, my focus is on metadialogical support.

support a thesis to the effect that two arguments stand or fall together, but also a thesis to the effect that the conclusion of the one argument stands, due to the virtues of the other argument. Or, for that matter, that it falls, due to the other argument's vices (in which case the result is, what Juthe (2009) calls a *refutation by parallel argument*). Second, they label these arguments meta-arguments, apparently because when writing out the basic structure of an analogical argument, two arguments are mentioned and talked about, rather than merely used:

> (1) Argument A possess a deep structure whose logical form provides that the premisses of A bear relation R to its conclusion. (2) Argument B shares with A the same deep structure. (3) Therefore, B possess a deep structure whose logical form provides that its premisses likewise bear R to its conclusion. (4) Hence, B is an analogue of A. A and B are good or bad arguments, by parity of reasoning, so-called. (Woods and Hudak 1989, p. 127)

Third, the deep structure or logical form that is alleged to be identical includes, according to the authors, both deductive patterns as well as non-deductive ones, Thompson's famous violinist analogy instantiating a non-deductive logical form.

With the aim of examining arguments from analogy as a contribution to an argumentative dialogue, I shall give a characterization of metadialogical arguments from analogy from the perspective of the theory of argumentation schemes, as developed by van Eemeren and Grootendorst (1992), and by Walton et al. (2008), and hypothesize that the following argumentation scheme underlies typical arguments from parallel reasoning (Fig. 6.1):

Conclusion:	You should accept proposition S.
Premise 1:	Because, proposition A in dialogical situation C did (or would) convince you of proposition B.
Premise 2:	In the current dialogical situation T you accept proposition R.
Premise 3:	Accepting B on the basis of A in C is comparable to accepting S on the basis of R in T.

Fig. 6.1 The argumentation scheme from parallel reasoning

Premise 1 presents the *comparison case* (Woods and Hudak 1989, p. 128). Premise 2 might be seen as giving the argument's main reason, for it is R that must convince the opponent of S, the other premises explaining *how* R should convince the opponent of S. Premise 3 presents a meta-dialogical analogy, which could be phrased abstractly thus: *Proposition B is to proposition A in dialogical situation C as proposition S is to proposition R in dialogical situation T.*[4]

We should deal in some detail with the intended interpretation of Premise 3. First, the comparison premise could be taken to express that the two cases are sufficiently similar. In other words, the similarity between the two cases of reasoning is

[4] According to a stricter analysis, a metadialogical argument from analogy would instantiate two, interlocked argumentation schemes. Argumentation scheme (1) "S, because in the current situation T you accept R, and if in T you accept R then you should accept S." Argumentation scheme (2) "If in T you accept R, then you should accept S, because A in a situation C did (or would) convince you of accepting B, and accepting B on the basis of A in C is comparable to accepting S on the basis of R in T." The conclusions that I shall draw, can easily be made to apply to an account that strives for individual argumentation schemes that remain as basic and simple as possible.

such that if the opponent's accepts of B on account of A in C, she cannot but accept S on account of R. In that case, the argumentation scheme is not a defeasible one, but any instance, according to this reading, expresses a logically valid argument, in the sense that it would be logically inconsistent to accept the three premises and yet raise criticism against the thesis. Note that, different from what some authors suggest, such case-based (see below for an elaboration of the claim that such an instance is really case-based), rather than principle-based, argument from analogy can be genuinely valid.[5]

Second, Premise 3 can be taken to express that the two cases are in some relevant respects similar, so that the opponent's acceptance of B on the basis of A in C provides a reason to accept S on the basis of R, in the case at hand, albeit not necessarily a compelling reason. In other words, the similarity between the target and the comparison cases is such that the opponent's acceptance of B on account of A is a relevant consideration, and a possible reason to accept S on account of R. Yet, in this version, the argumentation is a defeasible one, in the sense that it is possible for the opponent to accept all premises of an instance of this scheme, including the comparison premise, and yet resist, in a consistent and even plausible manner, the argument's conclusion. Given this reading, the opponent could explain the tenability of her position by indicating a relevant difference between the comparison case and the target case that raises doubts about whether thesis S follows from R.

In my view, it is not a task for argumentation theorists to tell a discussant what argumentation scheme he should adopt. Instead, they should develop repositories of argumentation schemes for which discussants can, as it were, choose their tools, as well as develop procedures for the proper use of these tools. In this paper, I shall deal with the second reading of the comparison premise, without wanting to discredit the other option in any way, in order to see what dialogical procedure fits it, in such a way that the argumentation is of use to the proponent, notwithstanding its defeasibility.

As a consequence, an instance of the above argumentation scheme allows an opponent to accept each of the argument's three premises, and yet to challenge the connection between the set of the three premises and the conclusion in the case at hand. We can implement this critical option by associating each argument with a connection premise that can be challenged. The connection premise will simply be a conditional statement, having the conjunction of the argument's premises as its antecedent, and its conclusion as its consequent, and this usually implicit premise expresses the proponent's claim that a commitment by the opponent to the argument's premises should bring, within the circumstances at hand, a commitment to the argument's conclusion. In our example, the connection premise would read: "If you allow cameras on satellites on account of their cost-effectiveness, and despite

[5] For example, Waller (2001) discusses so-called "deductive arguments from analogy" (and compares them with "inductive" ones), which he understand as having a premise that appeals to a principle, which, translated to the terminology of my Fig. 6.1, would read: "The most plausible reason for believing B is the acceptance of principle P" (p. 201), and any instance of his scheme is deductively valid in so-far as principle P implies conclusion S. As I am interested here in (meta-dialogical) case-based reasoning, I will disregard his principle-based version of argumentation from analogy.

privacy considerations, and if camera surveillance with drones for a police force is cost-effective, and if—also—these cases are comparable, then you should allow the Amsterdam police force to use camera surveillance with drones." The connection premise is fully particular, tied to the specific application of the argumentation scheme to the case at hand, and *if* the opponent commits herself to its acceptance, she can no longer consistently accept the three (regular) premises while refusing to accept the conclusion. The distinction between the analogy premise and the connection premise enables the opponent to challenge the application of the argumentation scheme's application in the current situation, without either challenging the analogy between the two pieces of reasoning, let alone that of challenging the appropriateness of the underlying argumentation scheme.

6.3 Criticism as a Driving Force

The Opponent as a Co-producer An argument, as understood here, is a piece of reasoning that is used by a proponent in an attempt to convince an opponent of his opinion by answering her critical doubts and objections, maintaining that this attempt fits the confines of a resolution-oriented, critical discussion. For example, within the pragma-dialectical theory, argumentation is an attempt to persuade an opponent (*antagonist*) who, within the normative framework of a critical discussion, interprets and evaluates the proponent's (*protagonist's*) standpoint and the arguments he puts forward in answer to previous critical reactions (van Eemeren and Grootendorst 2004). And within the model for *permissive persuasion dialogue*, a proponent of a thesis tries to construe a complex of reasoning, in an attempt to transfer the opponent's commitment to her initial concessions towards the proponent's thesis (Walton and Krabbe 1995).

Given that the proponent's argumentation is step-wise constructed in response to the critical inquiries by the opponent, it can be expected that the quality of this argumentation is influenced by the choices made by the opponent. Thus, the opponent has a responsibility here. In order to encourage the proponent to develop argumentation that starts from reasonable premises, that employs suitable reasoning schemes, and in which propositions are phrased sufficiently clear, the opponent should take care not to let him get away with unacceptable premises, implausible argumentative connections or vague and ambiguous formulations. Consequently, the opponent cannot remain passive, and should accept responsibility for steering the dialogue in a proper direction. I distinguish between three types of decisions that enable her to influence the development of the proponent's argumentation.

First, it is the opponent who decides what propositions she concedes, either at a preliminary stage of the dialogue or in the course of the dialogue, thereby determining the propositions that the proponent can use as the undisputed starting points of his argumentation. By making these choices, the opponent steers the development of the proponent's argumentation, and the more so if the proponent is sufficiently responsive, and eager to develop a successful, *ex concessis* argumentation.

Second, it is the opponent who decides what premises and what argumentative connections to criticize. Even a minimally informative challenge of the form "Why so?" directs the proponent in a particular direction by showing him what part of his position stands in need of defence. Walton discussed the responsibility or obligation to raise critical question in response to the proponent's argument as the *burden of questioning* (Walton 2003).

Third, the opponent may decide to inform the proponent about what underlies or motivates her critical stance, thereby giving some directions to the proponent about what kind of argumentation she would consider convincing. She can do so by providing the proponent with, what can be referred to as, a *counter-consideration*. The reasoning thus advanced by the opponent does not constitute argumentation, for it lacks the purpose of developing an *ex concessis* argument aimed at convincing the addressee. Instead, it exemplifies a kind of explanation for why the opponent considers it opportune or apposite to criticize the proponent's proposition, and she may motivate her criticism of a proposition P without taking any responsibility for the denial of P, or even for the proposition that constitutes her counter-consideration. The responsibility to offer counter-considerations, in addition to expressing one's critical stance (for example by a request for argumentation of the form "Why so?") is called the *burden of criticism* (van Laar and Krabbe 2013), and I shall go into some more detail about it, because, first, the opponent can request for an argument from parallel reasoning by means of particular kinds of counter-considerations, and, second, within some situations, the opponent can only challenge the connection premise of an argument from parallel reasoning (and in that way trying to defeat it) by incurring the obligation to provide a counter-consideration that explains why she does not regard the set of premises as sufficient ground for the conclusion.

The Burden of Criticism Given this role for the opponent, it is not surprising that she has particular responsibilities, and even obligations, so as to guarantee the soundness of the resolution process. Many of the rules pertaining to the role of the opponent have been examined and formulated by van Eemeren and Grootendorst (2004) in their 15 rules for critical discussion. These rules, however, can be extended by dialogue rules that specify a burden of criticism, i.e., a responsibility or obligation to elaborate on, and motivate one's critical stance, as a supplement to the responsibility to raise criticism in the first place (what Walton 2003 calls "the burden of questioning"). The question, thus, is: when has an opponent a responsibility or even a dialectical obligation to offer an explanatory counter-consideration?

Suppose that the proponent asserts that the use of drones by the Amsterdam police force should be allowed, and that in response the opponent offers *tenability criticism*, i.e., she poses a request for argumentation in support of the proponent's thesis, in this case an argument in favour of the correctness of the statement that drones are allowable. In such a situation, the proponent incurs a burden of proof with respect to the challenged proposition. But before discharging his burden of proof, he may first want to obtain information about what motivates the opponent not to accept his statement at face value, so as to enable himself to devise an argument that stands a serious chance at convincing his opponent by being genuinely responsive to her doubts. So, instead of giving a reason in support of the drones immediately, the proponent first puts forward a request for explanation: "Please, explain why you do not accept that drones are acceptable for the Amsterdam police?" A proponent should have a right to pose such a request for explanation, "Explain (Why A?)."

The proposition that the opponent puts forward in explanation of her critical stance is referred to as a *counter-consideration*, "Counter C." In the example, the counter-consideration might be the proposition: "No expert in privacy issues considers police drones acceptable." The opponent need not really *assert* that there is no expert in privacy issues who vouches for police drones, at least not in the sense that she incurs a burden of proof for this proposition. This counter-consideration can be presented by the opponent in two quite different, yet equally non-assertive ways to the proponent. When offering her counter-consideration, the opponent may stress *her* aim of showing the tenability of her critical position: "As far as you've shown, no privacy expert vouches for it." The very same message, however, can also be expressed more modestly, "How about the privacy experts? What do they say about it?" in which case the opponent, as it were, provides the proponent with a strategic advice, stressing *his* individual aim of persuasion.

In both cases, the appropriate response by the proponent is to refute the counter-consideration, by saying something to the effect that "This privacy expert considers police drones acceptable!," or to refute it by stating that his opinion stands, even if no privacy expert were to vouch for it. It would, however, not be an appropriate response for the proponent to request the opponent to argue in favour of the counter-consideration (a formal dialectical system that implements this norm has been proposed in Laar 2011). Rescher introduced the notion of a "cautious assertion," which clarifies the typical illocutionary force of a counter-consideration. According to Rescher, a cautious assertion of a proposition P, indicated by "†P", stands for: "P is the case for all that you (the adversary) have shown" or "P's being the case is compatible with everything you've said (i.e., have maintained or conceded)" (Rescher 1977, p. 6). Consequently, it is possibly for the opponent to raise a critical reaction that is highly informative to the proponent by conveying her motives for being critical and thereby giving him strategic advice, without, however, becoming committed to this counter-consideration.

The opponent can be assigned a mere responsibility to provide the proponent with a counter-consideration, if requested, in the sense of it being desirable that the opponent informs the proponent about her position, and makes her contributions more than minimally directive. Because the quality of the dialogue improves if the opponent, in addition to raising a mere challenge, also offers a counter-consideration, so that the proponent is assisted in developing an interesting *ex concessis* argumentation.

As stated above, counter-considerations are relevant for a dialogical theory of argument from parallel reasoning, for two reasons. First, because the opponent can request for such an argument from parallel reasoning by means of particular kinds of counter-considerations. In line with the speech-act oriented theory of van Eemeren and Grootendorst, a challenge or critical question by the opponent can best be conceived of as a request for an argument. Given that the opponent's counter-consideration also functions to advise the proponent to put forward an argument of a particular kind, the opponent may add a counterconsideration to her challenge in order to make the request more specific. By using counter-considerations, the opponent can make her request more and more specific, up to the level of requesting for, say, an argument from authority—"Why S?"; "Why S? Says who?"; "Why S? Says what privacy expert?" (the last one being equivalent to "Says who? As far as you've shown, there's no privacy expert who considers it acceptable"). Similarly, critical responses can be specified by the opponent by giving a counter-consideration that encourages the proponent to offer an argument from parallel reasoning. (See for a treatment of the dialogical norms for offering, and for responding to less specific and more specific requests for argument, J. A. van Laar "Criticism in need of clarification", 2014.)

Second, counter-considerations are relevant to a theory of argument from parallel reasoning, because if the opponent adopts the argumentation scheme From Parallel Reasoning as *prima facie* acceptable, and the proponent offers an instance of that very scheme, then the connection premise of that argument counts as a so-called *presumptive commitment* of the opponent (Krabbe 2001, p. 151). That a proposition P is a *presumptive* commitment means that the commitment is not *fixed*, and that it can be challenged. It also means that the commitment is not *free*, and cannot be challenged without further ado. Instead, if P is a presumptive commitment, the opponent can challenge it, albeit at the expense of incurring the obligation to explain her withdrawal of her commitment to P with a counter-consideration, if the proponent requests so (and to argue for the appropriateness of withdrawing this commitment to P, if the proponent requests so). Whether a proposition counts as such a presumptive commitment is typically highly dependent on the context of the dialogue. By entering the gym, even a philosophical sceptic incurs a presumptive commitment to having a physical body, whereas in the company of his professionally sceptical colleagues, challenging the existence of your physical body does not force him to explain himself (cf. Rescorla 2009). Similarly, if in the situation at hand the opponent happens to have adopted the argumentation scheme From Parallel Reasoning as prima facie acceptable, and she nevertheless challenges the connection premise of an argument that clearly instantiates it, then she must, upon request, provide an explanatory counter-consideration to the proponent. In this way, an adopted argumentation scheme is binding on the opponent in so-far as the opponent, when offered an instance of that scheme, must choose between on the one hand accepting the reasons—if true—as sufficient justification of the conclusion or, on the other, offering a counter-consideration against the argumentative connection.

6.4 Requesting for an Argument from Parallel Reasoning

Suppose that the proponent states his opinion, by uttering his standpoint "S", that the opponent subsequently challenges it with a fully unspecific request for argumentation "why S?", and that the proponent responds by saying: "explain (Why S?)." Then, the opponent may choose to direct the proponent to present an argument from parallel reasoning. Before turning to the issue of how she may make such a specific request for argumentation, let's examine the issue of why she would want to do so in the first place.

Why wouldn't the opponent request for a more straightforward argument, instead of for requesting for the indirect, roundabout way of directing the attention to a piece of reasoning in a comparable case? Govier (1989, p. 148) suggests an answer when writing that "[t]he trick about analogies—and their charm as well, I think—is that we are often able to see or sense important resemblances between cases without being able to spell them out exhaustively in just so many words". In line with this view, we can expect the opponent to request for an argument from analogy when, first, she surmises that an analogical argument is easier to grasp, either for herself or for the proponent. For one, one of them may not be very knowledgeable in the field, and the use of a well-adapted analogy might appeal to an area where they do have more well-developed intuitions about what to accept on the basis of what.

A different motive is the expectation that a different argumentative strategy (for example offering some universal statement from which the standpoint follows) will happen to be ineffective to the opponent, due to the unacceptability of one of the premises (such as the universal statement) that is needed for such a strategy to work (cf. Juthe 2009, p. 158).

Thus, arguments from parallel reasoning can portrayed in a negative way: it is by lack of more knowledge, more useful concessions, higher understanding, more consensus, and the like, that we should rest satisfied with an argument from parallel reasoning. But then, such situations can also be used to polish the value of argumentative analogies, for we might as well state that understanding in a new field, or the generation of new knowledge about a topic may properly commence with recognizing analogous patterns, so that the argument may come off the ground, without the need to appeal to more direct evidence, or to problematic universal claims.

There are various ways in which one may request for an argument from parallel reasoning. I conceive of these requests as challenges accompanied with a counter-considerations, steering the proponent towards discharging his burden of proof in this special manner. Some examples are:

> You know the positions I have defended in our earlier discussions. Why would someone like me accept your thesis S?
> Why S? As far as you've shown, someone like me can consistently question S!
> Why would a be B? With what could I compare a?
> Can you show me how you reason to your conclusion, by comparing it with how I would reason in a parallel case?
> Why would a be B? As far as you've shown, a is not relevantly similar to anything I accept as B.[6]

Suppose, a philosopher adopts the role of the proponent and defends, against his critical opponent (either a sceptical colleague, or he himself in his sceptical mo-

[6] Other terms that are useful for requesting for an analogy, or for making it clear that such a request is being complied with are: x is similar/parallel/corresponding to y, x resembles/correlates with/relates to y, there is a kinship between a and b, a and b are kindred/cognate/equivalent.

ments) that some person B has a mind. The opponent, at a loss of what kind of straightforward argument could convince her, makes a request for an argument from analogy: "Can you show it to me, by parity of reasoning?" Or she may even do some of the creative work for the proponent: "I have become convinced of myself as having a mind. Can you show me how I can reason, in a similar fashion, to your conclusion that this person B has a mind?"

When compared to a request for an argument from expert opinion (or for another straightforward argumentation scheme), a request for an argument from parallel reasoning is special. As we have seen, an argument from analogy makes reference to the reasoning in a comparable dialogical situation. As a result, one way of posing a request for an argument from analogy could be phrased thus: "I wouldn't know what kind of argumentation would convince to me, but please, present me with a convincing application of some argumentation scheme or other, so that I get some hunch about the kind of reasoning that could lead me to accept your current conclusion." Due to the metadialogical character of the argumentation scheme from parallel reasoning, it deserves a special position in any future classification of argumentation schemes.

6.5 Critically Testing an Argument from Analogy

Given that premise 1 in the argumentation scheme From Parallel Reasoning (see Fig. 6.1) mentions the reasoning in the comparison case, it is possible for the opponent to focus either on the premise (or on one of the premises) of the reasoning in the comparison case, as well as on the connection between premises(s) and conclusion in the comparison case, thereby giving rise to two quite distinct types of criticism. The more premises, and the more steps of reasoning, the more points of criticism are to be distinguished when targeting premise 1. Since each of these points of criticism concerns, albeit in a different way, the acceptability of premise 1, I categorize them as tenability criticisms.

Tenability criticism focusing on premise 1, by questioning the connection between premises and conclusion in the comparison case:

> Why would proposition A, in a dialogical situation C, convince me of proposition B?
> For all you've shown, A might be true and B false. You need to convince me that A would convince me of B, within situation C.

Tenability criticism focusing on premise 1, by questioning the tenability of the premises in the comparison case (only available if the dialogical situation if not hypothetical):

> Why would I accept proposition A, in a dialogical situation C?
> For all you've shown, A might false. You need to convince me that A, if you want me to accept that I would have become convinced of B on account of A, within situation C.

Tenability criticism, focusing on premise 2:

Why would I accept proposition R?
Your assumption is wrong: I do not yet accept R. For all you've shown, R is false. What's your argument for R?

Tenability criticism, focusing on the comparison premise (Premise 3), in short: comparison criticism:

Why would accepting B on the basis of A in C be comparable to accepting S on the basis of R in T?
For all you've shown, accepting B on the basis of A in C is not in any relevant manner similar to accepting S on the basis of R in T.

In Sect. 2, I stipulated that premise 3 expresses that the two cases are relevantly similar, but without necessarily being sufficiently similar. Consequently, an instance of this scheme is defeasible, and allows the opponent to accept each of its three premises and yet resist to accept its conclusion on ground of taking into account the possibility that S is false. Consequently, there is room to accept premise 3, and yet to challenge the connection premise.

Connection criticism:

Why would I accept S, if (a) proposition A in a dialogical situation C convinced me of accepting proposition B, and if (b) I accept proposition R, and if also (c) accepting B on the basis of A in C is comparable to accepting S on the basis of R in T?
For all you've shown, I need not accept S, even if proposition A, in a dialogical situation C, convinced me of accepting proposition B, and if I accept proposition R, and if also accepting B on the basis of A in C is comparable to accepting S on the basis of R in T.

The distinction between tenability criticism, focusing on the comparison premise (criticism 3) and connection premise, could, in the drone case, amount to the following:

Comparison criticism:

Agreed, drones are cost-effective for the Amsterdam police force. However, this is not a relevant consideration that helps you to convince me to accept drones for this police force. For this is a sensitive issue of public policy rather than a commercial decision.

Connection criticism:

Agreed, cost-effectiveness would could be a reason to accept drones for the Amsterdam police force. However, though comparable in relevant respects, there are also some relevant dissimilarities between the drone and the satellite cases. For one, I genuinely doubt that we can entrust the Amsterdam police force with the drone technology. For another, the privacy consideration in the case of police drones is simple more weighty as compared with those in the case of satellites.

Finally, the opponent may want to resist the use of argumentation from analogy by the proponent. She may consider this kind of argumentation for the kind of issue too weak, too indirect, or institutionally inappropriate. I label this kind of criticism *scheme criticism* (van Laar 2011):

Scheme criticism:

Why would I accept any instance of an argument from analogy?
As far as you've shown, any argument from analogy is unreliable.

Two questions can now be answered. First, of what use is this defeasible way of arguing for a proponent? Let us consider the critical options in a situation where the opponent has requested more or less explicitly for an argument from parallel reasoning. Then we can expect the opponent to have committed herself to the *prima facie* acceptability of the argumentation scheme From Parallel Reasoning. As a consequence, in the discussion at hand the opponent scheme criticism focused at this very scheme would be inaccessible to her. In addition, the connection premise of any instance of this scheme would count as a presumptive commitment on her side. Given that arguments from analogy are defeasible, the opponent must be able to challenge such a connection premise, thereby trying to defeat the argument, albeit at the expense of incurring the obligation to *explain* her criticism with a counter-consideration, if the proponent requests so. If the opponent had, however, put forward a less specific challenge, the proponent probably would not have these advantages. Consequently, though highly defeasible, argumentation from analogy can be specially expedient for a proponent if the opponent is prepared to adopt the underlying argumentation scheme. Because, if the opponent is unable to offer any adequate explanation of her challenging the connection premise, or if she is but the proponent manages to refute the counter-consideration, then the proponent should have it his way.

Second, is argumentation from parallel reasoning, thus analyzed, genuinely case-based, or does it in some hidden way appeal to a universal claim? Each of these critical points, with the exception of scheme criticism, pertains to the target case, to the comparison case, or to the specific relations between them. In line with what Govier (1989, pp. 147–148) and Juthe (2009) have contended, it is possible to evaluate an argument from analogy without raising the issue of the acceptability of some universal claim that would underlie the similarity of the two cases, for the reason that the proponent does not appeal to any specific universal claim. Of course, the proponent may choose to put forward such a substantial universal claim in response to a connection criticism, alleging that this specific connection follows from a more general truth. (In a very specific sense, therefore, I agree with Govier's idea that such a universal claim is *implied*, although not *assumed* or *presupposed* or *premised*, by an argument from analogy). But then, he may also try to support the connection premise in a different way, being able to derive it from other particular propositions. Or, it may be the case that the opponent was presumptively committed to the connection premise but unable to explain her subsequent resistance to it, so as to enable the proponent to resolve the difference of opinion in favour of his position without supporting the connection at all.

Now that I have dealt with the various points of criticism of this kind of argument from analogy, I will turn to a more involved example of argument from analogy.

6.6 Mill's other Minds Argument

I shall consider Mill's famous argument from analogy used in support of his standpoint that other people have feelings (a mind). Though clearly making use of an analogy, the example much less clearly contains an argument, at least in the sense of an attempt to convince some addressee. One reason of choosing this example is to show that the dialogical account of arguments from parallel reasoning is quite flexible, and also is useful for analogical reasoning that, at least at first sight, does not involve two disputants involved in an argumentative conversation.

Mill's (1979) argument can, apparently, be used against the persona in anyone who feels the force of other-minds scepticism:

> By what evidence do I know, or by what considerations am I led to believe, that (…) the walking and speaking figures which I see and hear, have sensations and thoughts, or in other words, possess Minds? (…) I conclude it from certain things, which my experience of my own states of feeling proves to me to be marks of it. (…) I conclude that other human beings have feelings like me, because, first, they have bodies like me, which I know, in my own case, to be the antecedent condition of feelings; and because, secondly, they exhibit the acts, and other outward signs, which in my own case I know by experience to be caused by feelings. I am conscious in myself of a series of facts connected by an uniform sequence, of which the beginning is modifications of my body, the middle is feelings, the end is outward demeanour. In the case of other human beings I have the evidence of my senses for the first and last links of the series, but not for the intermediate link. I find, however, that the sequence between the first and last is as regular and constant in those other cases as it is in mine. In my own case I know that the first link produces the last through the intermediate link, and could not produce it without. Experience, therefore, obliges me to conclude that there must be an intermediate link; which must either be the same in others as in myself, or a different one: I must either believe them to be alive, or to be automatons: and by believing them to be alive, that is, by supposing the link to be of the same nature as in the case of which I have experience, and which is in all other respects similar, I bring other human beings, as phænomena, under the same generalizations which I know by experience to be the true theory of my own existence.

Mill's argument in favour of the existence of other minds is normally referred as his *argument from analogy* (Avramides 2001, p. 5). One preliminary comment. The text is a kind of a soliloquy, suggesting that any sceptic who starts investigating the issue of whether or not others have minds, should by such reasoning of the "I" persona come to the conclusion that other minds exist. Such internal reasoning might be seen as quite different from the kind of dialogue that I have assumed to be essential to argumentation. However, the dialogical account must be understood so as to include at least those kinds of reasoning that exhibit some kind of conscious reflection, rather than mere thinking. The terms *proponent* and *opponent* refer to dialogical roles, and one individual can play the parts of both roles. Thus, in those cases where the reasoning individual is examining whether or not she ought to be persuaded of the acceptability of a particular proposition on grounds she herself considers reasonable, can well be analysed with the concept of a critical dialogue.

The argument from analogy might be reconstructed as a ground-dialogical argument from analogy, along the following lines: "My first and last link stand to my intermediate link as another person's first and last link stand to his intermediate link. Well, my intermediate link is constituted by a causally connecting mind. Therefore, his intermediate link is constituted by a causally connective mind." However, we can add detail to the argument from analogy by conceiving of it as instantiating the Argumentation Scheme From Parallel Reasoning. In order to bring out all features of the dialogical theory of argumentation from analogy, I slightly modify Mill's argument so as to deal with a particular person B (Fig. 6.2).

Conclusion: I (in the role of opponent) should accept that person B's regular and constant sequences of modifications of his body and outward demeanour are causally mediated by a mind.
Premise 1: When I examine how the regular and constant sequences of the modifications of my body relate to my outward demeanour, I find that I experience them as causally connected by my mind, and on that basis I conclude that they are, really, causally mediated by my mind.
Premise 2: I accept that B has regular and constant sequences of modifications of his body and outward demeanour.
Premise 3: My reasoning from the regular and constant sequences of the modifications of my body and my outward demeanour to them being causally mediated by my mind is comparable to my reasoning from B's regular and constant sequences of modifications of his body and outward demeanour to B's sequences being causally mediated by mind.

Fig. 6.2 Mill's argument from analogy as an instance of the argumentation scheme from parallel reasoning

What kinds of criticism can be raised against this argument, if we follow the suggestions of the previous section (skipping scheme criticism)?

Tenability criticism, focusing on premise 1, by questioning the tenability of the premises in the comparison case:

> I am not convinced, as of yet, that there exist regular and constant sequences of modifications of my body that relate to my outward demeanour. As far as I (in the role of proponent) have shown, these patterns do not exist.

Tenability criticism, focusing on premise 1, by questioning the connection between premise and conclusion in the comparison case:

> I am not convinced, as of yet, that when I have found that I experience the regular and constant sequences of the modifications of my body and my outward demeanour as causally mediated by my mind, that, really, they *are* causally mediated by mind. As far as I (in the role of proponent) have shown, the experience might be illusory, and nothing can be deduced from it at all.

Tenability criticism, focusing on premise 2:

> For all that you've shown, B has no regular and constant sequences of modifications of his body and outward demeanour.

Comparison criticism:

> For all that I (proponent) have shown, the two cases of reasoning are not relevantly similar. For one, I consider my own judgements regarding whether I have a mind as incorrigible (because, if I conclude that I have a mind, I must have a mind, by necessity), but I do not regard my judgements regarding B's having a mind as incorrigible. Consequently, I cannot exclude the possibility that I am exceptional in having a mind.

Connection criticism:

> Without wanting to do detract from each of your regular premises' merits, I still want to resist your conclusion. To explain: I seriously take the possibility into account that this person B, is not really a person at all. Even if I were to concede your comparison premise, B might be an exception, for did you notice that he always reacts in a somewhat inflexible, if not machine-like manner, quite unlike myself. So I still wonder: could he possibly be a mindless robot?

To conclude my treatment of Mill's argument, I would like to point out that the meta-dialogical reconstruction has the advantage of making visible many more possible points of criticism as compared to a ground-dialogical reconstruction, due to its focus on the internal reasoning in the comparison case. From the perspective of critical testing, it would be preferable to interpret an argument from analogy as instantiating a metadialogical version if the textual evidence allows it, because it generates more detailed critical questions. And if the proponent is capable of specifying his argument so as to transform his ground dialogical argument into a metadialogical argument from parallel reasoning, we should applaud it, for inviting more detailed criticism, and thus facilitating the critical examination of the argument. Note, however, that a revision of his ground level argument from analogy so as to lead to a more straighforward kind of reasoning would, possibly, give an even better result.

6.7 Conclusion

In this paper, I have examined arguments from parallel reasoning as a special type of meta-dialogical argument from analogy. It has been contended that such arguments can be dealt with as instances of an argumentation scheme, giving rise to a specific set of evaluative questions, such that the resulting arguments are both case-based and defeasible yet profitable to their proponents. By applying the framework to Mills argument from analogy it was shown how the dialectical theory of arguments from parallel reasoning can also be made to apply to analogical reasoning that does not wear its dialogical character on its sleeves.

References

Avramides, A. 2001. *Other minds*. New York: Routledge.

Govier, T. 1989. Analogies and missing premises. *Informal Logic* 11 (3): 141–152.

Guarini, M., S. P. Smith, and A. Moldovan. 2009. Resources for research on analogy: A multidisciplinary guide. *Informal Logic* 29:84–198.

Juthe, A. 2009. Refutation by parallel argument. *Argumentation* 23:133–169.

Krabbe, E. C. W. 2001. The problem of retraction in critical discussion. *Synthese* 127:141–159.

Mill, J. S. 1979. An examination of William Hamilton's philosophy and of the principal philosophical questions discussed in his writings. In *The collected works of John Stuart Mill,* ed. J. M. Robson, Vol. IX. Toronto: University of Toronto Press/Routledge/Kegan Paul. (Originally published 1889).

Perelman, C., and L. Olbrechts-Tyteca. 1969. *The new rhetoric: A treatise on argumentation.* Notre Dame: University of Notre Dame Press. French edition: C. Perelman, and L. Olbrechts-Tyteca. 1958. *La nouvelle rhétorique: Traité de l'argumentation.* trans.: J. Wilkinson, and P. Weaver. Paris: Presses Universitaires de France.

Rescher, N. 1977. *Dialectics: A controversy-oriented approach to the theory of knowledge.* Albany: State University of New York Press.

Rescorla, M. 2009. Shifting the burden of proof? *The Philosophical Quarterly* 59:86–109.

van Eemeren Frans H., and R. Grootendorst. 1992. *Argumentation, communication, and fallacies: A pragma-dialectical perspective.* Hillsdale: Lawrence Erlbaum.

van Eemeren Frans H., and R. Grootendorst. 2004. *A systematic theory of argumentation.* Cambridge: Cambridge University Press.

van Laar J. A. 2011. Argumentation schemes from Hamblin's dialectical perspective. *Informal Logic* 31:344–366.

van Laar, J. A. 2014. Criticism in need of clarification. *Argumentation*, Online First. doi: 10.1007/s10503-013-9309-8.

van Laar J. A., and E. C. W. Krabbe. 2013. The burden of criticism: Consequences of taking a critical stance. *Argumentation* 27:201–224. doi 10.1007/s10503-012-9272-9.

Waller, B. N. 2001. Classifying and analyzing analogies. *Informal Logic* 21 (3): 199–218.

Walton, D. N. 2003. Is there a burden of questioning? *Artificial Intelligence and Law* 11:1–43.

Walton, D. N. 2012. Story similarity in arguments from analogy. *Informal Logic* 32:190–221.

Walton, D. N., and E. C. W. Krabbe. 1995. *Commitment in dialogue: Basic concepts of interpersonal reasoning.* Albany: State University of New York Press.

Walton, D. N., C. Reed, and F. Macagno. 2008. *Argumentation schemes.* Cambridge: Cambridge University Press.

Woods, J., and B. Hudak. 1989. By parity of reasoning. *Informal Logic* 11:125–139.

Chapter 7
A Systematic Review of Classifications of Arguments by Analogy

André Juthe

7.1 Introduction

This is a systematic review of the classification of analogical arguments. This is the third article in a series, that aim at explicating arguments by analogy (Juthe 2005, 2009). The reader should note this is an abridged article, the full version of which will be published at a later date (A. Juthe, "A comprehensive review of classifications of argument by analogy", forthcoming). The goal of this article is to provide a comprehensive and systematic overview of various classifications of argument by analogy. Over 600 journals and books have been reviewed in order to provide the material required to assess what various subtypes of analogical argumentation exist. Different variants of analogy (comparison and similarity) argumentation have been distinguished. The criterion for classification has been either the author's own claim (of which I have made a *prima facie* acceptance), or if an article lacks such a claim, my own assessment of what the basis is for the author's subdivision. The most salient feature that could best explain the subdivision is taken as the parameter. This judgement is based on a particular assessment of each material, whenever there has been ambiguity between different parameters I have given precedence to an interpretation that gives rise to a new parameter in order not to miss any parameter that has been employed. Graphs and tables are provided in order to make it easier for the reader to grasp the overview. This is a descriptive article, the normative question regarding how analogical arguments *should* be classified is a question that will be addressed in a subsequent article (A. Juthe, "How should analogical arguments be classified", forthcoming).

The working process can be described in the following three steps: first, a collection of articles and books that concern analogy in particular; second, a selection of

A. Juthe (✉)
Department of Speech Communication, Argumentation Theory and Rhetoric,
University of Amsterdam, Amsterdam, The Netherlands
e-mail: andre.juthe@gmail.com

H. J. Ribeiro (ed.), *Systematic Approaches to Argument by Analogy*,
Argumentation Library 25, DOI 10.1007/978-3-319-06334-8_7,

those articles that concern argument by analogy; thirdly, an election of those articles that are relevant for distinguishing various subtypes of argument by analogy.[1]

The article, although not exhaustive, strives to list work from different disciplines to deal with contrasting interpretations of arguments by analogy in a broad sense. The research examined includes, but is not limited to, work from argumentation theory, artificial intelligence (AI), cognitive science, linguistics, archaeology, mathematics, natural sciences, philosophy, psychology, and (other) social sciences. Many different types of argument by comparison have been referred to as analogies or as analogous, and analogy has been studied from a number of disciplinary perspectives. This work consolidates research from different fields to provide an overall picture of different ways of classifying arguments by analogy.

7.1.1 Scope and Limits

There is an important terminological issue involved, since the contemporary use of *analogy* does not always have the same meaning as in the classical uses. The classical Greek term for analogy (analogia or αναλογία) is sometimes translated as "proportion", which would include ratios (3 is to 6, as 4 is to 8). However, many of the contemporary uses of analogy just refer to some kind of comparison between similar things, in order to justify an inference based on the similarity. Terms like "proportion"; "similarity"; "same"; "figure"; "simile"; "metaphor"; and "comparison" may all refer to analogy in some sense. Analogy is sometimes used in a broad sense, referring to any comparisons of similarities between two or more objects, and sometimes in a more precise sense, as a certain kind of similarity.[2]

However, a mere reference to or *use* of analogy or any of these other concepts, is insufficient to be included in this overview. The work I have included attempts to theorize about, or otherwise explicate one or more of the uses of analogy as *arguments*; other kinds of analogical reasoning such as explaining something, or for the purposes of illustration or elucidation have been excluded. However, the

[1] An extensive literature search was designed to identify and retrieve primary studies relevant to the project's major research question. The database Philosopher's index was used to some extent but mostly the web search engines Google and Google Scholar. The search was very broad, the key words used was "analog*", or "analogy", or "argument"+"analog*" or "reasoning"+"analog*", or "argument"+"comparison" or "case-based reasoning", in order to not miss anything that could be relevant for the study. The following inclusion criteria were used: (a) accessibility—the study must be publicly available or archived; (b) relevancy—the study must contain arguments by analogy; (c) sufficiency—it must be fairly easy to identify what kind of classification an author implicitly or explicitly employs in his analogical arguments; (d) language—the material must be in English. I further made a search of "analog*" on the *Informal Logic* website and on the *Argumentation* website.

[2] I share Hoylak (2005, p. 118) view of analogy: "Analogy is a special kind of similarity: two situations are analogous if they share a common pattern of relationships among their constituent elements even though the elements themselves differ across the two situations."

exact distinction between these different kinds of reasoning is not entirely clear, and works that discuss analogical *inferences* might be included.

I have also made a distinction between different *applications* of the same type of argument and different *argument types*. If there are just contrasting applications of basically the same argument, it does not count as a subtype worthy of classification.

I have included other similar, but less comprehensive, attempts to review the literature of arguments by analogy, as well as their sources (because the reviewer's classification could differ from the original source). I have not analysed every possible article that *uses* an argument by analogy and from that discovered or extracted a new subtype of argument by analogy. Another limit is that the overview will be limited to literature in the English language. I have rejected articles that claim that argument by analogy can be reduced to some other type of argument, and assume that they are an irreducible type of their own. I have also avoided articles that explicitly discuss arguments from metaphor. The relation between metaphor and analogy is interesting and important, but not relevant to this article. I have only made an exception in the instances where *metaphor* is used in the sense of "figurative analogy" and not "genuine" metaphorical arguments. Analogical reasoning must also be distinguished from arguments that employ *extensive interpretation* in law.[3]

In general I have only classified arguments into one category, although the taxonomy may often cut across different parameters at the same time. These paramaters pertain to different levels of arguments and may relate to each other in various ways. Arguments that were subdivided based on their difference in function could sometimes arguably also have been divided based on their logical form. The relation between the parameters is discussed in the expanded version of this article. However, to provide an overview of all such possible relations would be unmanageable and counteract the purpose of giving an overview. I have made some exceptions to this rule, when the author himself can clearly be interpreted as advocating two parameters.

Furthermore, I have not discussed further specification of using a *combination* of parameters unless the author him/herself makes such distinctions. For instance, nothing in itself hinders one from initially distinguishing two types of argument by analogy by virtue of their different function in the discourse, and then in turn subdividing these subarguments by virtue of contrasting their logical structure, and so on.

I have not commented on every author named in the tables, but rather I have chosen to comment on those who were typical or adequate examples of proponents of the parameter used for classification. In the tables, one can see the label of each subtype, the author, and by which parameter the argument is classified. An empty cell in the table means that the author has not formulated any further subdivided argument, (although the author has used the parameter for those arguments that are in other cells). Arguments in the same row are the same type of arguments as classified by the same parameter, that is, given the actual, and presently used parameter, they belong to the same subtype of analogical argument. That does not, however,

[3] For a discussion about the difference and how it relates to the philosophy of law, see D. Canale and G. Tuzet, "Analogy and interpretation in legal argumentation" (published in this volume).

as stated above, exclude the fact that they could also be considered another type of argument if another parameter was applied.

7.1.2 Terminology

Various terms have been used by different authors for distinguishing the objects of comparison; examples are: Source vs. Target, Source-case vs Target-case, Primary Subject vs Analogue, Source domain vs Target domain, Case vs Parallel case, Source-case vs. Target case, and so on. My own preferred terminology is that the object that should be assigned a new predicate via the analogical inference is the *Target-Subject*, while the object which is used as the source for the new predicate, is the *Analogue*. It should, however, be clear to the reader that all these different terms are used by different theorists.

7.1.3 Goal and Research Questions

As stated, the major aim of this article is to give a comprehensive overview of different classifications of argument by analogy and the parameters used for this classification. The research questions are:

1. What different subtypes of argument by analogy have been suggested or used in the literature?
2. What parameter(s) have been used for this classification?

There are several challenges for this goal. One problem is that various philosophers may use the same term but mean different things; or vice versa they may not really name them at all, but rather merely describe them. Sometimes the terminology may be misleading. For example, several philosophers who think that arguments by analogy are irreducible to the inductive or deductive type of argument still subdivide argument by analogy into an "inductive" type and a "deductive" type, which has made others make faulty classifications.[4] Another problem is that various philosophers do not use the same criteria and contrasting taxonomical axes; different parameters are used in the classification and they focus on different features as criterion for classification. Moreover, some classifications coincide even though they have different parameters and criteria for the classification, whilst other cut across different classifications.

[4] For example, David Botting (2012) claims that Wreen, Govier and Waller think that one type of argument by analogy are an inductive argument, but this is not so. Talk about inductive argument by analogy could mean (1) being reducible to argument by induction without any reference to genuine analogy and (2) being irreducible to inductive or deductive argument but have a similarity with inductive probabilistic reasoning, with an analogical relation as a necessary part. Govier (1985, 2010) and Wreen (2007) and Waller (2001) believes in (2) not (1).

My review aims to help the reader to overcome these obstacles by providing an overview of the terminology, and the parameters that have been used by various authors. Moreover, I hope that the review can also be of value to readers without any particular interest in the classification of argument by analogy, as well as being a rich source of information that can be used for other means that concern arguments by analogy.

Previous Attempts

There have not been many attempts to produce any larger systematic taxonomy regarding arguments by analogy. The reason for this is, I think, because it has always been controversial whether or not arguments by analogy are a genuine class of arguments irreducible to the standard pattern of inductive or deductive arguments. Another reason is due to all the problems associated with such an attempt noted above. Doury (2009), is however, a recent exception. She has attempted to make a classification of argument by analogy (or comparative arguments, which is the term she uses for it as a general class). Her discussion is an overview and her goal is to provide a more systematic typology for the argument schemes of "comparative arguments", based on actual argumentative practices. Doury discusses various criteria used in the classification by different authors, which give rise to divergent ways of categorizing and classifying argument by analogy, depending on which criterion is used for differentiation. Doury found four main criteria used as ground for typology by authors in argumentation studies: (1) Domain constraint (whether the objects of comparison belong to the same domain or not); (2) Qualitative/quantitative orientation (whether the analogy concerns quantitative or qualitative considerations), (3) The epistemic status of premises (how the analogue is known), (4) The dialectical orientation of the argument (whether the argument aims at supporting or refuting something). In the next section I will discuss what parameters this current overview has discovered.

7.2 Result

7.2.1 Parameters Used for Classification

In order to make a classification, regardless of subject, one has to have some idea of what parameters should be used as the distinguishing criterion. A major challenge is that a subtype of an argument type may be classified by virtue of several parameters at the same time, or it may be difficult to distinguish exactly what feature is working as a criterion in distinguishing between types.

In my own investigation, I have found at least eight parameters used for classification. These are: (1) Epistemic status of the analogue; (2) Function or purpose; (3) Logical form; (4) Domain constraint; (5) Mode of inference; (6) Direction of vertical

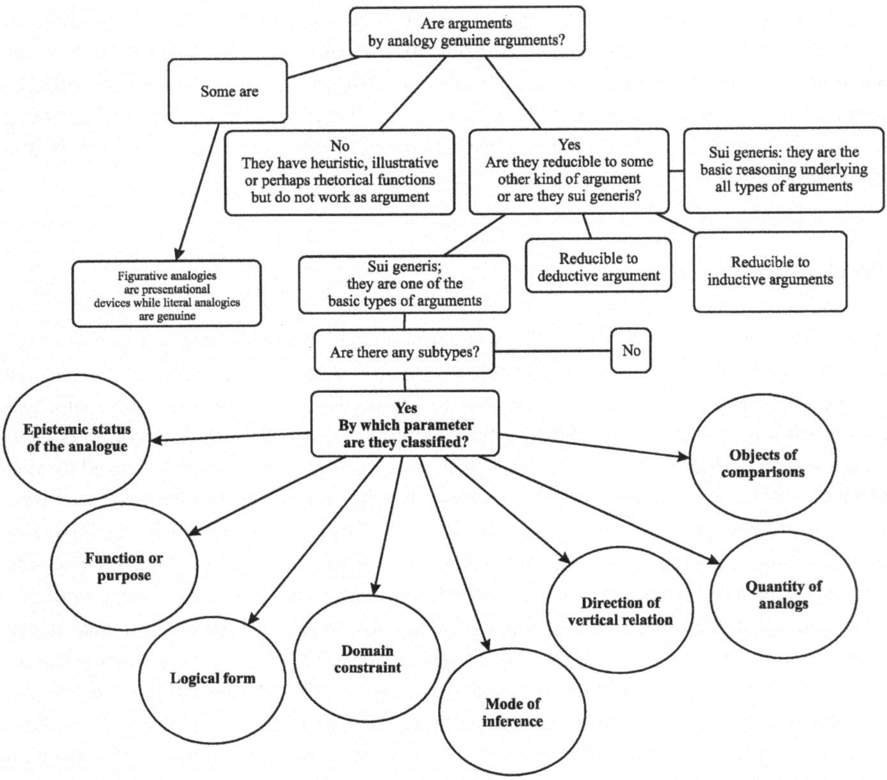

Fig. 7.1 Graphical overview

relation; (7) Quantity of analogs; (8) Objects of comparisons. This abridged version will only contain discussion about (1)–(4); those readers interested in (5)–(8) will find the relevant information in the forthcoming expanded version of this article (A. Juthe, "A comprehensive review of different classifications of arguments by analogy"). The tables and the information about each parameter are more developed in the enlarged version.

I will explain each parameter under separate headings. However, the main result can be seen in the graphical overview below. The graphic shows the relevant subdivisions contained in the literature of the 600 books and journals that were reviewed (Fig. 7.1).

7.2.2 The Subtypes

In this section, I will comment on the subtypes as well as the the parameter used for classification.

The Epistemic Status of the Analogue

This subdivision is based on how the premises of the analogue are known, and whether it has empirical content or not. For example, if the premises of the analogue are known by empirical means or if it is "*a priori*" a hypothetical, invented case. The analogy can involve two real facts/situations, or a real fact/situation and a hypothetical, invented one. According to Doury, this criterion is the reason for Govier's distinction between inductive analogies and *a priori* analogies (Doury 2009). Sometimes the distinction is based on whether the analogue makes a prediction or not. Stephen Barker's view is a good example of this parameter: he distinguishes between two types of arguments by analogy. These are inductive argument by analogy and noninductive argument by analogy. The inductive argument by analogy does not depend upon our being able to establish any generalization that all or most F's are G's, but rather upon a case being similar with other cases. Thus, inductive analogies have the following general structure (Barker 1989b, p. 175).

(1) a, b, c… each has been observed to have property F and G;
(2) n is observed to have property F;
(3) Therefore, probably n has property G

Inductive analogies are based on empirical experience, and always predict that the target subject also will have a certain property. Given that two or more objects share certain properties, it is expected that they also share another property. This is not the case with so called *a priori* argument by analogy where the relevant similarities between the analogue and target subject are often *invented a priori* independently of reality, *in order to make an appeal to treat or think about them in a similar way*. A certain class of analogical argument used in law falls under this category. Sunstein (1993, p. 745) summarizes the structure of legal argument by analogy, in four steps:

> (I) Some fact pattern A has a certain characteristic X, or characteristics X, Y, and Z; (2) Fact pattern B differs from A in some respects but shares characteristics X, or characteristics X, Y, and Z; (3) The law treats A in a certain way; (4) Because B shares certain characteristics with A, the law should treat B the same way. For example, someone asking for protection against domestic violence is requesting affirmative government assistance, just like someone asking the government for medical care; it is said to "follow" from the medical care case that there is no constitutional right to protection against domestic violence.

Thus, what Reidhav (2007) and Langenbucher (1998) call "Normative argument by analogy", and Sunstein (1993) calls "analogical reasoning in law", is basically what Govier (1989) calls "*a priori* analogy" and what Stephen Barker (1989a) labels "Noninductive argument by analogy", with the exception that it is employed in the context of jurisprudence. Several authors use different names, although they use the same parameter for the subdivision, as as shown in the table below (Table 7.1).

Table 7.1 Analogical arguments distinguished by their difference in epistemic status

Criterion for classification: whether the analogue has or lacks empirical content		Author
Has empirical content	Lacks empirical content	
Inductive analogy	A priori analogy	Govier (1989, 2010)
Predictive analogy	Normative arguments from analogy	Garssen (2010)
Everyday analogical reasoning	Analogical reasoning in law	Sunstein (1993)
Inductive analogy		Mill (2013)
Inductive argument by analogy	Noninductive argument by analogy	Barker (1989b)
Inductive analogical arguing		Johnson (1989)
Inductive analogy	(The non-inductive argument is reducible to a deductive argument)	Waller (2001)
Inductive argument from analogy[a]	Argument from analogy based on classification	Walton (2006, 2010, 2012); Walton et al. (2008)
Argument by empirical analogy	Normative argument by analogy	Langenbucher (1998)
Inductive arguments from analogy	Normative arguments from positive analogy[b] Normative arguments from negative analogy	Reidhav (2007)
	Statutory analogy	Peczenik (1971, 1989)
Inductive analogy	Noninductive analogy	Barker (1989a)

[a] This label is mine. Walton never really labels the argument. His argument could also arguably be classified on the basis of logical form, see Sect. 7.2.2.3. Sometimes he uses the term "basic form"

[b] Normative argument from positive analogy: (i) C1 (source case) ought to be treated as Q. (ii) C2 (target-case) is relevantly similar to C1. (iii) C1 ought to be treated as Q (Reidhav 2007, p. 40). Such an argument does not work from induction but from what Reidhav calls the "principle of formal justice": treat relevantly similar cases alike.

This parameter is, however, problematic; since several analogical arguments fall outside this taxonomic parameter, many analogies have an empirical content while simultaneously make no prediction and do make an appeal to treat or think about them in a similar way. An invented example is provided below:

> You say that it is wrong for the government to make abortion illegal because it will increase the total amount of deaths by increasing the number of women who die from botched, illegal abortions.. But that is like saying that the government in South africa should not have made apartheid illegal because it might inrease the total amount of deaths due to riots and increased racial conflicts.

This clearly is a analogical, normative argument that appeals to treat or think about two cases (that do have empirical content) in a similar way. Without the data from South Africa the argument would fail, or at least not be as strong as it is, but it nonetheless does not predict anything. (For more about this, see Guarini's position in the next section.) Therefore the same arguments can be classified according to what they do, which is discussed in the next section.

The Function or Purpose of Analogy

Some subtypes are classified according to a functional or teleological criterion. The philosophers who employ this parameter as a criterion for the taxonomy, classify the subtypes in accordance with the purpose or the function they have in the discourse (or how the function of the analogy works in the argument). For example, Brown (1989) asserts that there are two types of argument by analogy; *predictive* analogy and *proportional* analogy.[5] Arguments which utilize a predictive analogy make a comparison between two objects (events, ideas, classes of objects, etc.) and from the fact that the objects have attributes in common, infer that they most likely have some other attribute in common. If two Cadillacs are in the same price range, you might infer by analogy that they are on the same level of quality.

The proportional analogy states that two objects have the same (or similar) relation to each other as two other objects have to each other. For example: "As Porsche is to Volkswagen, so is Cadillac to Chevrolet." Although many variants of proportional analogy may be reduced and reformulated into predictive analogies, there are those that cannot be formulated as such, because the logical structure is essentially different. Therefore, according to Brown, there are at least two legitimate classes of arguments.[6] But even in those cases they *have* the same logical form; they cannot be used interchangeably, since they have different *functions* either in reasoning or in discourse (Brown 1989, p. 163). The function of predictive analogy is to *predict* that an object has a certain attribute, whereas the function of proportional analogy is to *point out a common principle* between two pairs of objects. It should be noted that this parameter can be used for division at several levels. For instance, the distinctive functions of *refuting* in contrast to *supporting* with an analogy, would yield more subtypes. Other authors have made the same distinctions as Brown has done but with different terminology. For example, Ehninger and Brockriede (1963) use "analogy" for "proportional analogy, and "parallel case" for "predictive analogy". Emiliano Ippoliti (2006) argues that there are two kinds of argument by analogy, demonstrative and non-demonstrative reasoning by analogy. The distinction, however, refers not to any difference in the nature of justification, but to the difference in function. Demonstrative reasoning by analogy is reasoning that is a means for justification, in particular, in the proving of theorems and in processes of corroboration of conjectures and hypotheses, while non-demonstrative reasoning by analogy is analogy used to formulate conjectures and hypotheses, i.e., having a purely creative function.

Guarini (2004) questions Govier's (1985) classification of argument by analogy. Govier's position (which several philosophers' have followed) made a distinction between argument by *a priori* analogies and argument by inductive analogies. He

[5] Brown (1989, p. 164) also mentions figurative analogy which he regards as a weakened version of proportional analogy. Furthermore, Brown claims that an analogy is never merely illustrative, explanatory, metaphorical, or literary. They always play *some* role in an argument.

[6] Brown (1989, p. 169) states: "I can think of no way to transform a proportional analogy involving an ordered pair of attributes into predictive form: 'As the Porsche surpasses the Volkswagen in speed, so does the Cadillac surpass the Chevrolet in luxury'. In fact, such a transformation is impossible because Porsche and Cadillac are not said to have any property in common."

accepts that some analogies can only be evaluated by way of empirical investigation, as well as that fact that such analogies make predictions (Guarini 2004, pp. 165–165). Thus, those two criteria that mark the difference in Govier's classification of inductive versus a priori analogies appear to hold. However, the third criterion, that *a priori* argument by analogy makes use of hypothetical cases, is faulty, according to Guarini. He points out, that the need for the analogue to be actual depends on *how* the analogy is *employed,* and Guarini gives an example of an obvious *a priori* analogy that appeals to consistency but which still must be actual in order to work.[7] (Thus, refuting Govier's classification with the method of counterexampling).

Guarini (2004) provides his own classification based on two criteria: whether the analogies support a judgement regarding how a case should be treated or classified or whether they support a prediction. The former he calls *classificatory* analogical arguments, and the latter, *predictive* analogical arguments.[8] This is clearly a functional/teleological taxonomy. Classificatory analogical arguments would in many cases coincide with what Govier and others call *a priori analogy,* although the taxonomical criterion is different. The same applies with inductive analogies; they would in many cases coincide with predictive analogies. Doury's (2009) criterion: *The Dialectical Orientation* falls within this category. This criterion is based on whether the argument has a positive purpose (supporting the arguer's standpoint) or negative purpose (refuting the opponent's argument). The negative use of analogy has been labelled "rebuttal analogy", or "refutation by logical analogy", or "refutation by parallel argument", "parity of reasoning" and is a kind of *ad absurdum* argument. This dialectical difference is the basis for Govier's (1985) type "refutation by logical analogy" as a separate class different from inductive and *a priori* argument by analogy (Table 7.2).

As the astute reader may notice, several of the arguments distinguished by the previous parameter (the epistemic criterion), could be classified by this parameter as well, as having a classificatory function. The reason that they are not put in that row of this table is because the author did not classify them that way. The review is intended to primarily display how different theorists have classified subtypes of argument by analogy, not to display how subtypes *may* be classified. An argument has been entered in the tables with different parameters, only in the case of an ambiguity.

Logical Form

This parameter distinguishes the subtypes by reference to the intrinsic logical structure of the argument scheme. Difference in logical form, means that the inferences of the argument flow in "different directions" or via different logical constants, like

[7] The example was an analogy that used discrepant treatment of real similar cases to argue for the actual problematic treatment of black women by the U.S: courts. Further, as Guarini remarks, one cannot claim that the difference is that *a priori* analogies can sometimes make use of hypothetical cases, while inductive analogies cannot, since some inductive analogies work well even when the source analogue is hypothetical.

[8] Classificatory analogies is what Govier (2002) would call "a priori" and what Waller (2001) calls "deductive", whereas they label predictive analogies as "inductive".

Table 7.2 Analogical arguments distinguished by their difference in function

Criterion for classification: function or purpose of analogy in argument							Author
Predictive function	Supportive function	Classificatory function	Refutative function	Creative function	Pointing out common principle	Heuristic function	
						Presumptive analogical argument[a]	Cummings (2004)
	Demonstrative reasoning by analogy			Non-demonstrative reasoning by analogy			Ippoliti (2006)
			Refutation by logical analogy; Counteranalogy				Govier (1985)
			Refutation by parallel argument				Juthe (2009)
	Normative arguments from *positive* analogy		Normative arguments from *negative* analogy				Reidhav (2007)
Predictive analogical arguments		Classificatory analogical arguments					Guarini (2004)
Predictive analogy					Proportional analogy		Brown (1989)
Parallel case					Analogy		Ehninger and Brockriede (1963)
			By parity of reasoning				Woods and Hudak (1989)
	Basic logical form		Argument by disanalogy				Brewer (1996)

Table 7.2 (continued)

Criterion for classification: function or purpose of analogy in argument							Author
Predictive function	Supportive function	Classificatory function	Refutative function	Creative function	Pointing out common principle	Heuristic function	
			Counterexampling parallel arguments				Hitchcock (1992)
			Refutation by logical analogy				Copi and Cohen (1990); Copi and Burgess-Jackson (1992)
			Rebuttal analogy				Whaley (1998); Whaley and Holloway (1997); Whaley and Wagner (2000);
			Method of logical analogy				Krabbe (1996)
			Arguments by Parallels				Pascale (2008)

[a] This label is mine.

the form of modus ponens differ from the logical form of modus tollens or from the disjunctive syllogism. For example, Prade and Richard (2009, 2010) distinguish between three types of analogical reasoning. The standard type of analogical reasoning is what they call analogical proportions, which are statements of the form a is to b, as c is to d, which implies that the way a and b differ corresponds to the way c and d differ. The next type is the reverse analogy, which states that what a is to b, is the converse of what c is to d. The third type is paralogical proportion, which states that what a and b have in common, c and d have in common as well.

These arguments are divided by virtue of having a separate logical form and employing different logical principles and/or "pathways of inference". For instance, analogical proportion utilizes (1) reflexivity; (2) central permutation; and (3) symmetry, while paralogical proportion utilizes (1) bi-reflexivity; (2) even permutation; and (3) symmetry.

Wreen (2007) distinguishes between two logical forms (none of which correspond to the logical forms distinguished by Prade and Richard (2010), and argues that it is wrong to think that there are two different types of analogical arguments that share the same form. It is rather a spectrum of a continuum of diverging argument schemes, with two clearly-identified contrasting logical forms at the end point of the spectrum. Thus, except in terms of logical form, there are no different "kinds" of arguments by analogy, only one and the same scheme which can be expressed in two differing logical forms. According to Wreen, the accepted opinion among philosophers is that there are two kinds of argument from analogy, which apparently have the same form, but are categorised on the basis of propositional content (e.g., future-oriented or not), differing modes of epistemic access (e.g., *a priori* or empirical), epistemic function (e.g., prediction or classification), or nature of inference (e.g., inductive or non-inductive). The different forms, Wreen simply labels Form *A* and *B* (Wreen 2007, pp. 221–222, 227).

Form A:	*Form B:*
(1) X has characteristics a, b, c…	(1) X has characteristics a, d, g…
(2) A has characteristics a, b, c…	(2) A has characteristics a, b, c
(3) A also has characteristic x	(3) A has characteristic x
(4) A's having x is caught up with its having a, b, c…	(4) A's having x is caught up with its having a, b, c
(5) B has characteristics a, b, c…	(5) B has characteristics d, e, f
(6) B also has characteristic x	(6) B has characteristic x
(7) B's having x is caught up with its having a, b, c…	(7) B's having x is caught up with its having d, e, f
(CI) Therefore, X has characteristic x'	(8) C has characteristics g, h, i
	(9) C has characteristic x
	C's having x is caught up with its having g, h, i
	(C) Therefore, X has characteristic x

Wreen (2007, p. 222) makes a critical examination of S. F. Barker's (1989b) view as a backdrop in order to identify and clarify the second argument form. Wreen has three critical objections to Barker's classification; the latter, which did not base it on the ordinary dichotomic distinction in the *kind of inference* (deductive vs inductive) but rather on a mixture of *content* of the conclusion (predictive vs non-predictive) and *relation* between premises and a conclusion (whether a conclusion goes beyond what is contained in the premises or not). The most important objection is that Barker's analysis does not result in any argument scheme for the assumed categorically distinct type of argument by analogy, which Barker claims is neither inductive nor deductive.[9] Wreen suggests that in reality the other argument Barker sought after was another *logical form* which Wreen names as "Form B". Walton has lately claimed that there are two distinct argument schemes for argument by analogy, based on contrasting logical form (see Walton, "Argumentation schemes for argument from analogy", published in this volume).

Brewer (1996) discusses argument by analogy in a legal setting where the main purpose of reasoning by analogy is to discover rules or to determine whether a rule applies or not. According to Brewer, arguments by analogy utilize a reasoning process that belongs to a broad family of example-based arguments that are irreducible to argument from rules (i.e, ordinary inductive, deductive/abductive arguments) (Brewer 1996, p. 163). The logical form of an analogy is thus:

(1) z has characteristics F, G...
(2) x, y, also have characteristics F, G...
(3) x, y, also have characteristic H
(4) The presence in an individual of characteristics F, G... provides sufficient warrant for inferring that H is also present in that individual. (AWR—Analogy Warranting Rule)
(5) Therefore, there is sufficient warrant to conclude that H is present in z

This basic formula can be changed (Brewer 1996, p. 963) by modifying some of the premises into a inductive analogy:

(4′) The presence in an item of F and G makes it (sufficiently) probable that H is also present (inductive analogy-warranting rule)
(5′) Therefore, it is (sufficiently) probable that H is present in y

or into a deductive analogy (pp. 969–971):

(1″) y has F and G
(4″) All items that have F and G also have H
(5″) Therefore, y has H

Brewer's argument by *disanalogy* has the following logical form:

(1) x and y both have F;
(2) X has G;
(3) y does not have G (y has not-G);
(4) x also has H;
(5) any F is H unless it also has not-G (all things that are both F and G are H) (DWR—disanalogy warranting rule)
(6) Therefore, the presence of F and H in x does not provide a sufficient basis for inferring the presence of H in y (Table 7.3)

[9] The other two objections argue that several arguments, which according to Barker's definition are non-deductive and non-inductive, are clearly inductive. However, his objection misses the fact that they could be said to be abductive, which would avoid the objection.

Table 7.3 Analogical arguments distinguished by their different logical form

Criterion for classification: logical form of argument											Author
Form A Form B											Wreen (2007)
						Argument by disanalogy[a]		Logical form basic formula			Brewer (1996)
						Inductive disanalogy*	Deductive disanalogy	Inductive analogy	Deductive analogy		
		Paralogical proportion	Reverse analogy		Analogical proportion						Prade and Richard (2010); Miclet et al. (2011)
	Analogy by rendition[b]	Predictive analogy[c]			Proportional analogy						Indurkhya (1989, 1992)
				Imperfect analogical deduction[d]	Analogy based on proportion[e]						Klug (1951); see Macagno and Walton (2009)
				Basic scheme						Inductive argument from analogy[f]	Macagno and Walton (2009); Walt on (2012); Walton (Chap. 2)

[a] Brewer never explicitly defines any argument by inductive disanalogy, but it seems clear that a version of that could be formulated following how it is done with mutatis mutandis with argument by deductive disanalogy.
[b] Also labeld "interpretive analogy".
[c] Also labeld "analogical inference".
[d] The label is mine.
[e] The label is mine.
[f] This label is mine. Sometimes he uses the term "basic scheme".
* The label is mine.

Domain Constraint

This parameter sub-classifies the arguments according to whether they belong to the same or different domains. The well-established distinction between figurative and literal comparison is based on this criterion. A same-domain-analogy is an analogy where not only the relations, but also the elements are from the same domain. In a different-domain-analogy, the analogy comes only by virtue of having the same relation between the elements of the different objects; the elements of the two objects belong to entirely different spheres of reality. For example, Juthe (2005) distinguishes between same-domain and different-domain analogies in which the Assigned-Predicate is transferred *mutatis mutandis* on the Target-Subject.

The difference is crucial since it determines what predicate one can infer from the analogy. The transference of the predicate that is assigned to the Target-Subject must be contained in the domain of the target-subject, regardless of the predicates that are contained in the domain of the analogue. If the comparison is between different domains such as, say, sex and food; then any predicate that is concluded *from* how society deals with sex *to* how society deals with food, will be about whatever *food* issue that *counterparts* how society deals with sex.

The concepts of figurative analogy, argument from metaphor and argument from parable may be terms that signify a very distant different-domain analogy. This is also Weitzenfeld's (1984) basis for distinguishing between two types of analogical inferences. According to Weitzenfeld, isomorphic inference is the basic analogical inference, which can be subdivided into: *homeomorphs* which are analogous of the same kind, and *paramorphs* which are analogous of different kinds. In a homeomorph, the determining structure is the same, although the exact properties may differ as in an analogue between two games of chess. In contrast, the paramorphs have different determining structures, although they are isomorphic, the variables are not the same. However, some authors also use figurative analogy to denote non-argumentatively reasoning by analogy (Waller 2001). In the table the reader can see that theorists have utilized this distinction to sub-classify argument by analogy, as well as which label has been used (Table 7.4).

7.3 Summary and Conclusion

In this paper I have attempted to provide a brief overview of different types of argument by analogy and the various classifications thereof. It is based on a comprehensive overview and review of different classifications and distinctions of analogical arguments. Over 600 articles and books have been reviewed in order to achieve this review. The results reveal that different authors use different criteria as means for classification, and that there is consensus neither on what types of

Table 7.4 Analogical arguments distinguished by belonging to the same or different domain

Criterion for classification: difference in domain			Author
When the objects of comparison are in the same domain	When the objects of comparison are in different domains		
Same-domain analogy	Different-domain analogy		Juthe (2005, 2009)
Argument by literal analogies	Argument by figurative analogy descriptive version	Argument by figurative analogy normative version	Kienpointner (2012)
Literal analogy	Figurative analogy		Perelman and Olbrechts-Tyteca (2008)[a]
	Argument from metaphor[b]		Santibanez (2010)
	Argument from parable		Govier and Ayers (2012)
Homeomorphs	Paramorphs		Weitzenfeld (1984)
Homeomorphs	Paramorphs		Weingartner (1979)
Within-domain analogy	Cross-domain analogy		Ruiz and Luciano (2011)
Intra-domain analogy	Inter-domain analogy		Kokinov (1996)

[a] This information is taken from Doury (2009) and Kienpointner (2012).
[b] It is not entirely clear whether this really is an example of a figurative analogy or whether it belong to some other kind of argument scheme.

analogical argument there are, nor on how to classify them. The review also revealed that several different parameters have been used as criteria for classifying various subtypes of arguments by analogy. Of these parameters, four have been addressed in this paper.

References

Barker, E. M. 1989a. Beardsley's theory of analogy. *Informal Logic* XI (3): 185–194.

Barker, S. F. 1989b. Analogy in Hume's dialogues. *Informal Logic* XI (3): 173–184.

Botting, D. 2012. The paradox of analogy. *Informal Logic* 32 (1): 98–115.

Brewer, S. 1996. Exemplary reasoning: Semantics, pragmatics, and the rational force of legal argument by analogy. *Harvard Law Review* 109 (5): 923–1028.

Brown, W. R. 1989. Two traditions of analogy. *Informal Logic* XI (3): 161–172.

Copi, I. M., and K. Burgess-Jackson. 1992. *Informal logic*. 2nd ed. New York: Macmillian Publishing Company.

Copi, I. M., and D. Cohen. 1990. *Introduction to logic*. 8th ed. New York: Macmillian Publishing Company.

Cummings, L. 2004. Analogical reasoning as a tool of epidemiological investigation. *Argumentation* 4:427–444.

Doury, M. 2009. Argument schemes typologies in practice: The case of comparative arguments. In *Pondering on problems of argumentation: Twenty essays on theoretical issues,* eds. F. H. van Eemeren and B. Garssen, 141–154. Dordrecht: Springer.

Ehninger, D., and W. Brockriede. 1963. *Decision by debate*. New York: Dodd, Meade.

Garssen, B. 2010. Comparing the incomparable: Figurative analogies in a dialectical testing procedure. In *Pondering on problems of argumentation: Twenty essays on theoretical issues,* eds. F. H. van Eemeren and B. Garssen, 133–140. Dordrecht: Springer.

Govier, T. 1985. Logical analogies. *Informal Logic* 7 (1): 7–33.
Govier, T. 1989. Analogies and missing premises. *Informal Logic* II (3): 141–152.
Govier, T. 2002. Should *a priori* analogies be regarded as deductive arguments? *Informal Logic* 22 (2): 155–157.
Govier, T. 2010. *A practical study of arguments*. 7th ed. Belmont: Wadsworth Cengage Learning.
Govier, T., and L. Ayers. 2012. Logic, parables, and argument. *Informal Logic* 32 (2): 161–189.
Guarini, M. 2004. A defence of non-deductive reconstructions of analogical arguments. *Informal Logic* 24 (2): 153–168.
Hitchcock, D. 1992. Reasoning by analogy: A general theory. In *The generalizability of critical thinking: Multiple perspectives on an educational ideal,* ed. S. P. Norris, 109–124. New York: Teachers College Press.
Holyoak, K. J. 2005. Analogy. In *The Cambridge handbook of thinking and reasoning,* eds. K. J. Holyoak and R. G. Morrison, 117–142. New York: Cambridge University Press.
Indurkhya, B. 1989. Modes of analogy. In *Analogical and inductive inference: Lecture notes in artificial intelligence,* ed. K. P. Jantke, vol. 397. 217–230. Berlin: Springer.
Indurkhya, B. 1992. Predictive analogy and cognition. In *Analogical and inductive inference: Lecture notes in artificial intelligence,* ed. K. P. Jantke, vol. 642, 214–231. Berlin: Springer.
Ippoliti, E. 2006. Demonstrative and non-demonstrative reasoning by analogy. In *Demonstrative and non-demonstrative reasoning in mathematics and natural science,* eds. C. Cellucci and P. Pecere, 1–24. Cassion: Universita Degli Studi Di Cassino.
Johnson, F. 1989. Analogical arguings and explainings. *Informal Logic* XI (3): 152–160.
Juthe, A. 2005. Argument by analogy. *Argumentation* 19:1–27.
Juthe, A. 2009. Refutation by parallel argument. *Argumentation* 23:133–169.
Kienpointner, M. 2012. When figurative analogies fail: Fallacious uses of arguments from analogy. In *Topical themes in argumentation theory: Twenty exploratory studies,* eds. F. H. van Eemeren and B. Garssen, 111–125. Dordrecht: Springer. (Argumentation Library vol. 22).
Klug, U. 1951. *Juristische logik.* Berlin: Springer.
Kokinov, B. 1996. Analogy-making: Psychological data and computational models. In *Perspectives on cognitive science,* ed. B. Kokinov, vol. 2. Sofia: NBU Press.
Krabbe, E. C. W. 1996. Can we ever pin one down to a formal fallacy? In *Logic and argumentation,* eds. J. van Benthem, F. H. van Eemeren, R. Grootendorst, and F. Veltman, 129–141. Amsterdam: North-Holland.
Langenbucher, K. 1998. Argument by analogy in European law. *Cambridge Law New Journal* 57 (3): 81–521.
Macagno, F., and D. Walton. 2009. Argument from analogy in law, the classical tradition, and recent theories. *Philosophy and Rhetoric* 42 (2): 154–182.
Miclet, L., H. Prade, and D. Guennec. 2011. Looking for analogical proportions in a formal concept analysis setting. In *Proceedings of the 8th international conference on concept lattices and their applications,* eds. A. Napoli and V. Vychodil, vol. 959, 295–307. Nancy: LORIA CNRS-Inria Nancy Grand Est-Université de Lorraine.
Mill, J. S. 2013. *A system of logic, ratiocinative and inductive, being a connected view of the principles of evidence and the methods of scientific investigation*, Chap. XX, 332–336. New York: Harper and Brothers. Originally first published 1843. http://ebooks.adelaide.edu.au/m/mill/john_stuart/system_of_logic/chapter35.html. Accessed 21 July 2013.
Pascale, H. 2008. Arguments by parallels in the epistemological works of Phya pa Chos kyi seng ge. *Argumentation* 22:93–114.
Peczenik, A. 1971. Analogia legis: Analogy from statutes in continental law. In *Le raisonnement juridique. Proceedings of the world congress for legal and social philosophy,* ed. H. Hubien, 329–336. Brussels: Établissements Émile Bruylant.
Peczenik, A. 1989. *On law and reason.* Dordrecht: Kluwer Academic.
Perelman, Ch., and L. Olbrechts-Tyteca. 2008. *The new rhetoric: A treatise on argumentation.* Trans. J. Wilkinson and P. Weaver. Notre Dame: Notre Dame University Press. (English translation of *La nouvelle rhétorique: Traité de l'argumention*, Paris, Presses Universitaires de France, first published in 1958).

Prade, H., and G. Richard. 2009. Analogy, paralogy and reverse analogy: Postulates and inferences. In *KI 2009, LNAI 5803,* eds. B. Mertsching, M. Hund, and Z. Aziz, 306–314. Berlin: Springer.

Prade, H., and G. Richard. 2010. Analogical proportions: Another logical view. In *Research and development in intelligent systems XXVI,* eds. M. Bramer, et al., 306–314. London: Springer.

Reidhav, D. 2007. Reasoning by analogy: A study on analogy-based arguments in law. Doctoral Diss., Faculty of Law, Lund: Lund University.

Ruiz, F. J., and C. Luciano. 2011. Cross-domain analogies as relating derived relations among two separate relational networks. *Journal of the Experimental Analysis of Behavior* 95 (3): 369–385.

Santibanez, C. 2010. Metaphors and argumentation: The case of Chilean parliamentarian media participation. *Journal of Pragmatics* 42:973–989.

Sunstein, C. R. 1993. On analogical reasoning. *Harvard Law Review* 106 (3): 741–791.

Waller, B. N. 2001. Classifying and analyzing analogies. *Informal Logic* 21 (3): 199–218.

Walton, D. 2006. *Fundamentals of critical argumentation (critical reasoning and argumentation).* Cambridge: Cambridge University Press.

Walton, D. 2010. Similarity, precedent and argument from analogy. *Artificial Intelligence and Law* 18 (3): 217–246.

Walton, D. 2012. Story similarity in arguments from analogy. *Informal Logic* 32 (2): 1–23.

Walton, D., C. Reed, and F. Macagno. 2008. *Argumentation schemes.* Cambridge: Cambridge University Press.

Weingartner, W. 1979. Analogy among systems. *Dialectica* 33:355–378.

Weitzenfeld, J. S. 1984. Valid reasoning by analogy. *Philosophy of Science* 51:137–149.

Whaley, B. 1998. Evaluations of rebuttal analogy users: Ethical and competence considerations. *Argumentation* 12:351–365.

Whaley, B., and R. Holloway. 1997. Rebuttal analogy in political communication: Argument and attack in sound bite. *Political Communication* 14 (3): 293–305.

Whaley, B., and L. S. Wagner. 2000. Rebuttal analogy in persuasive messages: Communicator lihability and cognitive responses. *Journal of Language and Social Psychology* 19:66–84.

Woods, J., and B. Hudak. 1989. By parity of reasoning. *Informal Logic* XI (3): 125–139.

Wreen, M. J. 2007. A second form of argument from analogy. *Theoria* 73 (3): 221–239.

Chapter 8
Messing Up the Mind? Analogical Reasoning with Metaphors

Eugen Fischer

Physicists, psychologists, and philosophers alike frequently make conscious and explicit use of metaphors in analogical reasoning. Much of this has been prominently acknowledged as helpful and productive (e.g. Hesse 1966; Gentner and Grudin 1985). On the other hand, philosophical students of metaphor (incl. Rorty 1980; Lakoff and Johnson 1999; Fischer 2011) have forcefully suggested that partially unwitting use of conceptual metaphors has led to utterly unsound but highly intuitive philosophical (proto-)theories—notably including introspective or "Cartesian" conceptions of the mind which are still influential at the level of intuitive reasoning. The apparent tension raises the question: Exactly when and why does the frequently helpful use of metaphor in analogical reasoning turn pernicious? More specifically (since we are less interested in haphazard slips than in systematic or predictable fallacies): What fallacies arise from the use of metaphors in analogical reasoning, in a systematic or predictable manner? And why do competent thinkers make them—in a systematic or predictable manner?

This paper will contribute to answering these two questions by building on an explanation of the prime example of fallacious reasoning mentioned: Elsewhere (Fischer 2014), I have argued that the unsound but intuitive introspective conception of the mind that has attracted so much attention in the philosophical metaphor literature is shaped by intuitions that result from the interaction of unconscious analogical reasoning (Day and Gentner 2007; Thibodeau and Boroditsky 2011) with routine information-integration processes in semantic memory, which rely on partial matching (Budiu and Anderson 2004; Kamas et al. 1996). The present paper will redevelop this explanation in a way that allows us to identify a fundamental fallacy and to understand why even competent thinkers are prone to commit it. By explaining how and why philosophers messed up the notion of "the mind", we will get clear on one important way in which the—frequently unproblematic—use of conceptual metaphors in analogical reasoning may mess with our minds.

E. Fischer (✉)
School of Philosophy, University of East Anglia, Norwich, UK
e-mail: e.fischer@uea.ac.uk

H. J. Ribeiro (ed.), *Systematic Approaches to Argument by Analogy*,
Argumentation Library 25, DOI 10.1007/978-3-319-06334-8_8,

First, we will introduce key findings about analogical reasoning from cognitive psychology, explain the notion of "conceptual metaphor", and see how analogical reasoning and conceptual metaphors contribute to an autocatalytic process: Simple analogical reasoning builds up conceptual metaphors that, in turn, facilitate more complex analogical inferences (Sect. 1). Then we will encounter evidence that such inferences, namely, analogical inferences using conceptual metaphors ("CM-inferences"), can be drawn automatically or at any rate without conscious awareness (Sect. 2), will familiarise ourselves with equally automatic information-integration processes that are routinely executed in semantic memory (Sect. 3), and will see that the interaction of automatic analogical CM-inferences with such routine processing can generate the influential philosophical intuitions to be explained (Sect. 4). Finally, we will see how the interaction of the processes analysed leads to a previously unidentified fallacy: the "realisation-defeating extension of linguistically realised conceptual metaphors" (Sect. 5).

8.1 Analogy and Metaphor

According to a framework now standard in cognitive psychology, actual analogical reasoning involves at least three steps, each guided by substantive constraints (Holyoak 2005). First, a suitable source-model is identified, and knowledge about it is retrieved from memory. To take a familiar example, Rutherford chose the solar system as model of the atom. Second, model and target are aligned and elements of the source-model are mapped onto elements of the target domain. In our example from physics, planets are mapped onto electrons, the sun onto the nucleus, and relations between celestial bodies (x orbits y, y attracts z, etc.) onto relations between sub-atomic particles. Third, the actual inferences are made.

The first two steps are actually executed in accordance with two kinds of constraints, which carry different weight at different stages (Gentner et al. 1993; Holyoak and Koh 1987; Ross 1989). The dominant constraint at the first stage of retrieval is *surface similarity*: In thinking about a target X (object, property, relation, etc.), we are the more likely to seize on a source model Y the more properties we take X and Y to share. The second constraint is *structural similarity*: In particular when several different source models share sufficiently many properties with the target to be potentially pertinent, subjects choose the one structurally most similar to the target (Wharton et al. 1994, 1996).

Similar constraints guide the second step, of alignment and mapping: According to an influential computational model of analogical inference (SME, Falkenhainer et al. 1989; Forbus et al. 1995), we first correlate elements from the source domain SD (e.g. planetary systems) with those elements from the target domain TD (e.g. atoms) which we take to fall under the same concepts, thus mapping elements we take to obtain in both domains (say, the orbiting-relation) onto themselves. We then prune these correlations and add new ones by imposing requirements of *structural consistency*: When a property or relation in the SD (say, "x orbits y") is mapped onto a property or relation in the TD, their arguments or relata (be they individuals—like planets and sun—or lower-level predicates or relations) have to be placed in correspondence too ("*parallel connectivity*"). Each element (individual, property, relation) in one domain must be placed in correspondence with at most one element in the other domain ("*one-to-one mapping*"). Finally, mappings are preferred when they "*enforce systematicity*" and map a whole system of lower-order relations as well as several higher-order (causal or logical, etc.) relations that link or constrain them. Experiments have confirmed various behavioural predictions derived from this computational model, about analogical reasoning (Clement and Gentner 1991; Markman 1997; Gentner and Markman 2005; Gentner and Kurtz 2006) and metaphor processing (Gentner and Bowdle 2008). This suggests that a process subject to these constraints actually occurs when we employ analogies.

In the third key step of analogical reasoning, the actual inferences are made from a set S of assumptions about the SD in line with the procedure of *copying with substitution and generation* (CSG) (Falkenhainer et al. 1989; Hummel and Holyoak 2003):

1. When a SD-element A has been mapped onto a TD-element B, all the relations in which A, according to S, stands in the SD, plus relevant relata, are attributed to B ("copied into the TD").
2. In the initial conclusions thus obtained, (representations of) relations and relata from the SD are replaced, as far as possible, by (representations of) those TD-elements onto which the SD-elements have been mapped ("substitution").
3. Where an element of the SD could not be mapped onto any element of the TD, a new element is postulated in the TD, to the extent necessary to render true the conclusions thus obtained ("generation").

People find these conclusions credible to the extent to which they rely on mappings of first-order relations that stand in some of the same higher-order relations (Gentner et al. 1993; Lassaline 1996).

Simple analogical reasoning forges *conceptual metaphors:* These are cross-domain mappings that preserve relations and thereby motivate the extension of linguistic terms from SD to TD (Lakoff and Johnson 1980; Kövesces 2002). To the extent to which terms are thus extended, the conceptual metaphor is said to be "linguistically realised". (Alternatively or in addition, it can be "pictorially realised", as by familiar pictures of advancing torchbearers who represent the progress of enlightening science helping humanity to new knowledge). Analogical reasoning forges conceptual metaphors by building up from a "basic mapping" like:

1. S sees x → S knows x

The first mappings made in analogical reasoning correlate elements of the different domains to which the same concepts apply (Falkenhainer et al. 1989; Forbus et al. 1995). They hence map relations obtaining in both SD and TD, onto themselves. In CSG, these relations get "substituted" by themselves (and are, in effect, simply copied). The most elementary CSG inferences involve only *copying with substitution (CS)* but no generation, and employ only such "mappings onto self" plus a basic mapping, while logical operators simply carry over. Such *elementary CS inferences*

Table 8.1 An elementary inference

	SD premise	Operation	TD conclusion
1	Not	Substitution (identical)	Not
2	S sees x	Substitution (basic mapping)	S knows X

can proceed from closed and open sentences. In the latter case, premises can be mapped onto conclusions (or, rather, the relations they stand for). Such analogical inferences can be conveniently represented by "grids" such as the following (Table 8.1).

Such inferences yield further mappings:

2. S does not see x → S does not know x
3. It's possible for S to see x, i.e. x is visible for S → It's possible for S to know x
4. It is not possible for S to see x, i.e., x is invisible for S → It is not possible (for S) to know x.
5. X makes it possible for S to see y, i.e., x makes y visible for S → X makes it possible for S to know y
6. X makes it impossible for S to see y, i.e., x makes y invisible to S → X makes it impossible for S to know y
7. S tries to get to see x, i.e., S looks for x → S tries to get to know x

The basic mapping and the mappings that can be obtained from it through elementary CS are jointly *constitutive* of conceptual metaphors like *Knowing as Seeing*.

Such metaphors can motivate the metaphorical extension of terms from their source to their target domains. Such extension is motivated by implications: We frequently say things by implying them without stating them, and rely on our interlocutor to draw the requisite inference. E.g. the ancient Greeks stereotypically associated strength, courage, and nobility with lions, and spontaneously inferred from "x is a lion" that x is strong, courageous, and noble. Hence they could say—Aristotle's textbook example—"Achilles is a lion" to state that Achilles is strong, courageous, and noble. They thus metaphorically extended the application of "x is a lion" from animals to heroes and humans. Metaphorical extension of relational terms to their stereotypical implications can motivate the basic mappings of conceptual metaphors: Typically, when you see something (happening), you know it (happens).

Conceptual metaphors facilitate a plethora of CSG inferences which forge fresh implications that motivate such metaphorical extension. Take a familiar fact about the source domain of visual search: When things stand right in the way, in front of us, they are, by and large, easily visible. Until the eighteenth century, the adjective "obvious" was used with the meaning "standing in the way, positioned in front of, opposite to, facing" (OED 2012). That things are "obvious" in this now forgotten literal sense hence implies that they are easily visible. CSG inference takes us from this premise to the conclusion that when things are "right before your nose" or "obvious", they are easily knowable (Table 8.2):

Table 8.2 Analogical inference grid

	SD premise	Operation	TD conclusion
1	X is obvious	Generation	X is obvious
2	Implies (1;3)	Substitution: identical	Implies (1;3)
3	X is easily visible	Substitution: mapping 3	X is easily knowable

This is an example of what we might call a "CASD-GASC inference": a CSG inference that proceeds from a conditional assumption about the source domain, "generates" or carries over the antecedent, and substitutes the consequent. Such inferences endow terms employed in talk about the source domain, which remain in the antecedent of the conclusion, with metaphorical implications about the target domain, which are stated by the substituting terms in the consequent. We can define:

> p has the *metaphorical implication* q* iff p→q* can be obtained through CSG from a truth p→q about the source-domain of a conceptual metaphor whose mappings license substitution of q by q* but none of p, where "→" designates de- *or* inductive inference.

To interpret the use of the "source-domain terms" in talk about the target domain, competent speakers can spontaneously seize on such metaphorical implications. They thus infer, e.g., from "the solution is obvious" that it is easy to get to know the solution, and say the former to state the latter.

Experiments on "metaphor consistency effects" have confirmed the hypothesis that, without necessarily being aware of them, speaker/hearers actually make analogical (CSG) inferences which employ conceptual metaphors when they encounter freshly minted metaphorical expressions (Boroditsky 2000; Gentner et al. 2002; Boroditsky and Ramscar 2002; Gentner and Bowdle 2008, pp. 113–115). In these experiments, different subjects read different texts, each of which consistently employs a given metaphor. However, different texts use different metaphors for the same target domain: e.g., where one employs the conceptual metaphor Debate as War ("The speaker had to use every weapon at his command"), the other uses the metaphor Debate as Race ("The speaker had to steer his course carefully"). Both texts are followed by a test sentence for which reading times are measured. For some subjects, texts are paired with test sentences which employ a metaphorical expression motivated by the same guiding metaphor; others are given sentences relying on the guiding metaphor of the other text. If cross-domain mappings are involved in understanding the metaphorical expressions used, subjects will read the test sentence more quickly when it continues to rely on the same mapping as the previously read passage, and more slowly when they need to switch to a new mapping. Such metaphorical consistency effects were found for unfamiliar or fresh metaphorical expressions—as well as for familiar spatial time metaphors, which involve closely inter-defined relational terms ("after", "before", etc.).

These findings have motivated the *career of metaphor* hypothesis (Bowdle and Gentner 2005; Gentner and Bowdle 2008): When freshly coined, metaphorical expressions are initially understood on the basis of the conceptual metaphor that motivates their introduction, and speaker/hearers make analogical (CSG) inferences which employ its constituent mappings, consciously or unconsciously. As speaker/

hearers keep being exposed to this metaphorical alongside the literal use, they come to form an abstract relational schema and to derive a new, wider category, under which elements from source- and target-domain can be subsumed. Once they have thus endowed the expression at issue with a new domain-general meaning, the same processes are involved in understanding the expression when used metaphorically as when used literally.

To sum up: Analogical reasoning and conceptual metaphor can mutually enhance each other. The basic mapping of a conceptual metaphor facilitates simple analogical reasoning, namely, elementary inferences with copying and substitution but without generation. These "elementary CS inferences" yield further mappings that flesh out the conceptual metaphor. These further mappings then facilitate more complex analogical inferences, viz. proper CSG inferences which also involve generation. These inferences endow terms with metaphorical implications that motivate their metaphorical extension, and are made, consciously or unconsciously, when speaker/hearers first encounter freshly introduced metaphorical uses motivated in this way.

We are thus looking at an auto-catalytic process in which conceptual metaphor serves as a catalyst for analogical reasoning that, in turn, extends them, thus adding fuel to its own fire: Recall from the beginning of this section (1) that thinkers are the more likely to seize on a source domain in thinking about a target domain, the more properties they take their elements to share, and (2) that thinkers are the more likely to draw analogical inferences based on a particular mapping, the more the mapping meets the consistency requirements of parallel connectivity and one-to-one mapping, and the more it enforces systematicity. (Re 2) CS inferences expand conceptual metaphors in a way that satisfies the consistency requirements and enforces systematicity ever more strongly—as higher-order relations between lower-order relations are preserved, parallel connectivity is ensured (Gentner and Bowdle 2008). (Re 1) The mappings obtained facilitate ever more CSG inferences which motivate the metaphorical extension of ever more terms, leading to the formation of ever more domain-general categories under which elements of source- and target-domain can both be subsumed, and thus lead thinkers to take these elements to share more and more properties. Hence the more CS and CSG inferences we make with the mapping CM that constitutes a conceptual metaphor, the more extensive, and extensively realised, this metaphor becomes; and the more this happens, the more likely we are (1) to make CSG inferences about the metaphor's target-domain from premises about its source domain, (2) using the mapping CM. This happens not only in language-development and-comprehension (above) but also in problem-solving (below, Sect. 2). The source-domains of extensively developed and realised conceptual metaphors are particularly likely to be employed as models in analogical reasoning—which may in turn extend them. Analogical inference and linguistically realised conceptual metaphor form part of an auto-catalytic process.

8.2 Automatic Inferences

Cognitive psychologists distinguish automatic from controlled cognitive processes. This is no neat dichotomy. Rather, cognitive processes are automatic to the extent to which they are effortless, unconscious, non-intentional, and autonomous (Bargh 1994; Moors and De Houwer 2006) .These gradable and independent properties have operational definitions. The first two generally suffice to earn a process the accolade "automatic" (Evans 2010, p. 314): A cognitive process is

- *effortless* iff its execution requires no attention or other limited cognitive resource—and is hence not impaired when the subject is distracted by tasks requiring such resources (say, keeping in mind long numbers), and
- *unconscious* to the extent to which the subject is unable to report the course of the process, as opposed to articulating its outcome (judgment, decision, etc.)

Automatic cognitive processes can *duplicate* rule-governed inferences from premises to conclusions: Under specifiable circumstances, they may lead to the same judgments as output that the rule-governed inferences license as conclusions from the same premises or information as input. Where automatic processes duplicate inferences governed by the rules of CSG, cognitive psychologists speak of "automatic analogical inferences".

Until about 15 years ago, most psychologists and philosophers alike took for granted that we draw analogical inferences only in conscious, controlled reflection. Since then, evidence of automatic, or at any rate unconscious analogical inference has been provided also by text-comprehension experiments (e.g. Day and Gentner 2007): Subjects read analogous texts, e.g. about two suspicious deaths of wealthy relatives, where a more detailed source was followed by a less detailed or ambiguous target text. Different subjects were given different versions of the source texts (containing e.g. variants A and B below, respectively):

Example 1: Prompts for analogical inferences

Source text [extracts]	Target text [extracts]
When the widow-heiress Margaret Haverty died suddenly, there were some who suspected foul play...	The death of wealthy old Alexander van Houten was abrupt and unexpected, and there were rumours that it might not be of natural causes...
(A) As soon as her death was announced, her niece Helena mysteriously booked a flight from Amsterdam, where she also lived, off to Naples	Surprisingly, when his death was announced, Mr. van Houten's nephew George immediately bought a ticket and flew to Rio de Janeiro
(B) As soon as her death was announced, her niece Helena respectfully booked a flight from Naples, where she lived, to Amsterdam for the funeral	

In a subsequent "recognition task" readers have to judge which of the statements on a list had been contained in a text they had read. These include statements consistent with, but not actually contained in, the target text, which can be obtained through analogical inference from more detailed or precise passages in the source text, such as:

Example 2: Analogical conclusions

From A	George had been in the same city as his uncle but left town when the death was announced
From B	George was among those who came into town for Alexander van Houten's funeral

In 72 % of the cases in which subjects could obtain a statement in this way from "their" previously read version of the source text, they misattributed it to a text they had read—significantly more often than other statements (25 %). When subsequently asked, "Did you feel that each of the passages was completely understandable on its own or did you find yourself referring to previous stories in order to understand later ones?", 80 % declared all passages completely understandable on their own. The experimenters inferred that analogical inferences were drawn without awareness.

We are now interested, more specifically, in analogical inferences which employ conceptual metaphors. Metaphor consistency effects provide evidence that *such* inferences are drawn without awareness in understanding fresh metaphorical expressions (above). More importantly, experiments on problem-solving evidence their wider relevance, beyond language comprehension. In one set of experiments (Thibodeau and Boroditsky 2011), participants were asked how to reduce crime in an imaginary city, after reading texts outlining its crime statistics and recent developments. The texts were consistently couched in either of two metaphors: *crime as (infectious) virus* or *crime as (raging) beast*. This metaphor frame had a stronger effect even than subsequently self-reported political affiliation on whether participants proposed remedial or bellicose measures. The frames exerted a significant influence even when subjects were presented with a comprehensive list of options. Experimenters concluded that metaphor-based analogical inferences influence not merely which answers occur to subjects first but also which they find most compelling. When subsequently asked to indicate which part of the text influenced their decision, subjects typically mentioned crime statistics, while only 3–15 % mentioned the metaphor used. The observed effects remained significant once these responses were disregarded. Experimenters inferred subjects' use of metaphors in analogical problem-solving was unconscious.

Cognitive and social psychologists seek to explain a wide variety of automatic inferences as the outcome of simple associative processes which can duplicate achievements of complex reasoning (Kahneman 2011; Uleman et al. 2008). According to the influential theoretical framework of *memory-based processing*, all spontaneous inferences subjects make in the absence of specific goals when hearing or reading texts result from automatic association processes in semantic memory (e.g. Gerrig and O'Brien 2005; O'Brien 1995). If this view is correct, also analogical inferences such as those studied by the above text-comprehension experiments should be duplicated by such processes: Their participants were not given any specific goal in advance, and subsequent experiment ruled out simple lexical priming but no other associative processes (Day and Gentner 2007, exp. 2). Since memory-based processing has been shown to draw not only on "contextual knowledge" about earlier parts of the text, or earlier texts (e.g. Albrecht and Myers 1998), but also on "general world knowledge" (e.g. Cook and Guéraud 2005), this point should extend from spontaneous analogical inferences that employ *ad hoc* models provided by carefully manipulated textual contexts (as in Day and Gentner 2007), to inferences which employ the sort of amply familiar models (like seeing medium-sized objects in our physical environment) that are provided through conceptual metaphors realised in ordinary language (like Knowing-as-Seeing).

Semantic memory is our memory for facts and meanings, as opposed to personally experienced events (McRae and Jones 2013). It is most commonly conceived as a semantic network which doubles as information-storage and inference-facilitator. Such a network consists of nodes representing concepts and links between them that can automatically pass on activation from stimuli, verbal and other. Co-occurrence forges links which grow stronger upon use (frequent activation) and atrophy upon disuse. Simultaneous activation of concepts can amount to the activation of a proposition made up of those concepts. An activated concept or proposition becomes conscious if—and only if—the activation exceeds a threshold. The associative process of spreading activation can therefore duplicate inferences, by spreading in sufficient strength from nodes representing one proposition to nodes that jointly represent another.

Current theories of how analogical reasoning emerges from associative processing (e.g. Leech et al. 2008) cannot yet explain how such processes can duplicate analogical inferences (Markman and Laux 2008). What matters for present purposes, however, is that, regardless of how exactly such inferences are duplicated by associative processes in semantic memory, their conclusions will be subject to further such processing. In particular, they will be subject to processes that constantly integrate new information we receive with information we already possess.

8.3 Information Integration in Semantic Memory

Associative processes in semantic memory are postulated on the basis of priming-experiments: Subjects are presented first with a stimulus or "*prime*" (word, sentence, short text) and then a "*probe*" word or string of letters, and have to either read out the word or decide whether the string forms a proper word. When subjects need less time for such 'naming' or 'lexical decision tasks' for prime/probe pairs of same length and complexity ("bank"-"money" rather than "bank"-"honey"), researchers infer that the prime "*activated*" the probe concept: made it more readily available for use (e.g. Peleg and Giora 2011). By varying the time elapsing between the presentation of the prime and the probe, psycholinguists can study the time course of activation.

Such work (comprehensively reviewed by Giora 2003) has revealed two different kinds of processes: *Stimulus-driven processes* are wholly determined by current and immediately preceding verbal input. *Expectation-driven processes* are influenced also by previously processed stimuli (say, earlier parts of a text or speech) and the deliverances of other cognitive processes (such as the simultaneous perception of a visual scene or illustration). These processes initially run in parallel. Their outputs are subsequently integrated, as the activation of the differently activated concepts is automatically maintained or enhanced, or unconsciously suppressed in a goal-sensitive manner.

Many category concepts ("bird", "bank teller", "accountant", etc.) are associated with stereotypical or prototypical properties (Rosch 1978): Competent speakers name these properties earliest and most frequently when asked to list properties of "a typical X" (bird, accountant, etc.), rate individuals with more of these properties as better examples of the category in question, and classify individuals possessing more of these properties more rapidly as belonging to this category. In response to a verbal stimulus, stimulus-driven processing activates property-concepts that are in this way stereotypically associated with the objects or people in question (Giora 2003): Nouns activate stereotypical properties of their bearers. Verbs activate stereotypical properties of their agents and patients as well as typically involved instruments, etc.: "manipulate", for example, primes the stereotypical victim-property "naïve" (Ferretti et al. 2001).

Such activation can lead to automatic attribution of stereotypical properties, as illustrated by this riddle (Giora 2003, p. 13):

> A young man and his father had a severe car accident. The father died, and the young man was rushed to hospital. The surgeon at the emergency room refused to operate on him, saying, "I can't. He's my son."—How is this possible?

Many students find this question difficult to answer. This difficulty is due to the fact that "surgeon" activates the stereotypical properties of surgeons—including their stereotypical (male) gender—which are then attributed to the speaker, unless the activation is suppressed in the subsequent integration stage, due to conflict with the outputs of context-sensitive expectation-driven processes. The more stereotypical the pertinent properties are, the more strongly they are activated, and the harder their activation is to suppress in inappropriate contexts. Thus, students who find the above riddle hard, take for granted that the speaker is male, even though it is easy to infer that, since the father has died, the speaker must be the remaining parent, the mother.

Since it facilitates automatic property attributions, the stimulus-driven activation of stereotypical properties (male, naïve, etc.) can be regarded as bringing to bear general knowledge or beliefs about agents and events (that most surgeons are male, that people who are successfully manipulated are typically naïve, etc.), in the interpretation of utterances, observations, and spontaneously drawn conclusions. We can hence regard associative processing in semantic memory as a two-pronged process of information integration: Stimulus-driven activation of stereotypical features brings to bear general knowledge, while expectation-driven activations brings to bear contextual information, on the interpretation of newly encountered statements and freshly drawn conclusions.

Stimulus-driven activation does not stop with stereotypical features. The nodes representing them pass on activation (if more weakly) to nodes representing prototypical bearers of those features. In this way, a verbal stimulus comes to activate at one go several concepts that are "semantically similar" (as cognitive psychologists put it in an idiom that will strike many philosophers as alien):

> A *concept* is *semantically similar* to another, for a subject S, to the extent to which S takes the things (individuals, stuffs, properties, etc.) they stand for to share the same attributes or to stand in the same relations. (E.g. Oostendorp and Mul 1990, pp. 36–37)

The more salient or available (first thought of or easily remembered) properties two things share, the more strongly the verbal stimulus denoting one comes to activate the concept of the other. Furthermore, activated concepts activate propositions in which they are embedded in the same thematic roles (agent, patient, verb, etc.).

This facilitates the use of a memory – and interpretation-heuristic that has been proposed to account for semantic illusions: After reading aloud the question "How many animals of each kind did Moses take into the ark?", over 80 % answered "2"—even though they knew that Noah, not Moses, is the protagonist of the ark story, and had been instructed to either answer questions *or* indicate that something is wrong with them, as appropriate (Erickson and Mattson 1981). In attenuated form (which may merely reflect word order effects), this "*Moses illusion*" survives the move from questions to statements (ibid.): When asked for true/false judgments, over 40 % of Biblically knowledgeable subjects judged true "Moses took two animals of each kind into the ark". Other examples include: "The circle is the shape whose circumference is pi-r-squared" and "Switzerland is famous for cuckoo clocks, chocolate, stock markets, and pocketknives" (cp. Park and Reder 2004, p. 277).

The "partial match hypothesis" (Barton and Sandford 1993; Kamas et al. 1996; Oostendorp and Kok 1990), which has been empirically more successful than proposed competitors (Park and Reder 2004), seeks to account for such semantic illusions by postulating a "simple heuristic" (Park and Reder 2004, p. 289). Heuristics are rules of thumb which usually give reasonably accurate results within their usual domains of application, but (in contrast with the normative rules of logic or probability theory) do not determine or constrain what answers can be regarded as true or reasonable (Tversky and Kahneman 1983; Goldstein and Gigerenzer 2002). Their application is rapid and effortless (De Neys 2006; Pachur and Hertwig 2006), and cognitive psychologists now try to explain it in terms of associative processing in semantic memory (Kahneman 2011; Morewedge and Kahneman 2010).

We can informally put the "partial match heuristic" thus: "When unsure how to understand a statement or conclusion, interpret it as stating the semantically most similar proposition you already believe true—provided the similarity exceeds a certain threshold." Here, semantic similarity between propositions depends upon the semantic similarity of concepts filling the same thematic roles (agent, patient, verb, place oblique) in the different propositions, and on the number of different such roles that get filled in either proposition (Budiu and Anderson 2004, p. 38).

The semantic similarity between concepts, in turn, depends upon the extent of feature overlap (above). The heuristic tells us to search the semantically most similar proposition already stored in memory and treat it as the content of the statement at issue, if similar enough. Since stimulus-driven activation tracks semantic similarity, thus understood, associative processing in semantic memory should be able to duplicate its application.

This proposal can explain the Moses Illusion: If the processes that routinely go on in statement comprehension duplicate the proposed heuristic, we are liable to treat "Moses took two animals of each kind into the ark" as stating a familiar fact about Noah, a semantically quite similar subject (Noah and Moses are both believed to be male Biblical leaders with a covenant with God), and are more likely to interpret that sentence thus than otherwise identical sentences with subjects "Adam" (also a male Biblical figure, but covenant-less and no leader) or "Nixon" (a former U.S. president). Experiments confirmed these predictions (Oostendorp and Mul 1990). Wherever we already hold a semantically sufficiently similar belief, it seems, the integration of information conveyed by a statement we hear or a conclusion we draw takes the shape of conflating the new with the old.

8.4 Integrating Analogical Conclusions

A computational model of the present heuristic is afforded by the computationally implemented theory of *information-based processing* (INP) (Budiu and Anderson 2004). This model processes new statements incrementally, beginning the moment the first semantic unit has been, e.g., read. As each such unit is read (i.e., more specifically, as each noun phrase, verb, or adverb is read, ignoring auxiliary verbs and prepositions), INP retrieves the then most strongly activated proposition from memory and uses it as "candidate interpretation" which specifies the content of the statement. In line with the scope of stimulus-driven processing, the model relies only on activation emanating from the present verbal stimulus and immediately preceding input. At each step, INP aligns the current candidate interpretation (e.g., *Moses led his people from Egypt*) with what is already available from the input sentence (initially "Moses…", then "Moses took", then "Moses took two animals of each kind…", etc.). The model then compares the freshly read unit (e.g. "took" in step 2) with the part of the candidate interpretation that occupies the same thematic role (*led*), for—subjective—semantic similarity. If they are sufficiently similar for the subject (if the read expression activates this role-filler sufficiently strongly to increase the activation of the candidate interpretation above a certain threshold), the interpretation is retained. Otherwise, the model retrieves as new candidate interpretation the proposition most strongly activated by the current and immediately preceding input, and aligns and compares as before.

If information-integration in semantic memory works along the lines set out (cp. Sect. 3), this process is bound to occur when fresh conclusions are obtained through automatic analogical inferences, including inferences which employ conceptual metaphors (Sects. 1 and 2). In this case, the process can lead thinkers to interpret wrong conclusions of automatic CSG inferences as truisms. Yet more perniciously, the alignment of such inferences' conclusions with familiar propositions can forge fresh mappings which are, in a sense to be explained, incompatible with those constitutive of the relevant conceptual metaphors. Predictable fallacies thus ensue where automatic analogical inferences lead to conclusions that are semantically highly similar to propositions thinkers already believe true.

We will explain this problematic interaction by considering the perhaps most prominently discussed example of unsound analogical reasoning with metaphors: Various scholars have attributed introspective ("Cartesian") conceptions of the mind to misuse of conceptual metaphors in conscious reflection or automatic cognition (Rorty 1980; Lakoff and Johnson 1999; Fischer 2011). In their classical early modern versions, these conceptions rely on two key developments: the transformation of the understanding from a *faculty* of reason, intellect, or understanding, into an *organ* of sense (which I examine through analysis of Locke (1975), in Fischer 2011, Chaps. 1 and 2) and the transformation of the mind from a purely spatial memory-metaphor into a space or field *of perception*, surveyed by that organ of sense. These transformations, I submit, involve several parallel and mutually reinforcing analogical inferences which employ distinct but related visual metaphors and proceed from source-domain premises about different acts and achievements of visual perception. All these inferences ultimately rely on the use of two new mappings alongside the mappings constitutive of those conceptual metaphors: the below mappings M and N which cannot be obtained through elementary CS inferences from the basic mappings of these metaphors.

In analogical reasoning, with or without metaphor, we routinely add new mappings, where (i) some relations linked by higher-order relations have already been mapped, (ii) the requirement of parallel connectivity demands that we map their relata, and (iii) the target domain contains suitably related elements. This can, I submit, account for the reconceptualization of the understanding. Consider, e.g., an inference from the premise

When we look at something, we use our eyes.

It employs the basic mapping of the metaphor *Thinking-about as looking-at* which motivates metaphorical talk of "looking hard at the problem", "looking at the issue from different angles", or "looking at the options available". The next verb, "x uses y" stands for a generic relation that obtains both in the visual source domain and in the target domain of intellectual activity. It is hence mapped onto itself. This leaves us looking for an element of this domain that corresponds to our eyes. The latter are introduced here as a relatum of the *use*-relation, as temporally linked to the *looking-at* relation that gets mapped onto *thinking-about*. The requirement of parallel connectivity hence has us look for something we use when we think—and settle for our "reason", "intellect", or "understanding", commonly used as different labels for the same faculty. We thus obtain the

Table 8.3 Analogical inference to organs of understanding

	SD premise	Operation	TD conclusion
1	S looks at X	Substitution: CM	S thinks about X
2	When (1) then (3–4)	Substitution: identical	When (1) then (3–4)
3	S uses Y	Substitution: identical	S uses Y
4	S's eyes (Y)	Substitution: parallel connectivity	S's understanding (Y)

New mapping N: eyes → understanding

and the conclusion: "When we think about something, we use our understanding" (Table 8.3).

Mapping N is *ad hoc* in that it is made in considering only the relations invoked by a single premise, rather than by a more comprehensive description of the source domain.

The other crucial new mapping is

Mapping M: visual field → mind

It cannot be obtained in the same way. Most ordinary uses of "the mind" are motivated by a spatial-inclusion metaphor of remembering and thinking-of which unfolds from the basic mapping:

X is inside a space belonging to S → S remembers/thinks of X.

This personal space is typically called 'the mind'. The conceptual metaphor thus motivates saying that we "keep" or "have" something "in mind" when we can think of or remember it, that things 'come to mind' when we actually think of them, and that they "slip" or (archaically) "go from our mind" when we forget, temporarily or permanently, etc. (Fischer 2011, pp. 41–45). While it is only used in talk about the TD of remembering etc., the term "the mind" is thus used to stand for an element of the SD of the conceptual metaphor used to talk about this topic, viz. for the space belonging to S that figures in this metaphor's basic mapping. Hence whatever mappings involving minds are made *ad hoc* in analogical reasoning with this conceptual metaphor would have to map *from* and not—like Mapping M—*onto* minds.

Instead, I submit, Mapping M is obtained through the interaction of automatic analogical reasoning with the information integration processes modelled by INP: An analogical (CSG) inference leads, e.g., from "When we look at things, they are in our visual field", to the conclusion

C_0 "When we think about things, they are in our visual field."

"Looking-at" gets mapped onto "thinking-about" (as above). The spatial-inclusion relation "x is in y" is arguably mapped onto a homonymous domain-general ordering relation that evolves from it in the career of metaphor (cp. Sect. 1). But this relation does not impose sufficient constraints to determine any relatum for things-we-think-about. Hence "visual fields" must be posited (or 'generated') in the target domain (Table 8.4).

Conclusions of analogical inferences strike us as credible to the extent to which they rely on meaningful mapped relations linked by some of the same higher-order

Table 8.4 Analogical inference to C_0

	SD premise	Operation	TD conclusion
1	S looks at X	Substitution: CM	S thinks about X
2	When (1) then (3–4)	Substitution: identical	When (1) then (3–4)
3	X is in Y	Substitution: abstract	X is in Y
4	S's visual field (Y)	Generation	S's visual field (Y)

relations (Sect. 1). Relying on nothing of the sort, C_0 is bound to strike us as dubious, as and when it is explicitly presented. However, we need not even become aware of it, as fresh conclusions are likely to trigger automatic execution of the partial match heuristic modelled by INP (Sect. 3): "When unsure what to make of a statement or conclusion, interpret it as stating the semantically most similar proposition you already believe true—provided the similarity exceeds a certain threshold."

Plain men and philosophers, early modern and contemporary, tend to accept a semantically highly similar claim as true, all along: "When we think of things, they are in our…" Few people have trouble completing this sentence with—"mind". The resulting sentence (labelled C_0^{INP} below) fills the same number of thematic roles as C_0 and fills all but one of them with the same terms. It therefore stands to be semantically highly similar to C_0, for the subject. Since C_0^{INP} employs different expressions than C_0 only in the last slot, INP will activate it throughout, and increasingly strongly. Hence already a comparatively low degree of semantic similarity for the concepts in the final semantic unit ("are in our visual field"—"are in our mind") will suffice for the overall proposition to be accepted as interpretation of C_0, provided no yet more similar proposition is already believed true. And we can indeed say some of the same things about minds and visual fields, making for the requisite degree of "feature overlap": Things can "be in" and "out" or "outside" either, can "drop out of" or "suddenly pop up in" them, etc. Indeed, the relevant parts of C_0 and C_0^{INP} seem to state such an overlap. Hence INP accepts the familiar proposition as interpretation of C_0:

C_0^{INP} "When we think about things, they are in our mind."

This re-representation of the conclusion leads to a remapping from elements of the initial premise, and facilitates a mapping onto minds: In interpreting the initial analogical conclusion C_0, INP has highlighted the multiple feature overlap between visual fields and minds, as "visual field" activates those several features, whose nodes, in turn, pass on activation to "mind" (cp. Sect. 3). In automatic analogical reasoning, we automatically first correlate the source- and target-domain elements which are semantically similar. Accordingly, the further processing in line with INP leads us to re-map the elements of the initial premise onto the elements of the proposition now accepted as content of the conclusion, and to map visual fields onto minds. This yields Mapping M—and moves minds from the source to the target domain.

Mappings M and N facilitate a plethora of CSG inferences from premises P to conclusions C, which include (non-identical substitutions underlined, generated elements in italics):

P1 When we look at things, things are before our eyes.
C1 When we think about things, things *are before* our understanding.
P2 When we look at things, things are in our visual field.
C2 When we think about things, things *are in* our mind.
P3 Things before our eyes are in our visual field.
C3 Things *before* our understanding *are in* our mind.
P4 When we look at things, we perceive things with our eyes, *in* our visual field.
C4 When we think about things, we perceive things with our understanding, *in* our mind.

To understand this last inference, namely, why "perceive" is not replaced by something else, recall that "to perceive" is "to apprehend with the senses or mind" (as the OED puts it): The verb stands for a generic epistemic relation that obtains in both source and target domain, so that the rules of CSG substitute it by itself (identical substitution).

These automatic inferences generate intuitive judgments (Evans 2010; Fischer 2014, Tversky and Kahneman 1983), commencing with C_1 to C_4, which jointly transform the understanding from an intellectual faculty into an organ of sense employed in thought, and the mind into this organ's perceptual field.

8.5 A Fallacy

The explanation of the intuitions that jointly effect this momentous transformation allows us to expose a fallacy, identify a systematic source of it, and understand why even competent thinkers commit it. The fallacy can be informally characterised as the "realisation-defeating extension of linguistically realised conceptual metaphors". It occurs in analogical reasoning, at the stage of mapping—for a start, in the inferences to all of C_1 to C_4. And it takes us from straightforward truths to conclusions which lack determinate meaning or content.

Recall (from Sect. 1) that conceptual metaphors motivate metaphorical uses of linguistic expressions by facilitating analogical inferences (specifically, CASD-GASC inferences) that endow expressions used literally to talk about a source domain (say, "x is before your eyes") with implications in the metaphor's target domain (of intellectual achievement): Things before our eyes are, by and large, easily visible, so CSG (without the new mapping N) yields "If things are before our eyes, they are easy to get to know". We seize on this metaphorical implication when interpreting the statement: "The solution was all along right before your eyes." Similarly, when something is beyond my range of vision ("ken"), I cannot see it, so CSG (without M) yields "If something is beyond my ken, I cannot know or understand it". You seize on this metaphorical implication when interpreting my admission that quantum physics is "beyond my ken".

CSG inferences which use visual cognition metaphors but do not employ the new mappings M and N take us from the premises of C_1, C_2, and C_4 to the rather different conclusions "When we think about things, things are before our eyes", "…

things are within our ken", and (re-representing "perceive with our eyes" as "see") "...we see things within our ken". These expressions include spatial terms but, in their entirety, have source-domain implications that facilitate metaphorical interpretation. On a straightforward such interpretation, these conclusions state that when we think about things, we can easily get to know things, it is possible for us to get to know things, and we get to know things we can get to know, while P_3 tells us that when it is easy for us to get to know things, it is possible for us to get to know them. All of these claims are about the intellectual target domain; none even appears to refer to spaces or organs of perception, of any kind or description.

The use of the further mappings M and N in analogical inference employing these conceptual metaphors makes such metaphorical talk impossible. In "...before my eyes", e.g., N has us substitute "eyes" by "understanding". But "x is before my understanding" has no implications in the visual source domain. And metaphorical implications accrue to terms through CASD-GASC inferences from their source-domain implications. Hence "...before my understanding" also lacks metaphorical implications, and cannot be given what we may call a "conceptually motivated metaphorical interpretation", namely an interpretation motivated by the conceptual metaphor employed. We thus come to "extend the conceptual metaphor in a way that defeats its linguistic realisation" (or "defeats it", for short). Such undue extension consists in the simultaneous use, in analogical reasoning, of mappings constitutive of a conceptual (here: visual) metaphor and of mappings that "defeat" it:

> A mapping *defeats* a conceptual metaphor to the extent to which it pre-empts CASD-GASC inferences licensed by the metaphors' constitutive mappings.

Mappings which thus defeat the visual cognition metaphors considered above include N, M, and the mapping of "perceive" onto itself (upon re-representation of "see").

The introduction of such defeating mappings can be haphazard or systematic: They can be *ad hoc* mappings like the mapping N, which we introduced as *ad hoc* mapping in the inference to C_0. The proposed explanation of C_1 to C_4, by contrast, exposes a systematic source of defeating mappings, namely the interaction of automatic analogical inference-making with routine information-integration in semantic memory. This interaction generates new mappings, like M, where thinkers already believe a proposition that is semantically highly similar to a conclusion they draw in analogical reasoning. Such fresh mappings are liable to be defeating, wherever the prior proposition is semantically similar to the conclusion in virtue of its use of a metaphorical expression (like "is in the mind") that is semantically similar to a part of the conclusion that uses some of the same words literally (like "is in the visual field").

The simultaneous use, in analogical inference, of a conceptual metaphor and mappings that defeat it, amounts to a fallacy in virtue of its immediate and further consequences. First, it takes us from straightforward facts about the source domain, such as "When we look at things, things are before our eyes", to conclusions which lack determinate meaning or content, such as (C_1) "When we think, things are before our understanding." The understanding is commonly conceived as a *faculty* (which the OED characterises as the "faculty of comprehending or reasoning" or "power or ability to understand"), and faculties cannot be placed in spatial relations (like "x is before y"). This rules out a literal interpretation of the conclusion. Since it also lacks a conceptually motivated metaphorical interpretation, its meaning and content remain unclear.

Second, the simultaneous use of conceptual metaphors and defeating mappings can lead thinkers to project a rich relational structure from a metaphor's source-domain onto a target-domain which in fact does not contain any elements standing in the projected relations, as linked by that structure. In the inferences we discussed, for example, the use of the defeating mappings mentioned has us generate or posit new relations between target-domain elements, in CSG inference: Due to mappings N and M, the predicates "x is before our eyes" and "x is in my ken" (or, rather, the subject-properties they stand for) cannot be carried over in their entirety, and the spatial relations "x is before y" and "x is in y" are generated, instead, e.g. in inferences to C_1 to C_3. Through inferences to conclusions including C_1 to C_4, *higher-order relations* between these *mapped relations* are then posited to obtain in the target- just as in the source-domain: *When* objects of sight/thought are *perceived with* the eyes/understanding, *then* they *are before* the eyes/understanding, *and in* the visual field/mind, etc. Of course some of the mapped first-order relations do not actually obtain between the target-domain relata. E.g., neither my faculty of understanding nor the problem I think about are party to the spatial relations. But once these relations are posited to obtain between target-domain elements, and are duly correlated with their source-domain homonyms, in further analogical inferences, these inferences rely on mappings of comprehensively linked relations. And deeply integrated mappings endow analogical conclusions with high subjective plausibility (Gentner et al. 1993; Lassaline 1996; see Sect. 1). We thus arrive at subjectively plausible conclusions whose lack of determinate meaning further prevents their immediate rejection as false.

To sum up, we have seen that the use of conceptual metaphors in analogical reasoning is autocatalytic and unproblematic in and of itself (Sect. 1). But it systematically gives rise to persuasive conclusions which are not true, where conceptual metaphors are used in conjunction with mappings that defeat them. One non-random source of such mappings is the interaction of automatic analogical inference-making (Sect. 2) with routine information-integration in semantic memory (Sect. 3). By examining this interaction (Sect. 4), this paper has identified a previously undescribed fallacy (Sect. 5), and explained when and why competent speaker/thinkers may commit it: when and why competent speaker/thinkers may extend linguistically realised conceptual metaphors in a way that defeats their linguistic realisation.

References

Albrecht, J. E., and J. L. Myers. 1998. Accessing distant text information during reading. *Discourse Processes* 26:87–107.

Bargh, J. A. 1994. The four horsemen of automaticity. In *Handbook of social cognition,* eds. R. Wyer and T. Srull, vol. 1, 1–40. Hillsdale: Earlbaum.

Barton, S. B., and A. J. Sandford. 1993. A case study of anomaly detection: Shallow processing and cohesion establishment. *Memory and Cognition* 21:477–487.

Boroditsky, L. 2000. Metaphoric structuring: Understanding time through spatial metaphors. *Cognition* 75:1–27.

Boroditsky, L., and M. Ramscar. 2002. The roles of body and mind in abstract thought. *Psychological Science* 13:185–188.

Bowdle, B., and D. Gentner. 2005. The career of metaphor. *Psychological Review* 112:193–216.

Budiu, R., and J. R. Anderson. 2004. Interpretation-based processing: A unified theory of semantic sentence comprehension. *Cognitive Science* 28:1–44.

Clement, C. A., and D. Gentner. 1991. Systematicity as a selection constraint in analogical mapping. *Cognitive Science* 15:89–132.

Cook, A. E., and S. Guéraud. 2005. What have we been missing? The role of general world knowledge in discourse processing. *Discourse Processes* 39:265–278.

Day, S. B., and D. Gentner. 2007. Non-intentional analogical inference in text-comprehension. *Memory and Cognition* 35:39–49.

De Neys, W. 2006. Automatic-heuristic and executive-analytic processing during reasoning: Chronometric and dual-task considerations. *The Quarterly Journal of Experimental Psychology* 59:1070–1100.

Erickson, T., and M. Mattson. 1981. From words to meaning: A semantic illusion. *Journal of Verbal Learning and Verbal Behaviour* 20:540–551.

Evans, J. S. B. T. 2010. Intuition and reasoning: A dual-process perspective. *Psychological Inquiry* 21:313–326.

Falkenhainer, B., K. D. Forbus, and D. Gentner. 1989. The structure-mapping engine: Algorithm and examples. *Artificial Intelligence* 41:1–63.

Ferretti, T., K. McRae, and A. Hatherell. 2001. Integrating verbs, situation schemas, and thematic role concepts. *Journal of Memory and Language* 44:516–547.

Fischer, E. 2011. *Philosophical delusion and its therapy*. New York: Routledge.

Fischer, E. 2014. Philosophical intuitions, heuristics, and metaphors. *Synthese* 191:569–606.

Forbus, K. D., D. Gentner, and K. Law. 1995. MAC/FAC: A model of similarity-based retrieval. *Cognitive Science* 19:141–205.

Gentner, D., and B. Bowdle. 2008. Metaphor as structure-mapping. In *The Cambridge handbook of metaphor and thought,* ed. R. Gibbs, 109–128. New York: Cambridge University Press.

Gentner, D., and J. Grudin. 1985. The evolution of mental metaphors in psychology. *American Psychologist* 40:181–192.

Gentner, D., and K. Kurtz. 2006. Relations, objects, and the composition of analogies. *Cognitive Science* 30:609–642.

Gentner, D., and A. Markman. 2005. Defining structural similarity. *Journal of Cognitive Science* 6:1–20.

Gentner, D., M. Ratterman, and K. Forbus. 1993. The roles of similarity in transfer: Separating retrievability from inferential soundness. *Cognitive Psychology* 25:527–575.

Gentner, D., M. Imai, and L. Boroditsky. 2002. As time goes by: Evidence for two systems in processing space-time metaphors. *Language and Cognitive Processes* 17:537–565.

Gerrig, R. J., and E. J. O'Brien. 2005. The scope of memory-based processing. *Discourse Processes* 39:225–242.

Giora, R. 2003. *On our mind: Salience, context, and figurative language*. Oxford: Oxford University Press.

Goldstein, D., and G. Gigerenzer. 2002. Model of ecological rationality: The recognition heuristic. *Psychological Review* 109:75–90.

Hesse, M. 1966. *Models and analogies in science*. Notre Dame: University of Notre Dame Press.

Holyoak, K. J. 2005. Analogy. In *The Cambridge handbook of thinking and reasoning*, eds. K. J. Holyoak and R. Morrison, 117–142. Cambridge: Cambridge University Press.

Holyoak, K. J., and K. Koh. 1987. Surface and structural similarity in analogical transfer. *Memory and Cognition* 15:332–340.

Hummel, J. E., and K. J. Holyoak. 2003. A symbolic-connectionist theory of relational inference and generalization. *Psychological Review* 110:220–263.

Kahneman, D. 2011. *Thinking, fast and slow*. London: Allen Lane.

Kamas, E. N., L. M. Reder, and M. S. Ayers. 1996. Partial matching in the Moses illusion: Response bias not sensitivity. *Memory and Cognition* 24:687–699.
Kövesces, Z. 2002. *Metaphor*. Oxford: Oxford University Press.
Lakoff, G., and M. Johnson. 1980. *Metaphor we live by*. Chicago: University of Chicago Press.
Lakoff, G., and M. Johnson. 1999. *Philosophy in the flesh*. New York: Basic Books.
Lassaline, M. E. 1996. Structural alignment in induction and similarity. *Journal of Experimental Psychology: Learning, Memory, and Cognition* 22:754–770.
Leech, R., D. Mareschal, and R. P. Cooper. 2008. Analogy as relational priming. *Behavioural and Brain Sciences* 31:357–414.
Locke, J. 1975. *An essay concerning human understanding*. 4th ed. Oxford: Clarendon Press. (P. Nidditch ed., First published 1770).
Markman, A. B. 1997. Constraints on analogical inference. *Cognitive Science* 21:373–418.
Markman, A. B., and J. B. Laux. 2008. Analogical inferences are central to analogy. *Behavioural and Brain Sciences* 31:390–391.
McRae, K., and M. Jones. 2013. Semantic memory. In *Oxford handbook of cognitive psychology*, ed. D. Reisberg. Oxford: Oxford University Press.
Moors, A., and J. de Houwer. 2006. Automaticity: A theoretical and conceptual analysis. *Psychological Bulletin* 132:297–326.
Morewedge, C. K., and D. Kahneman. 2010. Associative processes in intuitive judgment. *Trends in Cognitive Science* 14:435–440.
O'Brien, E. J. 1995. Automatic components in discourse comprehension. In *Sources of coherence in reading*, eds. R. F. Lorch and E. J. O'Brien, 159–176. Hillsdale: Earlbaum.
OED. 2012. *The Oxford English dictionary*. Oxford University Press. http://www.oed.com/. Accessed March 2012.
Pachur, T., and R. Hertwig. 2006. On the psychology of the recognition heuristic: Retrieval primacy as a key determinant of its use. *Journal of Experimental Psychology: Learning, Memory, and Cognition* 32:983–1002.
Park, H., and L. M. Reder. 2004. Moses illusion. In *Cognitive illusions*, ed. R. Pohl, 275–291. New York: Psychology Press.
Peleg, O., and R. Giora. 2011. Salient meanings: The whens and wheres. In *Salience and defaults in utterance processing*, eds. K. M. Jaszczolt and K. Allan, 32–52. Berlin: Gruyter.
Rorty, R. 1980. *Philosophy and the mirror of nature*. Oxford: Blackwell.
Rosch, E. 1978. Principles of categorisation. In *Cognition and categorization*, eds. E. Rosch and B. Lloyd, 27–48. Hillsdale: Erlbaum.
Ross, B. 1989. Distinguishing types of superficial similarity: Different effects on the access and use of earlier problems. *Journal of Experimental Psychology: Learning, Memory and Cognition* 15:456–468.
Thibodeau, P. H., and L. Boroditsky. 2011. Metaphors we think with: The role of metaphor in reasoning. *PLoS ONE* 6:e16782. doi:10.1371/journal.pone.0016782.
Tversky, A., and D. Kahneman. 1983. Extensional versus intuitive reasoning: The conjunction fallacy in probability judgment. *Psychological Review* 90:293–315.
Uleman, J. S., S. A. Sairbay, and C. M. Gonzales. 2008. Spontaneous inferences, implicit impressions, and implicit theories. *Annual Review of Psychology* 59:329–360.
van Oostendorp, H., and I. Kok. 1990. Failing to notice errors in sentences. *Languages and Cognitive Processes* 5:105–113.
van Oostendorp, H., and S. de Mul. 1990. Moses beats Adam: A semantic relatedness effect on a semantic illusion. *Acta Psychologica* 7:35–46.
Wharton, C. M., K. J. Holyoak, T. E. Lange, T. D. Wickens, and E. R. Melz. 1994. Below the surface: Analogical similarity and retrieval competition in reminding. *Cognitive Psychology* 26:64–101.
Wharton, C. M., K. J. Holyoak, and T. E. Lange. 1996. Remote analogical reminding. *Memory and Cognition* 24:629–643.

Part II
Applied Approaches to Argument by Analogy

Chapter 9
How to Make Figures Talk: Comparative Argument in TV Election Night Specials

Marianne Doury

Most of the researches on comparative arguments focus on a leading subtype within this broad category, namely, figurative arguments from analogy. Figurative arguments from analogy "associate situations or cases resulting from two heterogeneous domains of knowledge" (Govier 2001, p. 350), and are generally based on shared non gradual properties. The purpose of this paper however is to examine arguments which also belong to the general category of comparative arguments (in that they are "based on a comparison"; van Eemeren et al. 2002, p. 173); but they are literal comparisons, paralleling elements drawn from the same domain (van Eemeren et al. 2002, p. 100; Brown 1995, p. 90), and the comparison they are based on has a quantitative dimension: it involves properties that are numerically quantifiable. Thus, the entities they apply to may be ranked against each other.[1]

My main concern will be empirical: my aim is to describe the form and to clear up the function of a specific argument of that kind (the argumentative sequences based on a comparison between different scores during TV election night specials), as well as the critical discourse it may elicit; I will conclude on the difficulties raised by its analysis[2].

Typically, election night specials focus on announcing the results of an election and on commenting them. The comments usually reveal two stages. The first stage consists in assessing the scores ("it's a good/poor result"); the second stage is explanatory (it involves statements such as "this poor score reflects the voters' disappointment of the outgoing president" or "this high score shows the voters' longing for change").

[1] For a systematic inventory of the parameters used to establish subtypes within comparative arguments, see Doury (2009).

[2] This paper is part of a research, initiated in collaboration with Assimakis Tseronis, which deals with various argumentative devices aiming at making figures talk (and more specifically, at making electoral scores talk) during election night specials on TV (Doury and Tseronis 2014).

M. Doury (✉)
French National Center for Scientific Research (CNRS), Paris, France
University of Paris 3 (New Sorbonne), Paris, France
e-mail: marianne.doury@cnrs.fr

H. J. Ribeiro (ed.), *Systematic Approaches to Argument by Analogy*,
Argumentation Library 25, DOI 10.1007/978-3-319-06334-8_9,

The present paper will focus on the assessment process. One usually feels that, at least to some extent, the assessment of a score is determined by an objective reality: the figure that expresses it. Nevertheless, it is hard to settle the numeric threshold beyond which a score will clearly be considered a good one or a bad one. French citizens may remember Georges Marchais's unintentional sally in 1981. During the 1981 legislative elections, the number of communist deputes had collapsed from 86 to 43. It didn't prevent Georges Marchais, the Communist Party's leader, from claiming: "for me and my party, it's a great victory".

Marchais's case may be considered an atypical illustration of political bad faith: it calls for contest from political opponents—or for laughs from the audience, as it was the case on the TV set of TF1 after Marchais's claim. Nevertheless, the lesson it gives holds for any electoral score assessment: the observation of election night specials during the last decades in France suggests that an electoral result is not good or bad *in itself*, but is *discursively constructed* as such.

9.1 Presentational Devices

The present research is based on an analysis of the transcript of two TV specials after the first round of French presidential elections (April, 22nd, 2012) from two national TV channels (TF1 and France 2).

A first exploration of the data, attentive to the discursive choices of the participants, shows that the use of what could be called, in pragma-dialectic terms, presentational devices (van Eemeren and Houtlosser 2006), orients the scores towards a specific assessment. For instance, the choice of an ordinal presentation rather than that of a cardinal presentation (in other words, the choice of mentioning the rank of the candidate rather than indicating the percentage of the votes he obtained) has clear strategic implications. As far as François Hollande is concerned, such a choice orients towards a positive assessment of his score (example 1), while it orients towards a negative assessment of Sarkozy's result (example 2):

Example 1
Ségolène Royal^{FH}: c'est le candidat socialiste qui arrive euh: (…) *en tête* (*versus* "le candidat socialiste obtient 28 % des suffrages").[3]
SR^{FH}: the socialist candidate *comes first* (…) (*versus* "the socialist candidate wins 28 % of the votes").

Example 2
Pierre Moscovici^{FH}: [NS] est devancé au premier tour (*versus* [NS] "obtient 27 % des voix").
PM^{FH}: [NS] is left behind in the first round (*versus* "[NS] wins 27 % of the votes").

A second presentational device is the choice of absolute values rather than percentages. It orients towards a positive assessment of the score. This device is mostly

[3] Superscript FH, NS, MLP or JLM indicates that the politician whose name has just been mentioned supports François Hollande, Nicolas Sarkozy, Marine Le Pen or Jean-Luc Mélenchon respectively.

used by the candidates who obtained rather low percentages of the votes. For instance, Eva Joly, the ecologist candidate, whose score is about 2 %[4], starts her official televised statement as follows:

Example 3
Eva Joly: *Je tiens à remercier avec chaleur (...) le million de Françaises et de Français (...) qui m'ont apporté leurs suffrages (...) et ce faisant (...) ont défendu (...) par leur vote (...) l'écologie (...) l'Europe (...) et la République (...) exemplaire.*
EJ: I want to thank warmly (…) the million French people (…) who gave me their vote (…) and thus supported through their vote Ecologie (…) Europe (…) and the exemplary (..) Republic.

Another example of presentational devices influencing the argumentative orientation of the scores is the use of what Ducrot calls "argumentative operators" such as "only", "less than" or "close to", which orient a claim towards a specific set of conclusions.

Thus in

Example 4
Ségolène Royal^{FH} : (…) Monsieur Sarkozy qui *ne* recueille *que* vingt-cinq pour cent des voix (…).
SR^{FH} : (…) Mister Sarkozy who *only* polled twenty-five per cent of the votes (…).

"only" orients towards a negative assessment of the score. In

Example 5
Journalist: *Monsieur Mélenchon vous faites* moins de *douze pour cent [11,7 % à ce moment de la soirée]. Est-ce que vous êtes déçu?*
J: Mister Mélenchon you win *less than* twelve per cent of the votes. Are you disappointed?

"less than" has the same argumentative orientation, whereas in

Example 6
Journalist (J): Marine Le Pen fait un score *proche de* vingt pour cent [18,6 % à ce moment-là de la soirée] est-ce qu'on peut considérer qu'vous avez perdu votre bras d'fer avec elle?
J: Marine Le Pen obtains a score *close to* twenty per cent can we say that you lost your tug-of-war game against her?

"close to" orients to a positive set of assessments.

Such presentational choices give the score a discursive form which makes it possible for it to serve as a premise for a specific conclusive assessment. They orient the numerical results and prepare them to support preferentially certain conclusions over others.

9.2 Comparisons

Beyond the presentational devices, the discursive evaluation of a result is often integrated within argumentative sequences that aim at justifying it. In this section, the function of comparison in such argumentative sequences will be investigated.

[4] Later on during the election night special, Gilbert Collard, an extreme-right politician, calls her disdainfully "Mrs Two-per-cent".

As will be shown below, the assessment of the scores relies on various comparisons: between the results obtained by the different candidates within the same election; between the results obtained by one political party in successive presidential elections; between the results obtained by the leaders of different countries confronted with similar economic crisis; between the results predicted by polling organizations and the actual results. The argumentative use of such comparisons will be highlighted, as well as the associated conditions of acceptability in context.

The argumentative comparison we will focus on may be described, at the most superficial level, as a shift, from the relative assessment of two scores, to the absolute assessment of one of them:

S1 > S2 → *S1* is a good score
S1 < S2 → S2 is a poor score

Such a scheme results in various specific comparisons, according to the nature of the *phoros*.

9.2.1 Comparisons Between the Scores of the Candidates in the Same Election

The most obvious comparison in the context of a presidential election first round is between all the candidates that took part in this round. Such a comparison allows for the ranking of the candidates with regards to the scores they obtained.

Objectively, the main political relevance of such a ranking is to identify the first two candidates as opposed to all the other ones: they, and only they, will take part in the second round of the presidential elections 2 weeks later. The observation of former presidential elections in France shows that the ranking of the first two candidates after the first round does not presage of the final result of the election. Hence this ranking has only a symbolic importance. Nevertheless, as suggested by examples 1 and 2, François Hollande's supporters, rather than specifying the score obtained by their candidate, prefer only mentioning that he is the leader of the election over his challenger, whom he "distinctly gets ahead of":

Example 7
Jean-Marc Ayrault^{FH}: C'est clair, c'est un désaveu incroyable du président sortant (…) il [Nicolas Sarkozy] arrive *en deuxième position* (…) en plaçant *nettement* François Hollande en (…) *en première place* (…) parce qu'il incarne (…) le changement (…) et le redressement de la France.
JMA^{FH}*:* Clearly it's an amazing disavowal for the Past President (…) he [Nicolas Sarkozy] *comes in second* (…) placing clearly François Hollande *in first position* (…) because he incarnates change and recovery for France.

There are two possible reactions to such an argument.

The first one consists in minimizing the difference between the score obtained by François Hollande and that obtained by Nicolas Sarkozy, as in examples 8 and 9.

Example 8
Nadine Morano^{NS} : Ils sont arrivés (…) dans un mouchoir de poche.
NM^{NS} : It was a close finish [French expression is literally: they arrived in a pocket handkerchief].

Example 9
Henri Guaino^{NS}*:* Il [NS] arrive pas loin hein?
HG^{NS}*:* He [Nicolas Sarkozy] does not come far behind, does he?

Such reactions suggest that for the arguer, the order of arrival of the candidates does not suffice to conclude to a positive or a negative absolute assessment of their scores: an important difference between the scores is needed (and of course, Sarkozy's supporters consider that the difference between their candidate and Hollande is not important enough to support Jean-Marc Ayrault's conclusion that "it's an amazing disavowal" for Sarkozy).

The second possible reaction to such a comparative argument, which is clearly unfavorable to Sarkozy, is to propose another comparison favorable to him, as in example 10. In reaction to Hollande's supporters' emphasis on the fact that Hollande has overtaken Sarkozy, Valérie Pécresse claims that:

Example 10
Valérie Pécresse^{NS}*:* Nicolas Sarkozy (…) a réussi à devancer le Front National.
VP^{NS}*:* Nicolas Sarkozy (…) has succeeded in overtaking the National Front.

Valérie Pécresse thus illustrates a property common to all comparative argument schemes: they can always be opposed another comparison orienting towards a different, if not opposite, conclusion.

However, the strategic possibility of choosing another reference candidate in order to make the comparison favorable to one's candidate is limited by the requirement that the comparison should be politically significant. It is the case when Marine Le Pen's supporters congratulate themselves that her score is two times Jean-Luc Mélenchon's score: as Jean-Luc Mélenchon made defeating Marine le Pen a stake of the elections, the comparison makes sense. By way of contrast, Marine Le Pen's score is a hundred times Jacques Cheminade's score, who obtains 0.2 % of the votes; though it would undoubtedly have been spectacular, the comparison is never raised by Marine Le Pen's supporters because it definitely lacks any political relevance. Hence political relevance should be considered another requirement for such a comparison to hold.

9.2.2 Comparison between a Candidate's Score and His (or His Party's) Previous Scores During Former Presidential Elections

Another kind of comparison consists in comparing the score of a candidate to the previous scores he or his party obtained during former presidential elections. Such a comparison still aims at justifying an assessment of the score, which constitutes the conclusion of the comparative argument. This comparative device may be used by a politician in order to enhance the result of his favorite candidate (example 11), or in order to depreciate that of his opponent.

Example 11
Ségolène Royal[FH]: Ce score (…) est exceptionnel [conclusion] puisqu'il dépasse en effet le score de deux mille sept (…). [Argument]
SR[FH] : This score (…) is exceptional [conclusion] in that it exceeds the two thousand and seven score (…). [Argument]

It also is a means for journalists and commentators to exhibit their political analyst's expertise, and to demonstrate that they are depositories of the political memory of the country; therefore they often base their commentaries on such diachronic comparisons.

Besides the mechanism shared by all the comparisons described here, the diachronic dimension of this one allows the arguer to endow the score obtained by a candidate with a positive or a negative dynamics, and to suggest that he or she is on an upward or downward path—which is particularly important at the night of a first round election in prevision of the second round coming soon.

Such comparisons allow politicians whose results are deemed disappointing by commentators to evade a negative absolute assessment owing to the evocation of a positive relative evaluation. Thus Pierre Laurent, from Front de gauche (radical leftist coalition), invited to comment on Jean-Luc Mélenchon's relatively poor score, answers as follows:

Example 12
Pierre Laurent[JLM]: C'est à la fois un très bon résultat [conclusion] parce que je rappelle que (…) pour la gauche: que nous représentons (…) c'est le meilleur résultat ET de loin depuis trente ans [argument] (…) c'est un très beau résultat. [Conclusion].
PL[JLM]: At the same time it is a very good result [conclusion] because I remind you that (…) for the left we represent (…) it's been by far the best score for thirty years [argument] (…) It's a very beautiful result. [Conclusion].

The same kind of comparison, when applied to Nicolas Sarkozy, suggests a reverse evolution—that is, an evolution that follows a downward path. Hence Arnaud Montebourg, one of Hollande's supporters, does not hold back from using it:

Example 13
Arnaud Montebourg[FH]: Euh d'abord un président sortant sanctionné et très lourdement [conclusion] euh cinq à six points en moins qu'il y a cinq ans (…). [Argument (FR2)]
AM[FH]: Uh first a Past President severely penalized [conclusion] uh five or six points below the score he obtained five years ago (…). [Argument (FR2)]

Once again the comparison is used as an argument to support an interpretation of the first round results as a penalty against Nicolas Sarkozy.

A recurring strategy in order to resist such an argumentation consists in contesting the comparison by claiming that you can compare only what is comparable. In this specific case, the comparison between the results obtained by Sarkozy and those obtained by any former outgoing president would not hold because of the economic context: the present exceptional situation of crisis would make it impossible to compare the present election with any previous one.

The examination of the two election night specials also shows that a comparison may be used by journalists to excite rivalries between members of the same political camp when a party presented different candidates to successive elections. If the comparison is favorable to one candidate, its evocation may be uncomfortable for the others.

It is particularly the case when the comparison involves two candidates connected by personal links, like Marine Le Pen, the present candidate of the extreme right Party, and Jean-Marie Le Pen, her father and former candidate of the National Front:

Example 14
Journalist (à JMLP): Elle [MLP] fait un score encore plus important qu'vous en deux mille deux/ est-ce que vous avez l'impression qu'elle vous éclipse.
J (to Jean-Marie Le Pen): The score she [Marine Le Pen] obtains is even more important than yours in two thousand and two don't you feel like she's eclipsing you.

Jean-Marie Le Pen's reaction consists in challenging the relevance of the comparison: according to him, he and his daughter should not be considered as rivals (as a comparing process, according to him, would imply) but as team-mates in a relay race: he ran first, she took over, and what counts is the result of the team, not that of each runner:

Example 15
Jean-Marie Le Pen^{MLP}: Pas du tout (…) c'est un relayeur Marine (…) je lui ai passé le bâton (…) elle court, elle court plus vite tant mieux [sourire].
JMLP^{MLP}: Not at all (…) Marine is a relay runner (.) I gave her the baton (…) she runs, she runs faster all the better [smile].

He thus claims for the shared responsibility of Marine Le Pen's high score, and accordingly suggests that a comparative process does not fit the way the situation should be framed.

A very similar script may be observed as regards Ségolène Royal, the former socialist candidate to the 2007 presidential elections, and François Hollande, her former partner and candidate in 2012:

Example 16
Journalist: Pardon de vous poser cette question, mais c'est une soirée un petit peu particulière j'imagine pour vous, puisque (…) votre ancien compagnon arrive en tête il fait un meilleur score que vous aux à la dernière élection présidentielle (…) est-ce que vous en avez parlé avec lui est-ce que vous l'avez eu au téléphone ce soir?
J: Sorry for asking you this question, but this evening is quite special for you I guess because (…) your former partner comes in first he gets a better score than you did to the last presidential election (…) did you talk with him about that did you talk to him by phone tonight?

The journalist's comparison clearly aims at tickling Ségolène Royal's pride (if the comparison orients to a positive assessment of Hollande's score, it also orients to a negative assessment of Royal's former score). Ségolène Royal reacts as follows:

Example 17
Ségolène Royal^{FH}: Oui, bien sûr (…) et d'ailleurs c'est précisément pourquoi je suis bien placée pour dire que ce score (…) est exceptionnel puisqu'il dépasse en effet le score de

deux mille sept (…) et en même temps (…) euh il y a un score du Front National qui double (…) par rapport à deux mille sept (.) ce qui fait que le combat (…) euh de l'entre-deux tours va être un combat (…) decisif que nous devons gagner pour les Français.
SR[FH]: Yes, of course (…) and it is precisely the reason why I am in a good position to state that this score (…) is exceptional for it overtakes indeed the 2007 score (…) and at the same time (…) uh we have the score of the National Front that doubles (…) with regard to 2007 (…) it follows that the fight between the two rounds will be a decisive fight and we have to win it for the French people.

The comparison by the journalist between Royal's and Hollande's scores is introduced as an argument for the vague conclusion "this evening must be quite special for you", conclusion which might easily be specified as "it must be a hard blow for you tonight". Royal turns the comparison into an argumentatively opposite direction, making an argument out of it that increases the legitimacy of her positive assessment of Hollande's performance. Then she turns to another comparison (the National Front doubling its former score) which is much more spectacular and thus downgrades the progress performed by Hollande. Besides, it diverts the positive assessment induced by Hollande's progression on to an anxious concern about the dramatic rise of the National Front.

It is worth noting that in the context of the first round election night specials, the stability of the scores obtained by one candidate or one party from one election to another is seen as a sign of stagnation and is integrated within disqualifying strategies. Thus, Jean-François Copé claims that the left obtains the same results as in two thousand and seven (c'est "la même chose qu'en 2007") in order to downgrade François Hollande's first position; and stability from one election to another is never presented as a positive outcome by the candidates and their supporters. Alain Juppé adopts the same disqualifying strategy:

Example 18
Alain Juppé[NS]: Deuxièmement (…) il n'y a pas de poussée de gauche (…) hein, quand on totalise toutes les voix d'gauche on est à quarante-deux et d'mi pour cent (…) comme (…) en deux mille sept.
AJ[NS] : Second (…) there is no upsurge of the left (…) when you add all the votes of the left you get forty-two percent point five (…) as (…) as in two thousand and seven.

Contrary to what this example illustrates, most of the time during the two electoral night specials studied here, Sarkozy's supporters content themselves with claiming that "there is no upsurge of the left" without mentioning any precise score. This may be due to the fact that the comparison of the scores obtained by the left in 2007 and 2012 does indeed indicate an unquestionably ascending dynamics (from 36.7 % in 2007 to 44 % of the votes for the left in 2012): hence there is a clear interest for Sarkozy's supporters to remain vague when assessing that "there is no upsurge of the left", and to leave unspecified which left they are talking about, or which former election they refer to.

9.2.3 *Comparison Between a Candidate's Score and the Results Obtained by the Leaders of Different Countries Confronted with Similar Economic Crisis*

As mentioned before, an argumentative comparison which does not serve one's position can always be opposed another anti-oriented comparison. Thus Arnaud Montebourg's former diachronic comparison, which shows Sarkozy disadvantage (example 13), is opposed Jean-François Copé's alternative synchronic comparison, which allows him to assess positively the past President's score:

Example 19
Jean-François Copé^{NS} : Vous savez (…) moi, je vais vous dire une chose (…), euh, c'est (…) dans cette période de crise (…) j'ai vu (…) dans *tous* les grands pays où y a eu des élections (…) euh, ils, les responsables sortants, ont été balayés rappelez-vous en Espagne Monsieur Zapatero (…) Monsieur Gordon Brown en Angleterre (…) balayés (…) là (…) y a quoi (…) un point et demi d'différence entre les deux.
JFC^{NS}: You know (…) I'll tell you something (…) uh, it's (…) in this period of crisis (…). I saw (…) in *all* big countries where elections have taken place (…) uh the outgoing leaders have been swept away remember Mr Zapatero in Spain (…) Mr Gordon Brown in England (…) swept away (…) here (…) there's let's say (…) one point and a half between the two candidates.

The score obtained by Nicolas Sarkozy is poor if compared to the previous presidential elections; but it is superior to the results obtained by the past leaders in the European countries undergoing similar economic crisis; and in this light, Sarkozy's score is a *good* score.

9.2.4 *Comparison Between the Results Predicted by the Very Candidate and the Actual Results*

The comparison is ensured to escape any refutation of this kind when it compares the actual score of a candidate to the score that was explicitly aimed at by this very candidate (or by his camp).

This argument is used by Hollande's supporters to make Sarkozy's second place meaningful: such a second place is synonymous with defeat, since Sarkozy himself explicitly ambitioned to arrive first:

Example 20
Ségolène Royal^{FH}: C'est la première fois qu'un: candidat non sortant (…) euh, arrive en tête (…) donc c'est c'qu'il faut retenir, puisque monsieur Sarkozy nous avait annoncé qu'il était en tête là (…) c'est le candidat socialiste qui arrive, euh (…) en tête.
SR^{FH}: It's the first time that a non-outgoing candidate (…), uh, arrives first (…) so it's what should be remembered since Mr Sarkozy had announced that he would come first here (…) it's the socialist candidate who comes first.

Sarkozy's own ambitions are frequently evoked all along the night in order to justify a negative assessment of his actual score, as in examples 21 to 23:

Example 21
Ségolène Royal[FH] *(à AJ):* Mais vous l'avez placé comme objectif d'être premier au premier tour.
SR[FH] *(to AJ):* But you had stated it as an objective to come first at first round.

Example 22
Journalist: Nicolas Sarkozy (…) est beaucoup plus bas qu'il ne l'espérait.
J: Nicolas Sarkozy (…) is much below what he hoped.

Example 23
Marie-Georges Buffet[JLM/FH] : Encore hier vous disiez que Sarkozy serait premier Monsieur Copé.
MGB[JLM/FH]: Yesterday you still claimed that Sarkozy would come first Mr. Copé.

The same strategy applies to other candidates who imprudently set themselves objectives to reach. This is the case for Mélenchon, who aimed at overtaking Marine Le Pen and who failed, as Louis Alliot (who supports Marine Le Pen) stresses:

Example 24
Louis Alliot[MLP]: [à Clémentine Autain[JLM]] C'est un véritable échec de Jean-Luc Mélenchon (…) vous le reconnaissez ou pas (…) Le seul défi du Front d'gauche, c'était de faire plus que Marine Le Pen ben c'est loupé complètement.
LA[MLP]: [to CA[JLM]] It is a real failure for Jean-Luc Mélenchon (…) do you admit that or not (…) the only challenge for the Front de gauche was to get a better score than Marine Le Pen so it's a complete failure.

Such comparisons are based on an *ad hominem* argument in Perelman's sense (Perelman and Olbrechts-Tyteca 1988, p. 148), that is, an *ex concessis* reasoning: the conclusion is all the more solid since the premises are drawn from the opponent. Such a result is bad with regards to the standard the opponent himself proposed.

In such cases, the only solution left for the attacked politicians to counter such comparisons is to suggest that the candidate had to fight headwind (because of the economic crisis, because of a shameful campaign, etc.): it's a way of invoking mitigating circumstances, but it does not contest the acknowledgment of failure.

9.2.5 Comparison Between the Results Predicted by Polling Organizations and the Actual Results

A fifth kind of comparison used to make figures talk during election night specials is somewhat puzzling. It consists in comparing the actual results of a candidate with the results that were predicted by polling organizations and that were spread by the media.

In France in recent years, criticizing the accuracy and the political effects of the surveys achieved by polling organizations has become a national sport. This sport is intensively practiced during election night specials such as the ones studied here. The present paper proposes to connect poll criticism during election night specials with general argumentative strategies and local political stakes.

Examples 25 to 27 below are nothing but additional illustrations of the argumentative mechanism at the core of this paper, which consists in shifting from the relative assessment of two scores, on the basis of a comparison, to an absolute assessment of one of them.

Here Alain Juppé and Xavier Bertrand, who support Nicolas Sarkozy, attempt to downgrade the results of one of his opponents (Jean-Luc Mélenchon, the leader of the Front de gauche). Comparing Mélenchon's score with his party's former score would be favorable to him (it would show a spectacular uprise); thus such a comparison must be avoided. On the contrary, polling organizations often predicted that the Front de gauche's score would be higher than it actually is. So such a comparison is of interest to Sarkozy's supporters, who often use it in order to justify the negative assessment of Mélenchon's score:

Example 25
AJ^{NS}: Moi je dirais que (…) l'élection ne ressemble pas à ce qu'on nous avait annoncé (…) *le score mirifique annoncé à monsieur Mélenchon*/ (…) *n'a pas été au rendez-vous*.
AJ^{NS}: personally I would say that […] the election does not look like what was announced (…) *the fantastic score predicted for Mister Mélenchon* (…) *has not materialized*.

Example 26
XB^{NS}: [Sur Nicolas Sarkozy] le score (…) est un score qui est solide (…) et d'ailleurs on l'voit bien (…) beaucoup pensaient que c'était déjà joué ; *rappelez-vous voilà* quelques *semaines* (…) *il serait même pas qualifié au second tour paraît-il* (…) *il) serait même pas* (…) *dans le duo de tête* (…) et là aujourd'hui (…) j'ai juste de la mémoire.
XB^{NS}: [On Nicolas Sarkozy] the score (…) is a solid one (…) and besides you can see it (…) many people thought everything was already settled remember a few *weeks ago (...) he would not even qualify for the second round they said (...) he wouldn't even be one of the top two* (…) and now today (…) I just have a good memory.

Example 27
AJ^{NS}: Enfin il faut quand même se souvenir (…) que *il y a trois mois* (…) *Nicolas Sarkozy était donné absent* (…) *du deuxième tour* (…) *on le mettait à vingt pour cent* (…) et il a fait une campagne qui lui a permis de progresser d'façon très significative (…) c'est assez exceptionnel pour un chef d'Etat dans une période de crise (…).
AJ^{NS}: Now one should remember (…) that *three months ago (...) Nicolas Sarkozy was predicted absent (...) from the second round (...) he was assessed at about twenty per cent* (…) and owing to his campaign he progressed in a significant way (.) it is quite exceptional for a head of state in a period of crisis (…).

In these examples it is not always clear if the polling organizations are said to have been mistaken (it seems to be the preferred interpretation of example 25) or if the predicted score was a correct reflect of public opinion at the time the poll was made, but the electors' voting intentions have changed (example 27). In the latter case, the argumentative comparison resembles a former case of comparison: that between the successive scores of the same candidate or party.

At any rate, the comparison between the actual scores and those announced by the polls obeys the same argumentative logic as the one described so far. Jean-Luc Mélenchon's score is inferior to what was predicted: it can thus be deemed a bad score. Sarkozy's result is superior to what was announced: in this regard, it may be considered a good score.

The same process is applied to François Hollande by Rachida Dati in

Example 28
RD^NS: Tout d'abord moi je trouve que aujourd'hui il faut rendre hommage aux Français qui euh qui se sont mobilisés (…) avec gravité/responsabilité (…) *ils ont déjoué tous les pronostics* (…) *des sondeurs mais aussi des médias* (…) d'abord *on passe pour Monsieur Hollande de trente-huit pour cent à vingt-huit pour cent* (…) euh, monsieur Teinturier (…) dans les sondages (…) depuis le mois de novembre (…) Hollande n'était pas à vingt-huit pour cent il y a quelque temps.
RD^NS: First of all personally I think that we should pay homage to the French people who joined forces (.) with gravity/ responsibility (…) *they thwarted all forecasts (...) of the polling organizations but also of the media* (…) *first it goes for Mister Hollande from thirty-eight per cent to twenty-eight per cent* (…) uh, Mister Teinturier [a pollster from IPSOS] in opinion polls since November (…) Hollande was not given twenty per cent some time ago.

In this example as in the previous ones, the opinion polls are not explicitly connected to a specific polling organization or to a specific media, and are not assigned specific dates; such characteristics reinforce the hypothesis that their evocation is merely meant to produce a strategic upgrading or downgrading effect on the score of a candidate the speaker wants to support or to attack, but it is not sincerely laden with any deep political significance.

Such a vague account of the opinion poll's reference makes it difficult for Rachida Dati's targets to refute her claims. Example 29 shows how Brice Teinturier, the pollster from Ipsos who was mentioned by her, contests her attack, and how she reacts in turn:

Example 29
Brice Teinturier: Soyons très précis et très factuels. D'abord aucun sondage n'a donné, euh (…) François Hollande à trente-six pour cent. Nous étions à vingt-neuf pour cent au début janvier (…) trente-deux pour cent au moment du Bourget mais tout cela est (…) parfaitement vérifiable (…) et vingt-neuf pour cent dans l'dernier enquête (…) il ferait vingt-huit et demi. On est très près.
RD: Mais c'est au moment des primaires en fait.
BT: Let's be very accurate and very factual. First no poll gave uh (…) François Hollande at thirty-six per cent. We were about twenty-nine per cent in early January (…) thirty-two per cent at the time of the Bourget Meeting, but all this can easily be checked (…), and twenty-nine per cent in the last survey (…) now he obtains twenty-eight point five. We're very close.
RD: Actually I was referring to the primary election period.

In France as in many countries, opinion surveys aiming at assessing the intentions of vote before important elections are so numerous that one can probably always find a support for the comparison to work by simply altering the date or the source of the poll which is being invoked.

When introducing this fifth kind of comparison, I described it as "puzzling". All previous comparisons may be questioned and challenged to some extent; but this one seems hardly reasonable. How can one consider that the fact that an electoral result is better than what the polls predicted makes this result better "in the absolute" (specifically when the difference between the predicted results and the actual ones are due to an error of the polling organizations, as suggested in example 25, rather than to a change in public opinion)?

9.3 Critical Discourse on Comparison

This last remark opens the discussion to the issue of the critics of comparison.

I will first handle it from the point of view of the arguers, and I will recapitulate the various reactions aroused by the comparisons we've been examining. I will then endorse the analyst's perspective and try and match the actual examples with specific comparative argumentative schemes—and in particular, *a fortiori* argument.

I will first propose to consider the arguer's reactions as reflecting a spontaneous normative stance towards this kind of comparative argument. These reactions may be listed as follows:

- A first reaction to comparisons consists in contesting the truth of the premises, and particularly, the score used as a *phoros* in the comparison (example 29). Of course, such a critical strategy is not specific to comparative arguments, in that the rebuttal of many other argument schemes may follow this line; nevertheless, it makes sense as far as inductive analogies (that are empirically based; Govier 1989, p. 141) are concerned, but it is bluntly irrelevant as regards *a priori* analogies (in which the *phoros* may be fictitious; Govier 1989, p. 142).
- Another reaction is to suggest that the difference between the compared scores is not "significant enough" to warrant the soundness of the conclusion: Sarkozy's supporters' claim that the two top candidates arrived shoulder to shoulder in order to contest any positive conclusion about Hollande's leadership over Sarkozy (example 8–9).
- Challenging the comparison may amount to suggesting that important differences prevent the comparison from being conclusive (an outgoing president is being compared to an outgoing prime Minister, elections in a situation of economic crisis are being compared to elections in a much more favorable context):

Example 30
Valérie Pécresse^{NS} : La dernière fois qu'vous avez gouverné la France *c'était pas* (…) *avec une crise mondiale* (…). Vous n'étiez pas qualifié pour le second tour. Nicolas Sarkozy (…) a réussi sa qualification pour le second tour (…). Il a réussi à devancer le Front National.
VP^{NS}*:* Last time you governed France *it was not* (…) *in a situation of worldwide crisis* (…). You were not qualified for the second round Nicolas Sarkozy (…) did succeed in qualifying for the second round of the elections (…) he succeeded in getting ahead of the National Front.

- A very common reaction to comparisons consists in proposing an anti-oriented comparison (examples 10 and 19), presented as more conclusive.
- At last, another way of handling the issue is to suggest that comparative arguments reflect an erroneous framing of the political stakes of the election (example 15).

Some of these reactions echo the critical questions associated with comparative arguments (see for instance van Eemeren and Grootendorst 1992, pp. 101–102). This is why, even if I agree with Perelman's claim that what he calls "arguments from comparison" (or what Plantin (2011) calls an "analogy of comparison" [*une analogie de comparaison*]) show important differences with arguments from analogy, I don't follow him when he considers them as "quasi-logic arguments", that is, as belonging to a radically different category of arguments than arguments from analogy (which according to Perelman belong to arguments that establish the structure of reality; Perelman and Olbrechts-Tyteca 1988, p. 326). In other words, I claim that the arguments from comparison studied here are a subcategory of comparative arguments, as arguments from analogy *strict sensu* are.

9.4 Reconstructing Such Arguments

Reconstructing empirical arguments along the lines of classically identified argument schemes makes their description more accurate, and, in a normative perspective, makes it possible for a systematic and rigorous assessment to proceed.

Hence the superficial initial description of the mechanism studied here (an argument which allows to depart from a relative assessment of two scores to the absolute assessment of one of them) should be connected to a structural description according to specific argument schemes identified within Argumentation Studies.

van Eemeren et al. (2002) propose a very general description of comparative arguments, or arguments based on a relation of analogy in the broader sense of the term:

Y is true of X
Because: Y is true of Z,
And: Z is comparable to X.

When applied to the examples examined here, such a description produces the following reconstruction:

S2 is a good/bad score
Because: S1 is a good/bad score
And: S2 is comparable to S1

An obvious flaw of such a reconstruction is that it misses the specific orientation of the comparisons studied here, which more often than not focus on the *difference* between S1 and S2 rather than on their closeness. The arguments studied here do not presuppose that S2 is similar to S1: they claim that S2 is superior, or inferior, to S1, as a premise for a conclusive assessment of S2. In that, they echo Brown's penetrating, though unexploited remark, that "although usually not mentioned (…), differences would seem to be as susceptible as similarities to analogical treatment" (Brown 1989, p. 162).

9.4.1 What About an a fortiori Reconstruction?

Hence, as the comparisons studied here involve some kind of hierarchical organization (a score is said to be superior or inferior to another one, not only "similar"),

Fig. 9.1 Ducrot's argumentative scale

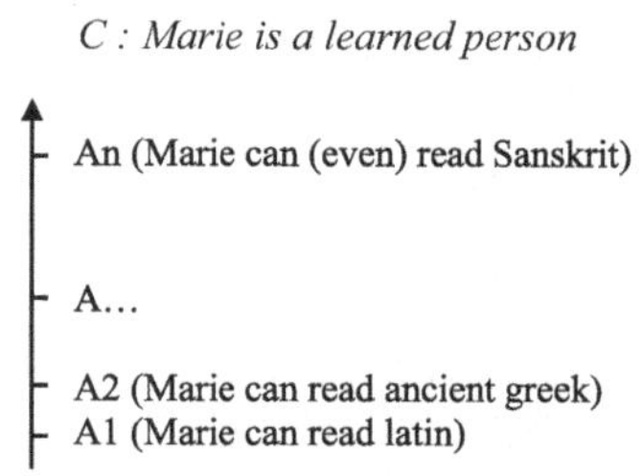

Fig. 9.2 Election scores' simple argumentative scale

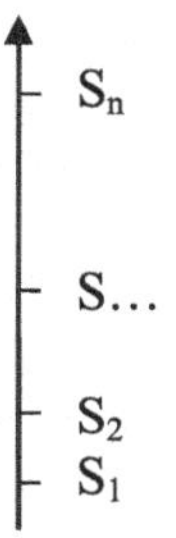

the *a fortiori* argument, which is often presented as a subtype of comparative arguments, and which implies a gradual dimension, might well be a more relevant frame for the analyst to characterize the structure of our examples.

In connection with the *a fortiori* argument scheme, the description of the argumentative mechanism involved in the examples we've been examining so far requires that one uses Ducrot's notion of argumentative scale (Ducrot 1973, p. 229). An argumentative scale is a set of arguments oriented to supporting a conclusion; these arguments are ordered according to their argumentative strength (Fig. 9.1).

An argument A_n is stronger than an argument A_1 means, in Ducrot's perspective, that if one accepts to conclude from A_1 to C, then (*a fortiori*) he must also accept to conclude from An to C.

Hence the connection between Ducrot's definition of an argumentative scale and the *a fortiori* argument is direct. The argumentative scale corresponding to our data is (Fig. 9.2):

The *a fortiori* argument based on such an argumentative scale would run as follows:

S_2 is a good score
Because: $S_n > S_1$
And: [S_1 is a good score]

Unfortunately, such an argumentative structure cannot always be applied *as it is* to our examples. As it stands, the description of the *a fortiori* argument presupposes that the lower claims on the scale (here, S_1), even if weaker than the arguments at the top of the scale, still have to be seen as arguments for C.

Such a presupposition fits some examples of the data. For instance, when Marine Le Pen's score is compared to her father's previous score in 2002, it is clearly consensually assumed that her father's score was deemed a high score (example 31), and sometimes even made explicit (example 32):

Example 31
FN: Bien (…), ce qu'on retiendra, euh (…), surtout ce soir au soir du premier tour c'est le score (…) impressionnant de Marine Le Pen, euh, vingt pour cent des voix c'est'à dire (…) bien au-delà du score réalisé par son père (…), euh, au soir du premier tour du vingt-et-un avril deux mille deux.
FN: Well (…), what we will retain, uh (…), especially tonight after the first round is the (…) impressive score of of Marine le Pen, uh, twenty per cent of votes that is (…) far beyond the score that her father had obtained (…), uh, at the first round evening of the twenty-first of April two thousand and two.

Example 32
Sympathisant: Elle explose le score historique (…) du Front National (…) et effectivement c'est un très, très grand soir (…) pour les patriotes pour les souverainistes.
A supporter: She sweeps away the historical score (…) of the National Front (…) and in fact it is a very very great evening (…) for patriots for sovereignists.

In this example the positive assessment of Marine Le Pen's score is secured by the comparison with her father's previous score, and by the positive assessment of the latter: if Jean-Marie Le Pen's 2002 score is deemed a good score, then Marine Le Pen's score, which is superior to it, may *all the more* be deemed so.

The relevance of the evaluative premise [S1 is a good score] is confirmed *a contrario* by the fact that when such a premise is clearly unacceptable for all participants, the inference from the comparison to the conclusion is held up. This is how example 33 should be understood:

Example 33
Claire Chazal (journaliste) [À Cécile Duflot] : Vous faites un peu plus de deux pour cent; c'est légèrement mieux qu'la dernière fois, mais c'est un score qui reste faible.
Claire Chazal (journalist) [To Cécile Duflot, an ecologist activist] : You win a little more than two per cent it is slightly better than last time but it is still a low score.

In a Ducrot's style analysis, the use of "but" signs the fact that "it is slightly better than last time" would normally point to a conclusion like "it's a good score" as long as the phora score can be considered a good one—or at least, not too poor a score. But in the case of the Ecologist party, the former score (1.57 %) was so low that the fact that the present score is superior to it does not suffice for concluding that "it's a good score".

Along the same line, if S1 is deemed an extremely high score, a comparison unfavorable to S2 (stating S2's inferiority relatively to S1) can still authorize a positive absolute assessment of S2—as long as the presentational devices used to phrase the comparison fit the argumentative objective (for instance "tonight Candidate X almost makes it as well as he did during previous elections", as opposed to "tonight Candidate X does not even reach the score he obtained during previous elections").

But most of the time, the second premise ("S1 is a good/bad score") is left implicit. And reconstructing it as an implicit premise would sometimes unduly "force" the arguer's reasoning into a pre-established argument scheme whereas nothing, in the very phrasing of the argument, points to the relevance of such an interpretation.

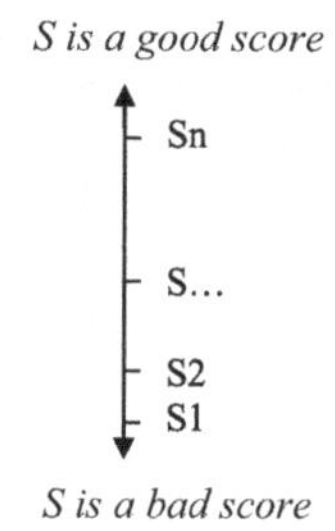

Fig. 9.3 Election scores' multi-directional argumentative scale

In these cases everything runs as if the comparison argument were based on a multi-directional argumentative scale as in (Fig. 9.3).

In such cases the only important premise to conclude that S2 is a good score is that S2 > S1 (or to conclude that S2 is a poor score is that S2 < S1), whatever position S1 occupies on the scale.

It is the case when Sarkozy's score is deemed a good one in comparison with the poorer scores obtained by the leaders of different countries confronted with similar economic crisis. The comparison shows at best that Sarkozy's score is less disastrous than the other European outgoing leaders' scores; but it is bluntly used to conclude that Sarkozy's result is good.

In most cases, the score taken as a reference in the comparison is neither clearly disastrous, nor clearly exceptional: its assessment seems to be somewhat irrelevant to the arguers, for whom the only thing that counts is the relative assessment of S2 with regard to S1.

To conclude with the analytic account of the comparative structures studied here, one should add that the *a fortiori* reconstruction of the examples sometimes requires that the enunciative, polyphonic dimension of discourse be taken into account. It is the case for example 34, which runs as follows:

Example 34
Gilbert Collard[MLP]: Bon (…) vous avez entendu m'sieur Mélenchon dire qu'avec onze virgule six (…) il est la clé du futur (…) alors (…) que sera (…) Marine Le Pen avec dix-neuf euh virgule: six à l'heure actuelle hein (…) la la le serrurier de la vie politique (…) euh la clé de l'avenir (…) à droite (…). C'est Marine Le Pen.
GC[MLP] : Well (…) you heard Mr Mélenchon saying that with eleven point six (…) he is the key of the future (…) then (…) what will be Marine Le Pen with nineteen uh point six at the moment (…) the the locksmith of political life (…) uh the key of the future (…) to the right (…). Is Marine Le Pen.

This example fits to some extent the usual description of *a fortiori* arguments. It suggests that within the set of the arguments for the conclusion "Candidate X is the key of the future", "to get 19.6 of the votes" is stronger than "to get 11.6 of the votes"; if one accepts to conclude from "candidate X got 11.6 of the votes" to "candidate X is the key of the future", then, *a fortiori*, one also must accept to conclude from "candidate X got 19.6 % of the votes" to "candidate X is the key of the future".

The problem lies in the absolute phrasing of the conclusion: "to be THE key of the future". This claim cannot be true simultaneously of Jean-Luc Mélenchon and

Fig. 9.4 Election scores' polyphonic argumentative scale

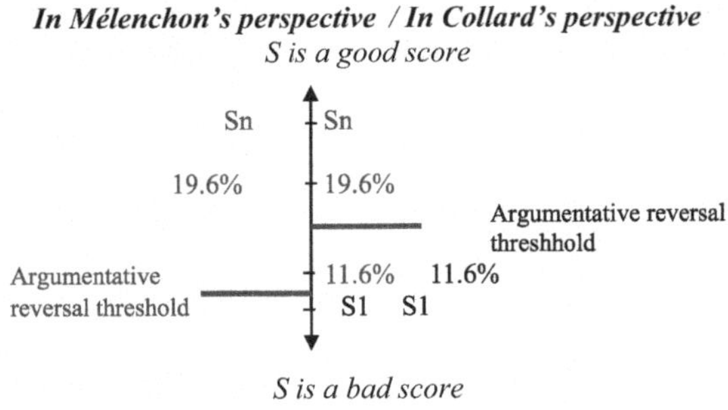

of Marine Le Pen. Hence the *a fortiori* argument reconstruction can be understood only resorting to a polyphonic interpretation of it: the inference from "candidate X got 11.6 % of the vote" to "candidate X is the key of the future" is attributed to Mélenchon's supporters, whereas the inference from "X got 19.6 % of the votes" is endorsed by Gilbert Collard himself. Collard's argument seems to be based on an enunciatively complex argumentative scale, as represented in (Fig. 9.4).

Undoubtedly, the present paper proposes a systematic account of an argumentative device (the argumentative use of comparisons between scores during election night specials) which is so specific that it might well seem anecdotal; but such a judgment would be mistaken, insofar as resorting to comparisons is a very common strategy used in order to make sense of quantitative data in all sorts of circumstances. The examples we've been through suggest that whereas the conclusive evaluations ("it's a good score"/"it's a bad score") that follow from the comparisons between different scores sometimes seem to be reasonable—at least to some extent—in other cases the comparisons seem to have a merely mechanical upgrading or downgrading effect that is more attached to the superficial comparative structure than to any reasonable political reasoning; in this sense, the argumentative comparisons studied here illustrate the complex connection between linguistic phrasing and the logical base of argumentation.

References

Brown, W. R. 1989. Two traditions of analogy. *Informal Logic* XI:161–172.

Brown, W. R. 1995. The domain constraint on analogy and analogical argument. *Informal Logic* 17 (1): 89–100.

Doury, M. 2009. Argument schemes typologies in practice: The case of comparative arguments. In *Pondering on problems of argumentation: Twenty essays on theoretical issues,* eds. F. H. van Eemeren and B. Garssen, 141–155. Dordrecht: Springer.

Doury, M., and A. Tseronis. (2014). Les faits et les arguments: La mise en discours des scores électoraux. In *Actes du colloque "Le langage manipulateur: Pourquoi et comment argumenter?", Arras, 13–15 septembre 2012*, eds. J. Goes, J.-M. Mangiante, F. Olmo, and C. Pineira. Arras: Artois Presse Université (APU).

Ducrot, O. 1973. *La preuve et le dire*. Paris: Mame.

van Eemeren, F. H., and R. Grootendorst. 1992. *Argumentation, communication, and fallacies: A pragma-dialectical perspective*. Hillsdale: Lawrence Erlbaum Associates.
van Eemeren, F. H., R. Grootendorst, and F. Snoeck-Henkemans. 2002. *Argumentation: Analysis, evaluation, presentation*. Mahwah: Lawrence Erlbaum Associates.
van Eemeren, F. H., and P. Houtlosser. 2006. Strategic maneuvering: A synthetic recapitulation. *Argumentation* 20:381–392.
Govier, T. 1989. Analogies and missing premises. *Informal Logic* 11 (3): 141–152.
Govier, T. 2001. *A practical study of argument* . 5th ed. Belmont: Wadsworth.
Perelman, C., and L. Olbrechts-Tyteca. 1988. *Traité de l'argumentation: La nouvelle rhétorique*. Bruxelles: Éditions de l'Université de Bruxelles. First published 1958 by Presses Universitaires de France.
Plantin, C. 2011. Analogie et métaphore argumentatives. *A Contrario* 16:110–130.

Chapter 10
Analogical Argumentation in Text Genres: Empirical Studies

Rosalice Pinto

10.1 Introduction

This paper focuses on the description of some linguistic and non-linguistic resources which participate in *analogical argumentative movements* in persuasive text genres. In the first part a text linguistic approach is presented: some different perspectives on *text genre,* considering that non-verbal and verbal communications (or *multimodal communication*[1]) are mainly influenced by social contextual aspects. In the second part the use of argumentation in persuasive text genres is highlighted. I point out some linguistic approaches of argumentation. This overview will be important in order to show what kind of semiotic resources may be used as argumentative strategies in specific text genres. In the third part I briefly outline the definition *of analogical argumentation* that will be relevant to this work. In addition, some methodological aspects will be presented and finally the analysis of empirical texts that circulate in different social practices. To summarize, this study provides some evidence on the influence of contextual aspects on both the *multimodal argumentative materialisation of texts* and on the varied *analogical argumentative movements.*

10.2 Text Genres—Different Traditions

Within the last three decades a number of researchers have been interested in genre as a framework for analyzing the form and function of nonliterary discourse, as well as a tool for developing educational practices. Hence, genre studies have been

[1] As Kress et al. (2001, p. 7) state: "Language—whether as speech or as writing—becomes simply one of several modes through which the business of science is done (…). We use the term *multimodality* to describe that approach".

R. Pinto (✉)
Research Centre for Linguistics, New University of Lisbon, Lisbon, Portugal
e-mail: rosapinto1@netcabo.pt

H. J. Ribeiro (ed.), *Systematic Approaches to Argument by Analogy,*
Argumentation Library 25, DOI 10.1007/978-3-319-06334-8_10,

conceived distinctively by researchers in different scholarly traditions, in different parts of the world (for more details, see Hyon 1996).

On one hand, English, American and Australian studies have been interested in genre as a tool for developing L1 and L2 competences; on the other hand, French and Swiss studies based on Circle's work have focused on analyzing the form, the function, and the social constraints in literary and non-literary discourses.

Researchers in English for specific purpose (ESP) have been interested in genre as a tool for analyzing and teaching the spoken and written language required of non-native speakers in academic and professional settings. However, many ESP scholars have paid particular attention to detailing the formal characteristics of genres focusing less on the specialized functions of texts and their surrounding social contexts.

New rhetoric studies describe a body of North American works from a variety of disciplines concerned with L1 teaching including: rhetoric, composition studies, and professional writing. Their focus is on the functional and contextual aspects of genres rather than on linguistic aspects.

Australian approaches to genre have been centered within a larger theory of language known as systemic functional linguistics, developed by Halliday. Broadly speaking, SFL is concerned with the relationship between language and its functions in social settings. They have differed from both ESP and New rhetoric researchers in their focus on primary and secondary school genres and nonprofessional workplace texts rather than on university and professional writing.

In fact, as our interest here in this paper is to analyze empirical texts that circulate in different social practices, the analyses of text genres will be based on French and Swiss traditions (Maingueneau 1996, 1999; Rastier 1989; Bronckart 1999), that were based on the work of the Bakhtin's Circle. However, it is important to emphasize that I will focus on some descriptive aspects developed by the Anglo-Saxon tradition to analyze typography, colors and images in texts, based on a Social Semiotics[2] approach. I argue that these elements are important argumentative strategies in some persuasive text genres.

In this paper text/discourse genres are defined as *textual/discursive forms in socio-ideological communication*.

[2] From the framework of social semiotics, the works of Kress and van Leeuwen (2006); Kress et al. (2001); Kress and van Leeuwen (2001) based on Halliday (1985) are pioneers in the construction of a theoretical framework able to study communication situations in their semiotic complexity. Language (written or spoken) is simply one of the modes that are always and simultaneously in use in some activities. Language, whether in speech or writing, has always existed as just one mode in the totality of modes involved in the production of any text, spoken or written. A spoken text is not just verbal but also visual, combining with "non-verbal" modes of communication such as facial expression, gesture, posture and others forms of self-representation. A written text, similarly, involves more than language: it is written on something, on some material (paper, wood, stone, metal, etc.) and it is written with something (…). The multi-modality of written texts has, by and large, been ignored, whether in educational contexts, in linguistic theorizing or in popular common sense. Today, in the age of "multimedia" it can suddenly be perceived again as Kress and van Leeuwen (2006) state.

Fig. 10.1 Text genre diagram—contextual and pluri-semiotical aspects

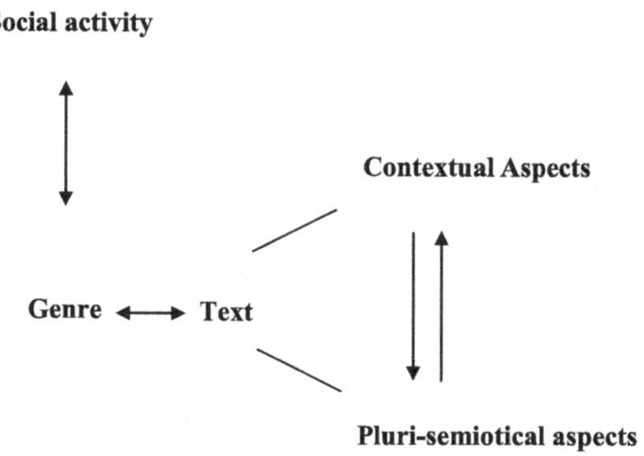

We stress that when agents produce texts, they must do so in accordance with the representations that they have of the production situation and the socio-historically indexed text templates, which have a certain degree of stability. The latter correspond to the *text genres* present in the *architext*.

Consequently we can affirm that texts are necessarily integrated into a text genre and proceed from an adaptation/or adoption of a text and/or genre template present in the long term memory of the producer agent. This outlook leads us to conclude that the empirical text describes not only the natural characteristics of the textual genre to which it belongs, but also the salient features that define its status as a unique object. It is the dialectic nature of relationships between the social/collective order and those pertaining to the individual order that add to *the complexity* of our object of analysis.

As a result, we can affirm that the empirical text is a *global communicative unit* (see Bronckart 2004, p. 115) and its materialisation will incorporate various generic aspects. Therefore, we can consider that the empirical text has two aspects that are inherent to it:[3] on one hand, the contextual aspects and on the other pluri-semiotical aspects. The former corresponds to contextual constraints that will influence the textual materialization. The latter is constituted by aspects pertaining to the micro and macro-textual organisation, which according to the textual genre, show different characteristics. These *two sides of the same coin* are in constant interaction in a dynamic process. The following diagram, which is purely didactic-methodological, tries to explain what has been described (Fig. 10.1):

---

[3] Components of the genre have been developed by several authors. Maingueneau (1996) has developed 5 components: *place and moment of realisation, legitimacy and status of partners, aim, material support and text plan.* Whereas Adam (2001) has defined eight levels: the *semantic*, the *enunciative*, the *pragmatic,* the *stylistic and* the *phraseologic,* the *compositional,* the *material,* the *peritextual* and the *metatextual.* Bronckart (1999) defines three levels: the *text plan*, the *textualisation mechanisms* and the *enunciative mechanisms*. According to our *corpora*, we have defined eight components (Pinto 2010). For the contextual aspects, we have the components *metatextual*, *intertextual*, *architextual*, *peritextual*, *language activity*, *situational (aim, interlocutive instances*, *support*, *time of circulation*, *place of circulation*). For linguistic-textual questions, we have the components *organisational*, *stylistic* and *extended enunciative*.

We underline that the diagram shown above, which duplicates the description of the empirical text, was developed to analyse the internal organisation of texts using a descending methodology of analysis, as recommended by Socio-discursive Interactionism (Bronckart 1999, 2004, 2008). This approach supports that the empirical text is a psycho-social-plurisemiotic object. However, what really interests us is the materialisation of the language action through texts. It is from the latter, as they are circulated, that we can really study the semiotization of this action and thereby certify how the various textual components incorporate the generic aspects. Having said that, we prefer textual analysis in the perspective of the *Linguistics of genres*[4]. This means that for analysing texts, we cannot disregard the contextual aspects that are still *dynamically* indexed with them.

It is important to note that in this paper we work with specific *text genres*—persuasive text genres—whose intent is to *persuade* people to agree with a certain point of view, in order, for instance, to vote for a candidate or to buy a product. I would like to argue that these text genres may present a *multimodal materialisation*[5] acting as *argumentative strategies*. This study will also illustrate the use of a multi-theoretical perspective (socio-interactionism discourse, textual linguistics, discourse analysis and social semiotics) to arrive at a comprehensive and critical view of multimodal empirical texts.

10.3 Argumentation—Text-linguistic Studies on a French-Swiss Approach

We all know that the notion of argumentation in French linguistic studies has arisen from the works of Ducrot and Anscombre (1983) in semantic pragmatic, and was developed in textual linguistics (Adam 1999), and in socio-discursive interactionism (Bronckart 1999).

In a more restricted sense, Ducrot and Anscombre studied the argumentation at the utterance level. According to these authors all the verbal utterances that lead people to a certain conclusion involve argumentative relations. Their descriptive approach is characterized by a special interest in words such as "only", "but", "even", "still" and "so", which can serve as argumentative "operators" or "connectors" and give the utterances a certain argumentative force and argumentative direction.

From the textual linguistic viewpoint, Adam (1999) points out that the text is composed of packets of propositions (macro-propositions). For this author the relatively regular types of utterances are cognitive models and their compositional regularities of which Bakhtin (1984) speaks, are at the basis of the sequential regularities. For Adam, there are five sequences (argumentative, narrative, descriptive, dialogue and explicative) that have typical properties of the category (sequence) to which they belong. In other words, each category has characteristics that correspond

[4] Expression used by Rastier (2001, p. 265) and taken up by Bouquet (2004, p. 5) and Coutinho (2005, pp. 73–88).

[5] For more details about the multimodal materialization in text genres, see: Leal (2011) and Pinto (2010, 2013).

to diagrams or mental images of the abstract prototype-object. While establishing a comparison between the sequence that we are studying and the mental image that we have of this sequence, we are capable of recognising an example as prototypical of a category or even of a determined sequence.

It is important to note that the description of argumentative sequence is based on Toulmin's model: the special feature of the argumentative sequence resides in the fact that it is translatable to an inference, involving a relationship between data, reasons or arguments leading to a conclusion (Adam 2001, p. 104). Narrative or descriptive sequences may also have an argumentative function.

On the other hand, Bronckart (1999) understands the textual sequences (including the argumentative sequence) differently. Although he underlines the importance of textual sequences in empirical text he points out that they are not cognitive models, but are socially constructed and re(constructed).

Bronckart (1999) considers that sequences (including the argumentative sequence) do not constitute a *biological competence*, supported for example by authors still focused on cognitivism, like Adam. The truth is, the prototypical sequences, according to Bronckart, are influenced by situational questions where they interact and modify themselves constantly. When producer agents select prototypes of determined sequences, they do so based on the representations that they have from the recipient and finalities of the text. In this manner the sequences for Bronckart, necessarily do have a *dialogal status*.

However it is important to note that our interest in this work, conceived by *Linguistics of genres*, is to provide us with a semiology that leans towards some stability of concepts. Therefore, the term *argumentation* corresponds to all the multimodal aspects (linguistic elements—implicit or explicit—, typography, image, colours) present in persuasive text genres. These elements, from a compositional point of view, may participate in *argumentative sequences* in the sense depicted by Bronckart (1999).

10.4 Analogical Argumentation

Quoting Walton et al. (2008, Chap. 2), there are two different schemes for *argument from analogy*. One is based on similarity while the other is based on *properties shared* or not shared in the two cases that are being compared.

As the author points out, the first scheme for *argument from analogy* is the following (Table 10.1):

Therefore the scheme for argument from analogy offered by Guarini and suggested by Walton is shown below (Table 10.2):

Moreover, it is interesting to note that according to the *text genre* analyzed the process of analogy can be motivated by *metaphors*.[6]

[6] In this case "analogy, in turn, is a process of classification: x is like y (in criterial ways). Which metaphors (and, ´behind´ the metaphors, which classification) carry the day and pass into the semiotic system as conventional, and then as naturalized, and then as ´natural´, neutral classifications, is governed by social relations of power" (Kress and van Leeuwen 2006, p. 8).

Table 10.1 Scheme for argument from analogy—Walton (Chap. 2, p. 48)

Similarity premise	Generally, case *C1* is similar to case *C2*
Base premise	A is true (false) in case *C1*
Base premise	A is true (false) in case *C2*
Conclusion	A is true (false) in case *C2*

Table 10.2 Scheme for argument from analogy—(Guarini 2004, p. 161; *apud* Walton Chap. 2)

Premise 1	*a* has features *f1, f2, ... fn*
Premise 2	*b* has features *f1, f2, ... fn*
Conclusion	*a* and *b* should be treated or classified in the same way with respect to *f1, f2 ... fn*

However, it is important to note that the text genres we analyze in this paper are strategically placed in different social practices presenting different multimodal aspects. How do these elements participate in an *analogical argument*? Are these elements influenced by very different contextual aspects embedded in documents belonging to different activities?

10.5 Methodology: Definitions and Criteria

Here we analyze texts from different persuasive text genres: a political poster, a commercial advertisement, and an advertisement from a non-profitable association. These documents were produced in the context of specific purposes and interests in 2002 and 2009. The aim of the first text genre is to promote a Portuguese political party. The second points out some advantages of a new product of an airline in order to convince people to buy it. The third intends to convince people to participate in a social campaign.

We know that some of the approaches to visual, linguistic or texts analysis are based on the analysis of collections of texts/images, and others on the analysis of single visual/linguistic texts. Here we selected one *prototypical text* (single text) from different persuasive text genres in order to compare the *argumentative strategies* employed in different social practices.

Let us now become more technically precise in defining *prototypical text*. The term *prototype* (for an extensive study, see Pinto 2009) corresponds to the idea that each text genre has normal traits ingrained with some stability, and others that are quite unique in indicating their singularity. These characteristics depend on the production conditions (historical-socio-cultural) typical to the analysed text genre. Consequently, in this paper the *prototypical text* will correspond to the *empirical text* that has a family resemblance to the text genre to which it belongs, but at the same time, this same text has very unique aspects. However, we insist on the fact that *prototype*, as highlighted by Bronckart, should only be considered from the viewpoint of its *dialogical status*. Having said that, we must admit that it is produced based on multiple representations and it can be modified (based on miscellaneous contextual aspects) in accordance with the degree of stability of the text genre in which it fits.

Consequently, the study of an empirical object implies a multi/pluri/interdisciplinary perspective.

10.6 Analysis

The theoretical approach adopted in this article derives from Socio-Discursive Interactionim (SDI): *texts are global communicative units*. Consequently, all the textual components depend upon the properties of the interactive situations and those of the general activities that they comment on, as well as the socio-historical conditions of their own making. We then argue with a top-down analysis of the texts. Firstly, we will contextualize the texts (text 1—political poster; text 2—advertisement from commercial activity; text 3—advertisement from a non-profitmaking association). Then we proceed to the analysis of multimodal resources describing how they may act in these empirical texts as *argumentative strategies participating in different analogical relations*.

It is important to note that for the analysis we considered essentially the *multimodal aspects* that participate in the argumentation of the texts, pointing out the elements that play a part in the analogical argumentation.

10.6.1 Text 1—Political Poster[7]

In December 2001, António Guterres, then Prime Minister of Portugal with the Socialist Party (PS) decided to leave the government after the defeat of his party in the local elections. This brought forward the general elections that would ultimately define which party would run the country as of March 2002. The two most important parties in Portugal (Socialists and Social-Democrats) were therefore competing for the post of Prime Minister of Portugal in 2002. The Portuguese legislative election of 2002 took place on March 17.

The political poster chosen is one of a series of 5 posters that were used by the Socialist Party (PS) in this election process. The socialist government suggested that they could find solutions to the critical social problems in the country and the poster emphasizes this attitude: they had to have determination to help overcome problems.

The following text is one of the political posters displayed by the Socialist Party (Fig. 10.2).

In the example under analysis, the text unit—"Determinação/*Determination*" is inserted in a political/advertising campaign, in a genre that is well-known by all: a *political billboard*. According to the representations that we already have in our

[7] In earlier works (Pinto 2010, 2013) other multimodal aspects concerning this political poster were described.

Fig. 10.2 Political poster from the Socialist Party (PS)—Portuguese Legislative election—2002

long-term memory concerning models of texts pertaining to this genre, we can already foresee some characteristics that are peculiar to them. Normally, the texts display a photo of the candidate for the elections, accompanied by lexical/enunciation impact units. The artistic (typographic and chromatic) appearance also demonstrates the enormous importance of these texts that seek, fundamentally, to convince the voter to vote for a specific party/candidate. It is also worth stressing that temporary and spatial situational aspects are important coercive factors in examples of this genre. As these posters are normally exhibited along highways with a great deal of traffic or on roundabouts, areas where they are legally allowed, the reader/voter has little time to interpret all of textual universe and be persuaded by the contents of the poster. These situational questions obviously influence the linguistic or non-linguistic choices made by the producer when designing the poster.

In the case under analysis we may think that the TU[8] "Determinação/*Determination*" displays an *epistemic value* associated with it, which indicates the speaker's degree of certainty in relation to the announced proposal. However, when considering that this TU is introduced in an example of this genre, the most suitable marker of modalization would be, for example, the modal adverb "obviously" and the correct assertion to *inferentially* translate the idea conveyed in the enunciation would be the enunciation itself:

- [Obviously, the candidate is determined and ambitious]

This way, it could be claimed that the inference is conveyed through an *interpretative path* exercised by the reader. By viewing the generic aspects of the genre, the reader establishes an association between the verbal TU and the photograph of the candidate, based upon the various enveloping inter-texts. The fact is that the updating of the verbal TU sense stems not only from the established relationships with other elements that are present in the textual universe—candidate's photo, the party's abbreviation and slogan—but also from the various inter-textual aspects of a generic nature. As Rastier (2001, p. 118) states (my translation):

[8] A textual unit may be defined as an implicitly or explicit lexical, a propositional unit (verbal or non-verbal) that presents a unit of sense within a text (Pinto 2010, p. 201).

> Meaning is not constituted in the text, but in the modes of interpretation. As such it must be related to them. (...) All interpretation consists of a path: thus to pass from one interpreted word to its neighbour, still to be interpreted, it is necessary to make a shared assumption regarding current traits and/or return to interpretations deriving from the *doxa* (the topoi, which are normative axioms), or other known texts in the corpus. A text appears legible and clear when the three types of interpretation, stemming from previous passages of text (of topoi) and the intertext become totally accessible and not contradictory.

One should also emphasize that the verbal TU under analysis works, in the textual genre in question, as an argument to support the thesis proclaimed on the poster: *Vote for the Socialist Party (PS)*. There is an encircling *topos* that establishes this: "the more determined the greater the possibility of being a good candidate". We, as readers, inferentially, establish a relationship between the two texts units through the *topos* mentioned.

Still in this textual universe we observe that the verbal TU "Determinação/*Determination*" works as an argument for other textual units present in the text. In this manner, we can establish, inferentially, various debatable arguments in this textual universe. There will be an argumentation materialized by the verbal TU "Determinação/*Determination*", and a thesis or conclusion, highlighted by the other textual units that make up the textual universe, as can be seen below:

- [If you want a candidate with determination, vote for Ferro Rodrigues (represented by the candidate's name)].
- [If you want a candidate with determination, vote for the Socialist Party (represented by the party's symbol)].
- [If you want a candidate with determination, vote PS (represented by the initials of the party)].
- [If you want a candidate with determination vote PS] (represented by the party's website)].

As we have seen from the verbal TU *Determination*, this example of text genre presents an epistemic modal value, whose *interpretation* will depend on the relationship established with other textual elements. However, the *persuasive potential* associated with this modal value should be stressed above all, since the TU in question is enclosed within a genre that has a well-defined objective: to persuade the voter to vote for a specific party. The TU thus assumes a persuasive role in the text. Furthermore, when referring to the persuasive potential of the modalities in some textual genres, Pinto (2010, p. 215) states:

> In genres where persuasion is more relevant, as in the case of the political billboard, we have modalities with *a high degree of persuasive potential*. Consequently, the modalities inserted in this genre will have a heightened persuasive effect. In other genres, on the other hand, the modalities will reflect lesser degrees of *persuasive potential*, and consequently, will have a lesser *persuasive effect*.

Now we can emphasize the importance of the analogical argumentation in this empirical text (Table 10.3):

Table 10.3 Scheme for argument from analogy in the PS political poster

Premise 1	"*An individual as Prime minister*" is supposed to have as features: *Courage, determination, and honesty*
Premise 2	*Ferro Rodrigues'* features are: *courage, determination and honesty*
Conclusion	*a* and *b* should be treated or classified in the same way with respect to *f1, f2 ... fn*

Evidently, the "verbal" features that are mentioned below were employed in all the socialist party campaigns. However, it is important to note that the image of the candidate confirms the idea shown by the verbal part of the poster. Just as image-producers, in depicting human or quasi-human participants, I must choose to make them look at the viewer or not.[9] In this case the candidate looks directly at the viewer. Contact is established by the eyes. The *demand image* tries to convince people to vote for the party and it sends out a message of confidence. Concerning social distance, we have a *close personal distance* because we can see the head and the shoulders. Distance is used in this case to show *respect* for authority. We know that the selection of an angle implies the possibility of expressing subjective attitudes towards represented participants, human or otherwise. In this empirical text we observe a frontal angle. The represented participant is depicted as someone we can trust.

10.6.2 Text 2—Advertisement (Commercial Activity)

In 2008 the Portuguese aviation company TAP developed a marketing campaign to compete with low cost airlines. Until then, TAP had only two products to sell (business and tourist classes). Later, it started to sell products in order to attract passengers from low cost airlines. The following advertisement is one of the documents produced for this campaign (Fig. 10.3).

It is important to note that the commercial activity and its objective constrain either the choice of argumentative strategies in this persuasive text genre or the analogical argumentative "movements" that can be implicitly inferred.

---

[9] As we know, according to Halliday, spoken and written texts always, and simultaneously, fulfill three broad communicative forms of metafunctions. The ideational function is the function of construction representations of what is going in the world and in our minds (see van Leeuwen (2006, p. 142). It is in the ideational function that the text-producer embodies in language his or her experience of *the phenomena of the real world* (see Halliday 1973, p. 106). The interpersonal function is the "participatory function of language". It allows for the expression of attitudes and evaluations. It also allows the expression of a relation set up between the text-producer and the text-consumer (Halliday and Matthiessen 2004, p. 7). The "textual" metafunction, allows us to use language to marshal individual representations and specific linguistic resources. Specific lexico-grammatical and discourse level systemic can be matched to each of these three metafunctions. Kress and van Leeuwen (2006) have shown that image can fulfill these metafunctions, too. As our interest is to study persuasive text genres we emphasize the interpersonal metafunction (or the interactive meanings) in this image. This is the function of language to constitute social interactions and express attitudes towards what is being represented.

Fig. 10.3 Advertisement from TAP Portugal (the Airline of Portugal)—2008

Some factors must be taken into account when analyzing this empirical text:

- TAP boasts some advantages: at the same price as a low cost airline people do not need to carry a "lunch bag". Moreover, they have more legroom and a 20 kg baggage allowance.
- TAP shares some characteristics with the Low Cost airlines. They are both airline companies that sell tickets and promote good prices for the customer.

Taking into account the argumentative construction of this text we can sustain the following compositional scheme:

- [TAP has] More legroom (when it is compared to other carriers)]—argument 1.
- [flying TAP the client has] 20 kg of free luggage (when compared to other carriers]—argument 2.
- [Consequently the client must buy tickets from TAP]—thesis.

In fact some argumentative strategies used to attract clients from Low Cost Airlines are represented by linguistic aspects, for instance:

- The use of intertextuality (dialogue between this text and other texts)—shown, for instance, in argument 1–2.

Table 10.4 Scheme from argument of analogy in the advertisement from TAP Portugal

Premise 1	"*With Low cost carriers*" passengers do not have enough leg room, passengers can only carry one small bag (less than 20 kg), *passengers have to bring their own lunch bag, the tickets are cheap*
Premise 2	"*With TAP*" passengers can carry more than 20 kg, passengers do not have to bring a lunch hag and the tickets are cheap
Conclusion	*a* and *b* can be compared because they share one important feature for this professional price: both sell *cheap* tickets

- The use of intertextuality with the topicalization of the local adverb (strategy used in oral texts)—"With TAP, it is not necessary to bring your own meal".
- The use of intertextuality with the 2nd person singular and the lexical choices contribute to the construction of the potential customer: [excusa de levar farnel] [you don't need to bring a meal].

The implicit intertextuality in this text can be viewed mainly by *analogical inferences*. The interpreter has to be aware of the characteristics of low cost airlines in order to reconstruct the *interpretative path* of the message.

By focusing on the importance of intertextuality in this professional practice, we can emphasize the implicit analogical arguments that can encourage people to buy TAP products (Table 10.4).

All these elements are used because the producer of the advertisement bears the characteristics of the potential customer: someone who wants to pay less for a ticket and does not want to purchase food on the plane. And it is by the association made between the representation that the producer has from the customer he wants to attain, and the representational meaning of the linguistic resources that the text is constructed.

As states Bhatia (2008, p. 163), *professional discourses have their own specific characteristics that constrain their use and interpretation*. In this case, as the case study points out, *the use of analogical argumentation through intertextuality* is an important strategy to persuade clients: they can pay the same price buying a better product.

Different Semiotic Modes Moreover, different semiotic modes (linguistic forms, typography, colors) interact dynamically in the text. In the special case of typography,[10] Van Leeuwen refers to the existence of a *metaphorical meaning-potential*.

Typographical metaphor is based on a principle of similarity between the visual form of the signifier (the letterforms) and the signified. In describing how *this special metaphor* comes about, Van Leeuwen, based on the work of Lakoff and Johnson (1980), talks about the *experiential metaphor of typography*: "The idea (…) is that a material signifier has a meaning-potential that derives from our physical experience of it, from what it is we *do* when we articulate it, and from our abil-

[10] For an extensive system network of the distinctive features of letterforms, see van Leeuwen (2006, p. 151).

ity to extend our practical, physical experience metaphorically, to turn action into knowledge" (van Leeuwen 2006, pp. 146–147).

According to van Leeuwen, increased weight of the letterform is used to increase salience. The bold function can be used to mean *daring, assertive, solid, substantial, and its opposite can be made to mean timid.*

It can also signify attitudes to what is being represented, or affect readers in some way. Bold, for instance, can typographically 'hector' readers and the smooth rounded letter forms can simultaneously signify the idea of indulgence and symbolically pamper and soothe the reader.

However, it is important to note that typography is a semiotic mode and interacts with other semiotic meanings to attain the objective of communication.

In this advertisement the focus is to show that people who fly with such a company do not need to carry a lunch bag (a criticism of low cost airlines where we would have to buy a meal).

All the features of the letterforms: *lighter characters, condensed in an upright position, vertical orientation, angular curvature* suggest that all the information listed is important and corresponds to an advantage for the customer (when this product is compared to other airlines). These advantages are placed at the bottom of the advertisement with a special punctuation mark: *bullets*, lending a coherent organization to the text.

Continuing the analysis, we observe that the destination and the price presented are in a different letterform with other characteristics: *bold characters, more expanded, rounded, horizontal orientation.* Typography realizes *textual meaning*. It demarcates these elements, foregrounding key elements of the message: the price of the ticket and the destination.

All these features contribute to a fast interaction with the public, conveying pragmatism to the message. It is important to emphasize that in our culture we get used to associating the features of these letterforms to this meaning.

In fact, we have to consider an analogical movement:

As experienced producers of written texts we know that *lighter characters, condensed in an upright position, vertical orientation, and angular curvature* can be associated with pragmatism and modernity. In this text genre, where the producer intends to highlight the advantages of the product (TAP) when compared to others (low-cost airlines), the pragmatism of the communication is highlighted.

10.6.3 Text 3—Advertisement (Non-governmental Organization)

In 2008, the Portuguese Food Bank, which is responsible for collecting and distributing food to a needy population, by avoiding the waste of food, produced a marketing campaign trying to persuade people to become volunteers for the Food Bank campaign. To do so, they had to participate either as a donator or as a collaborator (trying to convince people to donate food in the supermarkets).

Fig. 10.4 Advertisement from a Non-governmental organization—Food Bank from Portugal

The following text is one of 4 advertisements that were used by the Portuguese Food Bank in this campaign. This one in particular circulated within Portuguese universities and schools during the year 2008 and the textual construction (Fig. 10.4).

In this advertisement the argumentative movement starts at the top of the text and continues with the image:[11]

- "O banco alimentar precisa do heroi que há em si"—The food bank needs the hero within you.
- "Contribua e seja super por um dia"—Contribute and be super for a day.
- [Seja um super-heroi como o superhomem]—[be a superhero like Superman (inferred by the image).

One should emphasize that the first verbal TU works, in the textual genre in question, as an argument to support the thesis proclaimed on the poster, represented by the last textual unit. There is an encircling *topos* that establishes that "People

[11] Our choice for the analysis was mainly the top part of the advertisement. The characters of the typography shown at the top of this text and the importance of the image were important factors in this decision.

who contribute in social campaigns even for one day are heroes" inferentially we establish a relationship between the two *text units* through the *topos* mentioned. Moreover there is another *interpretation path established* between the lexical unit "heroi"—*hero* in the first example, the adjective "super"—*super* in the second one and the image that represents superman.

Still in this textual universe we observe that the verbal TU *The food bank needs the hero within you* works as an argument for other textual units present in the text. In this manner, we can establish, inferentially, various debatable arguments in the textual universe highlighted by the other textual units that make up this textual universe, as can be seen below:

- [As the food bank needs the hero within you, participate in collecting food on 5th and 6th May] (inferentially determined by the link between the argument and the details of the food collection at the bottom of the poster).
- [As the food bank needs the hero within you, be a superman] (inferentially determined by the link between the argument and the image).
- [As the food bank needs the hero within you, help the Food Bank against Hunger] (inferentially determined by the link between the argument and the logo of the institution).

The *social voices* portrayed in this document play an important argumentative role. The brand of the non-governmental organization (BA) is presented by the logo (*Food bank against hunger*) at the bottom-right hand part of the poster and by the nominal syntagm (*Food bank*) is repeated three times, combined twice to a deontic modality: (*the Food bank needs the hero within you*) and (*the food bank needs your super qualities*). Most important is *the multimodal representations* of the volunteer: by lexical units—"herói"—*hero*; by verbs in the imperative form ("contribua"—*contribute*; "seja"—*be*); by the image of the superhero. The responsibility of acting does not depend on the Food Bank, but it depends on the volunteers. They can be transformed into a hero if they accomplish the purpose of the campaign. As state Perelman and Olbrechts-Tyteca (1988, p. 72), acting is an important aspect for the argumentation. It is by acting that a previous stage can be changed.

Moreover we have to emphasize that the image plays an important role for the construction of the analogical argumentation in this document. As we can see in the example, the formation of the meaning of this image does not respect current disciplinary borders. We have to convoke other situations to understand what this image represents—*intermediality*[12].

Now we can emphasize the importance of *two movements of analogical argumentation* inferred in this empirical text (Tables 10.5 and 10.6):

Some Reflections From what has been described in this paper, we feel that it is important to state first, that the *analogical argumentation inferred from different*

[12] The concept of *intermediality* has been used with different meanings. For this paper, it is viewed as the *co-relations between different media, which result in a redefinition of the media that are influencing each other, which in turn leads to a refreshed perception*, as per Kattenbelt (2008, p. 7).

Table 10.5 Scheme (1) for argument from analogy in the non-governmental advertisement

Premise 1	*The superman depicted in movies is shown as having a special appearance, special power*
Premise 2	*The superhero depicted in this document is shown with a special appearance, special power*
Conclusion	*a and b should be treated or classified in the same way with respect to the characteristics shown above*

Table 10.6 Scheme (2) for argument from analogy in the non-governmental advertisement

Premise 1	*The superhero depicted in this document is shown with a special appearance, special power*
Premise 2	*You (as volunteer) represented in this document may have a special power (if you work as a volunteer in the social campaign)*
Conclusion	*a* and *b* should be treated or classified in the same way with respect to *the characteristics of a superhero, if some conditions are respected*

semiotic modes is an important tool for the description of persuasive text genres. Second, that their "textual linguistic materialization (or multimodal materialization)" depends on the social practice in which they are situated.

I have suggested, persuasively, that either the *(re)construction of the argumentation* or the analogical argumentation may vary according to the text genre we are analyzing. In the *prototypical* political billboard, the image of the candidate associated with the linguistic aspects is responsible for the construction of the inferred movement argumentation. On the other hand, in a *prototypical advertisement from a commercial activity*, the intertextuality[13] and the typography highlight the argumentative and analogical movements. However, in the advertisement for the non-profitable organization, the intermediality portrayed by the image of the superhero and the social voices represented linguistically play an important role in the construction of the argumentative analogical movements in the document.

As we have indicated, the text in linguistics of genres "incorporates" aspects of a contextual nature in a dialogic and thereby dynamic manner. It is exactly because of belonging to a textual genre that it will have aspects that will be stable and others that have some minor variations, in accordance with various criteria.

I fully realize, of course, that what I have done so far covers only part of the study of some semiotic modes in these specific text genres. Further analysis might be explored for more generalizations.

[13] Based on Bhatia (2008, p. 165),"Interdiscursitivity in this context can be viewed as appropriation of semiotic resources (which may include textual semantic, socio-pragmatic, generic, and professional)", across any two or more text genres. As we work with text genres, we prefer the term "intertextuality".

References

Adam, J.-M. 1999. *Linguistique textuelle: Des genres de discours aux textes*. Paris: Nathan.

Adam, J.-M. 2001. *Les textes types et prototypes*. 4th ed. Paris: Nathan Université.

Bakhtin, M. 1984. *Esthétique de la création verbale*. Paris: Gallimard.

Bhatia, V. K. 2008. Genre analysis, ESP and professional practice. *English for Specific Purpose* 27:161–174.

Bouquet, S. 2004. Linguistique générale et linguistique des genres. *Langages* 153:3–14.

Bronckart, J.-P. 1999. *Atividade de Linguagem, textos e discursos: Por um interacionismo socio-discursivo*. São Paulo: EDUC.

Bronckart, J.-P. 2004. Commentaires conclusifs. Pour un développement collectif de l'interactionnisme socio-discursif. *Calidoscópio* 2 (2): 113–123.

Bronckart, J.-P. 2008. Genres de textes, types de discours, et "degrés de langue". Texto! http://www.revue-texto.net/index.php?id=86. Accessed 21 July 2013.

Coutinho, A. 2005. Para uma linguística dos gêneros de texto. *Diacrítica* 19 (1): 73–88.

Ducrot, O., and J. C. Anscombre. 1983. *L'argumentation dans la langue*. Liège: Mardaga.

Guarini, M. 2004. A defence of non-deductive reconstructions of analogical arguments. *Informal Logic* 24 (2): 153–168.

Halliday, M. A. K. 1973. *Explorations in the functions of language*. London: Edward Arnold.

Halliday, M. A. K. 1985. *An introduction to functional grammar*. London: Edward Arnold.

Halliday, M. A. K., and C. Matthiessen. 2004. *An introduction to functional grammar*. 3rd ed. Londres: Hodder Education.

Hyon, S. 1996. Genre in three traditions: Implications for ESL. *TESOL Quarterly* 90 (4): 693–722.

Kattenbelt, C. 2008. Intermediality in theatre and performance: Definitions, perceptions and medial relationships. http://www.e-revistes.uji.es/index.php/clr/article/viewFile/30/30. Accessed 21 July 2013.

Kress, G., and T. van Leeuwen. 2001. *Multimodal discourse: The modes and media of contemporary communication*. London: Edward Arnold.

Kress, G., and T. van Leeuwen. 2006. *Reading images: The grammar of visual design*. London: Routledge.

Kress, G., et al. 2001. *Multimodal teaching and learning: The rhetorics of the science classroom*. London: Continuum.

Lakoff, G., and M. Johnson. 1980. *Metaphors we live by*. Chicago: University of Chicago Press.

Leal, A. 2011. A organização textual do gênero cartoon: Aspectos linguísticos e condicionamentos não linguísticos. PhD thesis. Research Centre for Linguistics, New University of Lisbon (Portugal).

Maingueneau, D. 1996. *Les termes clés de l'analyse du discours*. Paris: Seuil.

Maingueneau, D. 1999. Ethos, scénographie, incorporation. In *Images de soi dans le discours: La construction de l'ethos,* ed. R. Amossy, 75–100. Lausanne: Delachaux et Niestlé.

Perelman, C., and L. Olbrechts-Tyteca. 2008. *Traité de l'argumentation: La nouvelle rhétorique*. 5th ed. Bruxelles: Éditions de l'Université de Bruxelles (First published 1958 by Presses Universitaires de France).

Pinto, R. 2009. Prototypicity and textual analysis. *Belgian Journal of Linguistics, New Approaches in Text Linguistics* 23:31–44.

Pinto, R. 2010. *Como argumentar e persuadir—Prática política, jurídica, jornalística*. Lisboa: Quid Juris.

Pinto, R. 2013. Les élections législatives portugaises de 2002 et 2009 à partir des affiches politiques portugaises: Un "regard" multimodal. *Mot: Les langages du politique* 101 (1): 47–60.

Rastier, F. 1989. *Sens et textualité*. Paris: Hachette.

Rastier, F. 2001. *Art et science du texte*. Paris: Presses Universitaires de France.

van Leeuwen, T. 2006. Towards a semiotics of typography. *Information Design Journal* 14 (2): 139–154.

Walton, D., C. Reed, and F. Macagno. 2008. *Argumentation schemes*. Cambridge: Cambridge University Press.

Chapter 11
Classical Fables as Arguments: Narration and Analogy

Paula Olmos

11.1 Narrativity, Argumentation and Analogy

This paper makes part of a wider inquiry regarding the so far neglected issue of the argumentative qualities of narratives. There have been, at any rate, some recent theoretical advances from the received idea of stories and narratives as characteristic *nonarguments* (Govier 2001, p. 14) towards an increasing interest in narrative argumentation which comprises both: (a) the examination of certain narrative-based argument schemes as well as (b) the more controversial and speculative exploration of narration itself as a form of argument.[1] Although I have recently tried to start facing the difficulties of this second aspect (Olmos 2014), the present paper will remain within the limits of the first of these issues.

There would be a number of widely acknowledged argument types in which narratives may be involved in significant ways. “Arguments from example” and “from analogy”, especially “practical reasoning from analogy” (Walton et al. 2008, pp. 314–316), are the first obvious choices and have been so recognized ever since Aristotle’s account of the rather confused conglomerate he gathers under the label *paradeigma*, including narratives taken from real events, fables and parables (*Ret.* 1393a27-1394a18). “Arguments from precedent” (Walton et al. 2008, p. 344) could also belong within this group. In these cases, the arguer may introduce, in an imaginatively argumentative way, a story[2] and, through the development of her argument, she should show how such story supports the conclusion she is aiming

[1] Within this renewed interest in the relationship between narration and argumentation, we find a significant number of references to W. R. Fisher’s (1987) narrative paradigm of rationality, although there is not yet a specific proposal for the integration of this theoretical framework within argumentation theory.

[2] Usually a *digressive* kind of narration, not immediately related to the case discussed. Cf.: Cicero *De inv.*, I 27.

P. Olmos (✉)
Department of Logic, History and Philosophy of Science, National Distance Education University (UNED), Madrid, Spain
e-mail: polmos@fsof.uned.es

H. J. Ribeiro (ed.), *Systematic Approaches to Argument by Analogy*,
Argumentation Library 25, DOI 10.1007/978-3-319-06334-8_11,

at. Sometimes, the alleged thesis is fully expressed, as, in principle, we should think it happens in the classical fables' *morals* and sometimes it is left to the audience to draw. Plumer's (2011) account of novel as a kind of implicit analogical argument counts on this second possibility.

Now, most of the recent literature on narrative-based arguments has focused on the identification and analysis of cases labelled, by this same literature, as analogical types of argument, although, not always using the same concept of analogy. The question they try to tackle is then: what is characteristic or remarkable of these *analogies* based on stories?

For Walton (2012), in such cases what we need is a specific way of evaluating the plausibility of the "similarity between stories" asserted in the "similarity premise" needed for the reconstruction of the argument as an *analogy* according to the following scheme:

Similarity premise: Generally, case C1 is similar to case C2
Base Premise: A is true (false) in case C1 (source case).
Conclusion: A is true (false) in case C2 (target case).

Walton's suggestion[3] is that we should and actually do compare stories by using "story-schemes", made up of elements, relations between them and specific sequences in which allegedly both source and target cases must fit. The factors that initially determine the acceptability of a story will be the story's coverage, coherence and uniqueness which, taken together with the propounded similarity between two stories, will allow us to evaluate the argument about the target case.

Now, the way Walton schematizes the argument does not really respond to a concept of analogy that would really go beyond what is actually an "argument by similarity or likeness". According to Perelman (Perelman and Olbrechts-Tyteca 1958, pp. 500–501, quoting P. Grenet), who supports a more specific concept of analogical argument, the characteristic of analogy is that it invokes not just a "relation of similarity" ("rapport de resemblance") but a "similarity of relations" ("ressemblance de rapports"), namely of *argumentative* relations. The analogy would be a form of meta-argumentation in which two arguments are compared and the similarity of their respective argumentative structures alleged as a reason supporting directly the acceptability of the target argument and indirectly that of its main thesis or standpoint (Cf. Woods and Hudak 1989; Marraud 2013a, pp. 271–274). Moreover, as Perelman points out, in order to talk about analogy, properly speaking, we also need two different "domains" or "fields" whose inner relations we will compare as analogous. If we just compare cases within the same domain, the analogy becomes just an argument by example or illustration with the "theme [target] and phore [source] offering two particular cases that fall under the same rule" (Perelman and Olbrechts-Tyteca 1958, p. 502).[4]

[3] Walton's paper draws on the work of F. Bex and others on "legal argumentation".

[4] Even though the distinction between cases with just one domain and cases with two distinct domains is not always an easy one, and there might be much interpretative work to be done, this is something that should be taken into account.

In the critical questions presented by Walton for the evaluation of his basic *analogical* scheme, there is some acknowledgement of this more elaborated characterization of analogy by talking about the compared aspects of both cases as "conclusions":

CQ1: Are there respects in which C1 and C2 are different that would tend to undermine the force of the similarity cited?
CQ2: Is A the right conclusion to be drawn in C1?
CQ3: Is there some other case C3 that is also similar to C1, but in which some conclusion other than A should be drawn?

But such "conclusion" (A) is presented, in principle, as the same in both cases and so both source and target are treated as supporting a general claim or rule and as particular examples or illustrations of it.[5] However, coming now to the examples provided and analyzed by Walton, we really find some elaborated analogies in Perelman's sense, with diverse and imaginatively comparable domains (car/political power; fire/terrorism) and parallel models of argumentation (as shown in his Fig. 4, p. 205, much better than in other "linear tree schemes" provided). What Walton wants to emphasize about these cases, though, is that in them the structures compared are not just any kind of argumentative structures but precisely those based on chronological (typically casual) sequences or stories (typically "arguments from consequences"). The unique "story scheme" that allegedly fits both sides of the analogy would serve as the argument's warrant for the analyst or the arguer in dialogue. But there is nothing that essentially links narration (or narrative-based arguments) and analogy in our more restricted sense; not even parallel narrations and analogy, as these may appear in more simple arguments "by similarity", "by example" or "illustrations" (more akin to explanations than justifications). The "story scheme" as a way to evaluate "story plausibility" is an abstract container that may invoke very different principles and not always the "argumentative comparability" ("by parity of reasoning so called" in Woods and Hudak's terms) proper to analogy.

However, the immediate recourse to the concept of analogical argument when talking about narrative-based arguments and most especially when fiction is involved is present in many different proposals. Plumer (2011), for example, presents the following scheme to talk about novels as "analogical arguments":

1. The story (complex) is believable.
2. This story is believable only if such and such principles operate in the real world.
3. Therefore, such and such principles operate in the real world.

Now, the supposed distance between the "real world" and the "world of fiction" may, in principle, support the idea of different domains; but the insistence of Plumer on a kind of "realistic believability" of the "thesis novels" he is interested in,[6]

[5] Later in the discussion, after presenting the basic scheme, Walton (2012, pp. 193–194) talks about the possibility of "parallel" or "comparable" conclusions but always alongside the basic standard of the "same" conclusion.

[6] And he explicitly avoids the complexities of other kinds of narratives as, namely, Joyce's literature (Plumer 2011, p. 1553).

transforms his proposed scheme into a kind of, more or less imaginative, "argument by example". If the *same* principles operate in both cases, a classical realistic novel is not really so unlike telling a real case for the public's enlightenment. The closer we come to Plumer's scheme and its proposed realistic believability the further away we go from analogy, properly speaking.

We also find certain fictions, much more related to our paper's topic, analyzed as *analogical* in Hunt (2009, p. 370), for whom "narration in the Aesopian mode is never simply telling a story". He starts, though, with a rather different version of *analogy* which is even more remote from Perelman's account and closer to "verbal classification arguments":

X has the properties p1, p2, p3, … and f
Y has the properties p1, p2, p3, …
Therefore, Y also has the property f.

Hunt, moreover, not at all happy with the logical reasonableness of such a scheme, proposes a further complication and refinement in which the first premise (regarding a kind of source case) would, in fact, already involve an "abductive argument" responsible for the attribution of f to X (as the "best explanation" of its having properties p1, p2, p3,…) This argument would then support (¿inductively?) a general conclusion about things having properties p1, p2, p3,… which could be consequently applied "deductively" to Y (the alleged target). Having construed this air-tight structure, he suggests this is the way fables work as logically reasonable arguments. I will not enter here into de polemics about whether there are "deductive analogies" (Bermejo-Luque 2012), but it seems to me that Hunt's proposal is a way of flattening all differences between argument schemes in order to finish up with deduction as the only way to support a thesis that is very remote from our current way of accounting for arguments in argumentation theory. The suggestion of treating fables within such a framework does not seem very promising and has little to do with the narrative aspects of such discursive resources.

We will finally review Govier and Ayers's (2012) article on the argumentative character of parables, a kind of "pedagogical" narration which is rather close to our topic, fables. These authors acknowledge something which I find rather useful. They criticize R. Munson's (1976) account and analysis of certain parables and apologues for his "unduly restricted" focus on analogy (Govier and Ayers 2012, pp. 170–173). He would have, thus, neglected other possibilities of "representation" (kinds of relationship between the alleged parallel cases) they claim to find in such narratives, namely "symbolism" and "instantiation" (Govier and Ayers 2012, p. 168). This variety is promising, but again, *analogy* is here equated with "similarity" and an argument by analogy with one that provides a "relevant similarity" responsible for the double applicability of a certain unique claim;[7] the difference with "symbolism" being precisely the fact that, in this latter case, no real resemblance is present. In Perelman's account though, the presence of symbolism would be a nice symptom (there being at least two separate discursive domains) of our being in the

[7] "The presumption underlying the argument is that the claim made about X can also correctly be made about Y", p. 168.

presence of a genuine analogy: if there is no evident "relation of similarity" what is propounded by the arguer must be something like a "similarity of relations".

Govier and Ayers analyze certain parables, for example the *Good Samaritan*, as a case of "instantiation". I agree that there is no real analogy here. Discourse keeps within the domain of human behaviour and directly comparable instances of it. If there is an argument in it, it would support a recommendation about charitable treatment of strangers just by seeing it working, with good results, in a concrete realistic story. The fictitious but credible account acts as a precedent and sets an example. Moreover, if we examine it within the larger discursive context of its insertion in S. Luke's Gospel (10, pp. 25–37), it is, in fact, a response to the question "Who is my neighbour?" made to Jesus by a lawyer who, in principle, agrees with the norm "love thy neighbour as yourself". It would convey, thus, an implicit definition of "neighbour" by means of an instance of neighbourly behaviour. After making the lawyer adhere to such "paradigmatic definition", Jesus states the practical conclusion, "go and do". It is a complex chain of dialogic argumentation involving different argument schemes, which is not really well represented by its single-argument and monological analysis in p. 177, but at least Govier and Ayers show a more open-minded approach to the discussion of the argumentative qualities and structure of this kind of short and exemplary stories.[8]

When it comes to classical fables,[9] though, a strongly plausible conjecture about their analogical character may serve us as a starting point. In principle, we typically count on two parallel domains to start with:

- The fabulous world of talking and reasonable animals (source domain or *phore*)
- The real world of human action (target domain or theme)

Moreover, this general idea about fables would have been supported by a millenary tradition explicitly endorsed by La Fontaine in his own versified prologue to his books of fables:

> Ce qu'ils disent s'adresse à tous tant que nous sommes.
> Je me sers d'animaux pour instruire les hommes.

However, as we will see in the next section, fables, although always acknowledged as argumentatively interesting resources and typical rhetorical means had always a somewhat problematic fit within argumentation treatises. Moreover, in taking a

[8] Govier and Ayers's paper does also focus on whether these narrative arguments are, in the end and by themselves, good or bad arguments. Their conclusion is not very sympathetic and one of their points has to do with the problems of the epistemic evaluation of fictitious (counterfactual) premises, problems that become rather insurmountable in cases of "symbolic representation": "Being unable to spell out a symbolic premise, we are unwilling to deem such a premise acceptable or unacceptable. Rather, we will deem it 'not amenable to logical assessment'" (Govier and Ayers 2012, p. 187). As my own views on evaluation belong to a more contextual and comparative framework I will not discus these points.

[9] I.e. those attributed to Aesop and Babrius as well as the tradition which directly derives from them, including the Latin fabulists and the enlightenment recreations of the genre, like La Fontaine's in France or Samaniego's in Spain.

look at certain real examples of traditional classical fables, in Sects. 3 and 4, we will be able to acknowledge an evident variety of discursive strategies in which the relative distance and structural qualities of the allegedly analogous domains plays an important role in ultimately determining the kind of argument they may be employed to support.

11.2 Classical Fables in Classical Argumentation Theory

Fables are a well known part of our classical heritage. We consider them a classical literary genre conveying certain lessons and prudential teachings. Fables do have a message (they are undisguised "thesis literature"), usually made explicit through a sententious *moral* and presumably "supported" or, at least, "explained" or "illustrated" by its narrative. That is why they are, in principle, interesting candidates for argumentative assessment. Now, taking in account that the origins of our own fabulist tradition are in the Greek culture as are those of our argumentation theories, the question is whether there was an interest in fables in the Greek treatises on argumentation. And the answer is: of course, and most noticeably starting with Aristotle's *Rhetoric* (1393a 26ff).

In Book II, Chap. 20, Aristotle is presenting and commenting on his systematic and rather innovative classification of generic types of rhetorical arguments, acknowledging two basic models: the enthymeme and the *paradeigma.*[10] Among the possibilities of *paradeigmata*, traditionally considered in a rather loose way as "arguments by example"—and rather more problematically branded, by Aristotle himself, as the rhetorical counterpart of induction (*epagōgē*, 1393a26-27)—, the philosopher mentions two species corresponding to two discursive resources and strategies:

i) Either telling events that have previously taken place ("*to legein pragmata progegenēmena*"). The argument, in this case, would be warranted by the maxim "for the most part what's coming will be similar to what's already happened".[11]
ii) Or inventing events/facts ("*to auton poiein*"). This is done in parables (*parabolai*), as the Socratic ones, says Aristotle,[12] or in *logoi* such as those by Aesop or the Lybians, that is, in what we call fables.[13]

Aristotle says very little about the examples based on facts, which he seems to consider rather simple, straightforward ways of arguing. Regarding parables and fables,

[10] Plus a subtype, the maxims, which he finally includes among the enthymematic modes of arguing (*Rhet.* 1394b17ff; cf. Olmos 2007, 2011).

[11] "*homoia gar hōs epi to polu ta mellonta tois gegonosin*" (1394a7). On the expression "*hōs epi to polu*", "for the most part", and "conjectural knowledge" in Aristotle, see Piazza (2012). On the advantages of the use of warrant as a verb and not just a propositional expression, see Klump (2006).

[12] He is not using the term "parable" as in Govier and Ayers (2012).

[13] They would be subsequently and more precisely called *logoi muthikoi*.

he starts giving some instances, which implicitly account for his classification, but then states no real differences in their rhetorical use. He says of both that they are good for public and popular (*dēmēgorikoi)* speeches and persuasion because it is easier (in principle) to construe them *ad hoc* than finding relevant real cases. But this is just so provided that we are trained in perceiving similarities, which is a capacity that philosophical training will make easier (1394a5-6).[14]

The distinction between parables and fables is just implicitly stated by means of the illustrations offered in the text. As an instance of parable, Aristotle chooses one attributed to Socrates in Xenophon (*Memorabilia*, I 2.9) in which it is claimed that magistrates should not be selected by lots; a thesis supported by comparing this case with those of athletes and ship pilots, who are not selected by lots but on account of their art and expertise. It is a rather simple "argument by similarity" between different cases all within the realm of human action and specifically grouped under the more specific practice of "selection for a job" (that they are similar in this way could be the argument's warrant if challenged).[15]

The two fables presented by Aristotle are rather more complex in argumentative terms. They are more narrative, more symbolic and involve, in principle, separate domains. Both include talking/interacting animals. The first one is attributed to archaic poet Stesichorus when counseling the people of Himera about their relationship with general Falaris. It is, thus, embedded in a political and popular speech as those envisaged by Aristotle as adequate for the efficacy of fictional *paradeigmata*. Stesichorus tells a tale about a man who finally enslaves a horse that has asked him for help to take revenge on a deer. He claims then that the same will happen to them, Himerians ("*houtō de kai humeis*"),[16] if they concede Falaris special powers to fight against the enemies: he will become a tyrant and enslave them. Even though we have here animals on one side and men on the other, the stories compared are so similar that no sophisticated analogy is really proposed.

The tale is told, moreover, as a kind of semi-mythical and genealogical explanation of why horses are domestic animals. The horse's enslavement is presented as a kind of "historical" event, the moment in which the horse accepted the bit and bridle

[14] The philosophical interest in perceiving similarities or likenesses is also mentioned in *Topics* 108a7.

[15] It is presented, though, with the argumentative and discursive complications of a *reductio*: selecting magistrates by lot would be similar to selecting athletes or pilots by lot and not by art or expertise, which is something *evidently* unacceptable. It is never an easy task to analyze arguments in real texts, but, in any case, I do not think this particular complication is very relevant for our concrete discussion.

[16] In both parables and fables the similarity warranting the argument is usually made explicit and marked by the use of formulae. In the instances offered by Aristotle, we find, for example: "in a similar way …" ("*homoion gar hōsper…*"), "so, also in your case…" ("*houtō de kai humeis*"), "thus, you as well …" ("*Atar kai humas*"). Another most typical and well known formula in classical fables is: "The fable teaches us that …" ("*ho logos<ho mythos> dēloi hoti…*"). This one is generally used, as we shall later observe, in cases where the "conclusive" moral, in the realm of human life and action, is made explicit just after telling the fabulous story, with no more explanations added. It would generally be a case in which the way the conclusion is supported by the story told in the fable would be left implicit.

and, in this sense, it is acting as a "quasi-realistic" example. The similarities (almost equation) between the slave state and the animal state made, furthermore, part of the Greek reflections about these themes as can be seen in Aristotle's *Politics*. It is rather consistent with this line of thought that both stories are placed in a very close parallel, using the one that has *in fact* already happened (the enslavement, *qua* domestication, of the horse) as setting a rather realistic example, or even "precedent", of what may happen in the case of the Himerians and Falaris.

In the second, more sophisticated fable, we find again a poet, in this case Aesop himself, advising the people from Samos about their attitude towards certain kind of individuals that may take advantage on them. So, here is again the same popular and political setting, and the same Greek obsession with tyrannical or individualistic government. The story tells us about a fox, who was wading across a river and was attacked by ticks that sucked her blood; a hedgehog felt pity for her and offered to take them out; the fox refused, saying that these ticks were already satiated and new ones would come to suck the rest of her blood.

Aesop uses the tale to advise the Samians not to sentence to death their already rich demagogue, because others would come to replace him who would not be yet satiated and would rob them the more. Here, the fable itself is less realistic and even a bit paradoxical (as is Aesop's awkward and rather desperate "defence" of the demagogue). Sucking blood is not, on the other hand, exactly plundering riches, and we can talk about an imaginative analogy drawn by the author between both processes[17] which, due to the more pressing character of the blood loss as compared to the money loss, would make assessment (and decision) easier in the phore case. Moreover, the fox makes an argument that is paralleled by Aesop's own. If we accept that the fox, at least, has a point in wanting to keep the attached ticks; for analogous reasons, we could accept that Aesop has a point in advising the Samians to keep their demagogue alive. I would therefore, admit that this particular fable, as voiced by Aesop in the setting described by Aristotle, could be reasonably analyzed as a meta-argument by analogy, comparing two "arguments by (negative) consequences", one of which is invented and fabulous (and uttered by a typically cunning fox), and requires a narrative setting to be understood (not the other because it is the audience's own situation), whose parallel conclusions are petitions for (in)actions, being thus, also, practical arguments with directive and not constative thesis. And I could complicate it even more, but of course, nothing of this complication is in Aristotle who seems happy to gather all these cases under the label of paradigm and to make it even more confuse by the mention of induction (*epagōgē*).

Aristotle, on the other hand, does not seem to be very concerned about the realistic or unrealistic aspects of fables and parables. He just presents the division between invented and real events, but treats *paradeigmata* based on facts, parables and fables as rather similar in argumentative terms. Yet, within classical tradition itself, and Greek rhetoric in particular, we find other more explicit reflections about the plausibility of the comparison drawn between the human and the fabulous

[17] Notice that the analogy is not so much in the use of "talking animals" which, as we are starting to notice, is a rather straightforward and naturalized resource in Greek discourse.

worlds. Classical rhetoric kept paying attention to this kind of composition, the fable, *muthos*, or *logos muthikos*, and its argumentative qualities by including it in the standard list of "preliminary rhetorical exercises" (*progymnasmata*) that every student should be able to construe by the end of his education. It made, thus, part of a literary and rhetorical training in which the student's skills for composition where mainly directed towards the goal of persuasion in civic life (Olmos 2012). In the earliest Greek extant treatise on rhetorical preliminary exercises that has come to us, Aelius Theon's *Progymnasmata* (1st c. CE), we find, consequently, a nice discussion about fables.

Theon seems here much more concerned than Aristotle with the possible problems posed by the unrealistic setting of this mythical genre. Theon's concerns make explicit some rather interesting points that will help us have a greater insight about the expected characteristics of fables from a rhetorical point of view, according to classical tradition.

In the first place, he refutes some extended ideas about a division of fables allegedly mentioned by Aristotle in his *Rhetoric* (1393a 30-31) between Libyan and Aesopic ones. Although the passage, as we know it, just mentions these two categories as well known references for identification purposes, traditional commentators would have talked about a explicit divide between fables in which just animals appear *vs.* fables with animals and men in them. Contrary to them, Theon claims that those where just different traditional collections of stories and that there was nothing interesting, in rhetorical terms, in such a division. Either with animals alone or with interacting men and animals, the setting would have been equally fabulous. We will see, though, that, even if Theon is probably right with respect to the literary history of the genre and its transmission, there might be some interesting variations, for our own purposes, between fables with men in them and all-animal fables, although, in the end, it would be better to talk about a certain gradation in realism and, therefore, in the possibilities of construing imaginative analogies. Different conceptions of speech and language use may also surface in these different kinds of fables, regardless of their being or not part of different traditions.

Theon mentions as well a rather typical initial formula used in the fabulist tradition he knew: "A man from Sybaris told that…", "A Libyan woman told that …" Theon claims[18] that this was a means to make the tale more palatable and minimize its implausibility as a remote event told by remote people.[19] This remark is a nice prelude to Theon's explicit concerns about the implausible character of fables which we will immediately review, but it does not seem a very promising suggestion. I would rather say that such formulae are part of the fable's literary metafictional setting, which, in many cases, also makes part of their transmission, and that they add nothing to the fable's credibility or plausibility. Many fables included contextual data about a specific situation in which they where supposedly told and used. In Aristotle's instances, we have seen how the fables mentioned include an attribution of authorship and an occasion that accounts for their conclusive and

[18] Theon attributes this idea to Aristotle, but it is not in the *Rhetoric* we have.

[19] In order, for the actual speaker, to avoid the onus or burden of proof.

persuasive character. We may interpret that Aristotle, writing a rhetorical textbook, is just giving us examples of the rhetorical use of the fables by certain "orators" in certain settings; but it is also true that such meta-fictional paraphernalia was, in many cases, part of the fables own literary transmission. So that arguers or orators could choose between a freshly new reuse of a certain fable, in their own setting for their own intended claim, or telling how a reputed person (Aesop, Stesichorus etc.) had used it in his own discoursive context. This latter case would add, to the complications we have already seen, a new layer of "argument by authority".[20]

In any case, notice that here we have made use of such "additional" and contextual data in order to analyze and ultimately assess the arguments potentially provided by the fables and that the conclusions drawn from them may have different degrees of concreteness or contextuality that will bear on the way the story supports them. Stesichorus and Aesop are represented as suggesting to their audiences specific conclusions for Himerans and Samians in their own situations, by alluding to simple similarities or more sophisticated analogies between the stories told and the real conditions surrounding their speeches. In contrast, well know fables with more general, fossilized and maximized *morals* could be finally used in contexts where the already earned reputation of such sententious conclusions could make of the attached story a mere illustration or explanation of how the principle works.

But going back to Theon's treatise, his already evident concern about the fable's plausibility and even, we could say, epistemic status is further developed in other claims. In *Prog.* § 72 he declares that "A fable is a fictitious story [i.e. false and invented] giving an image of [symbolizing] something which is true". In *Prog.* § 76, he specifies "the fablemaker himself acknowledges that what he writes is false and impossible, though plausible and useful". I will not go here into a detailed discussion of Theon's not very systematic doxastic vocabulary, but it is clear that he is trying to defend the argumentative appropriateness of the use of fables in spite of their initially suspicious epistemic assessment. Through the benefits of "symbolism" and "imagery", the fable presents to us something that ultimately might be critically evaluated as more or less plausible or better (in most cases) as more or less useful.

This should be taken into account when trying to contradict a fable. According to Theon, we cannot "use the topic of falsity" against the story, as it is openly false and most times impossible in its details.[21] We may just attack the fable by mentioning the "uselessness" or "impracticability" of its moral or gnomic saying (*logos gnōmikos*), or alternatively the "unlikely" character of its predictions (*Prog.* 77-78).

Now with all these epistemic cautions and interpretive complications, we may ask ourselves: why did fables kept being a privileged vehicle for prudent teaching and persuasion? Why choosing the impossible (animals talking and having reasonable attitudes) to represent the sphere of the plausible (humans behaving in their own real world) was considered a rhetorically and philosophically commendable

---

[20] Or "testimony" of an ancient, poetical and reputed source, as Aristotle puts it in *Rhet.* 1375b26-30.

[21] Although there are certain internal rules to the genre's acceptability that might have been clumsily violated: "for example if someone (…) called an ass wise or a fox stupid", *Prog.* 77.

means of arguing? We have seen that Aristotle did not see any problem at all, treating in almost the same way and under the same theoretical category real, invented and fabulous stories, as providing at least comparable standards to support or explain claims and recommendations applicable in civic life. Aelius Theon showed more concern about these issues, but tried to preserve the applicability and rhetorical significance of the genre while setting its limits.

Aristotle was, in any case, acknowledging a widespread ongoing and fully operational discursive phenomenon (probably as old as the species). Humans tell stories.[22] These narratives are partly explanatory of real events, partly invented, partly "based on the structure of reality", partly "founding the structure of reality" (Perelman and Olbrechts-Tyteca 1958). At any rate, stories cannot be a 1:1 scale picture of reality, which is, moreover, rather incomprehensible in its complexity, so there is always a principle of literary schematization involved, with all the possibilities of more or less stylized symbolism.

This is not the place, moreover, to make a full-fledged theory of the role humans chose for other animals in their narrative accounts, but it seems "totemic" ways of understanding human classification and stereotyping might provide us with some genealogical and naturalized explanation about the presence of animals in narratives regarding humans. At any rate, the *homo sapiens* seems to have, de facto, such kind of close relationship with animals: they are almost as animated as she is, and at the same time may seem less complicated and uniform within species, what makes stereotyping plausible. In socially stratified, diversified and complex societies, like Aristotle's own—and this is even more visible in much later writers like fabulist La Fontaine—the use of animals may also respond to a politically correct way of alluding to human types. Instead of mentioning nationalities, or social classes, one may always use animals.[23]

11.3 Fable Variety

But even taking storytelling and fable-making as a given, their use in persuasive speech (and in political speech in particular) is just a possibility that was, for some reason, fully developed within Greek culture.[24] But this does not mean that all fa-

[22] Let us think of the now pervasive denomination of our species as *homo narrans* (Niles 2010) or the more philosophically committed "narrative paradigm of rationality" endorsed by Fisher (1987). Victorri (2007) defends, moreover, the "role of narration in the emergence of human language".

[23] Cf. : La Fontaine, *Fables*, VII.1 "Les animaux malades de la peste".

[24] Political speech and practical decision making typically involve the kind of argumentation that Goodnight (2006) calls "Type II Complex Cases", in which a variety of criteria, belonging to different fields and standards (justice, honesty, feasibility, economy, etc.) might be used as reasons, with the subsequent difficulties in their relative weighing we are all so used to in our daily lives. That we deal with such cases by modelling possible scenarios and outcomes and imagining what it would be like in case of a certain step or decision taken is, therefore, rather reasonable.

bles look alike or work alike in argumentative or rhetorical terms. First of all, because, even within the genre, and within the classical collections of fables, there is a great variety regarding certain aspects that may play a role in shaping the kind of argumentation in which they might be involved.

We may assume that, in a typical fable, we find animals who act like human types in different situations and particularly talking and interacting among themselves and across species. It presents an ultimately "unrealistic", but usually very conventional and not at all arbitrary, fabulous setting and typically ends with a *moral* that might be more or less general or applicable within the realm of human life and action. In *The cat and the rooster* ([Aesop], Pe. 16), for example the animal protagonists talk, reason and argue, although what they do and say about themselves has a certain realistic touch to it.

The Cat and the Rooster

A cat had seized a rooster and wanted to find a reasonable pretext for devouring him. He began by accusing the rooster of bothering people by crowing at night, making it impossible for them to sleep. The rooster said that this was actually an act of kindness on his part, since the people needed to be woken up in order to begin their day's work. The cat then made a second accusation, "But you are also a sinner who violates nature's own laws when you mount your sisters and your mother." The rooster said that this also was something he did for his masters' benefit, since this resulted in a large supply of eggs. The cat found himself at a loss and said, "Well, even if you have an endless supply of arguments, I am still going to eat you anyway!"

The fable shows that when someone with a wicked nature has set his mind on committing some offence, he will carry out his evil acts openly even if he cannot come up with a reasonable excuse.

The *moral*—introduced by the typical formula "*ho logos dēloi hoti…*"—is a generalization, in principle for all-human cases, of the kind of situation showed in the story. It could be taken as a conclusion drawn from a fictitious and symbolic example or, reversely, the story could be interpreted as an explicative illustration of how the general principle works. It would depend on the real dialogue setting in which it is used and in which the speaker could also try to induce some more concrete lesson or advice related to her interlocutor's own situation. At any rate, the use of "instinctive" animals helps to maintain, more realistically than with humans, a presupposition working in this as well as in many other fables: i.e. that individuals have "fixed natures" according to which they will invariably act.

But we may find many variations on this model. First of all, not all fables feature all-animal interactions. However rarely, some include plants or objects.[25] More typical is the participation of human characters. And this poses an initial problem, because it is difficult to say beforehand whether these are or not closer to real cases. The imaginative interactions and dialogues between humans and animals showed in them may transport us to an even more fabulous setting. But sometimes it is just the opposite, as humans are shown in more or less realistic situations and their supposed dialogues with animals are not really essential to the plot, but represent certain aspects of their possible encounter, as we will later see.

---

[25] E.g.: *The oak tree and the reed,* [Aesop], Pe. 70; *The Trees and the Olive*, [Aesop], Pe. 262; *The Viper and the File*, [Aesop], Pe. 93; Cf. *Le pot de terre et le pot de fer*, La Fontaine, V.2.

Then, sometimes the original fable has reached us without a moral, or with a later added one (according to philological criticism); and with or without meta-fictional elements showing a certain discursive use of the apologue in a reported speech.[26] Another significant aspect we must examine about the *moral*—the usual suspect of acting as the argument's conclusion or claim—is whether it is itself intra-fictional or meta-fictional, i.e. if it is uttered within the story, by one of its characters, so that it is, in principle, a story about someone finally making an argument of any kind (which eventually, in another discursive setting, could be mirrored, more or less analogically, by a parallel argument presented by the fable's user, as in Aristotle's Aesopic example); or is expressed as a general claim or maxim, after the story is finished, typically dismissing the concrete story's details. In this latter case the whole fable with its moral might be presented as an argument in which the story, with its inner plausibility (be it realistic or symbolic), is put forward as a particular instance (an example or paradigm) supporting certain ideas about how things usually go.

11.4 Bear Fables

In order to further explore this complex variety in the Classical fable tradition, I will take advantage of an exploration I made some time ago, looking for fables with bears in them. My research reasons in such an occasion were rather disconnected to argumentation theory,[27] but the nice thing I learned is that the bear is not a typical animal in fables as are the lion, the fox or the omnipresent rook or jackdaw, and this is why bear fables are usually atypical. Moreover, it is very difficult to find a bear who really *talks*. It is considered a paradigmatically dumb and clumsy animal, although, on the other hand, very fierce and dangerous. We will therefore take a look at four bear fables in order to study their particularities and explore their argumentative possibilities.

The first one in my selection is called *The two friends and the bear* ([Aesop], Pe. 65; Avianus, 9) and is really the story of two men who simply find a dangerous bear along their route.

The two Friends and the Bear
Two fellows were travelling together through a wood, when a bear rushed out upon them. One of the travellers happened to be in front, and he seized hold of the branch of a tree, and hid himself among the leaves. The other, seeing no help for it, threw himself flat down upon the ground, with his face in the dust. The bear, coming up to him, put his muzzle close to his ear, and sniffed and sniffed. But at last with a growl he shook his head and slouched off,

[26] In most versions of the *The Swollen Fox* ([Aesop] Pe. 24; Babrius 86), for example, there is no explicit moral. Other versions add a traditionally attached one which is, nevertheless, rather awkward, as it really goes against the grain of the typical prudential wisdom associated with fables: "The fable shows that time solves all difficulties."

[27] My real aim was commenting on certain aspects of Werner Herzog's documentary film *Grizzly Man*, a film reviewing the real story of Timothy Treadwell who was attacked and devoured by a bear in the Katmai National Park (Alaska), during the summer of 2003 (Olmos forthcoming).

for bears will not touch dead meat. Then the fellow in the tree came down to his comrade, and, laughing, said "What was it that Master Bruin whispered to you?" "He told me," said the other, "Never trust a friend who deserts you at a pinch."

This is evidently a rather "realistic" fable. It is a story about two companions who find themselves in a dangerous situation and act differently. Although there are some words about what the bear has supposedly *said* to one of them, the bear, in fact, does not talk. We may even say that the second man, with his question about the bear's words, is just making an ironic allusion to fables, as a literary genre. There is no meta-fictional moral, but the protagonist himself utters a maxim which we may think acts as such inside the story, but there is not really any argument here. He has learned something about his companion, that he is capable of deserting him "at a pinch",[28] and he enunciates what seems to be a well known and reputed maxim (or *endoxon*) which will just be operative in his future dealings with him.

The fable seems almost an illustration of the pervasive relevance and widespread reputation of a more general claim which is, precisely, the principle to which Aristotle refers in relation with *paradeigmata* "based on facts": "What is coming will be for the most part similar to what has happened" (*Rhet.* 1394b5-6).[29] This principle could reasonably back the more concrete maxim: "Never trust a friend who deserts you at a pinch"; but this latter rule is not at all "supported" by the story as told, that would need at least a second instance of desertion to be relevant to such a claim. So the maxim, as uttered by the protagonist only announces his future intentions, as justified by his experience this time. If, in the future, someone would question his distrust towards this particular friend, he could use the event as a reason and probably warrant it with the maxim and even back it with Aristotle's principle. But that would be a different story.

The second of my bear fables belongs to the Latin collection written by fabulist Phaedrus and is called *The hungry bear* (Phaedrus CXXV). This one does not even look like a fable at all. It is absolutely realistic, almost a scientific, ethological note.

The Hungry Bear
Hunger sharpens the wits of animals. [Famen acuere animantibus ingenium]
If at any time sustenance is wanting to the Bear in the woods, he runs to the rocky shore, and, grasping a rock, gradually lets down his shaggy thighs into the water; and as soon as the Crabs have stuck to the long hair, betaking himself to shore, the crafty fellow shakes off his sea-spoil, and enjoys the food that he has collected in every quarter.
Thus even in fools does hunger sharpen the wits.

Neither is it exactly *narrative* as no concrete event is recounted. An animal habit is just described. But here we have, instead, a rather complete and self-standing argument (of a more theoretical import) which pretends to strengthen the plausibility of the supposedly reputed principle mentioned in its first line. By choosing to describe

[28] I personally do not see how he could have acted otherwise, but that is inconsequential here.

[29] I cannot see this principle, by the way, as any kind of empirical claim or statistical plausibility. As a prediction, it would randomly work out. I would rather consider it a prudential maxim to act "as if it were so", but Aristotle mentions it as warranting the use of real stories as precedents and examples supporting claims about present or future events.

not just any case in which the principle holds, but precisely one in which it could be expected not to hold, the fable proposes an *a fortiori* support to its main claim of the kind "*a maiore ad minorem*" (Vega 2012). If the claim is operative even in such a very difficult, *maior* case (hunger sharpening the wits of the stupidest of animals) it will plausibly be applicable in less demanding, *minor* cases, i.e. any other animal. Its dominion is thus enlarged and its general acceptability strengthened.[30]

In principle, we do not need to make any allusion to the world of men to interpret this fable which pretends to talk realistically about animals, although, the use of concepts such as "wits" or a "scale of *stultitia*" seems more akin to human experience and categorization than to zoological data. In the context of a collection of fables, with its moralistic and practical bent, this particular example could be read as presenting a case which would subsequently be used to establish parallels within the all-human world, with some more ethical or practical argumentative purpose in mind.[31] But, again, that would be a different story.

With the third example, we finally come to a more typical all-animal fable. In *The lion and the bear* ([Aesop] Pe. 147) these two animals fight for a prey and fall exhausted to see how a sly fox gets it without any effort.

The Lion and the Bear

A lion and a bear had found a fawn and were fighting to see who would keep it. In the protracted violence of the battle, they had both grown faint from fighting so they called a truce in order to rest. Meanwhile, there was a fox who had been pacing around them in circles. When she saw that they had fallen to the ground with the fawn lying between them, she dashed up, grabbed the fawn and took off at a run. The lion and the bear were not even able to get to their feet, so they sat there watching the fox disappear. "What fools we are," they said, "for having gone to so much trouble on that fox's behalf!"

The fable shows that while some people do all the work, others make off with the profit.

It is not very fabulous, though. The two fierce animals fight over a prey as they do in real life. Their more humanizing characteristics, "calling for a truce" or expressing their frustration in the final "shared" thought—not an utterance nor a real discursive interaction—are all very subtle. It could be read as a typical scene in a wild life TV documentary with a somewhat imaginative and rather poetic host and commentator, but there is nothing really extravagant in it.

The fable has come to us with an explicit meta-fictional moral containing a widely accepted claim about how things work in the world of human affairs. The narrative in the fable would, in principle, illustrate and explain more than support such an

[30] The "*a maiore*" clause is explicitly mentioned at the end of the text: "Thus even in fools does hunger sharpen the wits" ("Ergo etiam stultis acuit ingenium fames") as a conclusion directly extracted from the fable which, by means of the *a fortiori* principle, supports the "*ad minore*" clause which is the apparently more general but operatively less specific (and thus weaker) maxim. Note that this kind of argument does not work at all as an induction in which the more universal the claim, the stronger the theoretical commitment. The "*a fortiori* argument" presents different varieties, many of them close to analogies in being meta-argumentative (Marraud 2013a, pp. 242–244, 2013b).

[31] For example, in positively praising the capacity for survival and quickness of uneducated and underprivileged social classes or in proposing pedagogical methods based on creating at least intellectual and cognitive necessities to the privileged ones.

undisputed claim although it could also be analyzed as providing a naturalized and rather resigned account of it: if this is how it works in the natural world to which we also belong, it is an insurmountable condition. But, in such a case, there would be no parallel, nor similarity, drawn between a world of fable and the human world, but rather it would be precisely the *continuity* between both that would be emphasized as a reason for accepting the applicability of the principle in human affairs. In any case, this more elaborated interpretation would call for a suitable dialogical context in which the plausibility or applicability of the claim would be contested. And that is, of course, a very different story.

In my final example, coming from the second most important collection of Greek fables, those attributed to fabulist Babrius (Babrius 14, Pe. 288), we finally find a bear that talks and interacts discursively with its co-protagonist, the fox.

> **The Bear and the Fox**
> The bear boasted that he was exceptionally fond of mankind since, as he explained, bears don't pull dead people's bodies to pieces. The fox remarked, "I'd prefer that you mangled the dead ones, if you'd leave the living alone!"

Not only does the Bear talk, he makes a more complex and very *humanizing* "speech act": he "boasts"[32] that he "is exceptionally fond of mankind". Then, in support of his claim, he mentions one of his own characteristics: that he does not feed on dead bodies. So, the bear is, in fact, arguing and his interlocutor and respondent, the fox, will counter-argue by adding information to the premises (the bear may not touch human dead bodies but he attacks and kills humans when they are alive) and so undercutting the bear's argument (Pollock 1995).[33]

So the fable does not provide but portraits an argument, or better an argumentative exchange. In fact, more than a fable, it could be assimilated to another one of the classical rhetorical preliminary exercises or *progymnasmata*: namely, the *chreia* or anecdote in which, most times, an intellectual figure (typically a philosopher, a grammarian or a rhetor) expressed a witticism or made an ingenuous rejoinder in a given situation, usually a kind of dialogue of a more or less argumentative character. The fable is symbolic in its use of animals to play the roles of human types: the ignorant and strong boaster and the ingenious intellectual capable of beating him with a clever remark; but it is done in a very conventional, straightforward way, and it does not offer any sophisticated kind of analogy between different realms or fields.

The fable, moreover, has no meta-fictional moral, nor conclusion, what makes its formal features very close to those of the *chreia*. But an over-systematizing tradition provided, at some point, the following explicit *moral*, added to some of its versions: "If someone injures me while I am alive, do not let him weep over me when I am dead." This apocryphal moral is probably too simplistic and literal

---

[32] I.e. claims ostentatiously and vaingloriously, according to the Oxford English Dictionary.

[33] The way the fox expresses her counter-argument is, nevertheless, a little bit more complex, suggesting that the bear would be a better animal—and she would gladly grant his claim, i.e. that he "loves humans"—*if* he had opposite characteristics to those he really has, i.e. if he would devour the already dead and leave the living alone. As this is not so, and those characteristics are just ironically mentioned, the undercutting defeater makes its work.

as the appropriate lesson to be drawn from the fable. *The bear and the fox* does not talk, in my opinion, so much about hypocritical or pragmatically inconsistent behaviour as it does about hypocritical ways of self-justification. In supporting his claim that "he loves men" by mentioning, as evidence, his not disgracing their bodies when dead, the bear is, at the same time, suggesting that the correct explanation why he does not pull them to pieces is that he loves them; while a more realistic explanation is that he does not feed on dead flesh and, therefore, the human dead body is useless for him. So a better and more prudent practical lesson and advice extracted from this fable as a narrative example with negative consequences (for boasters) could be something like: "never boast that you do (not do) something out of goodness when it is (it is not) in your interest." Or, if what we want to counsel is the adoption of an intelligent and attentive attitude such as that of the fox, we could conclude something like "do not accept, or examine carefully, dubious justifications of deeds".

Another much more elaborate but conceivable use for this fable, with its intra-fictional argumentative exchange, could be the construction of a complete analogical and double, meta-argument plus meta-counter-argument in which a speaker would parallel the fox's successful rejoinder before a certain interlocutor, in her own setting and referring to a different case and field of reference. If, for example, someone would claim that "President Bush was very generous with the Iraqi people, because he employed many resources [e.g. expending public money and sacrificing soldiers' lives] to liberate them," the opponent could say something as "what you say reminds me of a bear that, in a certain occasion, boasted before a fox that etc…", making thus the first argument by analogy. As, expectedly, both arguments would be found equally weak and vulnerable, the speaker could go on mirroring the fox's undercutting strategy and counter-arguing (within a second analogy) "Bush would have been much more generous if he had kept the American resources instead of spending them in making available for his friends and cronies the riches of Iraq". But, of course, that would constitute a completely different argumentative exchange in a very different story.

11.5 Conclusions

In approaching the genre of the classical fable from an argumentative point of view, we started with two very basic ideas: that certain narratives may involve arguments in some way or another and that these traditional, short and typically prudential texts were appropriate candidates for such a kind of research. We saw, moreover, that within the field of argumentation studies there have been, in fact, some recent attempts to tackle this genre (or other very close ones such as the parables) albeit probably in too generalizing and abstract terms. Classical rhetorical textbook provided us with certain reflections on the argumentative and persuasive characteristics of the fables which were closer to the original usage, in diverse contexts, of these discursive resources.

We have seen, though, that the attempts to capture the way they worked in argumentative speech presented some difficulties. Aristotle's rather confused category of *paradeigma* as "rhetorical induction", while correctly reporting some significant and contextualized instances and reasonably admitting the pervasive and naturalized usage of fictive stories alongside more "realistic" paradigmatic arguments, established a unitary approach and vocabulary which, taken as a theoretical framework, could and did in fact hide a more interesting variety. Theon's epistemic concerns and clarifications and his insistence on the incredible and impossible character of the fabulous premises, while correctly stressing an interesting play between fiction and practicality, between useful imagination and symbolism, probably focused too much on a stark contrast between two allegedly separate worlds (that of the fictive story *vs*. that of the epistemically assessable moral or *gnomic saying*) whose boundaries are not so easy to establish when we come to the actual examples.

Because, if we start looking carefully at the traditional collections of fables, what we find is a much wider variety of literary and argumentative possibilities: settings, interplays, characters, etc. There are, of course, some generic traits but each piece is different and deserves a more or less particularized approach. Moreover, what we find in such collections are somewhat artificially preserved and fossilized literary fragments which, in order to be analyzed and evaluated from an argumentative point of view, should be set in an adequate argumentative context (just as Aristotle did with his own instances of different *paradeigmata*). Fables contain, in general, good material for argumentative usage in different settings but that does not mean that they are, as such, and as transmitted, always unitary and uniform arguments, least of all of exactly the same kind.

In this sense, we have seen the perils of too rapidly invoking the term analogy when dealing with fables. A more sophisticated and precise notion of analogical argument as something distinct from arguments by similarity, by example or generalizations (in Perelman's terms) might help us deal more carefully with our fabulist examples. These may, typically, make use of what we can still call an *analogical* understanding of narration.[34] Surely a narrative paradigm of reason, such as the one advanced by Fisher, might help us start looking at the way our narratives establish plausible theoretical and practical frameworks for the human understanding of the human world. However, these general ideas, calling for a more insightful philosophical treatment of certain basic and cognitive aspects of our narrative reasoning and discourse, should not drive us to even out our conveniently detailed and contextualized examination of the argumentative characteristics, specific schemes, possible dialogical interchanges and rhetorical uses associated to our rich and varied fabulist heritage.

[34] Cf. Woods and Hudak (1989, p. 125): "Analogy is rife in the lives of certain species. It scarcely seems possible that we ourselves could do without it. We have analogical predication, analogical pattern recognition, analogical explanation, analogical inference, and analogical argument (…) Some may find it surprising that analogical argument differs from analogical inference. More surprisingly still is the suggestion that analogical predication differs from analogical argument, not just in the way predication differs from argument, but in rather more striking ways that suggest the unlikelihood that they exemplify a single, unified idea of analogy".

Acknowledgments This research has been made possible by funds provided by both the UNED Research Project's Programme (Project 2012V/PUNED/0010, "Narrativity and Argumentation: Discursive Basis of Plausibility") and the Spanish Ministry of Economy and Competitiveness (Research Project: FFI2011-23125, "Arguing in the Public Sphere: Deliberation as a Paradigm").

References

Bermejo-Luque, L. 2012. A unitary schema for arguments by analogy. *Informal Logic* 32:1–24.
Fisher, W. R. 1987. *Human communication as narration: Toward a philosophy of reason, value, and action*. Columbia: University of South Carolina Press.
Goodnight, T. 2006. Complex cases and legitimation inference. In *Arguing on the Toulmin model,* eds. D. Hitchcock and B. Verheij, 39–48. Dordrecht: Springer.
Govier, T. 2001. *A practical study of argument*. Belmont: Wadsworth/Thomson Learning.
Govier, T., and L. Ayers. 2012. Logic and parables: Do these narratives provide arguments? *Informal Logic* 32:161–189.
Hunt, L. H. 2009. Literature as fable, fable as argument. *Philosophy and Literature* 33:369–385.
Klump, J. F. 2006. Warranting arguments, the virtue of verb. In *Arguing on the Toulmin model,* eds. D. Hitchcock and B. Verheij, 103–114. Dordrecht: Springer.
Marraud, H. 2013a. *¿Es logic@? Análisis y evaluación de argumentos*. Madrid: Cátedra.
Marraud, H. 2013b. Variedades de la argumentación *a fortiori*. *Revista Iberoamericana de Argumentación* 6:1–17.
Munson, R. 1976. *The way of words: An informal logic*. Boston: Houghton Mifflin.
Niles, J. D. 2010. *Homo narrans. The poetics and anthropology of oral literature*. Philadelphia: University of Pennsylvania Press.
Olmos, P. 2007. 'Las Sentencias de un renglón' (1586) de Pedro Simón Abril: Un repertorio al servicio de la gramática, la retórica y la dialéctica… sin faltar a la moral. *Pandora. Revue d'Études Hispaniques* 7:137–154.
Olmos, P. 2011. From laconic apophthegms to film quotations: Using testimonies from reputed authorities. In *The promise of reason: Semi-centennial studies in the new rhetoric,* ed. J. Gage, 223–235. Carbondale: Southern Illinois University Press.
Olmos, P. 2012. Two literary encyclopaedias from late antiquity. *Studies in History and Philosophy of Science* 43:284–292.
Olmos, P. 2014. Narration as argument. In *Virtues of Argumentation. Proceedings of the 10th International Conference of the Ontario Society for the Study of Argumentation (OSSA), 22–26 May 2013*, eds. D. Mohammed and M. Lewiński. Windsor: OSSA.
Olmos, P. forthcoming. Grizzly Man. ¿Qué enseña la fábula? In *Animales políticos. Ensayos sobre la figura del animal en la teoría política,* eds. J. Cano and F. Pezzoli. Madrid: Ediciones Clásicas.
Perelman, C., and L. Olbrechts-Tyteca. 1958. *Traité de l'argumentation. La nouvelle rhétorique*. Paris: Presses Universitaires de France.
Piazza, S. di. 2012. Stochastic knowledge: For the most part and conjecture in aristotle. In *Greek science in the long run,* ed. P. Olmos, 78–95. Newcastle upon Tyne: Cambridge Scholars Publishing.
Plumer, G. 2011. Novels as arguments. In *Proceedings of the 7th Conference of the International Society for the Study of Argumentation (ISSA 2010)*, eds. F. H. van Eemeren, et al. Amsterdam: Sic Sat.
Pollock, J. L. 1995. *Cognitive carpentry*. Cambridge: MIT Press.
Vega, L. 2012. A contrario/a fortiori/a pari/a simili, argumentos. In *Compendio de Lógica, Argumentación y Retórica,* eds. L. Vega and P. Olmos, 15–16. Madrid: Trotta.

Victorri, B. 2007. *Homo narrans*: The role of narration in the emergence of human language. http://halshs.archives-ouvertes.fr/halshs-00153724. Accessed 21 July 2013.
Walton, D. 2012. Story similarity in arguments from analogy. *Informal Logic* 32:190–221.
Walton, D., C. Reed, and F. Macagno. 2008. *Argumentation schemes*. Cambridge: Cambridge University Press.
Woods, J., and B. Hudak. 1989. By parity of reasoning. *Informal Logic* 9:125–139.

Chapter 12
Analogies in Scientific Explanations: Concept Formation by Analogies in Cultural Evolutionary Theory

Christian J. Feldbacher

12.1 Introduction

In this paper we investigate a paradigmatic case of introducing concepts into theories via analogies. We will do so by concentrating on the controversial discussion about the meme-gene-analogy in cultural evolutionary theory.

An almost self-suggesting question regarding theories of cultural evolution concerns their very basic notion: How could meme theories explain diversity in culture, if cultural evolutionary theorists disagree so widely about the meaning of the basic vocabulary of their theories, especially about the meaning of the expression 'meme'? A more explicit argument underlying this question can be stated as follows:

1. Gene theories allow us to explain diversity in nature.
2. Meme theories aim at an explanation of diversity in culture.
3. Some people think that memes are "the software of the brain".
4. Other people think that memes are all kinds of information stored in brains, libraries, computers, states of affairs etc.
5. Hence, since 'meme' is a basic notion of cultural evolutionary theories, this diversity in meaning prevents the theory of cultural evolution from providing an explanation of diversity in culture.

Obviously this is no logically valid argument, but one may consider the premises of the argument as providing convincing reasons for the conclusion of the argument. In the following sections we will argue against such a view by showing that, although the expression 'meme' is used quite ambiguously by cultural evolutionary theorists, the concepts of cultural evolutionary theories are introduced by analogies allowing such a diversity without lack of precision, but at the cost of specificity in the sense of high informational content.

C. J. Feldbacher (✉)
Duesseldorf Center for Logic and Philosophy of Science,
University of Duesseldorf, Duesseldorf, Germany
e-mail: christian.feldbacher@gmail.com

H. J. Ribeiro (ed.), *Systematic Approaches to Argument by Analogy*,
Argumentation Library 25, DOI 10.1007/978-3-319-06334-8_12,

In order to keep technicalities quite general, we limit our investigation to a very rudimentary description of concept formation by analogies (Sect. 12.2). We will then present the analogy between natural and cultural evolution used by cultural evolutionary theorists (Sect. 12.3). We will do so in a three-fold step: First we present a general form of the analogy (Sect. 12.3.1). Then we present a formalized form and discuss the analogy in more detail (Sect. 12.3.2). And finally we will show that the analogies drawn in this area allow for a quite diverse meaning of the expression 'meme' (Sect. 12.3.3).

12.2 Concept Formation by Analogies

In scientific explanations and descriptions analogies and conclusions by analogies are frequently used. Indicators for analogical reasoning and analogical use of language are comparing phrases as, e.g., "similar as", "likewise", "analogically" etc. A very common analogy within science is the comparison of water in a pipe with current in a conductor. A shortened analogical description of this example would be 'Electric current in a conductor is like water in a pipe.' Take, e.g., the law of Hagen–Poiseulle (L1) and Ohm's law (L2):

$$\text{L1} \quad p_1 - p_2 \equiv \frac{V}{c} \quad (V \ldots \text{volume of fluid}, c \ldots \text{speed}, p_i \ldots \text{pressure})$$

$$\text{L2} \quad v_1 - v_2 \equiv \frac{I}{k} \quad (I \ldots \textbf{amperage}, k \ldots \text{conductance}, v_i \ldots \textbf{potential})$$

As one can see, both laws run straightforward analogously. Now, it is well known that c varies indirectly proportional with the length of the pipe:

$$\text{L3} \quad c \sim \frac{1}{l_1} \quad (l_1 \ldots \text{length of the pipe})$$

Analogical to this fact it holds that k varies indirectly proportional with the length of the conductor:

$$\text{L4} \quad k \sim \frac{1}{l_2} \quad (l_2 \ldots \text{length of the conductor})$$

So there is also another regularity running straightforward analogously in the source and the target domain. Furthermore it holds that:

$$\text{L5} \quad V \sim r_1^4 \quad (r_1 \ldots \text{radius of the pipe})$$

And so the question arises whether there holds also a similar regularity in the target domain? But here one can show that it only holds (not similarly) that:

$$\text{L6} \quad I \sim r_2^2 \quad (r_2 \ldots \text{radius of the conductor})$$

Analogical usage of language about two different domains (e.g., physics of liquids and electromagnetism) is given here in the sense that some descriptions of regularities are syntactically isomorph, that is: $V \mapsto I, c \mapsto k, p_i \mapsto v_i$ and vice versa.

Already with the help of this example the main problem of analogical usage of language can be stated quite easily: Which descriptions of regularities within one domain of investigation are adequately adoptable for descriptions of regularities within another domain of investigation?

The simplest and up to now most accepted solution to this problem is a restrictive definition (cf. Hempel 1970, p. 434): Instead of defining "expression e_1 is analogue to expression e_2" one just defines "expression e_1 is analogue to expression e_2 with respect to regularity φ". According to this solution it holds, e.g., that I is analogue to V with respect to L1 and L2, but not with respect to L5 and L6.

To make a little bit more technical sense of such a characterization we define a (partial) one-one mapping is on the language under investigation. Let's assume a standard first-order language L, containing the usual connectives and logical signs: ~, &, (the other connectives are assumed to be introduced by the usual meta-linguistic conventions), $\forall, \equiv, x_1, \ldots$ as well as terms and predicate signs $t_1, \ldots, P_1^n, \ldots$ (for all $n \in N$) in the vocabulary. Then we characterize is for the descriptive vocabulary as follows (for all $n, m \in N$):

- $is(t_n) \in \{t_i : i \in N\}$ (where individual variables are mapped by the identity relation)
- $is(P_m^n) \in \{P_i^n : i \in N\}$

And then generalize is inductively:

- For all atomic formulas $P^n(t_1, \ldots, t_n): is(P^n(t_1, \ldots, t_n)) = is(P^n)(is(t_1), \ldots, is(t_n))$
- For all terms $t_1,\ t_2 : is(t_1 \equiv t_2) = is(t_1) \equiv is(t_2)$
- For all formulas $\varphi: \boldsymbol{is}(\sim \varphi) = \sim \boldsymbol{is}(\varphi)$
- For all formulas $\varphi, \psi : \boldsymbol{is}(\varphi \,\&\, \psi) = \boldsymbol{is}(\varphi) \,\&\, \boldsymbol{is}(\psi)$
- For all formulas φ and variables $x : \boldsymbol{is}(\forall x \varphi) = \forall x \boldsymbol{is}(\varphi)$

(We also assume that the signs of arithmetic stay, like the logical signs, unchanged by is .) According to such a mapping it holds for our example of fluid physics and electromagnetism above that $is(I) = V, is(v_i) = p_i, is(k) = c$ and $is(l_2) = is(l_1)$. And so we can describe the analogical relation between these two domains simply by the regularity claims: $L1 \rightarrow is(L1), L3 \rightarrow is(L3)$. And these analogical relations can be restated logically equivalent as:

$$L1 \rightarrow (is(L1) \leftrightarrow L1)$$

$$L3 \rightarrow (is(L3) \leftrightarrow L3)$$

which may be seen as conditionalized contextual definitions of: I, k, v_i and l_2. To generalize this formulation: If e_1 and e_2 are analogue with respect to $\varphi[e_2]$ (where the square brackets after a formula around an expression serves here just as an indicator for the occurrence of the expression in the formula), then e_1 is introduced with the help of e_2 and $\varphi[e_2]$ by partial contextual definitions of the form:

$$\varphi[e_2] \rightarrow (is(\varphi)[e_1] \leftrightarrow \varphi[e_2])$$

The concept formation by analogies is only contextual since the usage of an expression is not clarified at the level of the signs of the vocabulary, but only at the level of formulas. And the formation is only partial since the usage is only clarified in contexts for which the analogy is assumed to hold, so it is conditioned on the source analogy.

One may note that there are two main problems with such a characterization of concepts: Firstly, there is the problem of distinguishing contextual definitions from any other kind of non-definitional axioms. Since we provide no further analysis of the contexts of such characterizations, one cannot draw an exact borderline between these two kinds of creative and non-eliminative theory-extension. But for our purposes of an analysis of the gene-meme-analogy in cultural evolutionary theory we do not need such a further analysis of the context—we will point out very general structural properties characterized by the gene-meme-analogy here only. And secondly, there is the problem of a conditionalized multiple characterization of an expression by analogical concept formation. Take, e.g., the regularities L1–L4 of the example above. If L2 and L4 are regarded as a contextual definition of structural properties between concepts of electromagnetism, conditioned on the relevant regularities of fluid physics L1 and L3 respectively, then, e.g., the relational properties of conductance k are characterized multiple times. In cases where the conditions of such a characterization are logically exclusive, a multiple characterization does no harm to a theory's consistency. On the contrary, it even increases eliminability of k in more contexts. But in cases where the conditions are not logically exclusive, such a characterization my end up with inconsistencies within the expanded theory and by this is harmful. Also this problem will be not treated here further because in our application to the gene-meme-analogy we will have to do with a conditioning on exactly one regularity only.

12.3 The Gene-Meme Analogy

Richard Dawkins (1976) spends one highly influential chapter (Chap. 11) for a—also to his mind—quite speculative analogy in his book *The selfish gene* in which he elaborates the idea that the basic units for evolutionary investigations should be neither populations nor single organisms, but replicators like genes. The mentioned analogy is the so-called gene-meme analogy which was since then used widely and very controversial in cultural evolutionary theory. In the following three subsections we will give a general sketch of the analogy, provide a formalization of it and finally discuss the diversity of the analogical characterization of the expression 'meme' in the context of the given formalization.

12.3.1 General Form of the Analogy

In order to extract the general form of the analogy, we first have to characterize—although very sketchily—the source domain of the analogy, namely natural evolution.

One insight Charles Darwin achieved during his detailed investigations of lots of biological species is the idea that in constructing biological models for describing the development of species one should take care of at least three parameters, namely a parameter for replication, one for variation and one for selection:

> Darwinian theory's (...) essential elements are simply replication, variation and selection. If these requirements are met then evolution seems bound to happen. If organisms reproduce, passing their characteristics almost (but not always quite) accurately on to the next generation, and if their environment does not supply them with unlimited resources for their survival, then they will evolve (...). (Distin 2005, p. 2)

So, according to Darwin's theory of evolution (*The Origin of Species*, 1869) there are three conditions needed to be satisfied within a system in order to count as a system of evolution (cf. Schurz 2011, p. 192):

1. *Reproduction*: There are subsystems or organisms which reproduce themselves with respect to some important properties. These properties are called "reproduced or inherited properties" and every process of reproduction creates a new generation.
2. *Variation*: The reproduction leads to variation which is also inherited.
3. *Selection*: There is selection, because some variants are fitter under the given environmental circumstances than others, i.e.: They reproduce themselves faster than others. By this some other variants are eliminated in the long run. The selecting parameters of the environment are called "*selection parameters*".

So, the schema of the source analogy may be symbolized as in Fig. 12.1. Sometimes also another condition for a system to be an evolutionary system is stated: In order to establish some complexity and regularities in an evolutionary system, a further condition is needed:

4. *Stability*: For directed evolution also a fourth condition, the condition of stability of the selecting forces is needed. This means that the changing rate of the selecting forces is little with respect to the generation rate (cf. Schurz 2011, p. 192).

We will be quite undecided here whether this condition should hold for evolutionary systems or not since in the general discussion of the gene-meme-analogy this condition for the source domain is not expanded to the target domain.

Since we have indicated the most relevant parts of the source domain of the analogy here, namely that of natural evolution, we can try now to expand these parts to the target domain, namely cultural evolution! Dawkins' main idea in *The selfish gene* was to ground the investigations of the conditions for systems of natural evolution at the level of genes. Reproduction, variation, and selection (especially fitness) is not only considered with respect to whole organisms, but with respect to genes. So, in Dawkins' theory the replicators are of main importance. According to his view, organisms are their "devised survival machines".

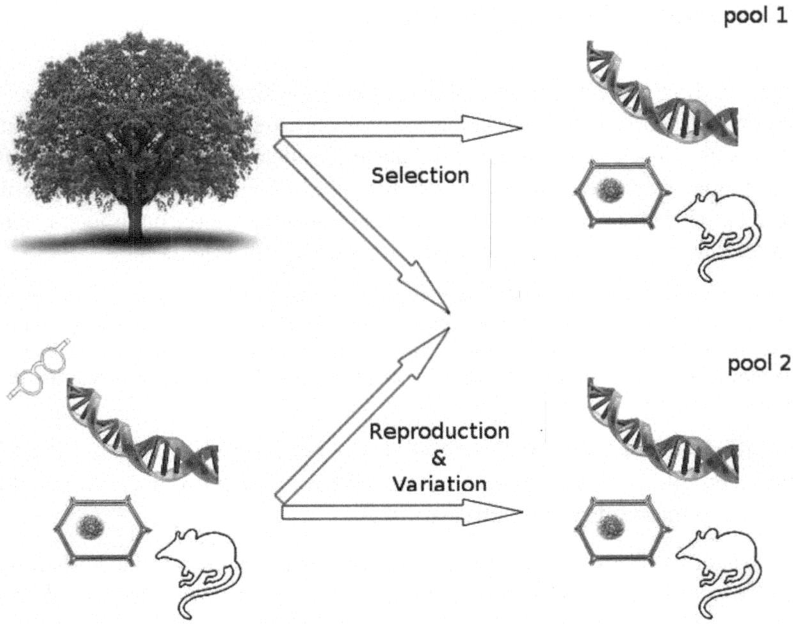

Fig. 12.1 Rudimentary schema of natural evolution The development of a population is influenced by a selection parameter (in general determined by the habitat the population lives in), a variation parameter (including variation through recombination and variation through mutation) and a parameter for reproduction (including information about the distribution of different properties among the species)

A typical way of expanding a successful theory is to expand its domain. In the words of Dawkins: "Darwinism is too big a theory to be confined to the narrow context of the gene." (Dawkins 1976, p. 191). But if the theory of natural evolution should be expanded to other domains as, e.g., the domain of culture, then, in the replicator-centered view of Dawkins, one also needs a more general and expanded form of a replicator. And especially in order to illustrate a universal and substrate-neutral replicator-centered theory of evolution, Dawkins introduced the expression "meme". So the idea was to widen the domain of evolutionary theory from $D = set\ of\ genes$ to $D = set\ of\ genes\ and\ memes$. Since then many philosophers and scientists interested in cultural theory joined the programme of expanding basic parts of the theory of natural evolution to a theory of cultural evolution. Important figures within this programme are, e.g.: Dawkins (1976), Dennett (1992), Blackmore (1999), Aunger (2000) and Schurz (2011).

We should also mention here that an expansion of the domain by new replicators is not the only possible and performed way of widening evolutionary theory. An alternative expansion of natural evolutionary theory to a theory of cultural evolution is attempted, e.g., within sociobiology. Alternatively to the introduction of new replicators it was tried to cope with cultural evolution by some kind of reductionism which allows one to reduce cultural phenomena to biological ones. Founding father of this movement was Edward Wilson with the main idea to try to find genetic patterns whose "extended phenotype" are cultural properties.

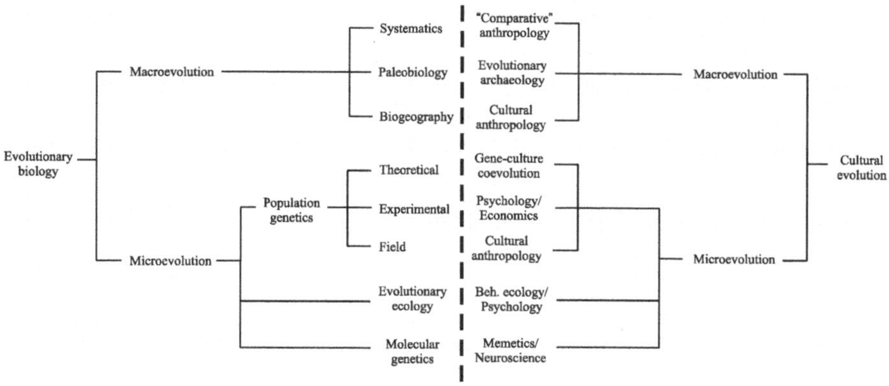

Fig. 12.2 Major subdivisions within evolutionary biology and corresponding disciplines of cultural evolution. (Mesoudi et. al. 2006, p. 331)

The main difference between sociobiology and meme-theories of cultural evolution is that whereas in sociobiology the phenotypes are settled at the neuronal level and the replicators within an evolutionary system are genes, in memetics the phenotypes are settled at the cultural level and the replicators are memes. Before we go on with the description of some more general parts of the target domain of the gene-meme-analogy, we just mention two important problems for the reductionistic programme of sociobiology: First, there is a shortage of material in the reductionistic programme, since genetically there are too less combinations possible to cope with electrochemical states of multiple neurons by base pairs. And second, there are too high differences in the speed of the processes going on in natural and cultural evolution in order to be adequately coped by the reductionistic programme, since cultural evolution is too fast in order to become manifest in natural evolution (cf. Distin 2005, p. 15).

As was pointed out by Mesoudi et al. (2006) and is depicted in Fig. 12.2, also in favour of the programme of meme-theories of cultural evolution is the fact that many more or less established disciplines of cultural theory can be mapped almost directly in analogy to a discipline of evolutionary biology.

The general form of the gene-meme-analogy consists in a mapping of the replicators of natural evolution, the genes, to the replicators of cultural evolution, the memes. Based on this mapping is the mapping of parameters. Whereas there is a parameter for reproduction, variation and selection in the source domain, there are also assumed analogous parameters for reproduction, variation and selection in the target domain. So, in constructing models for cultural phenomena one should seek for parameters of cultural reproduction, cultural variation and cultural selection acting on memes.

In order to find such parameters it is convenient to have a more or less concrete characterization of memes available. Although—and this is sometimes stressed by cultural evolutionary theorists against the criticism on the diversity of the interpretation of their basic concepts—also in natural evolutionary theory successes could be observed without a detailed knowledge of genes and their reproduction and variation behaviour, the natural evolutionary programme got a really boost since the gene-system was discovered and investigated on a chemical basis. Cultural evolutionary theorists hope to achieve a similar boost by clarifying the notion of a meme. But until now they are far away from a clear and concrete characterization of this notion—and this not only due to the diversity of an understanding of the expression 'meme'. Here is a list of the quite different meanings (and objections made against them) used by the most important followers of the cultural evolutionary programme:

- *Imitable entities*: Memes are all things that are capable of being imitated (cf. Dawkins 1976; Blackmore 1999):

  > We need a name for the new replicator, a noun that conveys the idea of a unit of cultural transmission, or a unit of imitation. "Mimeme" comes from a suitable Greek root, but I want a monosyllable that sounds a bit like "gene". I hope my classicist friends will forgive me if I abbreviate mimeme to meme. (…) It should be pronounced to rhyme with "cream". Examples of memes are tunes, ideas, catch-phrases, clothes fashions, ways of making pots or of building arches. (Dawkins 1976, p. 192)

  Blackmore:

  > Memes are not best understood as semantic information stored in brains, but rather, as whatever is imitated or copied in culture. (Susan Blackmore in her comment "Why we need memetics" to Mesoudi et al. (2006), p. 349)

  and: memes are independent of brain activity etc. because they are also "selfish":

  > Memetic evolution constructed human brains and is now building better, higher fidelity meme machines, including computers, the Internet, and digital media. For the moment we humans are essential to the further evolution of the memosphere, but there are already many memes created that never have contact with a human being, and there will be more. (Susan Blackmore in her comment "Why we need memetics" to Mesoudi (2006), p. 350)

- *Information*: Memes are acquired information, also storable outside of the brain, as, e.g., in books and computers (cf. Dennet 1992):

  > Equivalent to the genotype-phenotype (or replicator-interactor) distinction in culture (…) we can speak of culturally acquired semantic information stored in brains as replicators and the expression of that information in behaviour or artefacts as their interactors. (Mesoudi et al. 2006, p. 344)

  Contra: Meme-phenotype-distinction becomes vague.

- *Brain dispositions*: Memes are dispositions of the brain to store (represent) information and cause behaviour (cf. Schurz 2011, p. 213).

  Contra: Incoherent meme-histories:

  > if there were only minds and no external RS [Representation System] in which information could more permanently be stored, then memetic replication would lose much of its present stability. (Distin 2005, p. 90)

- *Brain software*: Memes are software parts of the brain (cf. Dawkins 1982, p. 109).

Contra: Too early stage of neuroscience.

- *Neuromemes*: Memes are electrochemical states of multiple neurons, so-called "neuromemes", i.e. configurations in one node of a neuronal network that is able to induce the replication of its state in other nodes (cf. Aunger 2000)

> Aunger (2000) has recently attempted to integrate memetics with neuroscience, arguing that a robust conceptualisation of the "meme" must specify its material basis in the brain. He proposes that memes should be seen as electrochemical states of multiple neurons, and offers a definition of a "neuromeme" as "a configuration in one node of a neuronal network that is able to induce the replication of its state in other nodes." (Mesoudi 2006, p. 343)

Contra: Too early stage of neuroscience.

Although there is such a diversity of meanings, almost all proponents of cultural evolution agree in the following desiderata for an explication of the "meme"-notion:

- *Reproducibility*: They must be reproducible, not only syntactically understood, which would be mechanistically, but also semantically, e.g. by imitation, but more generally by social learning activities as teaching etc. (cf. Distin 2005, Chap. 4). Compare also Dawkins' condition of *fecundity* of a replicator.
- *A not too high variation rate*: Their variation rate must not be too high. Cf. Dawkins' test: An order—e.g., in a drawing—must be recognizable (cf. Distin 2005, p. 104). Compare also his condition of *copying fidelity* of a replicator.
- *A not too low variation rate*: If the variation rate is too low, e.g. in almost perfect information copy machines as computers, then evolution comes to a standstill.

So the criticism that the very basic notion of cultural evolutionary theory is too diverse to be fruitful can be, at least for the moment, answered by a core meaning of this notion consisting in the—obviously very general—property of being reproducible and adequately variable. Nevertheless the programme of cultural evolutionary theory is not as uncontroversial as the "canonization" above might feign. Other and here not further discussed criticism of this programme can be summarized as follows (cf. Mesoudi et al. 2006, p. 343):

- *Discernibility*: Culture cannot be divided into discrete units (cf., e.g., Maurice Bloch).

Contra:

> However, the same putative "criticism" could equally be levelled at modern concepts of the gene. (...) The concept of the gene has undergone significant changes through the past 150 years. The classical view, held from the time of Mendel (1866) until the 1930s, [also] saw the gene as an indivisible unit of transmission, recombination, mutation, and function. (Mesoudi et al. 2006, p. 343)

And:

> Already, one can perceive the beginnings of what has been called a "social cognitive neuroscience" that aims to integrate all the required levels of analysis. (Mesoudi et al. 2006, p. 343)

- *Dissimilarities*: They outweigh similarities to a very high degree.
- *Generality*: Similarities are too general in order to be fruitful.
- *Terminology doubling*: Meme-talking is redundant. What we need is only to talk about the "phenotypes" as usual.
- *Inadequate Framework*:

> Mathematical models are potentially as useful for culture as for evolution, but cultural models must have different designs from genetic models. Social sciences must borrow from biology the idea of modelling, rather than the structure of models, because copying the product is fundamentally different from copying the design. (Bruce Bridgeman in his comment "It is not evolutionary models, but models in general that social science needs" to Mesoudi et al. (2006), p. 351)

To summarize this section we mention again that the main part of the gene-meme-analogy's source domain are the parameters reproduction, variation and selection in constructing models for the development of populations (considered at the level of genes). One extension of natural evolution to cultural evolution is the programme of sociobiology which tries to explain cultural phenomena reductionistically by showing that they depend on specific genetic patterns. Two main drawbacks of sociobiology are the problem of less material for genetically coding cultural information and the problem of adequately coding rapid cultural evolution by quite slow natural evolution. An alternative proposed by Dawkins is an extension of the domain of natural evolution to a domain also containing cultural replicators, namely memes. In favour of such a research programme is the fact that many disciplines of cultural theory can be mapped to analogous theories of biology. But when it comes to a clarification of the meme-concept, then the scientific community disagrees widely. Nevertheless there are two properties of memes it agrees on, namely the property of being replicable and the property of being adequately variable. Besides the critique that these are very general properties, there is also further heavy critique against the programme of cultural evolutionary theory as mentioned directly above.

Before we come to our formalization of the gene-meme-analogy in the next section, we make a short excursus that should—although only very marginally—support the programme of cultural evolution.

Excursus: Fruitfulness of the Expansion for Natural Evolution?

As we have mentioned already in the introduction, cultural evolutionary theorists hope to explain within this research programme cultural diversity and cultural phenomena similar successful as natural evolutionary theorists did explain diversity of species. Nevertheless it is very often criticised that this programme doesn't add anything substantial to cultural theory. So it is argued that cultural evolutionary theory is useless for cultural theory. In this excursus we will concentrate on another direction, namely on the question whether an expansion of natural evolutionary theory to a cultural evolutionary theory could be of some use for biology?

(This question concerns the topic of importing theses about the (originally) target domain of an analogy into the (originally) source domain of the analogy which is to invert the target and source domain of an analogy.)

It is not uncommon in the philosophy of biology to consider the most relevant part of a gene to be the information stored in it and the change of information to be the relevant place of seeking exact parameters for reproduction, variation and selection (for a critical discussion of this view and references cf. Mahner and Bunge (1997), Sect. 9.3.4). But this view of evolution seems to come concrete only in investigations that show how to parametrize models according to information stored in genes. One such an investigation is provided, e.g., in Vitányi et al. (2008, p. 53). The idea of Paul M. B. Vitányi et al. is to achieve a measure of semantic closeness via a complexity and information measure. For our purpose we don't have to go into much detail, but the procedure is as follows: Some data is binary coded and evaluated according to its complexity measure, where the complexity of a binary sequence is measured by the possibility of describing the sequence in a shorter way within a specific description (compression) system. The less short a description of a binary sequence is, the more complex it is (try, e.g. to describe the sequences $s_1 = 011011\ldots$ and $s_2 = 0101\ldots$ within a description system offering only operations for reading and writing a value (*val*), accessing the successor (′) of the nth place (starting: 0) and the boolean operations of negation (~) and conjunction (&)—solution in the footnote[1]). By measuring the distance between the complexity of binary sequences, one ends up with an information distance measure (assumption: the more similar the complexity of some data is, the more similar is the information stored in the data). And with the help of such an information distance measure one can try to cluster data. An interesting result of Vitányi et al. is that also by binary coding the chemical information of the DNA of different species, applying the above procedure of measuring the complexity as well as the information distance and then order the data according to these measures one ends up with an adequate tree about the origin of species. Figure 12.4 depicts such an ordering of species due to the provided information measure. Figure 12.3 depicts an ordering of music pieces with the help of this information measure.

The point to be highlighted here is that by inverting the source and target domain of the gene-meme-analogy one may also end up with new theses that are relevant for the theory of natural evolution. Memes, interpreted as (genetic) information, and reproduction, variation and selection parameters for informational content may serve somewhere along the way for clarifying, e.g., traditional classification problems of biology etc.

---

[1] The shortest description of s_1 within the description system is $val(0) = 0; \mathbf{val}(0') = 1; val(n'') = \sim(val(n)\&val(n'))$; with the length 46. The shortest description of s_2 within this description system is $val(0) = 0; \mathbf{val}(\mathbf{n}') = \sim\mathbf{val}(\mathbf{n})$; with the length 25. So s_1 is more complex than s_2.

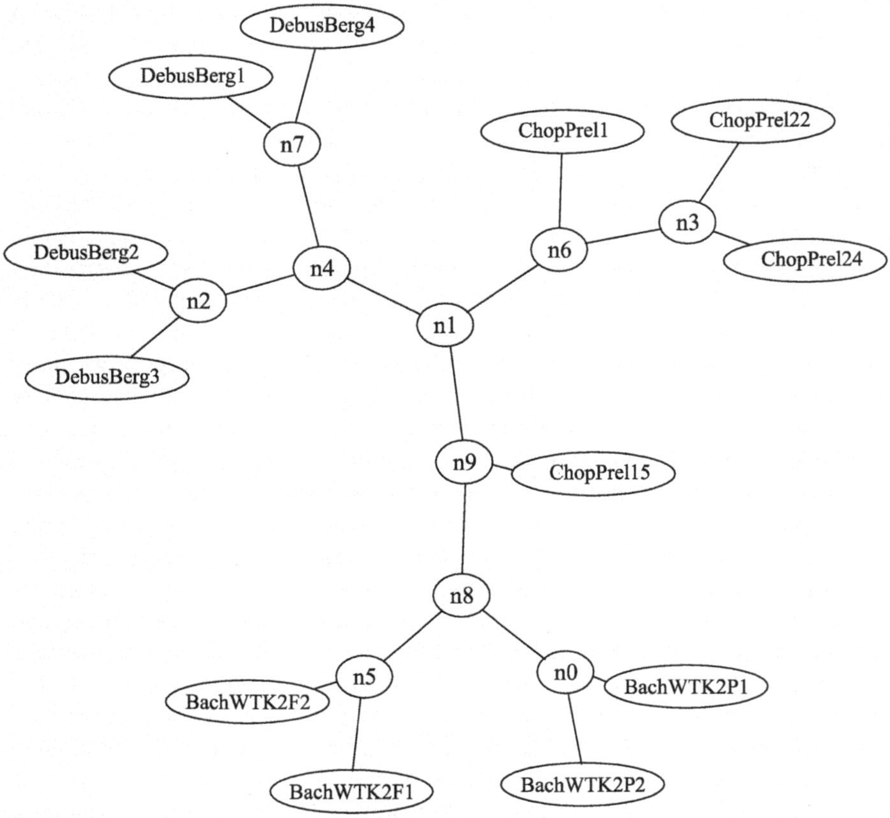

Fig. 12.3 Successful ordering of music pieces. (Vitányi et al 2008, p. 53)

12.3.2 Formalization of the Analogy

We have seen in the preceding section that the gene-meme analogy makes essential use of the reproduction, variation and selection parameters of natural evolution. In this section we will consider very briefly a formalization of the interdependence of these parameters. We start with a slightly modernized form of Mendelian genetics: According to Mendelian genetics inheritable properties of organisms are twofold: for every such property there is a phenotype representing the property in question which is based on a genotype. Take, e.g., the phenotype eye-colour which we consider her simplified in the sense that we distinguish only brown-eyed beings from blue-eyed beings. This phenotype is based on the genotypes AA, Aa (aA, the order doesn't matter) and aa via the genome and the diploid chromosome set (one part from the mother and one part from the father) as mapped in table 12.1:

A and a represent here the so-called alleles (located at the same genetic locus). An upper-case letter represents the dominance of an allele against its amending

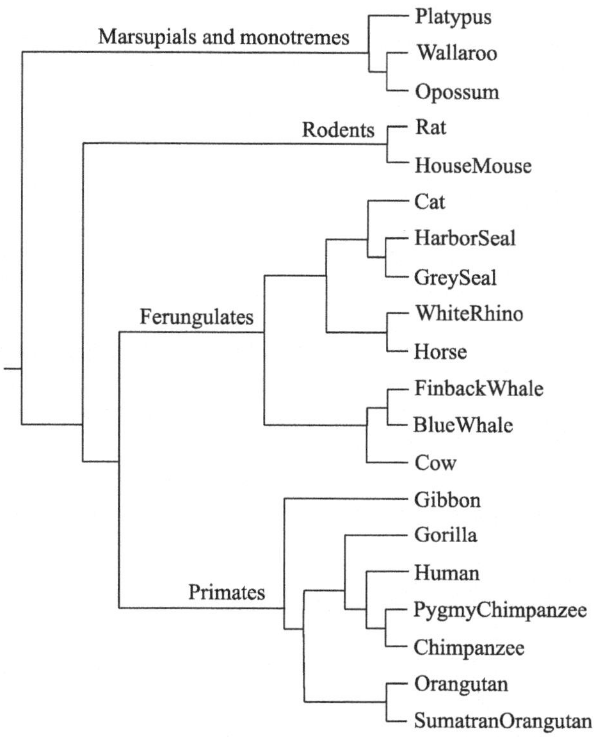

Fig. 12.4 Successful ordering of genetic dependency. (Vitányi et al 2008, p. 51)

Table 12.1 A simplified phenotype-genotype mapping

Phenotype	> Genome > Diploid chromosome set >	Genotype
Brown-eyed		AA, Aa
Blue eyed		aa

lower-case allele. So in our example A is dominant against a and a is recessive against A. Such a dominance was measured, e.g., by Mendel when he reared red and white homozygotic pea (via self-fertilization) and crossed them. Since every such crossing ended up with red offspring in the first generation he concluded that the red characteristic was dominant against the white one.

The mixture of genetic material of both parents is called 'meiosis'. Since meiosis is going on randomly (i.e. the frequencies are independent) it holds that the probability of each genotype is as follows: $p(AA) = p(A){\bullet}p(A), p(aa) = p(a){\bullet}p(a)$ and $p(Aa) = 2{\bullet}p(A){\bullet}p(a)$, where, e.g., '$p(AA)$' represents the probability that the genotype is AA and '$p(A)$' the probability that there is a dominant A–allele at the locus. With the help of this equation one can prove the so-called Hardy–Weinberg-law, namely the regularity that if there is no selective pressure, then these frequencies retain (Schurz 2011, Sect. 12.4):

Table 12.2 Implementation of a fitness factor for the selection of genotypes

	$Variation_1$	$Variation_2$	$Variation_3$
Genotype (V_i)	AA	Aa	aa
Fitness (f)	$1-s$	$1-s$	1

- $p_{n+1}(AA) = p_n(A)^2 = p_n(AA)$
- $p_{n+1}(Aa) = 2 \cdot p_n(A) \cdot p_n(a) = p_n(Aa)$
- $p_{n+1}(aa) = p_n(a)^2 = p_n(aa)$

Note that in these equations '*p*' represents the reproduction and non-mutational variation (recombination) parameter of natural evolution: The frequency of *AA*s (homozygotic) in the nth generation is such and such. Via recombination it is possible that, e.g., two non-homozygotic brown-eyed parents (*Aa* and *Aa*) have a blue-eyed offspring (since meiosis is randomly and from the four possible recombinations AA, Aa, aA and *aa* only the last one results in a blue-eyed phenotype, the probability is one fourth).

Note also that this holds only within systems with reproduction and non-mutational variation (recombination), but neither selection nor mutation. Selection may be introduced into the dynamics with a parameter for selection. Let's assume, e.g., a selection pressure s on brown-eyed people (such a selective pressure could, e.g., be the fact brought to the light by a Norwegian study according to which blue-eyed men significantly prefer blue-eyed women against brown-eyed ones; this phenomenon is sometimes explained with the fact that two blue-eyed parents (both *aa*) only can have a blue-eyed offspring and that therefore blue-eyed men have by such a choice a further indicator for fatherhood (cf. Laeng et al. 2007) such selection pressure is assumed, e.g., in table 12.2:)

Implementing a parameter for selection in the population dynamics changes the formulas above to the following one (here $k = 3$; (cf. Schurz 2011, Sect. 12.5)), where the second coefficient is just a normalization of the parameter for selection—the higher the fitness of a variant, the higher the relative frequency of the variant in the offspring:

$$p_{n+1}(V_i) = p_n(V_i) \cdot \frac{f(V_i)}{\sum_{j=1}^{k} p_n(V_j) \cdot f(V_j)}$$

Finally, to complete the evolutionary population dynamics one may implement the mutation of a variant V_i to another one V_j via a mutation coefficient m (frequency of V_i-mutations back or forth (cf. Schurz 2011, Sect. 13.1)):

$$p_{n+1}(V_i) = p_n(V_i) \cdot \frac{f(V_i)}{\sum_{j=1}^{k} p_n(V_j) \cdot f(V_j)} \cdot (1 - m(V_i))$$

So that's the formalization of the source domain of the gene-meme-analogy. But what about the target domain? As we have elaborated in the preceding section on the general form of the analogy, it's just a reinterpretation of the parameters and the variants for the cultural domain. We may express this as follows:

$$p_{n+1}(V_i) = p_n(V_i) \cdot \frac{f(V_i)}{\sum_{j=1}^{k} p_n(V_j) \cdot f(V_j)} \cdot (1 - m(V_i))$$

$$\downarrow$$

$$p_{n^*+1}(V_i^*) = p_{n^*}(V_i^*) \cdot \frac{f^*(V_i^*)}{\sum_{j=1}^{k} p_{n^*}(V_j^*) \cdot f^*(V_j^*)} \cdot (1 - m^*(V_i^*))$$

Where $is(V_i) = V_i^*, is(n) = n^*$ etc. The reinterpretation runs as follows:

- n : ancestor relation — n^* : generations/rounds
- m : mutation rate — m^* : variation rate of information etc.
- f : natural selection pressure — f^* : cultural selection pressure
- V_i : Genotypes — V_i^* : Memes

12.3.3 Why the Diversity of Meanings of "Meme" Fits into the Current Framework of Cultural Evolution

We have seen in Sect. 12.3.1 that there is a quite diverse usage of the expression "meme" within cultural evolutionary theory, but that cultural evolutionary theorists nevertheless share a core meaning of this concept as introduced via analogies, namely the property of being reproducible and adequately variable. In Sect. 12.3.2 we have seen that the meme-concept (V^*) occurs within the analogy in three important contexts, namely within the context of the cultural reproduction and (recombinational) variation parameter $p_{n^*}(V^*)$, in the context of the cultural mutation parameter $m^*(V^*)$ and in the context of the cultural fitness-parameter $f^*(V^*)$. Since m^* and f^* are quite general, the only constraints of V^* (i.e. the meme-concept) as introduced by a partial contextual definition is to be a possible value of these functions which is to say nothing else then being something reproducible, variable and selectable. This thesis about the current constraints on a characterization of the meme-concept is not new:

> [A] possibility is that such methods [that allow a clear characterization of memes] will reveal that certain aspects of cultural transmission are not [classical]. Even in this case, however, evolutionary models are still applicable (…). Indeed, Darwin formulated his theory of evolution with little understanding of genes or Mendelian inheritance. (Mesoudi et al. 2006, p. 344)

And:

> Although the neuronal interpretation of the expression 'meme' seems to me plausible, the theory of cultural evolution doesn't hinge on it. (My translation of Schurz 2011, p. 210)

Although the properties mentioned above which are the core of the meaning of the expression 'meme' are very general, in a more detailed characterization of the parameters of cultural evolution also the meme-concept may be clarified in a more informative way. Currently there are already some constraints for the fitness parameter of cultural evolution (f^*) formulated, but these constraints are also quite general:

- *Different kinds of fitness*: "Natural selection occurs when organisms differ in their *viability* and also when they differ in their *fertility*" (Sober 2000, p. 57), whereupon under the "fertility rate" the number of living born children of a parent and under the "viability rate" the number of children reproducing themselves is understood. For memes a similar distinction should hold wherupon the memetican fertility rate may be understood as operationalizable via first citations in a citation index and the memetican viability rate may be understood as re-citations in a citation index.
- A meme is the more reproducible, the less cognitive dissonant it is with respect to main stream ideas (cf. Schurz 2011, p. 230; Distin 2005, p. 61; and also Quine's web of belief where logic is at the core of our beliefs).
- One general selection criteria: The more a meme is organism self-defeating, the less fit it will be (cf. Schurz 2011, p. 231).
- Complexity theory: Hierarchical structure of repeatedly nested sub-units increases the reproduction rate of so-called memplexes (cf. Distin 2005, p. 41).
- Complexity theory: The more complex a system of memes, i.e. a memplex, is, the more unlikely it is that a meme/idea can be integrated. This is some kind of conservatism of complex systems (cf. Distin 2005, p. 59).
- It's also possible to model frequency dependent fitness (selection parameter s includes also the frequency of a variant)

Although such constraints on a selection parameter for cultural evolution are quite general, more specific constraints out of, e.g., complexity theory seem to be available. By increasingly specifying these parameters also the meme-concept will be more specified. But there are also heavy dissimilarities regarding important properties of natural evolutionary theory:

- The concept of species turns into a concept of quasispecies in cultural evolutionary theory since there are no reproduction barriers for memes. So also a genealogy of memes or ideas fails in the classical sense.
- There is no meiosis going on in cultural evolution. For this reason recombinational variation must come into play differently.
- There is no unguided or undirected selection and variation in natural evolution. A consequence of directed selection is fast evolution. In general it holds that in natural evolution there is a mean variation and high selection rate whereas in cultural evolution there is a high variation and low selection rate.

To conclude our investigation of the gene-meme-analogy we can say that the currently diverse meanings of the expression 'meme' fit the requirements for this concept as introduced via analogies partially and contextually, but in order to turn the research programme of cultural evolution into a fruitful one, there seems to be a need of further analogical relations and specifications.

12.4 Conclusion

Our starting question concerned the fruitfulness of the theory of cultural evolution: How can meme theories of culture cope adequately with cultural diversity if there is disagreement about the meme-concept? We named three necessary conditions for a natural system to be a natural evolutionary system: reproduction, variation and selection. In cultural evolutionary theory analogue processes are assumed whereupon the cultural processes of reproduction, variation and selection are based on the replicator meme.

We have argued that, although memes are seen quite diversly as imitable entities, information contents, brain dispositions, brain software or so-called neuromemes, there seems to be a core meaning of the concept with the main relevant properties of reproducibility and adequate variability. Our detailed analysis of the main gene-meme-analogy shows that these different understandings of 'meme' share these main relevant properties of memes (V^*) to such a degree that they are acceptable for the present descriptions of cultural fitness (f^*) and variation/mutation (m^*) parameters. So, the partial understanding of the expression 'meme' is at least currently unproblematic. But of course this hinges on the generality of f^* and m^* and in order to turn the theory of cultural evolution into a fruitful research programme, it needs some further analogies and specifications.

References

Aunger, R. ed. 2000. Darwinizing culture: The status of memetics as a science. Oxford: Oxford University Press.

Blackmore, S. J. 1999. The meme machine. Oxford: Oxford University Press.

Dawkins, R. 1976. The selfish gene. Oxford: Oxford University Press.

Dawkins, R. 1982. The extended phenotype. The long reach of the gene. Oxford: Oxford University Press.

Dennett, D. C. 1992. Consciousness explained. New York: Back Bay Books.

Distin, K. 2005. The selfish meme. Cambridge: Cambridge University Press.

Hempel, C. G. 1970. Aspects of scientific explanation and other essays in the philosophy of science. New York: Free Press.

Laeng, B., R. Mathisen, and J.-A. Johnsen. 2007. Why do blue-eyed men prefer women with the same eye color? *Behavioral Ecology and Sociobiology* 61 (3): 371–384. doi:10.1007/s00265-006-0266-1.

Mahner, M., and M. Bunge. 1997. Foundations of biophilosophy. Berlin: Springer.

Mesoudi, A., A. Whiten, and K. N. Laland. 2006. Towards a unified science of cultural evolution. *Behavioral and Brain Sciences* 29:329–383.

Schurz, G. 2011.*Evolution in Natur und Kultur. Eine Einführung in die verallgemeinerte Evolutionstheorie.* (Heidelberg: Spektrum Akademischer Verlag.) http://www.springerlink.com/content/978-3-8274-2665-9. Accessed 21 July 2013.

Sober, E. 2000. Philosophy of biology. Oxford: Oxford University Press.

Vitányi, P. M. B., et al. 2008. Normalized information distance. In *Information theory and statistical learning,* eds. F. Emmert-Streib and M. Dehmer, 39–71. New York: Springer.

Chapter 13
Analogy and Interpretation in Legal Argumentation

Damiano Canale and Giovanni Tuzet

13.1 Introduction

One of the distinguishing features of legal argumentation is the interplay between legal arguments supporting a conclusion and interpretive canons supporting a definite reading of the legal provisions that justify the conclusion argued for. On the one hand, a definite interpretation of the relevant legal materials aims to provide the normative premises of a legal argument concerning a case or a set of cases, but, on the other hand, interpretive choices are themselves in need of justification and therefore have to be supported by interpretive arguments (e.g. the argument from literal meaning of the relevant provisions, the argument from legislative intention, the argument from legislative purpose, etc.).

This kind of interplay becomes problematic in some circumstances. For instance, when different interpretive arguments justify different readings of the same provisions and therefore provide different normative premises. Or when, interestingly enough, argumentation and interpretation point to the same conclusion but the law prohibits the former and permits the latter. This is the case of criminal law when, to protect individual liberty, it puts a ban on analogical reasoning but at the same time, to protect society from crime, does not exclude the "extensive" interpretation of criminal legal provisions. The puzzling result is that the same conclusion can be accepted if argued for in interpretive terms but cannot if presented as the outcome of an argument from analogy.

The present work focuses on such tension between analogical reasoning and extensive interpretation in law. They are two techniques of judicial decision-making that permit to rule a case that is not explicitly considered by a legal provision

D. Canale (✉) · G. Tuzet
Department of Legal Studies, Bocconi University, Milano, Italy
e-mail: damiano.canale@unibocconi.it

G. Tuzet
e-mail: giovanni.tuzet@unibocconi.it

H. J. Ribeiro (ed.), *Systematic Approaches to Argument by Analogy*,
Argumentation Library 25, DOI 10.1007/978-3-319-06334-8_13,

and still is worth being regulated on the basis of it.[1] In most legal systems, as we said, reasoning by analogy is prohibited in criminal law (unless it is in favor of the accused) whereas extensive interpretation is not.[2] Hence, it is a crucial point in criminal adjudication to distinguish the two, although they seem to serve the same purpose (see e.g. Ross 1958, § 29; Silving 1967; MacCormick 1978, p. 155 ff.; Wróblewski 1992, pp. 223–227). Indeed, if a trial court justifies a criminal decision arguing by analogy, the decision will be reasonably quashed on appeal because it is contrary to the law. The same decision is justified, on the contrary, when it can be considered an extensive interpretation of a criminal provision, even when this is the same provision that the court could have used analogically. The problem is that in the legal practice one can hardly distinguish analogy from extensive interpretation. It is very unclear whether there is a real difference between the two and where it might be. On the one hand, some scholars claim that they differ from a theoretical point of view, since they do not have the same argumentative structure. On the other hand, analogical reasoning and extensive interpretation come to the same result starting from the same legal materials: they justify the extension of a regulation to a case that is not explicitly considered by the law.

As a consequence, one might have the suspicion that judges deploy these canons of argumentation strategically. When a judge intends for whatever reasons to punish a conduct that is not explicitly regulated by a criminal provision, then she justifies her decision as the compelling upshot of an extensive interpretation of the provision. On the contrary, when a judge is not willing to punish the same conduct, then she claims that the extension of criminal liability is not permitted, since this would be a case of analogical reasoning. As a result, these canons of decision-making would be susceptible of whatever manipulation for purposes of social protection and control: judges would make criminal law up as they go along on the basis of "what it seems to them a just society" (MacCormick 1978, p. 107).

All this being true, it is worth looking at whether there are any constraints on the judicial application of these argumentative canons in legal practice. If it were to turn out that no constraint is put on the judge, and the divide between analogical reasoning and extensive interpretation is *just* a matter of strategic maneuvering in argumentation, then the conceptual distinction we are considering is not consistent with the principle of legality and the rule of law. When constraints are given and

[1] Although "analogical reasoning" and "extensive interpretation" are often used in judicial discourse to denote two fungible techniques of decision-making, legal theory clearly differentiates the two classes of entities they refer to. As we shall point out in § 2, "extensive interpretation" makes reference either to the interpretive process that extends the standard meaning of an interpreted legal provision, or to the outcome of this process. On the contrary, "analogical reasoning" denotes an argumentative technique inferentially articulated. In this article we shall look at these subjects from the point of view of the theory of legal argumentation: those labels will single out two arguments that are used to justify a judicial decision.

[2] This is the case for instance of Spain, France, Germany and Italy: see e.g. Olivares (1989, pp. 136–139), Robert (2001, pp. 191–201), Hassemer (1992), and Caiani (1958) respectively. Common law countries face the same problem in the interpretation of statutes and precedents: see e.g. *McBoyle v. United States* (1931) and MacCormick (1978, Chap. 8). It is true that common law rules lack the canonical form of statutory ones: but even if they cannot be "interpreted extensively" in the same sense of statutory law, they can be construed extensively.

a straightforward line can be drawn between the two canons, then the legality of a criminal decision based upon them is not compromised.

To address these issues, we shall focus first on the theoretical distinction between analogical extension and interpretive extension, as it is traditionally conceived by legal scholars. Then we will concentrate on a recent Italian case (the "Vatican Radio Case") where the Italian Court of Cassation, in declaring that the accused could have been legally convicted of a criminal offence, claimed to argue from extensive interpretation and not from analogy. We shall assess, in this respect, whether the argumentation of the Court was sound. Finally, we will propose an original account of the distinction between analogical reasoning and interpretive extension, based upon the principle of semantic tolerance and its inferential structure in legal argumentation. In doing this, we will highlight the different constraints put on the interpreter who makes use of these techniques to underpin a judicial decision.

13.2 The Traditional Standpoint

In legal argumentation and practice, "restrictive" and "extensive" interpretations are often described as techniques that are used when the literal meaning of a legal provision (hereafter *standard* meaning) does not correspond to the intended meaning of the legislature. It may be the case that the legislature, by enacting a statute, says one thing but means another.[3] In the legal jargon, it is commonly claimed in these circumstances either that *lex magis dixit quam voluit* (the law said more than it wanted to say) or that *lex minus dixit quam voluit* (the law said less than it wanted to say). Now, when the standard meaning[4] of a legal provision differs from the intended meaning, a court that decides a case according to the former will fail to enforce the law that the legislature intended to make. Restrictive and extensive interpretation serve to address this issue. These interpretive techniques give the judge the opportunity to set aside the standard meaning of the statute in order to bridge the gap between what is said and what is intended. And they do this either narrowing the set of cases that the statute would have ruled if the judge had interpreted it literally, or expanding this set. In the latter circumstance, one or more cases that do not fall under the standard meaning of the statute will be ruled according to it nevertheless.

So, what does it happen when a legal provision is interpreted extensively? A case is not regulated by the law according to the standard interpretation of a legal text, but it becomes such on the basis of a second way of interpreting the same text.

C does not fall under N_1 obtained via I_1 of P.
But, C falls under N_2 obtained via I_2 of P.

[3] The distinction between what is said and what is intended has been pointed out by Grice (1989). Here we make abstraction from the ontological and epistemological worries about legislatures, namely whether there are such entities and how it is possible to know their intentions.

[4] We shall use the expression "standard meaning" to refer to the meaning that an expression assumes most times according to the rules governing the use of this expression in a given language.

I_2 is the extensive interpretation of provision P, according to which the content of norm N_1 is extended to N_2. For example, this happens when a provision about "vehicles" is about motor-vehicles according to I_1 and extends to devices that perform the same function even if they lack a motor (e.g. skateboards) according to I_2.

Given this explanation, it is clear that an interpretation is not "extensive" *per se* but with respect to some standard interpretation.[5] And it works like this: N_2 is a justified interpretive extension of N_1 when an interpretive canon permits to extend the standard interpretation of P. If I_1 is the standard (literal) interpretation, I_2 might be an extensive interpretation argued from the intention of the legislature, from the purpose of the regulation, from a legal principle, etc.[6] Therefore, strictly speaking, "extensive interpretation" and "restrictive interpretation" do not denote argumentative canons. These expressions simply qualify the upshot of interpretation: in particular, they mark the fact that the scope of the norm so stated is larger or narrower than it would have been had the provision been interpreted literally. In this sense, such interpretive techniques do not justify a judicial decision, although they are sometimes employed in legal argumentation as if they could. Extensive interpretation is in need of justification: it is not itself an argumentative tool. In fact, it simply brings into operation those argumentative canons that justify giving up literal interpretation, and thus leads the judge to defeat the principle of strict construction in criminal law. By making reference to the intended meaning of the legislature, which can be determined using different argumentative tools, the range of criminal liability may be both expanded and cut down.

What happens instead in analogical reasoning? A gap in the law is filled by arguing analogically from a source case to a target case (see Holyoak and Thagard 1995),[7] and thereby a new norm is created. To put it differently, a first norm regulates a source case which is relevantly[8] similar to a target case that lacks a legal regulation. On the basis of the relevant similarity and the lack of relevant dissimilarities, the regulation of the source is extended to the target. In this way, the gap is filled by the judge by generating a second norm that goes beyond the first, and hence can be seen as created by the judge.

[5] "Extensive interpretation (interpretation by analogy) is the term used when pragmatic considerations result in the application of the rule to situations which, regarded in the light of 'natural linguistic reading', clearly fall outside its field of reference" (Ross 1958, p. 149; note that Ross does not distinguish between analogy and extensive interpretation).

[6] Ross (1958, p. 150) claims that extensive interpretation has two presuppositions: (1) that a legal evaluation is in favor of applying a rule not only to sphere (a) but also to sphere (b); (2) that there is no difference between (a) and (b) that could justify a different treatment of the two cases. See also Silving (1967, p. 313): "though words have outer limits of social meaning, beyond which their extension might appear absurd, their meaning in a statute is very often sufficiently flexible to include or to exclude certain items, depending on purpose."

[7] On analogy in the law cf. Golding (1980, part III), Sunstein (1993), Brewer (1996), Kloosterhuis (2005), Kaptein (2005). It might also happen that the inference is drawn from multiple sources: see Guarini (2010).

[8] Relevance is determined by legal purpose (*ratio legis* in civil law systems), as we tried to show in Canale and Tuzet (2009). Cf. Cardozo (1921, pp. 28–30, and 1924, pp. 79–80) on analogy and *ratio decidendi* in case law.

C_1 falls under N_1.
C_2 does not fall under any actual norm of the system (there is a gap in the law).
There is a relevant similarity between C_1 and C_2.
C_2 falls under N_2 obtained by analogical reasoning (filling the gap).

In this scheme, C_1 is the source case, whose regulation is extended analogically to the target case C_2. N_2 is a new norm created by analogy from N_1. For example, to use the famous American decision *Adams v. New Jersey Steamboat Co.* (1896), the issue of the liability of steamboat companies for the loss of money or other personal effects of their passengers (target case) is treated by analogy with the liability of innkeepers for such losses of their guests (source case), considering that a steamboat is a "floating inn" in the light of such purpose as the protection of guests or passengers from "fraud or plunder" from the proprietor.[9]

13.3 Different Traits, and Common Ones

What are the distinguishing traits of extensive interpretation and analogical reasoning? According to the theoretical demarcation we just outlined, they have at least four different features (see e.g. Bobbio 1994: Chap. 1; Carcaterra 1988, pp. 16–18; Gianformaggio 1997; Peczenik 2005, pp. 20–24). First, analogical reasoning presupposes a given interpretation of the relevant provisions, which is at stake in extensive interpretation. Interpretation comes first. That is, one argues analogically after having interpreted the relevant provisions and having established that the case is not regulated, despite the interpretive method the judge could call on. On the contrary, extensive interpretation is precisely about the way in which such provisions ought to be interpreted, or have been construed as a matter of fact.

Secondly, analogical reasoning presupposes a gap, which is absent in extensive interpretation. This gap actually depends on the interpretive process itself: the case at hand in not regulated by the law in the sense that no available interpretation of a valid legal provision has been able to set up a norm covering it.

Thirdly, analogical reasoning creates a new norm to fill the gap, whereas extensive interpretation extends the content of the standard reading of the relevant provision. Let us say that N_1 regulates cases of type A and B: with extensive interpretation N_2 regulates cases A, B and C. With analogical reasoning, on the contrary, N_1 regulates cases A and B, whereas N_2 regulates cases C. The scope of N_2 with extensive interpretation is necessarily greater than that of N_1, which is not the case with analogical reasoning.[10]

[9] As scholars know, a disputed question was whether the relevant similarity of steamboats was with inns or with trains; in the former case companies were liable for such losses, in the latter they were not. See e.g. Weinreb (2005) and Posner (2006). For a similar problem see Sunstein (1993, p. 772): is hate speech analogous to physical assault or to political dissent?

[10] But analogical reasoning presupposes a principle or a value related to the *ratio* and covering all those cases.

Fourthly, as is the case in almost every contemporary legal system, analogical reasoning is prohibited in criminal law while, as we already pointed out, extensive interpretation is not. A basic legal principle lays behind this: it is the "rule of law" principle in common law countries and the "legality" principle in civil law ones. It is the shared idea that judges shall not create new law in criminal matters, but just decide on the basis of already established and cognizable norms. As the slogan has it, they have to apply the law. This idea is commonly represented by the maxim *nullum crimen sine lege, nulla poena sine lege.* But this is not meant to exclude all margins of judicial appreciation and discretion; flexibility is a felt need of law in general and also, with more caution, of criminal law. So both laxity of construction and vagueness of criminal statutes may sometimes be useful or even necessary.[11] As a consequence, legal scholars in general think that extensive interpretation is admissible in criminal matters, provided that judges do not create new law but confine themselves to the admissible interpretations of given provisions.[12] This view is reasonable if the two techniques at stake are different indeed. The different traits we outlined above seem to support the view that they are not the same, and rule out as a theoretical confusion the label "analogical interpretation".[13]

But extensive interpretation and analogy have common traits too. First, they share the need of settling, one way or another, the case in hand. A decision must be made and an argument must be given in favor of it. In particular, they deal with a case that is not explicitly regulated by a legal provision, i.e., that does not fall under its standard meaning but needs to be regulated for reasons of social protection and control.

Secondly, and more importantly, extensive interpretation and analogy have the same practical outcome. For N_2 (either obtained by extensive interpretation or by analogy) extends the regulation to the case in hand. The practical outcome for the parties involved is the same, either if you argue from extensive interpretation or from analogy. Let us consider our previous examples. A skateboard might be qualified as a vehicle according to an extensive interpretation of the provision "No vehicles in the park" whose standard meaning covers motor-vehicles, to the effect that skateboards are not allowed in the park (N_2). But one might also argue in the following way: "vehicles" is to be read as referring to motor-vehicles (because of some interpretive argument to be specified, like the argument from literal meaning or from legislative intent); so the norm does not cover the case of skateboards entering the park; so there is a gap in the law; but there is also a relevant similarity between motor-vehicles and skateboards (both represent a threat to the safety of pedestrians

[11] "Overly precise *statutes* invite the criminally inclined to frustrate the intent of legislation by skirting the inflexibly precise language. As a result fairness only requires that a statute put law-abiding non-lawyers on reasonable notice that their intended conduct runs a reasonable risk of violating the statute" (Dressler 1987, p. 28).

[12] In Italy, for instance, the positive law explicitly prohibits analogy in criminal matters (art. 14 of the "Preleggi"), but is silent on extensive interpretation; scholars in general claim that the latter is admissible.

[13] But MacCormick (1995, p. 474) argues that analogy can work as an *interpretive* argument, extending the interpretation of one provision to another.

in the park); therefore the gap is to be filled by analogy extending to skateboards the regulation on motor-vehicles, to the effect that skateboards are not allowed in the park (N_2). The same outcome that was arrived at by interpreting extensively the given provision could be reached by arguing analogically after having interpreted non-extensively the same provision. Or, the other way round, one could turn an analogical argument into a form of extensive interpretation. The Court of *Adams* argued there was a gap in the law and, because of the relevant similarity between steamboats and inns (a steamboat is a "floating inn") the gap was filled by analogy. Now, assuming there is a provision about "inns", one might also argue that the word "inns" is to be interpreted extensively (because a steamboat is a "floating inn") to the effect that the regulation about inns extends to steamboats. It is perhaps for this common traits that some scholars, in the context of systemic interpretation and with reference to the issue of legal gaps, use the labels "analogy *extra legem*" (analogical reasoning) and "analogy *intra legem*" (extensive interpretation).[14]

All of this might not be a problem for thinkers who love theoretical distinctions as such. It is indeed a problem for pragmatist thinkers who are more interested in outcomes than in the ways they are arrived at. It is a pragmatist principle that, if the application of two concepts has the same practical consequences, they are the same concept under different names.[15] Now, if "extensive interpretation" and "analogical reasoning" produce the same practical consequences, one could say that they are the same argument and that it does not make any sense to permit the one and prohibit the other. Same consequences, same arguments.

We shall discuss this core issue by considering the Vatican Radio Case, where our concerns as to the distinction between interpretive and analogical extension come directly into play. Indeed, the proof of the pudding is still in the eating.

13.4 The Vatican Radio Case

Vatican Radio transmission towers emitted electromagnetic waves that, according to the public prosecution, threatened the population nearby. A first disputed issue was whether the emissions were within the environmental limits fixed by Italian administrative law, and a second was whether the case had also a criminal profile.

Article 674 of the Italian Criminal Code sanctions the "dangerous throwing of things" (*getto pericoloso di cose*), while no article of the Code mentions electromagnetic waves. Was the emission of such waves a "dangerous throwing of things"?

[14] "The problem of the completeness of a legal system is linked with that of extra-statutory analogy ('analogy *extra legem*'), where legal consequences are ascribed to facts, which are not singled out in enacted legal rules. In interpretation, there is a problem of using analogy *intra legem*, where one does not go 'outside the valid law' but only tries so to fix the meaning of the legal rules that they constitute the most harmonious whole possible. Thus interpretation by analogy is singled out according to the reasoning it uses" (Wróblewski 1992, p. 103).

[15] It was, in particular, Peirce's pragmatic maxim. See e.g. Haack (2005, pp. 75–77).

The Court of Cassation (III Criminal Sec., decision n. 36845/2008) decided it was and claimed to argue from extensive interpretation and not from analogy.

Was the decision of the Court really the result of an interpretive extension of the regulation, or rather the hidden upshot of analogical reasoning? That case raised two interpretive problems in particular: (1) the meaning of "throwing" and (2) the meaning of "things". Is an emission an act of "throwing" according to the law? Are waves "things" according to the law? And, in conjunction, is the act of emitting such waves a "dangerous throwing of things"?

Note that these questions, put in this order, imply a semantics that follows the "principle of composition": first one has to determine the meanings of single words, then one has to put them together to determine the meaning of a whole sentence or complex expression. A semantics following the "principle of context" would do the other way round: first you determine the context, that is the meaning of sentences or complex expressions, then you extract from it the meaning of single words (cf. Searle 1978; for an inferentialist picture of these issues, see Canale and Tuzet 2007). In our case the Court follows rather a compositional semantics, cutting the expression at stake into pieces and determining the meaning of its parts in order to establish the meaning of the whole.

13.4.1 On "Things"

To be sure, waves are not "things" according to the linguistic standard uses. So an argument is needed to support that interpretive conclusion. A significant argument provided by the prosecution and then used by the Court makes appeal to another norm of the system: art. 624 (c. II) of the Criminal Code, on theft, states that electric power, as any other energy with economic value, legally counts as a thing; so electromagnetic waves are "things" according to the law. Against this argument the defense contended that, according to the intention of the legislature of 1930, when the Code was enacted, "things" in art. 674 refers to material things. To that argument the Court added some scientific considerations as to the physical nature of waves.

Now, to be sure, both interpretations seem admissible. The first is supported by a form of systemic argumentation (making appeal to other norms of the same legal system); the second is supported by a psychological argument (the argument from legislative intent). The first claims that taking waves as "things" is an extensive interpretation justified by systemic considerations; the second claims that to treat electromagnetic waves as material things is to make an analogy, since a psychological argument justifies a strict interpretation of art. 674 and the interpretive conclusion that there is gap: as a matter of fact, the 1930 legislature didn't care about such waves at all.

Note that if both interpretations are admissible there seems to be space for taking the extensive interpretation thesis as correct: there is no need to argue from analogy, it is sufficient, to settle the case, to select one of the admissible interpretations of "things", namely the extensive one (on "things" in ancient and modern law see also Silving (1967), pp. 313–314). This for the object of the conduct in question. What about the conduct itself?

13.4.2 On "Throwing"

Again, the argument of the prosecution and the Court about "throwing" is that art. 674 can be interpreted extensively. An emission falls under the notion of "throwing" because there are linguistic uses of the latter referring to the former; for instance, says the Court, to describe the act of emitting a cry one can use the expression "throwing a cry". You might also think at the phrases "throwing light" on something and "throwing suspicion" on somebody, which share with "throwing a cry" the fact of extending the meaning of the expression.

The defense replies that according to standard uses "throwing" refers to the act of flinging something, for instance out of the window, with some physical effort, and that a "dangerous throwing of things" refers to the act of dangerously flinging some material things into the public space; metaphorical uses are not at stake here and no interpretive canon permits to construe the provision as referring to an emission of waves. So there is a gap in the law, which could be filled only by analogy; but analogy is prohibited in criminal law.

It is worth noting that the interpretive argument of the defense seems to be inspired by a contextualist semantics: the meanings of "throwing" and "things" cannot be determined in isolation and should be fixed with reference to the whole meaning of the sentence in that context. As a result, the term "things" is referred to material things only, and the meaning of "throwing" is restricted to non-metaphorical senses.

Finally, note that if both interpretations are admissible there is room for thinking also here that extensive interpretation is a right solution. But one may have legitimate doubts about the admissibility of such an extensive interpretation of "throwing". The Court says there are linguistic uses of "throwing" that refer to the act of emitting something, for instance a cry. Dante's poetic language is taken by the Court as an example of this. Now you may wonder if a line of a poet who lived eight centuries ago is among the uses that determine the admissible interpretations of a provision in a legal controversy nowadays.

But the Court contended that the emission of electromagnetic waves can be a dangerous throwing of things and, after settling this interpretive issue, it quashed the appellate decision and ordered a new appeal trial for two Vatican Radio's officials, in order to settle the relevant factual question, that is, to ascertain if the waves were indeed dangerous for the people living nearby.

13.5 Legal Interpretation, Vagueness, and Semantic Tolerance

On the basis of the arguments provided by the Court of Cassation, it is actually far from being clear that its decision was the result of an interpretive extension and not instead of an undeclared extension by analogy. Actually, it is the standard account of the distinction between the two that seems to be unsatisfying or even lacking. In particular, the distinctive features of extensive interpretation in the standard picture seem to provide little or no guidance at all to legal interpreters, thereby giving rise to misuses of this interpretive technique.

In this section we shall put forward a different explanation of the interpretive practices we are focusing on in order to throw some light, as it were, on the issues considered in the outset.

As the Vatican Radio Case clearly shows, the question whether a legal provision is to be interpreted extensively presupposes that the content of such a provision is vague.[16] This is actually true by definition. Extensive interpretation is possible if, and only if, the interpreted legal provision admits some changes in the cases to which it can be meaningfully applied. In other words, to be interpreted extensively a legal provision shall yield borderline cases. The words "things" and "throwing" are a good example of this phenomenon, at least according to the Italian Court of Cassation. On the Court's view, it is not immediately clear whether the term "things" applies to electromagnetic waves, nor whether the word "throwing" applies to their emission. Consequently, art. 674 of the Italian Criminal Code is vague: it is not definitely true that electromagnetic waves are things nor that they are not; similarly, it is not definitely true that waves emission is a kind of throwing nor that it is not.

Now, it is well known that the notions of "borderline case" and "definiteness" are strongly controversial in the philosophical literature on vagueness (see Shapiro 2006, p. 2).[17] Regardless of this, one may outline the linguistic problem faced by the Italian Court by means of the following uncontroversial scheme (Fig. 13.1).

This scheme represents the extension and antiextension of a legal provision such as art. 674 of the Italian Criminal Code.[18] Let A be the set of cases that clearly fall under the legal provision according to its standard meaning and which thus belong to its extension. Similarly, let C be the set of cases that clearly do not fall under the standard meaning of the same provision, i.e., that belong to its antiextension. Finally, B is the set of the borderline cases that come between clear "positive" and "negative" ones (see Endicott 2000, p. 55; cf. Hart 1961, Chap. 7). When x is a borderline case, the task for legal interpretation is determining whether x ought to be treated as a "positive" or "negative" case from the legal point of view. In the first

[16] Some authors claim that vagueness is a property of (some) words, others claim it is a property of (some) contents. See below for some references.

[17] As a matter of fact, most theorists claim that vagueness involves a form of ignorance, so that the different accounts of this phenomenon depend on what such an ignorance amounts to. For instance, epistemicists claim that with borderline cases we are ignorant of facts that actually we cannot know (Williamson 1994); a supervaluationist holds that we are ignorant because a vague sentence is neither true nor false (Fine 1975); an incoherentist claims that we do not know whether a vague term applies to a case because our language sometimes is incoherent (Dummett 1975); a contextualist assumes that we are (apparently) ignorant of the conditions of application of vague terms because these conditions shift with context (see Raffman 1994, and Soames 1999). For a discussion of these accounts of vagueness as to legal language see Endicott (2000), Jónsson (2009) and Poscher (2012).

[18] The extension and antiextension of a sentence S shall not be confused here with the extensive interpretation of S. The extension of a sentence is the set of objects, events or states of affairs S refers to, whereas the antiextension is the complementary set thereof. An extensive interpretation of S actually modifies the standard extension and antiextension of it.

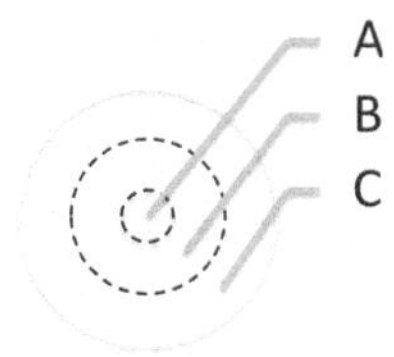

Fig. 13.1 Vagueness Scheme

circumstance, the content of the provision shall be extended so that to include *x*: the boundary between A and B moves to include *x* within the meaning of the provision. In the second circumstance, the content of the provision will be restricted: the boundary between C and B is shaped so that to include *x* in C. Obviously, all this requires that the boundaries between A, B and C be flexible in the sense that they lack sharp cutoff-points.[19] By interpreting the legal provision for decisional purposes, however, the judge is called upon to set up these boundaries and to determine where the case at hand is located. As a result, *after* legal interpretation *x* shall be qualified as belonging to A or C as a matter of fact.

Now, the crucial point is determining whether *x* belongs to A, B or C according to the standard meaning of the legal provision. If *x* is located in B, then extensive interpretation can be worked out from a semantic point of view. On the contrary, if *x* is located in C, extensive interpretation is not semantically admissible. This does not imply that the regulation provided by the legal provision cannot be extended to *x* by a court, being *x* located in C. The case could be so regulated by means of analogical reasoning, when legally permitted. But the starting point of analogical extension is quite different. Indeed, if *x* is located in C it is definitely not covered by the interpreted legal provision. Case *x* could still be regulated according to the law on the basis of its relevant similarity to the standard cases of application, although the interpreted legal provision does not rule *x* at all.

We shall label the problem just outlined "the location problem". The divide between extensive interpretation and analogical extension depends first of all on it. If we had some criteria for locating a given case within A, B or C, it would be possible to determine under what conditions extensive interpretation is admitted and analogical extension is not. Do such criteria exist?

To answer this question, let us return to the features of vague terms or contents. We have seen that a vague term admits of some content changes in the cases to which it can be meaningfully applied, i.e., the term is "tolerant" as to its application conditions.[20] Now, semantic tolerance is a matter of degree and depends on context: turning back to our example, when a case is slightly different from the standard one in the light of the contextual constraints put on the use of "things" and "throwing", these terms apply to it nevertheless. On the contrary, if the difference is contextually

[19] This claim is countered, however, by the epistemic theory of vagueness and by supervaluation theory as well. Cf. Williamson (1994). On supervaluationism and its logics cf. Varzi (2007).

[20] The tolerance metaphor is used here to point out that certain terms or expressions are less precise than others in a given context, so that they can be meaningfully used to denote cases that do not fall under their standard meaning. See Dummett (1975) and Wright (1975).

relevant, these terms do not apply. Given this, we might state the following principle (*Tolerance Principle*): being AC the application conditions of term T in context C, when two cases differ only marginally in the respects on which T is tolerant, so that they both satisfy AP in C, if a competent speaker judges the first case to be covered by T, then she cannot competently judge the other case in any other manner (cf. Shapiro 2006, Chap. 1). The Tolerance Principle sets out the conditions under which the extension of a regulation to a borderline case is justified. These conditions depend on the characteristics of the subject of regulation that are taken to be relevant, within a given context, as to the application conditions of a given legal term.

One might ask here: Why are those characteristics relevant? Now, the relevance criterion cannot be determined by the standard meaning of the vague term. Relevance is rather a function of context: contextual constraints put on language uses determine what characteristics of a given case are relevant in adjudication. These constraints are typically made explicit by means of legal arguments: the argument from intention, the argument from purpose, the argument from legal history, and the various sorts of systemic argument used in legal practice highlight different contextual constraints that the judge can take into account in interpreting a statute, which in turn make some characteristics of the case relevant according to the law. When interpreting the term "things" so that to include in its extension the case of electromagnetic waves, for instance, the judge is committed to give a reason for content extension, which sorts out the characteristics of the case: some of them will turn out to be relevant according to the argument that the judge resorts to, others will not. If this commitment is satisfied from the point of view of the participants in the argumentative practice according to the accepted argumentative standards, then the word "things" correctly applies to electromagnetic waves, since the latter are taken to have the same relevant characteristics of the standard instances of things. In this sense, the sort of tolerance we are focusing on can be called "semantic tolerance". The argumentative process aims at determining the semantic content of a vague term in a borderline case on the basis of the contextual constraints that are made explicit by legal arguments.[21]

As to analogical extension, on the contrary, the starting point of judicial reasoning is that the case is not within the meaning of the legal provision and thus no interpretation can include it in the extension of the provision. The tolerance principle does not hold as to the case at hand, which in fact is not a borderline case. In this sense, the argument from analogy takes for granted that extensive interpretation has failed: analogy is a remedy to the lack of success of interpretive effort. Despite this, there might be further reasons justifying the extension of the regulation. In this respect, the argumentative process does not seek to determine the semantic content of an interpreted term or expression: the content is taken for granted and the case falls under the antiextension of the interpreted term or expression. Argumentation aims to flesh out whether the purpose of the interpreted legal provision justifies the analogical extension of the regulation beyond the semantic boundaries of language.

[21] In the light of this, the semantic content of a legal provision can be conceived of as the set of inferences the provision is involved in legal argumentation. We have discussed this idea in Canale and Tuzet (2007).

One might object that analogical reasoning is based upon a relevance criterion too. Analogical extension of a given regulation is admitted only if there are relevant similarities between the source and the target, i.e., if the two cases share the same relevant characteristics. This being true, in what does analogical extension differ from interpretive extension?

The difference rests upon the source of relevance. As far as interpretive extension is concerned, relevance has a *semantic* source: it depends on the rules governing the uses of language and the contextual constraints put on them. In the case of analogical extension, on the contrary, relevance has a *pragmatic* source: relevance conditions are fixed by the purpose of the law in its standard circumstances of application. When analogical extension achieves the same goal that the provision was assumed to achieve in standard cases, then the extension is justified. These conditions, therefore, are fixed by the legislature or by the legal system as a matter of policy; they do not merely depend on language and context of use. As a consequence, pragmatic relevance might vary from semantic relevance. And these are precisely the circumstances in which analogical reasoning comes into play.

To sum up our analysis, the two argumentative games considered in this paper are similar (on interpretive games cf. Chiassoni 1999). First of all, they pursue the same goal: extending a regulation to a case that is not explicitly considered by the law. Moreover, some argumentative constraints are pretty alike. For instance, relevance is a necessary condition for getting the regulation extended in both games. Notwithstanding this, they are not the same game: they display a quite different argumentative path in theory and practice. In order to justify a judicial decision, it is up to the judge to decide what game to engage in, assuming that extensive interpretation comes first and analogical extension is (normally) not allowed in criminal law.[22]

On the basis of these findings, one may claim that analogical reasoning and interpretive extension actually do not have the same upshot. Their outcome is the same in the sense that they justify the extension of a regulation to a case that is not explicitly considered by it. But this is only one part of the story. With extensive interpretation one claims that the case is within the meaning of a legal provision: there is no gap in the law as to the case at hand, and it is so on the basis of a certain reconstruction of legislative intent, the considered legal system, or the goal pursued by the interpreted legal provision. Engaging in this argumentative game commits the interpreter to a systemic picture of the regulation. On the contrary, analogical reasoning assumes that the case is beyond the meaning of the interpreted legal provision: the court faces a gap that has to be filled. And this follows from an alternative systemic picture of the same regulation, a picture where purposes or principles certainly play a significant but different role.[23]

[22] "'Extensive interpretation' may not be distinguishable from 'analogy' in the sphere where the inclusiveness or exclusiveness of a word is uncertain. But where the outer limits of word meaning are exceeded, only 'analogy' can be said to be applicable if the statute is to be extended to conform to its apparent purpose" (Silving 1967, p. 315).

[23] "The decision whether to interpret a statute restrictively or extensively, or the decision whether to explain and distinguish or follow by extending a case-law rule is, as a matter of observation, in

13.6 Conclusions

On the basis of the framework just proposed, one can critically assess the justification provided by the Italian Court of Cassation in the Vatican Radio Case.

In this case the Court did not provide sufficient elements to justify its decision according to our analysis. The Court claimed that the emission of electromagnetic waves falls within the extended meaning of the expression "dangerous throwing of things". As far as the word "things" is concerned, the Court satisfied its argumentative commitment to extensive interpretation providing suitable reasons. The Court argued that the case of electromagnetic waves falls under the extension of the predicate "things" according to a systemic argument that relies, in turn, on scientific considerations as to the physical nature of waves. The counter argument provided by the defense, according to which the legislature intended the term to be referred only to material things, was not complete, since the defense provided no evidence of this fact. The argument from legislative intention was not properly used, since its premises were lacking: the defense just expressed its own intuition, not unwarranted in itself, about what the 1930 legislature intended to say. As a consequence, the Court was entitled to claim that "things" applies to the electromagnetic waves released by Vatican Radio according to the interpretive standards accepted in the Italian judicial community. These standards, in particular, single out the relevant characteristics of the subject of regulation and thus the conditions of application of the term "things" as to the case at hand.

Conversely, the qualification of waves emission as an act of "throwing" was highly questionable. The Court merely claimed that the standard uses of the term "throwing" cover a number of different actions, so that the content of this term is not vague but general: it does not yield borderline cases being its extension highly inclusive. As a consequence, the emission of electromagnetic waves would clearly fall under the meaning of "throwing", according to the Court, as supported by the poetic use of the term in the thirteenth century.

It has to be noticed, however, that the term "throwing" is not highly general as assumed by the Court. The judges simply mentioned an idiomatic and metaphorical use of the term ("throwing a cry") that is not sufficient to assess its extension in ordinary language. Moreover, the poetic use of the term in the thirteenth century is not an accepted canon of argumentation and statutory construction in Italian adjudication, since it does not single out a semantic standard neither at the time in which the law was enacted (original meaning), nor at the time in which the law is applied (current meaning). Notwithstanding Dante's greatness and his majestic use of the thirteenth century Italian, if even poetic and marginal uses fall within the framework of admissibility (together with ordinary and legally technical uses), one can suspect serious violations of the rule of law or of the principle of legality in criminal law.

part at least based on arguments from legal principles, as that we can't tell whether the case we are faced with is easy or hard until we have reflected on the principles as well as on the prima facie applicable rule or rules" (MacCormick 1978, p. 231).

References

Bobbio, N. 1994. *Contributi ad un dizionario giuridico*. Turin: Giappichelli.
Brewer, S. 1996. Exemplary reasoning: Semantics, pragmatics, and the rational force of legal argument by analogy. *Harvard Law Review* 109:923–1028.
Caiani, L. 1958. Analogia. b) Teoria generale. In *Enciclopedia del diritto,* vol. 2, 348–378. Milan: Giuffrè.
Carcaterra, G. 1988. Analogia. I) Teoria generale. In *Enciclopedia giuridica,* vol. 2, 1–25. Rome: Treccani.
Cardozo, B. N. 1921. *The nature of judicial process*. New Haven: Yale University Press.
Cardozo, B. N. 1924. *The growth of the law*. New Haven: Yale University Press.
Canale, D., and G. Tuzet. 2007. On legal inferentialism. Toward a pragmatics of semantic content in legal interpretation? *Ratio Juris* 20:32–44.
Canale, D., and G. Tuzet. 2009. The a simili argument: An inferentialist setting. *Ratio Juris* 22:499–509.
Chiassoni, P. 1999. Interpretive games: Statutory construction through Gricean eyes. In *Analisi e diritto 1999,* eds. P. Comanducci and R. Guastini, 79–99. Turin: Giappichelli.
Dressler, J. 1987. *Understanding criminal law*. New York: Matthew Bender.
Dummett, M. 1975. Wang's paradox. *Synthese* 30:301–324.
Endicott, T. 2000. *Vagueness in law*. Oxford: Oxford University Press.
Fine, K. 1975. Vagueness. Truth and logic. *Synthese* 30:265–300.
Gianformaggio, L. 1997. "Like"—"Equal"—"Similar": Are they to be treated alike? In *Normative systems in legal and moral theory,* eds. E. Garzón Valdés, W. Krawietz, G. H. von Wright, and R. Zimmerling, 251–277. Berlin: Duncker & Humblot.
Golding, M. P. 1980. *Legal reasoning*. New York: Random House.
Grice, P. H. 1989. *Studies in the way of words*. Cambridge: Harvard University Press.
Guarini, M. 2010. Understanding blended multi-source arguments as arguments from partial analogies. *Ratio Juris* 23:65–100.
Haack, S. 2005. On legal pragmatism. *The American Journal of Jurisprudence* 50:71–105.
Hart, H. L. A. 1961. *The concept of law*. 2nd ed. Oxford: Oxford University Press.
Hassemer, W. 1992. Richtiges Recht durch richtiges Sprechen? Zum Analogieverbot im Strafrecht. In *Rechtkultur als Sprachkultur. Zur Forensischen Funktion der Sprachanalyse,* ed. G. Grewendorf, 71–92. Frankfurt a. M.: Suhrkamp.
Holyoak, K. J., and P. Thagard. 1995. *Mental leaps: Analogy in creative thought*. Cambridge: MIT.
Jónsson, O. P. 2009. Vagueness, interpretation and the law. *Legal Theory* 15:193–214.
Kaptein, H. 2005. Legal progress through pragma-dialectics? Prospects beyond analogy and e contrario. *Argumentation* 19:497–507.
Kloosterhuis, H. 2005. Reconstructing complex analogy argumentation in judicial decisions: A pragma-dialectical perspective. *Argumentation* 19:471–483.
MacCormick, N. 1978. *Legal reasoning and legal theory*. Oxford: Clarendon.
MacCormick, N. 1995. Argumentation and interpretation in law. *Argumentation* 9:467–480.
Olivares, G. Q. 1989. *Derecho penal. Parte general*. Madrid: Marcial Pons.
Peczenik, A. 2005. *Scientia Juris. Legal doctrine as knowledge of law and as a source of law*. Dordrecht: Springer.
Poscher, R. 2012. Ambiguity and vagueness in legal interpretation. In *Oxford handbook on language and law,* eds. L. Solan and P. Tiersma, 128–144. Oxford: Oxford University Press.
Posner, R. 2006. Reasoning by analogy. *Cornell Law Review* 91:761–774.
Raffman, D. 1994. Vagueness without paradox. *Philosophical Review* 103:41–74.
Robert, J.-H. 2001. *Droit pénal général*. Paris: Presses Universitaires de France.
Ross, A. 1958. *On law and justice*. London: Stevens & Sons.
Searle, J. R. 1978. Literal meaning. *Erkenntnis* 13:207–224.
Shapiro, S. 2006. *Vagueness in context*. Oxford: Oxford University Press.
Silving, H. 1967. Analogy and extensive interpretation. *Revista Jurídica de la Universidad de Puerto Rico* 36:311–316.

Soames, S. 1999. *Understanding truth*. Oxford: Oxford University Press.
Sunstein, C. 1993. On analogical reasoning. *Harvard Law Review* 106:741–791.
Varzi, A. 2007. Supervaluationism and its logics. *Mind* 116:633–675.
Weinreb, L. L. 2005. *Legal reason. The use of analogy in legal argument*. Cambridge: Cambridge University Press.
Williamson, T. 1994. *Vagueness*. London: Routledge.
Wright, C. 1975. On the coherence of vague predicates. *Synthese* 30:325–364.
Wróblewski, J. 1992. *The judicial application of law*, eds. Z. Bankowski and N. MacCormick. Dordrecht: Kluwer Academic Publishers.

Chapter 14
Analogia Legis and *Analogia Iuris*: An Overview from a Rhetorical Perspective

Giovanni Damele

14.1 *Analogia Legis* and *Analogia Iuris*: An Apparent Distinction?

The argument from analogy, or *a simili* argument, has a great importance in legal practice, both in common law (because of the *stare decisis* principle, which implies that a Court should use precedents to guide new decisions) and in civil law. Particularly in the civil law tradition, two versions of legal analogy can be distinguished. The *analogia legis* (or the *a simili* argument properly or strictly so-called) ultimately based on drawing resemblances between two statutes, on the grounds of similarities considered "relevant" or "material" for the purpose of the case, and the *analogia iuris*, or "argument from general principles". In this latter case the interpreter, in order to fill a gap, establishes an analogy not according to norms, but rather, to the so-called "general principles of law".

In this paper, I will consider both types of analogy (and analogy in general) as a rhetorical argument. Obviously, analogies can also have a heuristic role in legal practice, helping judges or jurists in finding new premises. However, considered as legal arguments, they play a crucial role, first of all, in the justification of legal decisions. In Sect. 4., I will discuss Judge Posner's opposition between "legal thought" and "legal rhetoric", and I will briefly analyse the reasons Judge Posner provides for including legal analogy in the realm of rhetoric. This opposition, as we will see, seems to be grounded on two aspects: a basic distinction between, let say, "process of discovery" and "process of justification", and, consequently, a characterization of analogy as a "surface" (rhetorical) phenomenon. Then, I will discuss another characterization of analogy (*legis* and *iuris*), made by Giovanni Tarello in his book on legal interpretation. Also in this case, the rhetorical dimension of the analogical argument is emphasized, albeit in a rather different way. Finally, I propose a "reductionist" approach to legal analogy, based on the consideration of the rhetorical nature of legal (judicial) argumentation as a whole.

G. Damele (✉)
Institute for Philosophy of Language, New University of Lisbon, Lisbon, Portugal
e-mail: giovanni.damele@fcsh.unl.pt

H. J. Ribeiro (ed.), *Systematic Approaches to Argument by Analogy*,
Argumentation Library 25, DOI 10.1007/978-3-319-06334-8_14,

Thus, this paper can be considered as a first step toward an analysis of the use of the term "rhetoric", as used in the context of legal argumentation theories.

14.2 Analogies in Law

Legal analogies, such as the argument *a simili* and its counterpart the argument *a contrario*, analogies starting from general principles, extensive interpretations (that is, interpretations that "extend" the meaning of one or more particular legal terms included in a given statute), and argument from precedents are hardly distinguishable. As a matter of fact, authors such as Alf Ross do not distinguish between analogy and extensive interpretation: "Extensive interpretation (interpretation by analogy) is the term used when pragmatic considerations result in the application of the rule to situations which, regarded in the light of 'natural linguistic reading', clearly fall outside its flied of reference" (Ross 1958, p. 149). According to Ross the extensive interpretation can be described as follows: "if a rule in the 'natural linguistic sense' applies to sphere (a), its extension to sphere (b) presupposes (1) that legal evaluation is in favour of applying it also to the sphere (b) (…); (2) that there is no difference between (a) and (b) that could justify the different treatment of the two cases" (Ross 1958, p. 150). In the same vein, referring to the Italian legal context, Giovanni Tarello suggested that the argument from (statutory) analogy, when considered as an interpretive argument, appears as an extension of the meaning of a legal term in order to cover a new case (Tarello 1980, p. 354). Thus, the reason for the distinction between analogy and extensive interpretation basically has to do with the prohibition of analogy in criminal law or its limitation in areas of law such as tax law or civil law.[1]

Conversely, authors such as, among others, Damiano Canale and Giovanni Tuzet differentiate the two techniques (considered as "two techniques of decision-making"). From their point of view, extensive interpretation "makes reference either to the interpretive process that extends the standard meaning of an interpreted legal provision, or to the outcome of this process", while analogical reasoning "denotes an argumentative technique inferentially articulated" (Canale and Tuzet 2014, forthcoming, p. 1). According to Neill MacCormick (1995) (who includes analogies in the category of "systematic arguments"[2]) "if a statutory provision is significantly

[1] "La ragione per la quale sovente l'analogia viene distinta da una 'interpretazione estensiva' va ricercata nei divieti di analogia che talune organizzazioni giuridiche pongono in taluni casi (ad esempio in materia di norme penali, in materia di norme speciali)." See also *infra* n. 6.

[2] MacCormick and Summers includes in the category of systematic arguments, among others: (a) "arguments invoking precedents already interpreting the statute at hand"; (b) "arguments based on statutory analogies. For example, when a case is not provided for in the statute, the case is to be treated in the same fashion that closely analogous cases are treated in the statute"; (c) "arguments appealing to general principles potentially or actually operative within the field in which the interpretational issue arises" (MacCormick and Summers 1991). As Harm Kloosterhuis underlined,

analogous with similar provisions of other statutes, or a code, or another part of the code in which it appears, then even if this involves a significant extension of or departure from ordinary meaning, it may properly be interpreted so as to secure similarity of sense with the analogous provisions either considered in themselves or considered in the light of prior judicial interpretations of them". Particularly, "the argument from analogy appears to be stronger on the second hypothesis, where it incorporates a version of the argument from precedent" (MacCormick 1995, p. 474) (Canale and Tuzet 2014 forthcoming, p. 5 n. 16, noted that this construction is more complex than mere extensive interpretation, defining it as an "analogical extensive interpretation").

The enormous amount of literature on this topic has provided detailed investigations into the (possible) differences between analogy and extensive interpretation, as well as the logical and argumentative structure of the argument and its soundness, rationality or reasonableness. Ulrich Klug (1983) distinguished between three different kinds of analogy (as a conclusion following from two premises by means of a syllogistic inference; as an inference from a particular premise to a particular conclusion, by means of reasoning that cannot be classified as deductive or inductive; analogy as a kind of imperfect reasoning, leading to only presumptive conclusions) while Alexy's (1983) and Weinreb's studies (2005) focused on the imperfect inference leading to presumptive conclusions (Macagno and Walton 2009, p. 155). From a "material" (not merely formal) point of view, Wróblewsky distinguishes between analogy "*extra legem*" and analogy "*intra legem*". He states, "The problem of the completeness of a legal system is linked with that of extra-statutory analogy ('analogy *extra legem*'), where legal consequences are ascribed to facts, which are not singled out in enacted legal rules. In interpretation, there is a problem of using analogy *intra legem*, where one does not go 'outside the valid law' but only tries so to fix the meaning of the legal rules that they constitute the most harmonious whole possible. Thus interpretation by analogy is singled out according to the reasoning it uses" (Wróblewski 1992, p. 103).

Descriptive approaches have explained the use of analogy in real cases, while normative approaches have identified criterion for the acceptability of the argument. Douglas Walton has explored the persuasive force of analogical argument, starting from the example of the case of Silkwood v. Kerr-McGee corporation (Walton 2013). Other authors, starting from a normative point of view, have proposed rules for choosing or analysing analogies, like Peczenik's (1989) "ten reasoning norms" (for choosing between *a simili* and *a contrario* argument),[3] or like the criteria for evaluating analogies within the pragma-dialectical framework, proposed by Kloosterhuis

"this means that analogy argumentation is only relevant when a linguistic reading of the norm is unacceptable (in case of the interpretation of a norm) or impossible (in case of a gap) (Kloosterhuis 2000, pp. 178–179).

[3] Peczenik's definition of (statutory) analogy argumentation reads as follows: "One applies a statutory rule to a case which, viewed from the ordinary linguistic angle, is included in neither the core nor the periphery of the application area of the statute in question, but resembles the cases covered by this statute in essential respects" (Peczenik 1989, p. 392; Kloosterhuis 2000, p. 177)

(2000). Interesting enough, Kloosterhuis distinguishes between two approaches to the analysis of analogies in legal contexts. According to the "monological approach", represented by authors such as Tammelo (1969) and Klug (1983), analogy argumentation is a "specifically legal argumentation form" which "does not meet the requirements of logical validity", but which "can be reconstructed as a logically valid argumentation". This reconstruction, however, "abstracts from the discussion context and aims at the final product of the discussion process". Conversely, the "dialogical approach", represented by authors such as Aarnio et al. (1981) and Aarnio (1988), "regards argumentation as a part of a discussion". Thus, "the acceptability if the argumentation" depends "on formal and procedural requirements applying to the discussion process in which a standpoint is defended (Kloosterhuis 2000, p. 177). In order to complete this coupled analysis, a third approach can be added. From a rhetorical perspective, arguments are evaluated according to their effect on a particular audience, or, to put it simply, according to their rhetorical efficiency. Different approaches can be useful in addressing different aspects of legal argumentation, for example the *heuristic* or the *justificatory* role of the analogical argument. However, because of the requirement of justification of legal decisions in the context of the rule of law, the rhetorical approach seems to play a central role.

14.3 The *A Simili* Argument

From a *heuristic* point of view, the analogical argument can be characterized, roughly speaking, as a general strategy for reducing vagueness in norms, identifying the so called *ratio legis* (that is the purpose of a statute) and drawing an analogy between the case in question and the *ratio* of the statute. Even if *ratio legis* appears to be a fuzzy concept, this strategy of "extensive interpretation" based on the argument from analogy seems to be useful in order to reduce the penumbra of the "peripheral" cases not explicitly foreseen by a given statute. Beside the notion of *ratio legis*, a judge can also resort, in order to fill a legal gap, to another (strictly related) strategy: he can make reference to a "general" principle considered as foundational for a complex of norms (for example for a given legal code or for the whole legal system). This second strategy of gap filling, which presents a more axiological dimension, is the so-called *analogia iuris* (Guastini 2011, pp. 276–282). In short, the main difference between these two versions of the analogical argument has to do with how the interpreter fills a gap: whether according to a rule or to a principle, or, better, to a "particular" (the *ratio legis*) or a "general" principle. Beyond this difference, the main characteristic of the two interpretive techniques seems to be the same, consisting in an extension of the legal consequences to cases not (literally) foreseen by a given statute, on the ground of "relevant" or "material" resemblances. From this point of view, the legal analogy can be divided into two stages: a bottom-up process, from the expressed norm to an implicit principle, and a top-down process, from the (now explicit) principle to the (before unexpressed) norm, containing the case "analogous" to the cases explicitly foreseen (Vassalli 1957, p. 159).[4] Thus, statute law is regarded, in this case, as a source of (particular or general) legal principles.

Both in the case of a general or a particular (*ratio*) principle, such as a reference to the "consequences" of a statute (consequentialist argument), the rationale of the analogical argument is, ultimately, more abstract than the statute itself since it is the result of the aforementioned bottom-up process aimed at identifying an implicit criterion of relevance obtained by abstraction starting from the "literal meaning" of the statute. Or, as Neill MacCormick succinctly pointed out, to elucidate what is relevant in the likeness between two cases is to formulate a legal principle,[5] and this can be characterized as a form of inductive reasoning (MacCormick 2005, pp. 208–207).

According to MacCormick, analogies "are relevant to what the judges call 'developing the law'", that is, extending or restating a legal rule or principle to make it cover, or to show how it covers, novel situations of a kind of that Joseph Raz suggests calling "unregulated cases". This "can also be thought of a using analogy to fill 'gaps' in the law". In this case, "it can be taken as signifying that a situation fits with an acknowledged principle (or with a freshly statable principle) that covers the very rules which themselves do not cover this case, or that accounts for the analogous case which this one is found relevantly to resemble" (MacCormick 2005, pp. 206–207).

If considered with this (very general) structure, legal analogy can be intended as a technique used not simply for interpreting or reinterpreting statutes, but for reworking or extending their meaning.[6] Or better (considering that many different techniques in legal reasoning can be regarded, in general, as techniques for reworking or extending the meaning of a statute), legal analogy as an extensive interpretation hides a process of the creation of a new norm, previously unexpressed (Guastini 2011, p. 324). As Joseph Raz pointed out, the analogical argument is, ultimately, a form of justification of new rules drawn by courts in the exercise of their law making discretion (Raz 1990).

Starting from this point of view, although with the aim of criticizing its use, Richard Posner has argued that the analogical argument "belongs not to legal logic, but to legal rhetoric", and that as a persuasive device it is especially used in order to obscure the policy grounds that determine the outcome of a case because it directs attention to the cases being compared rather than to the policy considerations that connect or separate the cases (Posner 2009, pp. 186–187).

---

[4] See also MacCormick (2005, pp. 208–209): "Of course, to spell out what is relevant in the likeness between case A and C is, in effect, to formulate a legal principle, and this can be characterized as a form of inductive reasoning. For once it is articulated in this way, the procedure works from individual instances to explanatory or justificatory generalizations of these, then returns to the now coherently connected decision about the current problem".

[5] "Our capability to find or to see similar patterns in different stories explains our ability to formulate broad abstract statements of principle that cover the cases. Principled reasoning presupposes analogical thinking, not vice versa" (MacCormick 2005, p. 207).

[6] "A principle that can be shown to be itself anchored in established law it is then relevant to legally justifying the decision in the instant case, albeit the decision is one that in this restricted sense 'extends the law'" (MacCormick 2005, p. 211).

14.4 "A Rhetorical Device": Judge Posner on Analogy

Reviewing the book written by Weinreb (2005), Judge Richard A. Posner made a number of interesting comments on analogical argument defining it as a "surface phenomenon" that belongs not to legal thought, but to legal rhetoric. According to Posner, Weinreb "has confused how judges think with how they talk" (Posner 2006, p. 765).

For Weinreb, "the choice of which analogy to prefer is not like a flip of the coin" (Weinreb 2005) but ultimately relies on the judge's knowledge and experience of the law. An experience that includes, as Posner emphasizes, knowledge "of the polices that animate legal rules and doctrines" (Weinreb 2005, p. 130). In other words, the choice of the "good" analogy is, for Weinreb, matter of coherence, since "within a legal order, the body of rules provides the criteria of relevance" (Weinreb 2005, p. 105) through a "test of consistency and coherence" (p. 138).

On the contrary, Posner argues that the "analogical argument" can be intended only in the rhetorical sense. For Posner, legal thinking in cases not ruled by clear statutory text or unchallenged precedents, something that Posner significantly identifies like "conventional legal sources", is clearly driven at best by policy, at worst by "prejudice, temper, ignorance, or whim" (Posner 2006, p. 768). Leaving the role of other legal arguments in cases "not ruled by clear and statutory text or unchallenged precedents" (such as the consequentialist argument, which can be used in order to identify the policies behind the statute or the case) aside for the moment, we may note that what seems to be implicit in this statement is the (somewhat controversial) distinction between easy and hard cases. This distinction seems to appear in the definition that Posner gives of "unchallenged precedent" as a precedent "rationally indistinguishable from the case at hand" (Posner 2006, p. 768). In other words, considering the issue from the point of view of "legal thought", analogy is either useless (in "clear" or "easy" cases) or misleading (in "hard" cases), working as a kind of "smokescreen" which serves to distract attention from the policies behind the decision. Incidentally, it is worthy to pay attention to the fact that almost every legal argument can be successfully used with this deceptive purpose. For example, the use of arguments such as the systematic argument, the historical argument, the psychological argument, and the appeal to the (both chronological and topographical) coherence of the legal system, can be part of a strategy to emphasize the consistency of the normative corpus, even where there is no such consistency. In other cases, political or ideological preferences can be disguised into an appeal to the consequences (teleological argument) or to the "nature of things" or the "common sense" (naturalistic argument), and so forth (Damele 2011).

More generally, we may note that regarding the distinction between easy and hard cases it is possible to repeat what Posner said regarding the distinction between law (that apparently drives the decision-making process in easy cases) and policy (which guides decisions in hard cases): that there is a line, albeit not a clear one. Moreover, any good lawyer is able to transform an easy case into a hard one. Therefore, it does not seem so simple, also for the purpose of an analysis of the use of analogical arguments, to distinguish between a case driven by "conventional legal sources" and a case driven by policy (when not by "prejudice, temper, ignorance or whim").

In any case, what is relevant here is Posner's characterization of the analogical argument as essentially a rhetorical device, which ultimately serves a deceptive function. In fact, the use of analogical arguments, Posner says, "tends to obscure the policy grounds that determine the outcome of a case, because it directs the reader's attention to the cases that are being compared with each other rather than to the policy considerations that connect or separate the cases" (Posner 2006, p. 765). According to Posner, "reasoning by analogy has no traction unless considerations of policy are brought into play to determine whether a pair of cases shall be deemed analogous whether, in other words, they share a relevant similarity" (p. 766). Thus, this intellectual process shall be reinterpreted under the so-called "purposive approach", by which a court, in order to decide a novel case, "excavates the purposes behind or policies underlying" cases (or statutes) relevant to the case at hand, "and asks what decision would serve those purposes or policies" (p. 765). For Posner, what is really involved in reasoning by analogy "is a method of cautious, incremental judicial legislating". Legal gaps, along with judges' duties to decide cases, force the judge to legislate, but since judges have no legitimacy as legislators, this "judicial legislating" has to be, precisely, "cautious and incremental" (p. 773). As a rhetorical device, legal analogy helps to attenuate the impact of judicial law-making, showing the (alleged) inner coherence between the novel decision and the precedents, or the legal system. In this sense, the use of the analogical argument can be deceptive: policies can be obscured, often, by the shadow of legal technicalities.

14.5 "Legal Rhetoric" and "Legal Reasoning": Some Distinctions

Summarizing judge Posner's analysis, we may identify two main aspects: a basic distinction between "legal thought" and "legal rhetoric", and, subsequently, the inclusion of the analogical argument in the realm of pragmatic rhetorical expediency (while the "purposive approach" has much more to do, apparently, with "legal thought").

The rhetorical nature of the analogical argument, like any other legal argument, is due to the need for persuasive justification, which induces judges to write decisions consistent with the consensus of their peers (and possibly with the consensus of the jurists). In this sense, analogical argument magnifies the beneficial effect of this process precisely by showing the coherence between the novel decision and the legal system, or precedents. Briefly speaking, the analogical argument, like any other legal argument, is rhetorical first of all because it is context-dependent. From this point of view, explicitly showing the purposes or the policies behind the decision can make the justification of a decision much clearer, but doesn't make, *per se*, the same justification less rhetorical (as Posners seems to suggest).[7] The consequentialist argument, for instance, is just one among the many "traditional" legal arguments (Tarello 1974, pp. 425–474, 1980, pp. 341–396),[8] and has precisely the same persuasive dimension as any other legal argument including the analogical one. Furthermore, the analogical argument rarely appears alone. Indeed, since the relevance or similarity between the two poles of the analogy need to be further justified, analogical arguments tend to be associated with other arguments, which support this relevance or similarity. For example, one of the possible strategies for the (analogical) extension of the meaning of a statutory statement is showing the coherence between the *new* meaning and the real "will of the legislator" (*lex minus dixit quam voluit*) (Guastini 2011, p. 278). For this purpose, the judge can resort, in his justification, to the "psychological argument" (appeal to the real intention of the legislator, for example, through the analysis of the "travaux preparatoires"). Moreover, other strategies can include resorting to the "naturalistic argument" or, precisely, the "consequentialist argument", among others.

On the other side, the distinction made by Posner between legal thought and legal rhetoric seems to suggest a parallel distinction between the so-called "process of discovery" and "process of justification". As is fairly obvious, the analogical argument, as Harm Kloosterhuis emphasized (and as we noted before), is not only *heuristic*, helping in finding new premises, but also *justificatory*, being part of the grounds of the decisions (Kloosterhuis 2000, p. 174). It goes without saying that the problem of the persuasiveness of legal arguments concerns justification and that the persuasive dimension of legal discourse, taking for granted the distinction between "process of discovery" and "process of justification", belongs to the latter. In theory it is certainly possible to distinguish between "discovery" and "justification" while analysing legal reasoning and to give priority to the first (logically and/or chronologically) over the second. However, this distinction is far from a clean or neat division, particularly in judicial decisions (Mazzarese 1995). In order

[7] Obviously, there is a difference between using the expression "rhetorical argument" in a technical argumentative sense, and using the expression "rhetorical device", as Posner seems to do, in the lay sense of "not based on fact" or "deceptive". However, even considering this different use of the term "rhetorical", with the expression "surface phenomenon" Posner suggests a two-level model and distinguishes between a superficial "rhetorical" dimension and a deeper structure ("legal reasoning").

[8] This category includes the classic legal arguments, which find their most complete formulation in the work of Tarello: psychological argument (appeal to the will of the legislator), historical argument (assumption of continuity: hypothesis of the conservative legislator), *a contrario* argument, literal argument (syntactical and grammatical considerations), coherency of the legal system argument (horizontal: between statutes; vertical: interpretation according to the Constitution and to supranational and international law), argument from the completeness of the legal system, economical argument (hypothesis of non-redundancy of the legislator), *ab absurdo* argument (apagogical argument), systematic argument (*sedes materiae* or topographic argument, argument from terminological consistency, conceptualistic or dogmatic argument), naturalistic argument (hypothesis of the powerless legislator, reference to common sense), *a simili* argument (*analogia legis*) and argument from general principles (*analogia juris*), teleological argument (hypothesis of the legislator with purposes), *a fortiori* argument (*a minori ad maius*, *a maiori ad minus*), authoritative or *ab exemplo* argument (reference to *opinio doctorum*, reference to precedents, reference to other jurisdictions, etc.), argument from equity (principles of justice used to select the meanings of provisions), naturalistic argument. (Tarello 1974, 1980; Damele et al. 2011)

to clarify, the parallel differentiation emphasized by Guastini between "motives" and "reasons" holding up the decision can be useful. The motives are "mental" or "psychic states" inducting a decision: instincts, emotions, attitudes, sentiments, interests etc. The reasons are statements, which publicly justify a decision. They are, in sum, premises of arguments. Thus, "motives" are part of the psychological process leading to a decision. "Reasons", on the contrary, form the (public) process of argumentation for, and justification of, the decision. The two processes do not necessarily coincide and the justificatory discourse may not coincide with the psychological process that leads the judge to make a decision. It is—at least—possible that the justificatory discourse represents an ex post rationalization of an ultimately irrational decision-making process. Now, what is relevant for our purpose is that the analysis of legal reasoning has to do only with the available material, that is the justificatory discourses, and not with the mental state or psychological process of the judge. Ultimately, the "process of discovery" remains to a large degree obscure to us, having much more to do with psychological circumstances than with rational procedures. Thus, going beyond Guastini's thesis, we may say that when we analyse a legal argument (like the analogical one), the distinction between context of discovery and context of justification, although theoretically possible, is practically useless because the issue at hand is the justificatory dimension of the arguments. And justificatory discourses always have to do with their persuasive force. Briefly speaking, from the point of view of the analysis of legal discourses, what the judge thinks *is* what the judge says, and what the judge says, in the context of a justificatory discourse, is relevant mainly for its persuasive force.[9]

14.6 Giovanni Tarello: Analogy as a "Rhetorical Scheme"

As Neill MacCormick underlined, there are many possible illustrations of the process of developing lines of legal doctrine by analogical extension of an originally narrow base (MacCormick 2005, p. 207). As a matter of fact, there are different types of analogy based on different logical structures: the analogical argument, *strictu sensu* (the *analogia legis*) and its counterpart the *a contrario* argument, the argument from general principles (*analogia iuris*), the extensive interpretation, the argument from precedents, etc. In general, they are all based on statements of resemblance, which grounds their persuasive force. As Frederick Shauer pointed out, the analogical argument is a form of persuasion based on the identification of some characteristic between the *source* (an example, a precedent, a case clearly expressed in a statute), and the target, the current case. If the audience accepts this similarity, it will therefore be persuaded that the similarity justifies treating the target in the same way that the source was (or would be) treated (Schauer 2009, pp. 87 ss.).

---

[9] "As is fairly obvious, judges' opinions in the legal reports of problem cases concern mainly justification, and the question how and why this judicial reasoning is persuasive addresses particularly the issue of its persuasiveness in the process of justification (…). As Bruce Anderson says, the claim to have made a 'discovery' must remain a contestable claim until a satisfactory justification can be stated" (MacCormick 2005, pp. 208–209).

The *analogia legis* and, in many cases, the argument from precedent, can be interpreted as an argumentative manoeuvre of this kind. What about the *analogia iuris*?

According to Tarello, *analogia legis* and *analogia iuris* hide different rhetorical arguments. In general, the analogical argument can be interpreted both as a productive argument (motivating or justifying law-making) and as an interpretive argument. Intended as an interpretive argument, the *a simili* argument (*analogia legis*) works essentially as a vehicle of an extensive interpretation, extending the meaning of the statute to other objects previously not included (Tarello 1980, pp. 351–352).[10] In this case, it can be considered as a kind of defeasible reasoning or an imperfect deduction, whose deductive pattern is a *Quaternio terminorum* (with the following scheme: M is P/S is similar to M/Therefore S is P) (Macagno and Walton 2009, p. 157). As Macagno and Walton pointed out, because this consequence cannot be considered a valid syllogism, the main problem is that M and S are presented not as identical, but only as similar, relative to some unstated properties (Macagno and Walton 2009, p. 158).

In a similar vein, Tarello (following the Aristotelian tradition) presents the analogical argument as a kind of counterpart, in the field of legal interpretation, of the proportion of geometrical type (a:b = c:d). From a rhetorical perspective, Perelman and Olbrechts-Tyteca also considered analogy as a proportion or similarity between two pairs: a relationship whose simple scheme reads "A is to B as C is to D". The first pair (A/B) forms the *theme* of the analogy, the second (C/D) the support or *phoros* (Perelman and Olbrechts-Tyteca 1958; Kloosterhuis 1997).[11] For Tarello, however, the main difference between analogy and geometrical proportion is that the first allows one to *analitically* identify the unknown term, while the second *rhetorically persuades* of the unknown term. For these reasons, the unknown term, which is necessary in the mathematical proportion, is only presumptive in the analogy, and for this reason the audience has to be persuaded of its existence. Thus, while the mathematical proportion finds *analytically* the unknown term, the analogy *persuades rhetorically* about its existence (Tarello 1980, p. 352).[12]

[10] "Nella nostra cultura, esso funziona come regola (e relativo argomento) di interpretazione, e precisamente come la regola secondo cui: essendo dato un enunciato normativo che predica una qualificazione normativa di un termine dell'enunciato che sta per un soggetto o una classe di soggetti, si deve estendere il significato di quel termine a comprendere soggetti o classi di soggetti anche non strettamente e letteralmente inclusi, e che però presentino con i soggetti letteralmente inclusi una somiglianza o 'analogia' assunta come rilevante in ordine alla identità di disciplina giuridica (almeno per quanto concerne la qualificazione in questione) (…). "L'argomento *a simili* funziona, in sede interpretativa, come veicolo di interpretazione 'estensiva'".

[11] Interesting enough, in his analysis of the argument from analogy considered from a rhetorical perspective, Peter Mengel concludes that Perelman and Olbrechts-Tyteca (1958) fail to formulate criteria for the validity of analogy argumentation because they mistake validity for rhetorical efficiency. However, from a rhetorical point of view, persuasive efficiency is more important than "logical" validity. In point of fact, the normative criterion, introduced by Perelman and Olbrechts-Tyteca, of the "universal audience" is itself a matter of rhetorical efficiency (Mengel 1995; Kloosterhuis 1997).

[12] "Il modello della analogia (…) è la *proporzione matematica*. (…) La differenza tra la proporzione matematica (che permette di individuare *analiticamente* il termine incognito) e l'analogica (che persuade retoricamente del termine incognito) risiede ovviamente nel carattere necessario del termine numerico incognito da un lato, e nella mera persuasione dell'esistenza del termine incognito dell'analogia dall'altro lato."

When used in legal contexts, the analogical argument tends to become an argument based not on two couples of terms, but only on three terms. According to this scheme, the analogical argument can be a "productive" argument (that is, an argument dealing with judicial law-making) when used in order to show the existence of a new norm (a norm that q is Z, when before only a norm that p is Z existed). When considered as an interpretive argument of a normative statement "p is Z", the analogical argument appears as an extension of the meaning of "p" in order to also cover "q", and ascribe to the normative statement "p is Z" the normative meaning "p and q are Z" (Tarello 1980, p. 354)[13].

The difference between "productive" and "interpretive" uses of the analogy can be interpreted as coinciding with the distinction between the *analogia legis*, considered as an interpretive argument used in order to ascribe or motivate the attribution of meanings to normative statements and the *analogia iuris*, considered as a productive argument used in order to fill legal gaps (Tarello 1980, p. 384).

This distinction has become traditional in legal doctrine. However, it seems to be somewhat weak. Indeed, if the *analogia iuris* is conceived of as a reference to principles deduced from the "natural law" or from the laws shared by the "civilized nations", then it is ideologically dependent on a peculiar cultural point of view (i.e. the natural law school or traditional legal liberalism) and ultimately appears as a pure rhetorical trick used in order to cover judges' ideological principles (Tarello 1980, p. 385). Nevertheless, "legal principles" can also be drawn from the legal system or from constitutional provisions. In this case, however, there is no apparent difference with the *analogia legis* (Tarello 1980, p. 385). In other words, either the *analogia iuris* is a rhetorical device, which is hardly controllable in a reasonable public dialogue and is used in order to cover an ideological position or it is an interpretive schema, which is not different from the statutory analogy. Or, briefly speaking, either the *analogia iuris* can be reduced to an *analogia legis*, or is a vide scheme (Tarello 1980, p. 385)[14], not susceptible to interpersonal control.

Finally, the persuasive force of the analogical argument relies on the inclination of the audience towards the relevance of the "similarity ratio" (or resemblance) between p and q. as we already noted, since the relevance or similarity between the two poles of the analogy needs to be further justified, the analogical arguments tend

[13] "(…) negli impieghi giuridici l'argomento analogico è presto divenuto uno schema basato non già su due coppie di membri, bensì su una serie di tre soli membri (…). In questi usi giuridici, lo schema dell'analogia è argomento produttivo di norme nuove solo in quanto lo si consideri come volto ad asserire l'esistenza di una norma che *q* è Z mentre esisteva solo la norma che *p* è Z; ma se lo si considera un argomento *interpretativo* di un enunciato '*p* è Z' esso appare come una *estensione* del vocabolo rappresentato da *p* a coprire anche *q*, in modo da attribuire all'enunciato normativo '*p* è Z' il significato normativo che *p* e *q* sono Z".

[14] "Il ricorso ai principi di 'diritto naturale' o 'comuni a tutte le nazioni civili' serve a poco data la evidente dipendenza ideologica di tali nozioni e data la divisione culturale della cultura e degli operatori giuridici; l'induzione dei principi generali dal complesso degli enunciati del diritto positivo si risolve o in *analogia legis* (o *materiae*) ovvero in mera 'estensione' di enunciati ben 'particolari', talché non v'è ragione di individuare un argomento ulteriore (…). Insomma, l'argomento a partire dai principi generali è uno schema vuoto, che serve a coprire di volta in volta disparate operazioni".

to be associated with other arguments, which support this relevance or similarity (Tarello 1980, p. 354)[15].

14.7 Provisional Conclusions

Both Posner (2006) and Tarello (1980) regard the analogical argument as an essentially rhetorical device, albeit in differing ways. The characterization of analogy as a "surface phenomenon", made by Posner, suggests the existence of a deeper level ("legal thought") in which policies are taken into consideration before a new case. The judge can choose to make his policy analysis explicit or to hide it with analogical arguments. Choosing the later amounts to, as Posner suggests, just a rhetorical device – a type of argument which belongs to the realm of "mere" rhetoric and which is "perhaps even self-serving judicial rhetoric" (Posner 2006, p. 762). In short, the term rhetoric has, here, a pejorative sound.

On the other hand, Tarello regards the analogy (both as a *analogia legis* and as *analogia iuris*) as a rhetorical argument because all arguments used by judges or lawyers in the context of judicial argumentation are "rhetorical schemes" used with the aim of persuading an audience (the jury, the judges, the higher court etc.). Obviously, in this context analogy can be used as a manipulative or deceptive device just as every other traditional "legal argument"[16] can (Damele 2011), including those arguments used in order to show the "policies" involved in a judicial decision, or perhaps the "consequences", the "objectives", the "purposes" of a decision or a statute. Thus, the main question is, again, the way in which judges and lawyers use arguments in the judicial context, which is eminently rhetorical in the sense that, mainly in controversial topics, such as in new cases not covered in a statute, the persuasive purpose seems to overcome any other consideration, including the argumentation's inner coherence. Resorting to two military metaphors, we may say that sometimes judges use arguments like the artillery resorts to canister shot: not a single shell directly to the target, but a cluster of many bullets that spread the impact, in the hope that at least one will reach its target. The quantity of arguments sometimes prevails over the quality and the inner coherence of argumentation. In other cases, arguments have the function of smoke screens, hiding under more "technical" or "juridical" arguments (coherence of the legal system, reference to the *travaux préparatoires* and so forth), political or morally based considerations. It may happen that analogies are used, as Posner thinks, precisely in this latter way. However, like analogy, every legal argument can be used as a kind of "smoke screen", hiding, as Posner would say, at best policies, at worst prejudice, temper, ignorance or whim. More generally, rhetorical requirements shape the structure of legal argumentation. An aspect that can explain more generally the link between how judges think and

[15] "La forza persuasiva dell'argomento analogico dipende dalla propesione dell'uditorio ad accettare la *rilevanza* della somiglianza o analogia di *p* e *q* al fine di disciplinarli egualmente. Poiché questa rilevanza ha bisogno di essere argomentata a sua volta, l'argomento analogico tende a venire associato ad altri argomenti (…) che funzionano come supporti della detta rilevanza".

[16] See *supra* § 4.

how they talk. Or, in other terms, that can show the permeability, at least in legal contexts, of the borders between "context of discovery" and "context of justification". As Patricio Fernandez and Giacomo Ponzetto pointed out, "at the same time as he looks for rhetorical support for his decision, the judge will choose a rule that is easier to support" (Fernandez and Ponzetto 2012, p. 11). Put more simply, legal interpretation itself has a strong rhetorical imprint.

Perhaps Weinreb and Posner are both right: the analogical argument may be at the same time the "essence of legal reasoning" and a "rhetorical device". Perhaps, the answer to Posner's question about what is the essence of legal reasoning, if analogy is just rhetoric, is that the question itself is misleading, because the essence of legal reasoning, and least in a judicial context, *is* rhetoric.

References

Aarnio, A. 1988. *The rational as reasonable: A treatise on legal justification*. Dordrecht: Reidel.

Aarnio, A., R. Alexy, and A. Peczenik. 1981. The foundation of legal reasoning. (2): 133–158; (3): 257–279; (4): 423–448.

Alexy, R. 1983. *Theorie der Juristischen Argumentation. Die Theorie des Rationalen Diskurses als Theorie de Juristischen Begründung*. Frankfurt: Suhrkamp.

Canale, D., and G. Tuzet. 2014. Analogical reasoning and extensive interpretation. In *Analogy and exemplary reasoning,* ed. H. Kaptein. London: Ashgate. http://unibocconi.academia.edu/DamianoCanale. Accessed 21 July 2013.

Damele, G. 2011. Rhetoric and persuasive strategies in High Courts' decisions: Some remarks on the recent decisions of the Portuguese "Tribunal Constitutional" and the Italian Corte Costituzionale on same-sex marriage. In *Argumentation 2011: International conference on alternative methods of argumentation in law,* eds. M. Araszkiewicz, et al., 81–93. Brno: Masaryk University.

Damele, G., et al. 2011. On legal argumentation techniques: Towards a systematic approach. In *From information to knowledge. On line access to legal information: Methodologies, trends and perspectives,* eds. M. A. Biasiotti and S. Faro, 105–118. Amsterdam: IOS.

Fernandez, P. A., and G. A. M. Ponzetto. 2012. Stare decisis: Rhetoric and substance. *Journal of Law, Economics and Organization* 28 (2): 313–336.

Guastini, R. 2011. *Interpretare e argomentare*. Milano: Giuffré.

Kloosterhuis, H. 1997. Book review—Mengel, Peter, *Analogien als arguments*, Frankfurt Peter Lang, 1995. *Argumentation* 11 (1): 135–138.

Kloosterhuis, H. 2000. Analogy argumentation in law: A dialectical perspective. *Artificial Intellingence and Law* 8:173–187.

Klug, U. 1983. *Juristiche Logik*. Berlin: Springer.

Macagno, F., and D. Walton. 2009. Argument from analogy in law, the classical tradition, and recent theories. *Philosophy and Rhetoric* 42 (2): 154–182.

MacCormick, N. 1995. Argumentation and interpretation in law. *Argumentation* 9:467–480.

MacCormick, N. 2005. *Rhetoric and the rule of law*. Oxford: Oxford University Press.

MacCormick, N., and R. S. Summers, eds. 1991. *Interpreting statutes. A comparative study*. Darthmouth: Aldershot.

Mazzarese, T. 1995. Scoperta vs. giustificazione. Una distinzione dubbia in tema di decisioni giudiziali. In *Analisi e diritto 1995. Ricerche di giurisprudenza analitica,* eds. P. Comanducci and R. Guastini, 578–616. Torino: Giappichelli.

Mengel, P. 1995. *Analogien als Arguments*. Frankfurt Peter Lang Europäischer Verlag der Wissenschaften, Europäische Hochschulschriften, Reihe XX Philosophie.

Peczenik, A. 1989. *On law and reason*. Dordrecht: Kluwer.

Perelman, C., and L. Olbrechts-Tyteca. 1958. *Traité de l'argumentation. La nouvelle rhétorique*. Paris: Presses Universitaires de France.
Posner, R. A. 2006. Book review. Reasoning by analogy. *Cornell Law Review* 91:761–774.
Posner, R. A. 2009. *How judges think*. Cambridge: Harvard University Press.
Raz, J. 1990. The politics of the rule of law. *Ratio Juris* 3:331–339.
Ross, A. 1958. *On law and justice*. London: Stevens & Sons.
Schauer, F. 2009. *Thinking like a lawyer*. Cambridge: Harvard University Press.
Tammelo, I. 1969. *Outlines of modern legal logic*. Wiesbaden: Franz Steiner.
Tarello, G. 1974. *Diritto, enunciati, usi*. Bologna: Il Mulino.
Tarello, G. 1980. *L'interpretazione della legge*. Milano: Giuffré.
Vassalli, G. 1957. Analogia nel diritto penale. In *Novissimo digesto italiano*, eds. A. Azara and E. Eula, vol. I. Torino: Unione tipografico-editrice torinense.
Walton, D. 2013. Argument from analogy in legal rhetoric. *Artificial Intelligence and Law* 21 (3): 270–302.
Weinreb, L. L. 2005. *Legal reason: The use of analogy in legal argument*. Cambridge: Cambridge University Press.
Wróblewski, J. 1992. *The judicial application of law*, eds. Z. Bankowski and N. MacCormick. Dordrecht: Kluwer.

Chapter 15
Analogical Reasoning in Clinical Practice

Nino Guallart

15.1 Introduction

There are three basic uses in which we can explore the relationship between clinical thought and analogy:

- The first one is the use of analogy in everyday medical thinking. More specifically, the use of analogical thought in clinical diagnosis. This is going to be the object of study of this paper, but we can also understand this relationship in other ways, which will be summarized briefly.
- The second one is the use of analogy as a tool for *teaching* medicine. It has been shown its effectiveness in clinical teaching, both with theoretical and practical analogies. It deserves a separate study and, therefore, it will not be covered here.
- Furthermore, a third one could be a mixture of the two previous, the teaching of medical thinking, which should include the teaching of analogical clinical reasoning.

Medical thinking has been studied since the late '50s with two basic approaches:

- Psychological study of medical expert reasoning, that is, the study of how real doctors think in their daily work and what kinds of reasonings they use in order to achieve their goals.
- Modeling of clinical reasoning, that is, how AI systems should work in order to simulate expert human clinical reasoning properly. This approach has received a lot of attention since the late '60s for several reasons, including the use of expert systems software in medical training, but it will not be explored here (for further reading on this topic, see Price 1999).

N. Guallart (✉)
Department of Philosophy, Logic and Philosophy of Science, University of Sevilla, Sevilla, Spain
e-mail: nino@usal.es

H. J. Ribeiro (ed.), *Systematic Approaches to Argument by Analogy*, Argumentation Library 25, DOI 10.1007/978-3-319-06334-8_15,

This paper is going to focus on the first case, the study of the role of analogy in clinical thought. One of the main goals of this paper is to show the central role of analogical thought in the phase of diagnosis, that is, the phase in which physicians have to reach an accurate explanation for the symptoms and signs found in the patient.

In a very schematic way, doctors have two main tasks in their work; the first one is related to problem solving, and the second one focuses on decision making. The first task is the act of diagnosing diseases, which begins with a set of symptoms given by the patient and ends with a final diagnosis that explains these symptoms, whereas the second one belongs to the act of treatment. Occasionally there can be some other minor decisions, such as considering if the benefits of the treatment outweigh its side effects or choosing whether it is worthwhile making additional test or not in order to get to a more accurate diagnosis, that is, they are decisions subordinated to the main tasks. We will work with a conveniently simplified model of clinical work, and we will assume that the only goal of the physician in the phase of diagnosis is discovering the disease that causes and, therefore, explains the signs and symptoms in the patient. We will override practical considerations such as economical or ethical issues and we will consider this phase merely as a search for an explanation.

Just an additional comment in order to show how idealized this model is; although the diagnosis comes first and then the treatment in the schematic model considered here, in real practice patients can sometimes be treated without having a definite diagnosis. For example, it is possible that a doctor is not able to reach a satisfactory diagnosis and, therefore, is unable to give specific medication for treating it. However, he is still able to prescribe symptomatic medication, that is, medication to alleviate the symptoms in the patient. Since medicine is a very practical science, its main goal is not knowledge and, therefore, there can be medical practice without conclusive explanations although they are desirable.

The phase of treatment with its problems is very interesting and deserves a complete study, but we will focus on the phase of diagnosis as an expert system. Its importance is due to the fact that it is by far one of the most studied expert reasoning systems, and its characteristics make it a very interesting system of expert reasoning.

An *expert system* is a system oriented to the solving of complex problems within a certain field. It is often applied to artificial expert systems, such as computerized expert systems, that emulate expert humans, but in this paper we will focus on human expert systems reasoning, that is, systems in which human experts in a certain field apply their knowledge and skills in order to solve the problems of this field and to make the appropriate decisions.

Clinical reasoning is a classic example of an expert adult thought process, that is, a set of rules and knowledge that has to be properly learned since it doesn't come from the general thought process. Starting with an initial situation, when the patient arrives to the doctor's office, he/she must achieve a diagnosis which explains the signs and symptoms. Some of its more prominent features of clinical diagnosis are the following:

- It needs some previous professional training. Neither the knowledge nor the necessary attitude and mental schemes for clinical practice belong to conventional wisdom.
- It is context-dependent and heavily based on expert opinion and experience.
- It is goal-dependent, because its main purpose is achieving a successful diagnosis. Medicine is a very practical task and, therefore, its main goal is not only achieving a diagnosis, but also finding treatments. Diagnosis and treatment go together, but the first one is subsidiary to the second one.
- It combines several strategies, instead of being based on a single type of thought. In the search of a possible diagnosis, doctors do not use a single kind of reasoning, but a wide variety of them, and part of the wisdom they must possess lies on how and when to use each type of reasoning.

For the following discussion, the next definitions can be useful:

A *symptom* is a subjective condition noticed by the patient, a change in the normal function or appearance of some parts of the body, such as pain, nausea or anxiety, among others. A *sign* is an objective feature noticed by the doctor in the body of the patient by direct observation or by simple means. Examples of signs include marks, colouring, changes of form or function and many more features that for a trained health professional can be recognized and have meaning; in other words, a sign is an objective indication of some medical fact or characteristic that may be detected by a physician. Sometimes it is useful to distinguish subjective symptoms told by the patient from objective signs discovered by the doctor, although sometimes the terms "symptom" and "sign" are used quite loosely, almost as they were synonyms. A *syndrome* is a recognizable association of several symptoms and signs that usually come together and may be related to a certain disease or diseases, although sometimes their cause is unknown.

A disease is an abnormal, harmful condition that affects the body of an organism. As can be seen, this definition is more practical than theoretical, because the word "abnormal" implies a judgment, not only a neutral description, although the word "harmful" seems to be less controversial. Whether a condition is abnormal or just a neutral variation has to be determined by several non-theoretical reasons, and it is not always clear the neutrality of these (one can think, for example, of homosexuality, that was regarded as a disease in previous decades but now it not considered a disease anymore).

By *clinical practice* we understand several actions and processes which are performed by physicians and other clinical professionals in their work in order to achieve a specific diagnosis, and to treat the corresponding disease if possible. The practice of treatment involves several issues, such as the balance between primary effects and secondary effects, price, adequacy of the treatment to the disease and to the patient and many more, but it will not be discussed here. We are going to focus exclusively on the diagnosis phase.

By *clinical thought* we mean a cognitive process which has one main goal, achieving an accurate diagnosis. It implies not only having the corresponding clinical knowledge and skills, but also having the adequate motivation and the necessary reasoning schemes.

Anamnesis is the process of obtaining clinical information from the patient, both from spontaneous information or in response to specific questions. It should be thorough and should contain both general data and clinical information, and within the latter one both the aspects more directly related to the patient's symptoms and information about all organs and apparatus. It is supplemented with *clinical examination,* which is a process of examination of the patient's body in the search for signs. Along with the optional complementary tests, the doctor has to work with these sources of information.

Diagnosis is the process by which doctors arrive to the cause of the signs and symptoms in the patient. In other words, the process in which the doctors determine the nature of the patient's illness.

The definition of diseases It is very remarkable that diseases cannot be defined. Instead, they are *described*, but not with a complete accuracy since they may vary depending on the characteristics of the patient (cf. Cutler 1998, p. 26). Although in medical school diseases are described more or less exactly by giving their more common and more prominent signs, these descriptions are often a simplification over an idealized model of the patient, and in real practice things can be more complex, since each patient has his or her own traits and, therefore, a certain disease can have non-standard symptoms and signs, or a sign can have more or less importance due to the features of the patient. Doctors must take into account that symptoms vary according to each patient's circumstances: a young person and an old person are not the same case, nor a woman and a man. Therefore, diagnosis is not an exact process, not to mention a simple deductive process from symptoms to diseases. Patients can have more than one disease at a time, and sometimes this can be confusing, because the patient will show symptoms of both diseases. Knowing how to discern diseases is an important part of the medical art.

It has been said in the previous paragraph than diseases cannot be defined, but described. This point deserves a short explanation, because this is not only an epistemological problem but also an ontological one.[1] Diseases, like many entities and processes, are sometimes quite vague, but they need to have a certain degree of ontological concretion in order to be treated as real entities and not mere aggregation of traits. The main problem that arises here is that sometimes the relationship between the symptoms and the corresponding disease is not very clear. Defining a disease by its symptoms and signs would link these in a necessary way with the supposed disease, with no further explanation. It would mean that every time these signs are present, the patient has this disease. However, diseases are not just groups of symptoms and signs, they have a different status. In modern medicine diseases are not grouped by their signs, but by their causes, and that means that the bond

[1] We are considering that known diseases are the cause of signs and symptoms, and this is the most common situation. However, sometimes a group of signs has been identified as the manifestation of a well-described disease but the eventual cause of them is unknown and, therefore, the relationship between signs and a hypothetical cause is not possible. Mental illnesses are a typical case, because they can be described by their symptoms and signs, but there can be no known cause for them.

between diseases and symptoms is secondary, although not irrelevant. The link between diseases and signs is empirical and, therefore, contingent; it's possible that two or more diseases present similar signs or even the same signs, and it is possible for a disease to have different signs depending on the patient.

15.2 The Process of Clinical Reasoning

The process of clinical though has been studied systematically since the seminal work of Ledley and Lusted (1959). They proposed a two-stages-based model, the first stage being the generation of hypotheses and the second one, the evaluation of hypotheses. In 1961 Rimoldi conducted empirical research on clinical practice, in which he found several differences in the way novices and expert physicians reason, which will be subject of further study since it is a crucial aspect of this paper. Since the '70s, clinical reasoning has been studied in depth both from the field of psychology/epistemology and the field of artificial intelligence, and within the first field it is worth mentioning the works of Elstein et al. (1978), who suggested a scheme analogous to scientific hypothetic-deductive model that will be used here.

Types of reasoning in clinical thought Clinical reasoning cannot be understood as a single specific way of reasoning, but a complex amalgam of different kinds of thought, which have their goal in common, not their method. The main feature that allows us to classify them as clinical reasoning methods is not the way they operate, but the fact that they work together in the search for a clinical explanation. Therefore, instead of focusing on a specific method of reasoning, clinical thought combines a wide range of strategies, from deduction to induction and mainly different kinds of abductive reasoning (in this paper, analogical and causal reasoning). A crucial element of the art of diagnosis is knowing when to use each of them and how to combine them.

Sometimes it is useful to distinguish these kinds of reasoning in two basic groups, deductive reasoning and non-deductive reasoning, which comprises of both induction and abduction. The words "induction" and "abduction" have been defined in many ways depending on the author. For the purpose of this paper, "inductive method" will be identified with probabilistic and quasi-probabilistic reasoning, whereas abduction will mean other kinds of non-deductive thinking, mainly analogical and causal thought. Deduction has the distinctive trait of the relationship of necessity between the premises and the conclusion, although in real clinical practice it is very rare, and it is more common to use quasi-deductive schemes instead of real deductive ones, as will be seen later.

Although this paper will focus on analogical reasoning, it has to be examined in comparison and combination with other methods, mainly causal reasoning and inductive methods. Each of these methods has its own role in the group of clinical reasoning methods.

According to Kassirer et al. (2009), there are three basic kinds of medical reasoning, deterministic, inductive and causal. In this paper, we will consider a fourth kind, analogical and, therefore, we will consider four basic kinds of reasoning:

- *Deterministic/deductive reasoning*: Backwards from signs and symptoms to diseases. It is the simplest form of reasoning, and maybe it should be called quasi-deterministic, since real practice is based not in simple deductive rules but in terms of probabilities with a very high degree. However, in a simplified way this can be understood as a kind of weakened deduction.
- *Inductive reasoning* focuses on quantitative relationships between signs and symptoms and diseases, without explicitly stating the nature of their link. In this paper we will equate with probabilistic methods. It contrast with the following type of reasoning, it just specifies correlations between types of data, not causal bonds (cf. Braude 2012, p. 105 for a discussion about the differences between statistical and intuitive methods in medicine). For example, the correlation between the risk of having lung cancer and the amount of cigarettes smoked is relevant, but a simple probabilistic correlation cannot establish whether smoking is the cause of cancer, having cancer is the cause of smoking or if there is a third factor which is correlated to the previous two ones.
- *Causal reasoning* assumes that everything has a cause and, therefore, it focuses on looking for the cause of the signs and symptoms in the patient (cf. Higgs 2008, p. 67 for an explanation on causal assumption in medicine). Every clinical reasoning implies implicitly or explicitly some causal reasoning. Therefore, this kind of reasoning underlies every clinical reasoning, but it is not always present in an explicit way. It can be considered a kind of backwards reasoning from effects to causes, and due to this it is central in clinical reasoning, since every symptom has an eventual cause or causes. However, unlike the previous quasi-deterministic reasoning and inductive methods it assumes a kind of metaphysical bond between signs and diseases, a causal one, instead of merely establishing a rule of correlation. Nevertheless, sometimes the finding of this cause is irrelevant or impossible, but it is implicitly agreed that this search should be a goal in an ideal case.
- *Analogical reasoning* is the last one that will be considered here, and since it is the object of study of this paper, will be analyzed with more detail. Analogy can be understood as a kind of resemblance of one thing to another, thus assigning properties from one context to another. In this way, "clinical correlation", a term coined by Alvan Feinstein (1967), can be understood as a kind of analogical thought that, starting with a corpus of knowledge based on medical theory and past clinical experiences, is able to find resemblances in the present patient to prior cases, allowing one to not only identify each sign, but also to assign them a meaning and a value within a broader context and be able to reach a clinical conclusion.

Following King, we can distinguish between three types of analogy: declarative, illustrative and inductive (Braude 2012, p. 130). Declarative analogies are the simplest ones, since they only draw a similarity between two entities, with no further intention. An illustrative analogy shows the resemblance of an unknown entity to a known entity, but as in the previous case there is no further intention of a closer bond. The most significant one is the third one, the inductive analogy, since it has an inferential nature that allows not only to compare two entities and show their similarities, but also to infer further similarities in non-observed features (Braude 2012, p. 130). Clinical analogy belongs to this kind of analogy, because doctors don't just establish the resemblance of the present patient's signs to previous cases, but are also able to guess non-observed signs that can be found later, to infer links between these signs and, therefore, to establish possible causes, to establish a diagnosis and to predict the future evolution of the patient.

Sometimes *hypothetic-deductive reasoning* is considered another kind of reasoning strategy. However, we consider that instead of a distinct way of reasoning it is more exact to consider it a general strategy in which all the previous methods can be applied in the pursuit of a satisfactory diagnosis. In fact it is a complex method that is a subkind of applied scientific method to a practical discipline.

Clinical process as a subkind of scientific method Before moving to the next step, a few words about clinical method as a subkind of scientific method. We are going to study a simplified model of clinical reasoning with three stages:

- Anamnesis and physical examination. In this phase the doctor focuses on gathering information, discerning relevant features from irrelevant traits.
- Provisional hypotheses generation. From the collected information, the physician looks for a disease or a few diseases as a cause for the symptoms or in other words, he attempts to arrive to a diagnosis.
- Hypotheses evaluation and verification/rejection. Every provisional hypothesis has to be tested, since the link between signs and diseases is not of necessity and, if a hypothesis arises as the most successful one, it is considered the final diagnosis. If not, the doctor must keep on looking for more signs and making new hypotheses.

If we consider clinical practice a subtype of scientific practice in which the subject of study are patients and diseases, we can think of this kind of expert thought as a particular case of scientific reasoning. Therefore, the traditional method of generation and testing of hypotheses is applied here. It is very clear that this process is just an applied version of the well-known hypothetic-deductive model (Fig. 15.1):

However, we will see that reality deviates from this ideal model sometimes. Now let's focus on each stage of this ideal process.

Examination of the clinical process Let's consider the use of the aforementioned hypothetic-deductive model in clinical practice with three phases, data gathering, hypothesis generation and hypothesis testing. For didactical purposes we will explain them as separate stages, but actually they should not be considered completely separate steps since they interact constantly until the doctor arrives to a final diagnosis. For example, after the initial anamnesis, which is part of the data gathering phase/examination, the doctor may have some tentative hypothesis in mind in the second phase. In order to discern between them and in order to confirm or disconfirm them, he may look for additional signs, which means a return to the

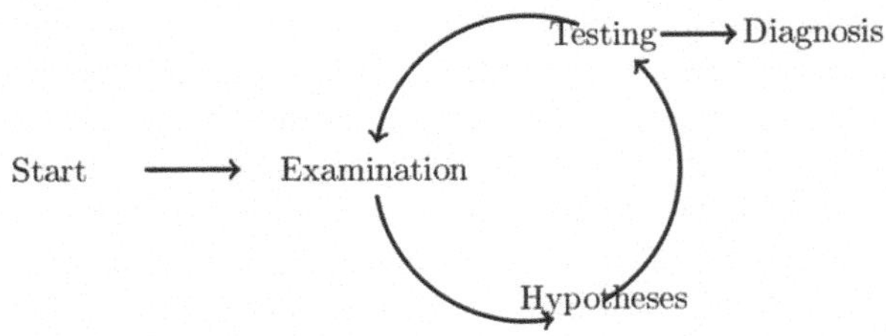

Fig. 15.1 Simplified model of the hypothetic-deductive model applied to diagnosis

examination phase. If this data disconfirm the previous diagnosis, he must reinterpret the data and make new hypotheses. Later we will see that this simplified model has several variations in actual practice, because it is not always linear and sometimes there can be shortcuts in it.

a. **Data gathering: Anamnesis and physical examination**

The first stage of clinical diagnosis is mostly based around on gathering information, which can be obtained from several sources:

- Complete anamnesis/clinical history. The doctor must start from the symptoms the patient mentions, both spontaneously or answering to the doctor's questions.
- Physical examination: the doctor must find relevant signs in the patient's body. Sometimes they appear at first sight, and sometimes the doctor must look for specific signs if he is thinking of a certain disease which has to be confirmed or disconfirmed.
- Complementary tests, such as ECG, laboratory tests, etc. In this paper, these tests can be grouped together with the physical examination.

A very important point of this process is that it is not a mere passive recollection of data, since the doctor must know what to look for and how to do it. Signs are not self-evident and a degree of knowledge is necessary to discover them. In other words, there is feedback, a dynamic relationship between exploration, hypothesis generation and testing.

Therefore, the doctor must examine each piece of relevant information, and depending of his level of expertise he will begin to make some provisional hypothesis. Since signs and symptoms have no meaning in an isolated context, it is problematic whether a certain symptom or sign is relevant or not, because it depends on the circumstances of the patient and on the illness he may have, and only the experience will indicate the possible relevance of it.

The problem of relevance of signs and symptoms As a general rule, a good diagnostic criterion must tackle the problem of relevance of symptoms in two ways:

- Relevance of each symptom and sign in the disease. Although a particular disease has a group of signs and symptoms associated with it, not all of them have the same importance. Signs may express themselves to different degrees, and doctors have to ask themselves if a particular sign can lead them to think of a certain disease or not, and to what extent.

- Importance of each symptom in the specific patient. The doctor has to decide whether a distinct feature of the patient is to be taken into account for the diagnosis or if it is an irrelevant trait, depending on the gender, age and other characteristics of the patient. For example, what can be irrelevant in an older patient can be very significant in a younger one, and so on.

These two problems can be summarized with a semantical approach: signs and symptoms don't have a specific meaning by themselves, but in a context given both by the patient's features and by a hypothetical disease. If we understand symptomatology as a semiology of clinical symptoms and signs, doctors face the task of determining their meaning, that is, the cause of what he notices in the patient's body. We can see that this is just an applied case of one of the classical problems in philosophy of science, the problem of relevance of evidence.

b. **Provisional hypotheses generation**

Doctors' experience helps them in their diagnosis, since it is primarily based on past cases they have seen rather than in pure theoretical knowledge. However, it is worth noting that it is a very systematic and organized experience which is set into a highly structured scheme. They begin with their academic background of anatomy, physiology and pathology, and they further add their own professional experience. Here we can understand the role of symptomatology, that is, how to explain symptoms.

Since the amount of hypotheses that can be managed is limited, doctors tend to focus only on relevant hypotheses, that is, hypotheses that can explain the symptoms in a realistic way. Knowing which hypotheses fit this condition is part of the medical training and, in fact, the more experienced the doctor is, the more accurate hypotheses he makes, leaving aside unsatisfactory ones. In contrast, novice doctors tend to make too many hypotheses, instead of focusing on a small group of them. In other words, in clinical practice making a few good hypotheses is by far better than making a lot of poor and doubtful hypotheses (cf. Dowie 1998, p. 216).

There are some relatively simple cases in which hypotheses generation is almost automatic. This is the case of *pathognomonic signs*, which are signs that are characteristic of a given disease. In other words, they are linked to that disease with an extremely high probability, almost certainty. Koplik spots are a typical example of this, since they are exclusive of the first stages of measles. Therefore, if they are present, the probability of having measles is practically equal to 100 %. However, this correlation is empirical and, therefore, subject to revision, and could change in the future. We can think of any yet unknown disease which causes Koplik spots too, for example, but this could be applied to any other sign we can think of.

In real clinical practice, although it is a complex process, achieving a result is relatively easy most of the time, since a high percentage of patients have more or less simple diseases and doctors are able to recognize them with more moderate ease, depending on the doctor's expertness. Since each disease has not a fixed pattern of symptoms and signs, but a group of probable signs that can be present with a high or low level of probability, reasoning backwards from signs to diseases is not always as easy as it could seem to be. In actual practice, things are more complex, because a patient can have several diseases at a time, or express his disease in different ways and degrees; age, gender and occupation may modify the way symptoms are shown, and doctors have to take these features into account.

c. **Hypotheses evaluation and verification/rejection**

When a doctor arrives to a diagnosis he should have to confirm or disconfirm his diagnosis by making additional tests. If the provisional diagnosis is compatible with these extra tests with very little room for doubt, the doctor may consider that his provisional diagnosis is well confirmed and, therefore, it can be considered the final diagnosis.

However, a very common case is that a group of signs is compatible with several possible diagnoses, although possibly with different degrees of probability. In this case, the task of the doctor is to discern between them, by doing a *differential diagnosis* (DD or Δ Δ in short), which is a process of decision between alternatives by looking for the particular differences between them. In a systematic way, this process has to identify a disease among several possible alternatives. There are several methods of doing that. Some of them make use of statistical methods. In this case, Bayesian probability is a good approach, since each new sign can increase the probability of the given diagnosis or to discard it in case of incompatibility. Other methods are analogical, by comparing the signs and symptoms of the patient both with an ideal case of the possible disease and with previous cases belonging to the doctor's experience. In this way, the more expert the doctor is, the more experiences he has to compare with the present patient. In the following pages, we are going to focus on the analogical way of reasoning.

15.3 Analogy in Clinical Practice

We have studied the reasoning foundations of diagnosis briefly. Now we can explore in depth the central thesis of this paper, which is that analogy plays a central role in medical diagnosis, and more precisely it plays decisive roles in the stages of data gathering and hypotheses generation, along with causal reasoning. Other kinds of reasoning such as deduction or statistical reasoning are complementary to them and may serve for testing the validity of the hypothesis and supporting the hypotheses, but they are not the chief methods of human-made diagnosis.

Doctors use several problem-solving strategies in their work, often mixing them. Pure uses of just one kind of reasoning can be useful for didactic purposes, for example, for showing the use of statistical methods or deduction in simple cases, but in actual practice using several methods together is more common most of the times. Causal reasoning underlies almost all diagnoses since the link between symptoms/signs and diseases must be of causal nature eventually. Inductive and causal reasoning often go hand in hand, since "[c]linical findings usually bear a probabilistic relationship to the underlying causes that produce them" (Dowie 1998, p. 116). Statistics are a good aid to the doctor's task (Ledley and Lusted 1959, p. 21), but most of the times they are not the core of his methodology other than laboratory tests, in which both statistical and deterministic methods are used more commonly. Nevertheless, in everyday clinical practice doctors usually work with causal and analogical reasoning, which can be considered their two main methods of his clinical work.

Analogical and causal thought Analogy and causal reasoning are grouped together as abductive method and, in fact, they are used together quite often. This is due to the following reasons:

- It is assumed that symptoms have a cause that must be found. In fact, causal reasoning underlies almost every clinical method, although not always in a clear way. However, causes are not visible traits, and they must be inferred from visible features and laboratory tests. In this task, analogy reveals itself as a highly useful way of linking visible signs and symptoms to possible causes, by comparing previous cases in which patients who had the corresponding features happened to have a certain disease which was the cause of these signs.
- Since every patient is a unique individual, he has his own personal history and each characteristic found in him can be considered the result of a personal story. The task of the doctor is to decide whether this is relevant or not for clinical purposes. In other words, he must focus on the possible illness that has brought the patient to the doctor's office and leave other features alone. Again, this decision is based on analogy both with previous patients and with healthy individuals of similar characteristics.

Therefore, analogy and causal reasoning are often used together, most of the times in an implicit way. However, this relation is not always so evident. This is the case with several diseases at a time, in which the doctor must know how to assign each sign to the corresponding disease and must consider the interaction of different causes.

Main uses of analogy Analogy plays a central role in two stages of the process:

- Pattern recognition during data gathering. Since signs are not always self-evident, the doctor must be able not only to perform the appropriate exams and tests, but also to discern signs and subsequently to assign them their correct weight of relevance. It may vary depending on the hypotheses that will be generated soon. Thus, depending on the hypotheses we are considering, a certain sign will have more or less relevance (cf. Cutler 1998, p. 11 for a wider explanation of this stage).
- It could be argued that pattern recognition is a process of particularization of general essential characteristics on specific patients. However, it is an oversimplification, because these theoretical models are just ideal cases, and in the long run doctors back up their decisions with previous experiences, not only with their theoretical knowledge. Therefore, it is more accurate to say that pattern recognition is based in both the comparison with theoretical models and with prior experiences, and the more expert the doctor is, the more use he will do of the latter ones.

- Generation of complex clusters of signs and symptoms linked to diseases. The whole hypothetic-deductive model we have studied before is very time-consuming. Therefore, if possible, it is more useful to abridge some steps by the immediate recognition of clusters of patterns which lead them to look in a hypotheses-driven way, back from the diseases they have in mind to additional signs to be found, instead of examining each relevant sign and then making some possible hypotheses that will have to be tested afterwards (cf. Patel et al. 2005). It is more likely to happen in trained physicians than in novice ones and, in fact, it can be said that the ability to recognize instantly these clusters is one of the main features that allow us to distinguish between experts and unskilled professionals.

The H-D model revisited Now let's consider a variation of the previous hypothetic-deductive model. Instead of considering each stage as an isolated phase, let's consider the process as a whole, in which doctors try to maximize their skills by identifying relevant, meaningful traits which lead them to a conclusion. We can study these stages, which are a variation from the standard model:

- *Identification of clinical signs*. The doctor has to have the appropriate perceptual skills to be able to recognize the signs present in the patient. This phase is the aforementioned data gathering phase, but in this case we add the emphasis on the ability of focusing on relevant traits from the beginning and on overall traits, instead of considering each isolated feature of the patient. Sometimes the recognition of signs is made in a *Gestaltic* way (Cutler 1998, p. 29) and leads to an immediate diagnosis instantly if the patient exhibits a remarkably evident group of signs. An example of this can be the recognition of Parkinson's disease, which is not made by detection of isolated signs that are put together later, but is recognized at first glance. In other occasions, things are not so evident, but doctors have to discern relevant clinical signs from irrelevant features with no particular clinical relevance. The importance of the context in these cases is crucial, and only the previous experience of the doctor can be a good guide to examination, and analogy to past cases allows not only to recognize signs, but also to assign them their corresponding weight of evidence.
- *Grouping them into clusters which make sense*. Isolated signs don't mean very much since a single sign can correspond to many unrelated diseases or even have no importance. As has been seen before, sometimes this clustering is immediate; sometimes, there are triads and tetrads of signs that come together very often and the diagnosis is almost immediate. Although things are inconclusive, clusters of signs tend to point in the direction of a certain disease, a group of related diseases or maybe a few non-related diseases. To know that, doctors must have a previous background in which signs can be understood, and this background that gives the signs a meaning comes in the first place from their theoretical formation and is later reconfirmed by their clinical experience. In other words, the relevance of a sign within its possible causes is reinforced or weakened by actual cases and, therefore, analogy to previous cases has an important weight in comparing the present case to previous ones.

- *Making a provisional diagnosis that explains the signs and testing it.* It is quite possible that a provisional diagnosis has been made by now. If not, the doctor must make an educated guess in the form of some explaining hypotheses from the signs he has found. In any case, every hypothesis must be tested. Sometimes this means looking for new signs that should be present in order to confirm/disconfirm the hypotheses, and sometimes this means making a differential diagnosis if signs are compatible with several diagnoses. In an ideal case, the hypothesis that explains the signs better should be considered the final diagnosis, if possible. Again, the use of analogy is very useful here, because the resemblance to previous cases in which patients with a certain group of signs had a certain disease most of the times can lead us to think that a patient with these signs has the corresponding disease with a high degree of probability. The appropriate additional tests that have to be made in order to test these hypotheses can also be suggested by previous experiences.

In this reformed model, we can see that each stage cannot work separately from the others, but they are interacting dynamically. Although examination, hypotheses' generation and confirmation are presented separately for the sake of clarity, very often they occur at the same time. Thus, some hypotheses may be formed while the doctor is examining the patient, and acceptance or rejection of them may occur almost at the same time, since every new sign can be used to confirm or disconfirm the hypotheses the doctor has in mind.

Expertness of the doctor. Backwards reasoning vs forward reasoning Although every research begins with the physical examination and anamnesis, unskilled doctors and expert doctors manage their data and hypotheses in a radically different way. The phenomenon of expert reasoning, not only medical expert reasoning but expert reasoning in general, has been widely studied in many sciences and even non-scientific fields such as chess (cf. Patel and Groen 1986). In short, non-experts tend to gather pieces of information first and then try to make sense from them, whereas experts are more able to see the whole picture and from this they focus on specific signs. Sometimes these ways of reasoning are described in terms of "forward" and "backwards" reasoning: Unskilled doctors reason "forward" from data to the diagnosis, whereas expert doctors reason "backwards" from diagnosis to the data, although this is of course an oversimplification:

- Students and unskilled doctors tend to use thorough methods. Their lack of experience leads them to need such an exhaustive exploration and hypotheses generation/testing, establishing quasi-deterministic and sometimes probabilistic relationships along with causal and more rarely analogical relations, forming several hypotheses and discarding unsatisfactory ones systematically in search of a conclusive diagnosis.
- Skilled doctors very often use abridged knowledge-based methods (cf. Patel and Groen 1986). Instead of following the standard H-D model, they use a lot of analogies to previous cases, grouped in clusters. They organize their prior experiences and make sense of them, learning how to discover similar cases. They are able to recognize at first glance complex patterns of signs that go together

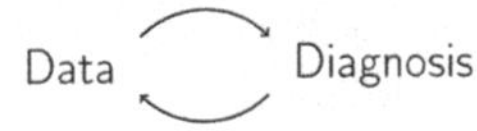

Fig. 15.2 Mutual feedback between physical examination and diagnosis

frequently and to discern between clusters of signs and symptoms, and they are also able to connect them quickly with the corresponding diseases, focusing on one or a small group of realistically possible causes, instead of having plenty of hypotheses to be tested. In short, skilled doctors have learned how to optimize their time and efforts.

As has been shown, that means that unskilled doctors begin focusing on *specific signs*, and from then they begin to make several provisional hypothetical diagnosis. In contrast, expert doctors begin focusing on the *general situation* and possible causes for it instead of isolated signs, are able to make a few accurate diagnosis and from them they look for additional signs that confirm or disconfirm their diagnosis (Fig. 15.2).

In other terms, this difference between expert and unskilled doctors can be expressed in terms of ability of maximizing their efforts. Skilled doctors are more efficient because they are able to use abridged methods, such as heuristics approaches.

Complexity of the disease We have focused on the use of analogy depending of the mastery of the doctor, now we are going the consider the relationship between the complexity of the case and the usefulness of analogy. Roughly speaking, the more complex the case is, the more prominent the use of analogy is:

- *Trivial and simple cases* comprise the vast majority of all actual cases. About 90 % of all patients have relatively simple diseases that can be diagnosed at first glance or after a few easy physical tests. Doctors can sometimes achieve their diagnosis by the use of quasi-deterministic and causal reasoning with not many doubts. In this case, the use of analogy is middle or low, and it can be grouped together with other kinds of reasoning although the more expert the doctor is, the more he will be able to use analogically and, therefore, the more efficiently he will perform his duties.
- *Mixed cases*, such as variations of known diseases or coincidence of several diseases in a patient, can be analyzed by the use of analogy, causal reasoning and induction in a successful way. There is a low level of deterministic reasoning because, in this case, the pathology cannot be studied in terms of simple rules of the form "symptoms → disease", but has to be scrutinized rigorously in order to consider all possible options. Statistical reasoning can sometimes be useful in differential diagnosis, but not always, and doctors have to make a more creative use of their skills. In these cases, the use of analogy reveals itself as particularly fruitful, since doctors have to examine the patient and compare his/her symptoms and signs with previous cases in order to arrive to a satisfactory final diagnosis. Since these patients are not typical, there are deviations from expected situations and several alternative diagnosis are possible, a high degree of clinical competence given by past experiences is necessary in order to arrive to a satisfactory result.

- *Unknown diseases*. This is the most interesting case of the use of analogy in clinical practice because it can be seen as the purest form of analogical medical thought. If the disease is unknown or the circumstances are radically different from usual, neither quasi-deductive reasoning nor probabilistic reasoning can be applied. Causal reasoning can be useful sometimes if there are some clues about the possible underlying disease, but of course it is not very useful if the possible causes are still unknown, which is the most common situation in this case. Analogy reveals itself as a powerful tool in the search of a possible explanation for the circumstances of the patient. Doctors must compare the patient with any case that have any resemblance to it, no matter in what way, and begin to work from that hypothesis. Therefore, these cases need a very high level of analogical reasoning. Since doctors have to make risky hypotheses, there must be a trade-off between creativity and accuracy. A purely analogical reasoning can be very uncertain since it assumes so many implicit hypotheses and these may be quite risky, although they may be tested afterwards. Since the other reasoning methods are of little help, the use of pure analogical thought in this extreme causes can lead to extremely innovative conclusions, at the cost of a high risk of failure.

15.4 Conclusions

We can reach a few conclusions from the previous pages. First of all, it has been shown that analogy plays a central role in the task of diagnosing, and sometimes a very important part in several stages of this process. It is not the only method of reasoning used in clinical practice, but along with causal reasoning it plays a central role in most clinical diagnoses. Since doctors are confronted with individual patients who exhibit different traits and peculiarities, doctors need to have the ability to reason in an analogical way to achieve a diagnosis because each patient is unique but at the same time shares characteristics with previous clinical cases. In this sense analogy is linked to creativity and the uncommoner the case is, the more analogy can play a central role in diagnosis.

It could be argued that diagnosis could be seen as process from the general to the particular, but this affirmation is quite incorrect. The difference between analogy and particularization is that the latter one compares the actual case with a theoretical general model of a certain disease, whereas the first one compares the actual case with previous patients along with the theoretical corpus, allowing more subtle and complex comparisons. Therefore, there is a crucial difference: analogy is dynamic, whereas the use of generalization is more static. As it has been shown, we can assign two main roles to analogical thought among the various kinds of clinical reasoning:

- The first one is a perceptual one, the recognition of significant patterns during the examination. Doctors do not look for isolated signs, but they try to see recognizable patterns, making sense of them within a context that includes the characteristics of the patient and some hypothetical diseases that could explain the signs in the patient.

- The second one is the generation of general pattern clusters linked to diseases that, if recognized in any patient, lead to quick diagnosis. It is more prevalent in skilled doctors than in novices, and it can be considered a kind of shortcut in the hypothetic-deductive model, as has been discussed when the difference between backwards and forward reasoning was explained.

These uses are crucial in the actual way physicians perform their work. Although statistical and logical approaches to clinical decision-making are very useful, they are not the core of real human medical diagnosis. In fact, doctor's diagnoses are usually based on the use of analogical and causal reasoning, and statistical and deductive methods are secondary to them.

Doctors make their own mental schemes from their past experiences, learning the importance of each symptom and creating clusters of symptoms linked to the diseases that are connected to them. One disadvantage of this method is that because the use of analogy relies on past experience, doctors tend to overdiagnose their own speciality's diseases. However, this feature is not exclusive of analogical reasoning because other models such as Bayesian inference tend to overrepresent the importance of diseases basing on previous experience. In order to balance diagnosis, each doctor must make up for his own experience with general data.

As stated before, diagnosis is part of a more complex system of medical decision-making which has as goals not only achieving an accurate explanation of the symptoms of the patient, but also finding a proper way for treating the disease. In this paper, we have just explored the cognitive aspect, but we should keep in mind that it is not an isolated process, but part of a wider work. Treatment has not been covered here, but a more thorough study should explore the links between diagnosis and treatment. To finish, there are several aspects that are worthwhile to emphasize:

- Clinical reasoning is dynamic because data must be searched for actively. It does not begin with a pure passive gathering of information but with an active search which is fed-back constantly with the hypotheses that are being formed.
- It is a non-purely-linear process, since its phases interact each with other constantly. Although the model starts with data gathering, follows with the creation of hypotheses and subsequent testing and ends with the final diagnosis, the actual process is less rigid.
- The more expert the doctor is, the more bypasses he will use in his reasoning, comprising the whole systematic scheme in an abridged method of recognizing patterns and diseases.

References

Braude, H. D. 2012. *Intuition in medicine: A philosophical defense of clinical reasoning*. Chicago: The University of Chicago Press.

Cutler, P. 1998. *Problem solving in clinical medicine: From data to diagnosis*. Philadelphia: Lippincott Williams & Wilkins.

Dowie, J. 1998. *Professional judgment: A reader in clinical decision making*. Cambridge: Cambridge University Press.

Elstein, A. S., S. A. Shulman, and L. A. Sprafka. 1978. *Medical problem solving: An analysis of clinical reasoning*. Cambridge: Harvard University Press.

Feinstein, A. R. 1967. *Clinical judgment*. Baltimore: Lippincott Williams & Wilkins.

Higgs, J., ed. 2008. *Clinical reasoning in the health professions*. New York: Elsevier.

Kassirer, J. P., J. B. Wong, and R. I. Kopelman. 2009. *Learning clinical reasoning*. Philadelphia: Lippincott Williams & Wilkins.

Ledley, R. L., and L. B. Lusted. 1959. Reasoning foundations of medical diagnosis. *Science* 130 (3366): 9–21.

Patel, V. L., and G. J. Groen. 1986. Cognitive knowledge based solution strategies in medical reasoning. *Cognitive Science* 10:91–116.

Patel, V. L., J. F. Arocha, and H. Zhang. 2005. Thinking and reasoning in medicine. In *The Cambridge handbook of thinking and reasoning,* eds. K. J. Holyoak and R. G. Morrison Jr. Cambridge: Cambridge University Press.

Price, C. J. 1999. *Computer-based diagnostic systems*. Berlin: Springer.

Chapter 16
The Role of Analogy in Philosophical Discourse

Henrique Jales Ribeiro

16.1 Introduction

In the conclusion of a first paper published in 1969 (11 years after *The New Rhetoric*), dedicated to the role of analogy in science, poetry and philosophy, Perelman highlights the crucial importance of reasoning through analogy in philosophical discourse in general, in contrast (at least in part) with an interpretation thereof, which would focus on the analysis and assessment of its purely "internal" or systematic structure, subordinating such reasoning to a merely external form of persuasion and argumentation:

> The history of philosophy could be rewritten entirely by laying emphasis not only on the structure of systems, but also on the analogies which guide philosophers' thought, the way they relate with each other, how they change one another and adjust to each other's point of view. There is analogical material that spans the centuries and which each thinker uses in his own way. (…) unquestionably, no philosophical thought may dispense analogies which structure it, make it intelligible and express, on a par with the philosopher's personal style, the tradition of which it forms part, which he extends and adapts to the requirements of his time. (Perelman 1989, p. 409, my translation)

Since analogical reasoning belongs unquestionably to the scope of the "reasonable", before the role that Perelman awards to such reasoning we are impelled to ask to what extent we may continue to accept, without reservations or questioning, his known theory, according to which Western philosophy—since ancient Greece—served the "rational" and, consequently, conviction and proof. This is a matter which I will address later. Essentially, what must be underscored is that from a perspective like that of this author—and which has been sustained by extensive and profuse literature on the subject—analogical reasoning is not merely an aid or an instrument of philosophical thought, but mostly it lays down the ground for it: structures it "internally", making it intelligible. This fundamental thesis—as we have just suggested—challenges the traditional conception, according to which philosophy

H. J. Ribeiro (✉)
Department of Philosophy, Communication and Information,
Faculty of Letters, University of Coimbra, Coimbra, Portugal
e-mail: jalesribeiro@gmail.com

H. J. Ribeiro (ed.), *Systematic Approaches to Argument by Analogy*,
Argumentation Library 25, DOI 10.1007/978-3-319-06334-8_16,

would be a purely rational, systematic and conceptual undertaking, which therefore would exclude from its own field basically everything which is not subject to conviction and proof, namely all that comes under the scope of what is vague and ambiguous, and which would provide substance for other forms of discourse, like poetry and literature. In some prominent circumstances, as is the case of the importance of reasoning through analogy in Plato, it actually leads us to paradoxical and disturbing consequences, which were highlighted by specialised commentators: the author who condemns poets and excludes them inopportunely from his "ideal city", in the dialogue *The Republic* (Plato 1992), is the one who ascribes to analogy and, under its scope, to poetic figuration an absolutely essential role (see Moore 2009).

Now, what is the nature and the role of reasoning through analogy in philosophical discourse in particular, what part the study thereof will play in argumentation theory is an issue which is far from being clear and is manifestly problematic. Most of the issues concern the following: apparently it does not fit into that framework, of ordinary language, which enables and justifies our analysis and assessment of argumentation in general and reasoning through analogy in particular, since such discourse would not be constitutionally argumentative, although it is obviously not unrelated to rhetoric, nor to its strategies and procedures. In other words, in philosophy stories are explained, narrated or, as has become a commonplace, told; one does not necessarily argue. Such objection does not mean nor imply that there is no room in philosophy for reasoning through analogy in all of its shapes (argumentative included), but it does affect substantially the scope of such reasoning—making it essentially disposable—and our assessment thereof. Herein, I intend to begin by analysing and discussing it in some detail, and to draw the possible consequences for the study of the ties connecting analogical reasoning in philosophy and argumentation theory. In the light of these consequences, I will be introducing and exemplifying a characterisation of the core features of such reasoning, within the historical framework of mostly modern and contemporary philosophy.

16.2 Is Philosophy Argumentative Discourse?

Before addressing the topic itself of the role of analogical reasoning in philosophy, I will start by asking whether philosophy is or not, generally speaking, an argumentative discourse. As we will see further ahead, this question is paramount not only for discussing such role, but also for understanding the status of other forms of discourse similar to the philosophical one, including argumentation theory itself. (As for the latter, the question we should be asking, *à la Wittgenstein*, is whether theory under which we define argumentative discourse is itself an argumentative discourse, or whether the requirements for that discourse are themselves the requirements for said theory.) My strategy is, thus, not to define philosophy *a priori*. The major issue with such definitions is that they are of little use to us to understand the nature of the philosophical discourse itself throughout history; that is if this discourse had or has specific and unique characteristics. (Personally, I believe it did and does have, but this is not the point now.) For example, to say that in philosophy we address one or the other type of problem, which triggers several broadly different standpoints, and, for this, we argue (and counter argue) about them, would allow us to link, from the beginning, philosophy to argumentation, but would not help us understand at all the nature of our own discourse. This is the greatest possible objection to the philosophical conceptions and philosophical argumentation, in particular of Popper (1963) and Cohen (1986) in the second half of the twentieth century.

So, allow me to introduce some definitions to clarify this matter. We speak of argumentative discourse when two parties have different opinions, at least about the subject they are discussing. Such difference must exist for there to be argumentation and not any other kind of discourse. As van Eemeren puts it: "Argumentation is basically aimed at resolving a difference of opinion about the acceptability of a standpoint by making an appeal to the other party's reasonableness." (van Eemeren 2010, p. 1) From this perspective, philosophical discourse is in principle an argumentative discourse: since Plato philosophers have discussed and argued among themselves precisely in this manner; but I do not find that the involved parties have to be physical and/or real ones, as most philosophical discussions—argumentation and counter-argumentation about a specific standpoint—are held between the philosopher and himself. The other part of the discussion is, thus, in most cases, fiction created by the authors themselves. I do not believe this is a real constraint on both rhetoric and dialectics, and on argumentation theory in general.

Before moving forward, please note that van Eemeren's definition, above quoted, applies, not only to dialectics, but also to rhetoric. But my problem here is not simply to understand philosophy *rhetorically*, in the traditional sense of the concept (in Perelman, for instance), that is, to discuss in what sense, or according to what kind of rhetorical devices and strategies a philosopher tries to persuade an audience. This is not at all my concern. My point is that we must (or we should) understand philosophy, not only rhetorically, but *argumentatively*, and that we must (or we should) study philosophical arguments in their own right, and analyse and evaluate them as, in principle, we do regarding any other kind of argument. M. Finocchiaro's (2005, 2010, 2013) approach to scientific arguments is an example of what I have in mind (I will come back to this example later). If we address philosophy from this perspective, I would say that I (we) am (are) precisely in the context of the five estates of the realm of argumentation studies, which are studied by van Eemeren and Grootendorst (2004, p. 11 ff.). However, I personally will not subscribe, without differentiating further, to the distinction between rhetoric and dialectics which was proposed in that book. (The main reason for this is that such distinction cannot be applied to an approach like that of Finocchiaro, for instance.)

Back to van Eemeren (2010), the second feature of argumentative discourse, on the other hand, according to the author, is quite problematic as far as philosophy is concerned: "The standpoints at issue in the difference of opinion can pertain to *any kind of subject* and they can be descriptive as well as evaluative and prescriptive." (p. 1, emphasis added) By "any kind of subject" we should also be thinking, for example, about the philosophical subjects in particular, but I do not see under which category the specific "standpoints" of philosophy in general can be included, since they apparently do not fall under any of the categories mentioned (descriptive, prescriptive, evaluative). Most philosophical issues are of the kind "What can I know?" (Kant 2010). These are definitely issues which can be argued by the philosophers in question (and they are, by both these and others), but they are metatheoretical "standpoints", as is in fact the case of most concepts used in philosophy. By "meta-theoretical" I mean here, in basic and introductory terms, the type of concept which does not refer to any particular object, but its core purpose is to provide the framework or organise the empirical concepts, in general, i.e. those which refer to the world of experience. Most philosophical concepts are concepts of this kind: "object", "subject", "substance", "reason", "experience", "intuition", etc.; and, from this standpoint, one could say that the differences between the philosophies throughout history include precisely the differences between meta-theoretical questions which are raised and the concepts which are chosen to answer these questions. Such concepts, since they are precisely metatheoretical in nature, do not correspond exactly to any state of affairs. For example, Kant's (2010) concepts of "subject" and "object", about which I will say something in the last section of my paper, do not correspond exactly or precisely to the subjects and objects of everyday experience (they are typically metaphysical), but they allow us to understand them. Therefore, they do not have a descriptive and/or declarative function, but we could say the same, in philosophical terms, about the other functions that van Eemeren (2010) had in mind when he wrote the introduction to that book. I will label the philosophy-specific standpoint "metatheoretical standpoints".

One of the most disturbing characteristics of arguing these "standpoints" is that we no longer have the real criteria for analysing and assessing them individually or in particular, i.e. in context, which should be the case of argumentation in general. They certainly are not arguments of that kind, nor do they really correspond to what Toulmin called "field independent arguments". Precisely because they are metatheoretical they are meta-arguments (or as M. Finocchiaro (2005) called them, "arguments about arguments"), and to decide about what is or is not a good argument in a given philosophy one must assess the standpoint as a whole of the systematic theses which provide the context thereof. It should be pointed out, in passing, that these philosophical meta-arguments are very different from the meta-scientific arguments which Finocchiaro addresses in his writings about Galileo Galilei. For Finocchiaro meta-scientific arguments can be analysed and evaluated having as basis an established and more or less universal discourse, i.e., scientific discourse. This is surely not the case of our meta-philosophical arguments. For example, whoever finds that what Kant (2010) or Wittgenstein (1933) discuss is argumentative discourse, and wishes to truly understand if only one of the fundamental theses of these books, he should start by analysing and assessing these theses in general, before doing so for each thesis individually.

One possible and pertinent counter-argument about the topic I have just mentioned would be to say that, in philosophy, we do not *argue* in general, but basically *we explain*, even when our philosophical discourse presents, if only apparently, all of the characteristics of an argumentative discourse, which is the case of linguistic indicators on the subject. A significant part of that philosophical discourse which we identify with metaphysics, for instance Wittgenstein's (1933) or Heidegger's (1962), is normally just that, an explanation. Consider, for example, this excerpt from the last mentioned book:

Example 1: Heidegger's discourse as explanation
All research—and not least that which operates within the range of the central question of Being—is an ontical possibility of Dasein. Dasein's Being finds its meaning in temporality. But temporality is also the condition which makes historicality possible as a temporal kind of Being, which Dasein itself possesses, regardless of whether or how Dasein is an entity "in time". Historicality, as a determinate character, is prior to what is called "history" (world-historical historizing). (Heidegger 1962, p. 41)

Now, this distinction between explanation and argumentation does not necessarily mean that, on the same subject, we cannot explain and argue at the same time; or, ultimately reconstruct as argumentation something which is presented to us as an explanation. In the case of Heidegger's text, quoted above, an expert would propose some fundamental definitions: (1) What Heidegger (1962) meant to say by "Being"; (2) What he meant specifically by "Dasein"; (3) What he meant by "temporality" and "historicality"; etc. Eventually, according to such definitions, we could reconstruct Heidegger's discourse as argumentative discourse (I am not sure that Heidegger's disciples and followers would accept this; in fact, I am convinced of the contrary). But, in the latter, the objection would be that we do not arrive at any consensus on different possible reconstructions; and, therefore, that such reconstructions are not finally useful for the aims of argumentation and critical thinking. To reconstruct a piece of metaphysical and ontological discourse (not only Heidegger's, but in general) would involve us in the same interpretation issues as reconstructing the message of a poem or a work of art.

On this (explanation and argumentation) we of course can always come back to the theory of Copi and Cohen (1994). This is the essential of the theory: in some forms of discourse, which is supposed to be the case of historiography, literature and philosophy, we are generally not arguing, but *explaining*. We *argue* when we deliver the reasons and/or the grounds (*P*) for a standpoint (*Q*) which is problematic, and we seek to establish the truth of *Q*. We *explain* when, on the other hand, we do not question nor discuss *Q*, and we wish to describe why *Q* is the case. This matches the conceptions of Perelman and Olbrechts-Tyteca (2008) about the difference between argumentation and evidence, because our understanding of "demonstrating" is only a specific case of the general and overarching case of "arguing" itself. As the authors state:

Example 2: Copi and Cohen's distinction between explanation and argumentation
If we are interested in establishing the truth of *Q*, and if *P* is offered as evidence for it, then "*Q because P*" formulates an argument. However, if we regard the truth of *Q* as being unproblematic, as being at least as well established as the truth of *P*, but we are interested in explaining *why Q is the case*, then "*Q because P*" is not an argument but an explanation. (…) Normally, if the purpose is to establish the truth of a proposition, it is an argument that is formulated. (Copi and Cohen 1994, p. 35)

Now, as they observe next, the distinction between arguing and explaining is problematic when applied out of context, because the essential difference resides in the speaker or writer's *intention*: if the intention is to persuade, convince, etc., what we have is an argument, because there is something that is problematic; but if that is not the case, then what we have is an explanation. Further ahead, I will suggest that this difference can be used to distinguish between two sorts of philosophical analogies. I am not completely sure that the distinction is pertinent and useful; further work is needed on this. But I would say that we do not have other theoretical tools, besides it, for interpreting philosophical discourse.

16.3 What Philosophers Say About Philosophers

That in the past philosophy was argumentative discourse, in the sense described in the previous section, is something which was only exceptionally acknowledged by philosophers in general, since Plato. In the twentieth century, Perelman and Toulmin were of course an exception, among others, albeit with some reservations which I should clarify. Lets recall the essential: both theorise that Philosophy, from the beginning of the Greek classical era, focused only on the "rational" and not on "reasonableness", in other words, it was at the service of the conception according to which what is fundamentally important for Philosophy is evidence and conviction (*episteme*). And these are, one way or the other, features of metaphysics and logic; not persuasion and/or doubt, "reasonableness", which are inherent to rhetoric and argumentation. This does not mean, however, that philosophical discourse itself—the very discourse which focuses on sustaining the "rational"—does not include the procedures and strategies which are characteristic of the "reasonable". In particular, what Perelman and Olbrechts-Tyteca (2008, p. 185 ff) call "argumentation techniques"; and from this perspective, such discourse—even when it takes place under the scope of what Copi and Cohen (1994) called *explanation*—is clearly argumentative. (The *logical* distinction between explanation and argumentation no longer makes sense for new rhetoric.) However, what we wish to understand—when we ask whether philosophical discourse is or is not argumentative—is what is its internal structure, how the propositions relate with each other in it to make it argumentative, and why this is the case or, ultimately (through the explanation), it is not the case; we seek to understand, for example, what Western philosophical tradition in the light of epistemological categories considered to be "deduction" and "induction" when applied to philosophy, and which must be somehow rhetorically reinterpreted. This is what M. Finocchiaro (2010) does with regards to scientific discourse in general and Galileu Galilei in particular. This issue does not require necessarily an overarching answer in the light of philosophy history; such an answer may at first apply to individual cases and be inductive, i.e. based on the interpretation of one or other case in hand which allows us to extend the relevant outcomes to several other cases and, possibly, introduce typologies. Now, while Perelman and Olbrects-Tyteca (2008) are far from being indifferent to or unconcerned about this issue, as is actually illustrated in their conception of argument through analogy, Perelman's concept of rhetoric is too broad and vague to that effect, to such an extent that, for the purpose of our issue, it is useless. As Johnstone (1965a) sustained, it does not focus enough on the study of rational argumentation itself in philosophy; the very same argumentation that formal logic partly addresses and which develops independently, so to speak, of the intention of persuading any audience. On the other hand, the formal argumentation model which Toulmin (1958, p. 94 ff) introduces cannot be manifestly applied to philosophical propositions.

Notwithstanding the above said, objections similar to the ones we have just presented could also be formulated to a conception of rhetoric like Johnstone's (1965b). The problem is not knowing how a philosophical argument can be refuted, but rather, *first* and according to the fundamental assumption that there is argumentation in philosophy, knowing what is its nature and how it may be represented and analysed. It is similar to the issue raised by Cohen (1986) about analytical philosophy, with the relevant difference that now it is about rhetoric and argumentation, and not epistemology as with Cohen; or, straight to the point, it is the question that Rescher (1998) raises and studies briefly, after concluding (Rescher 1985), somewhat pessimistically, that it is impossible to substantially define philosophy.

Such conclusions can be intellectually quite corrosive and harmful to the purposes of argumentation theory. Ongoing disagreement between philosophers, appeals to intuition, mysticism and similar kinds of irrationality, the lack of any kind of apparent progress or development in philosophy since classical Greece, among other aspects, can lead to the thesis that ultimately there is no true argumentation in philosophy and that it all comes down strictly to rhetoric, or at least that we do not have the tools to analyse such argumentation. Verene (2007) and others (Burrell 1973) drew these unacceptable conclusions, which match contemporary hermeneutics, and are disastrous, as they deprive argumentation theory of its principal matrix (philosophy). If there is no argumentation in philosophy, which is the rationality's paradigm since Plato and Aristotle to the present day, or if we cannot analyse nor assess it, how can there be argumentation in ordinary language and in the different branches of human knowledge, as is the case of science and law theory?

Now, allow me to come back to what I said in the beginning. The field of philosophy is not necessarily that of argumentative and/or arguable discourse in the everyday sense, i.e. that which can be outlined and may illustrate a difference in opinion about a matter or issue directly linked to the world of human experience broadly speaking, and the discussion or solution of which will ultimately guide our action. Of course this (the problematics of argumentation) arises usually when we address issues within the realm of ethics and/or moral, which is the supreme field of "reasonableness". However, as I began by highlighting, most philosophical questions are metaphysical and epistemological, and involve meta-historical and meta-conceptual standpoints which in principle are not immediately and manifestly linked to this world (which finally does not mean that they cannot become connected and that this link is not fundamental). Kant's questions: "What can I know?" or "What ought I to do?" thereafter, are questions of the sort. Furthermore, as a consequence of the nature of these views, the discourse and the concepts used in philosophy are inevitably ambiguous and confusing; in other words they are liable to produce different (or even contradictory) interpretations, which may make the interpretation of these arguments incredibly difficult. The best example of this kind of problems is the appeal for intuition and other escapes from reason and argumentation themselves. Consequently, the philosopher frequently ignores or even despises the argumentative or potentially argumentative nature of his own discourse, if not too often rejects it entirely. He *describes*, *analyses*, *compares* and *explains*, but does not necessarily argue. It is what Heidegger (1962) does. From this standpoint, and if we take current argumentative discourse as the benchmark, there will be no real argumentation in philosophy or, if it does exist, we still do not have the suitable means to analyse and interpret it.

16.4 The Role of Analogy: Explanation vs. Argumentation

Now coming back to the topic of my address and to what I said in the introduction, I propose the following essential distinction: an analogy is used in philosophical discourse, in the argumentative sense, where there is, from the standpoint of the philosopher involved, a structural connection between the thesis/standpoint he wishes to support and argue, and the analogical example (or comparison) which he uses for the purpose; and it is used as an explanation when this clearly is not the case, i.e., *when the purpose of such example is not to argue* per se (wherefore the speaker/writer's intention is paramount as I began to say), but it is the closure, albeit premature (as is the case of the different versions of philosophical, religious or other forms of mysticism), of a possible counter-argument. By "structural connection" I mean the kind of ties between the thesis/standpoint and the example provided, which enable us to establish a direct, more or less formal, link between several of the thesis's/standpoint's components and similar components of the example, and to closely analyse and interpret these ties; we can summarise it using a diagram or any other technique, like the ones Walton and others developed through the theoretical and conceptual framework of argumentation theory (see Walton et al. 2008, p. 48 ff). This differentiation, for which I will provide and analyse some examples further ahead, is fundamentally heuristic; I do not deny the fact that there is analogical reasoning which is both explanatory and argumentative; and where there is the urgent need to find out what really makes them different.

Analogical, explanatory or argumentative reasoning has been, since Plato, absolutely essential for philosophical discourse. It is used as the principal means of persuasion of theses/standpoints in general. The philosopher uses the analogy to convince the reader/audience of the originality and/or relevance of his thesis/standpoint, which can be done in several ways:

a. resorting to plays staged with his own discourse (cases in point, several allegories in Plato's dialogue *The Republic* (Plato 1992), the evil genius of Descartes's *Meditations on first philosophy* (Descartes 1996), the fictions conceived by Locke (1995) and other empiricist philosophers in regard to the genesis of ideas from sensitivity, etc.);

b. resorting to shows inspired by the need to compare and/or apply its conceptions to other fields of expertise, like science, law, art, etc. (a cross-cutting theme of philosophy since ancient Greece); namely science philosophy, law philosophy, art philosophy, etc.;
c. resorting to shows comparing their conceptions with those of other philosophers (once more a cross-cutting philosophical topic since the Greeks), i.e. using the analogy metatheoretically (for example, comparing Kant (2010) and Popper's (1959) conceptions, or the eidetic reduction of Husserl (1960) with that of Descartes (1996), etc.).

We are still missing a philosophical taxonomy of a), b) and c), i.e. a close analysis and classification of the arguments in question, for clarifying and deciding to what extent we are before real analogies and not other forms of discourse. The famous allegory of the cave in Plato's *Republic*, for example, is in my view a true analogy. It provides a close connection between Plato's philosophical thesis and the analogical example involved. But there is other more disputable philosophical reasoning, i.e. where we can discuss if we are (or are not) in face of an analogy. For instance, the famous example of "radical translation" presented by Quine (1969, pp. 26–68) with regard to the interpretation of the word "gavagai". Is the situation to which Quine alludes an analogy? Specially interesting is the analogical reasoning in philosophy of science, from Descartes and Kant to the present days, because philosophers, doing philosophy of science, are studying a subject-matter foreign to philosophy itself, but in some sense closely related to it; and this is the territory *par excellence* of analogical reasoning. Finally, of course, the meta-philosophical analogies, which consist in the comparison between different philosophies or philosophical approaches (Husserl and Descartes, Kant and Popper, etc.) are also fundamental for philosophical discourse in general.

Anyhow, the features I have mentioned should, in principle, hinder philosophical discourse significantly, i.e. it should make us question from the start the importance and legitimacy of analogical reasoning, because if philosophical discourse—explanatory at all times—is or can also be argumentative discourse, this is to say that it is a discourse founded on reasons or assumptions for whatever we wish to support (however problematic, philosophically speaking, these reasons or assumptions may be), this reasoning should be a weak or fragile form of argumentation. In other words, it should weaken or undermine, not strengthen, argumentation itself. The following could be said to object to a philosopher using analogical reasoning: we are not discussing the example and/or analogy, but rather the thesis! Analogical reasoning, specially when explanatory, induces most of the issues raised through the analysis and assessment of the arguments underlying the change in the agenda of a critical discussion, like the inappropriate appeal to authority (*ad verecundiam*), in this case an authority which is not and cannot be appropriately identified. Which is the authority in question in the recurrent analogies that characterise the different versions of philosophical mysticism? Which is the authority when we appeal to intuition as the source of evidence and proof of reasoning, as happened in the twentieth-century with Bergson or with Husserl, amongst others? When this happens, the burden of proof (at least apparently) is shifted and externalised; we no longer discuss nor argue what we were supposed to be discussing and arguing (the issue in question), and shift our focus to possibly entirely different problems. When the analogical reasoning is conducted as an explanation and the philosopher does not seek to argue (which is the case of mysticism), consequences like these are potentially perverse and disappointing. Consider, for example, the famous analogy between philosophy and a ladder made by Wittgenstein (1933, p. 189):

Example 3: Wittgenstein's ladder as a metaphorical analogy
6.54 My propositions are elucidatory in this way: he who understands me finally recognizes them as senseless, when he has climbed out through them, on them, over them. (He must so to speak throw away the ladder, after he has climbed up on it).
He must surmount these propositions; then he sees the world rightly.
7. Whereof one cannot speak, thereof one must be silent. (Wittgenstein 1933, p. 189)

Apparently, this is a true explanatory analogy: the human being (A), with regard to philosophy in Wittgenstein's approach to it (B), is like someone using a ladder to climb to the top (C), and, after doing so, does not need the ladder anymore (D). Wittgenstein's analogical reasoning, however is merely explanatory and metaphorical, not argumentative. There is no structural connection between Wittgenstein's philosophical thesis in the *Tratactus*, and a ladder. So, I would say that in the face of the objection: "Can you explain further your analogy between philosophy and a ladder?", Wittgenstein would reply: "This is only a metaphor! I had no other way of explaining what I meant, except through such a comparison!"

Often, philosophers since Plato have used analogical reasoning fallaciously, that is as a more or less radical change in the agenda being discussed and as a rather sudden closure thereof. *This reasoning closes the critical discussion.* However, what actually happens is that, far from being a mere expedient or supporting tool of rhetoric and philosophical argumentation, the analogy is its quintessential or fundamental medium. It is through it that philosophers in general finally seek to persuade or convince their audiences. A reasonable and relevant comment, when analogy is used in the argumentative sense, would be to say that this is not only unavoidable, but also welcome. Yet, I do not have any decisive or ultimate explanation for the explanatory use of analogy, other than the one supplied for the relation between philosophy and poetry, since ancient Greece; for example the interpretation on the matter suggested by historians and philosophers like Kirk and Raven (1957) about pre-Socratic philosophy: analogical reasoning refers us to the cosmic and ancestral genesis of philosophical thought; to a setting where the philosopher through his discourse (any discourse) gives in completely to the need to merge with the Universe.

A typical argumentative analogy is the one used by Kant (2010) to address the "Copernican revolution". Kant intends to submit the rationalist thesis which sustains that the requirements for knowing the object are in the subject, and not the other way around, as empiricism at the time sustained. By requirements, Kant means the forms *a priori* of space and time, and the categories and pure concepts of knowledge. If these requirements were established by the object or by the sensitivity in general, one could not explain the knowledge existing *a priori*, as is the case of maths and much of what was known at the time, in theoretical physics and mechanics in particular (for example, Newton's movement laws). According to him, this thesis was a completely new epistemological paradigm in the history of Western thought, a real revolution, only comparable to that which Copernicus introduced in astronomy with his theory that the Earth revolves around the Sun, and not the other way around. The analogy is precisely the following:

1. as in Copernicus's theory where it is the Earth (the spectator) that revolves around the Sun and the other stars, in philosophy and epistemology, it is the subject (the spectator) who revolves around the object; i.e.,
2. it is the subject, the spectator, who establishes the requirements for knowing the object (the "laws of thought").
3. The assumption of the opposite thesis (empiricism) leads inevitably to incoherence and contradictions (as shown by Kant, later, both in "transcendental aesthetics" about space and time, and in "transcendental logic" about the categories).

Example 4: Kant's "Copernican Revolution" as an argumentative analogy
We here propose to do just what Copernicus did in attempting to explain the celestial movements. When he found that he could make no progress by assuming that all the heavenly bodies revolved around the spectator, he reversed the process, and tried the experiment with the assumption that the spectator revolved, while the stars remained at rest. We may make the same experiment with regard to the intuition of objects. If the intuition must conform to the nature of the objects, I do not see how we can know anything of them *a priori*. If, on the other hand, the object conforms to the nature of our faculty of intuition, I can then easily conceive the possibility of such an *a priori* knowledge. (Kant 2010, pp. 13–14)

This analogy has a clearly argumentative meaning and at the time, when it was submitted, it was extremely powerful, considering the success and popularity of Newton's physics (see Whistler n.d.). It was the "Copernican revolution" of philosophy. Kant's analogical argument was, in effect, a macro-argument, an argument about arguments (as M. Finocchiaro would say). It was supposed to provide the essential framework of all arguments in general which can be drafted in their light; one can redesign it in the form of arguments, using as philosophical context, not only Kant's (2010) conceptions, but actually most philosophy at the time. However, its most remarkable feature is that it can be analysed and assessed not only as a whole, but also according to any of its assumptions in particular. Anyone disagreeing with the meta-theoretical presupposition (of the show) that involves differentiating "subject" from "object", which is actually philosophical fiction built to justify the fundamental theses of the *Critique* (the counter-argument being that the "subject" and "object" are always provided as a whole in the experience, and never separately), will not acknowledge the originality and pertinence of the analogy as a whole. That, however, means that the analogy is arguable.

Note that Kant's argument with his "Copernican analogy" can be applied meta-historically and can provide the model for metatheoretical analogies, as has been recurrently done in the past in the history of philosophy. That is: having as basis such argument, we can compare Kant's philosophy with that of Karl Popper, or with the philosophy of the logical positivists, for instance. Metatheoretical analogies can be very important tools for philosophical justification; they play in regard to philosophy a role similar to that of analogical reasoning in scientific explanation. In fact,

I would say that all that E. Nagel wrote in regards to analogy in scientific explanations, and specially all that he said about the distinction between "substantial" and "structural" analogies, can be applied to meta-theoretical analogies in philosophy (Nagel 1974, pp. 109–117).

Yet not all analogical comparisons are necessarily argumentative. On the contrary, most of them are explanatory or explicative; although, as I mentioned before, analogies like these can be presented (and reconstructed) as conclusions of macro-arguments. Take the following comparison made by Quine (1966), and which is very close to Kant's analogy mentioned above. The philosopher is interested in sustaining in philosophical terms the thesis which he will call, years later, "naturalized epistemology" (Quine 1969, pp. 69–90), i.e. the idea that only those entities who address mathematics and physical-natural sciences in general really exist, and that to appeal to any other, like traditional, foundationalist, epistemology (Kant's epistemology here included, and the metatheoretical concepts of the "subject", "object", etc.) no longer makes sense. From his point of view, to speak about "the world of human experience" as something that would be different and independent of the subject or the human being (as in Kant) is unacceptable. The world is a whole composed of inseparable pieces, a continuum from top to bottom, i.e. from the entities I mentioned to the philosophical and more refined mathematical discourses, which are themselves somehow made of these fundamental entities. Considering that it is impossible to talk about this world with all of the constraints and obvious difficulties implied by ordinary language, Quine is thus forced to represent himself analogically as a mere "physical object", not like that subject which Kant (2010) mentions:

Example 5: Quine as physical object
I am a physical object sitting in a physical world. Some of the forces of this physical world impinge on my surface. Light rays strike my retinas; molecules bombard my eardrums and finger-tips. I strike back, emanating concentric air waves. These waves take the form of a torrent of discourse about tables, people, molecules, light rays, retinas, air waves, prime numbers, infinite classes, joy and sorrow, good and evil.
My ability to strike back in this elaborate way consists in my having assimilated a good part of the culture of my community, and perhaps modified and elaborate it a bit on my own account. All this training consisted in turn of an impinging of physical forces, largely other people's utterances, upon my surface, and of gradual changes in my own constitution consequent upon these physical forces. All I am or ever hope to be is due to irritations of my surface, together with such latent tendencies to response as may have been presented in my original germ. And all the lore of the ages is due to irritation of the surfaces of a succession of persons, together, again, with the internal initial conditions of the several individuals. (Quine 1966, pp. 228–229)

Quine's comparison has all of the characteristics of a real analogy: **A** (the subject, i.e., the individual) is for **B** (the object), like **C** (an object) is for **D** (another object). And what the philosopher does is describe how the alledged "objects" connect among themselves according to a naturalized epistemology (without beliefs, representations and similar concepts, introduced by the metaphysical fiction of a subject of knowledge). Now, how can a mere "physical object" talk with itself without becoming one way or the other the "subject" mentioned by Kant (2010)? How can an "object" be *understood* by another (any other) "object"? Quine's analogical example is generally explicative and/or explanatory; (alone) it does not include reasons or grounds for the naturalist thesis which is supported by the philosopher, about the origins and the nature of human knowledge. The fact is, however, that the example appears right in the beginning of the paper mentioned as the most general conclusion of a philosophical macro-argument about that thesis (which Quine will continue after all to focus particularly on, in publications like Quine 1969). Had I more time for this, I would redesign, analyse and assess Quine's macro-argument as a whole. I, otherwise, suggest that Quine's analogy is both explanatory and argumentative.

The same, in my view, could be said about analogical reasoning in Wittgenstein (2001). It is a very interesting and curious fact that Wittgenstein's philosophical discourse, in that book, can be analysed and interpreted precisely as analogical reasoning. In the end, the book (*Philosophical Investigations*) could also be called "Philosophical Analogies". A comparison could be made with Quine: (1) Quine and Wittgenstein are interested in showing that all human knowledge can be interpreted in physical and behavioural terms; (2) Quine's strategy, in the paper quoted above, consists in provoking his reader with the following show: "let me show how a mathematical object (say, a prime number) would talk with other prime numbers" (amazing analogical reasoning!); (3) Wittgenstein's (2001) "shows" consist in comparing, provocatively, the shows of the traditional and foundationalist epistemology (that is, the shows of the epistemology regarding knowledge and its philosophical foundations) with what can really be said, philosophically speaking, according to a behavioural epistemology and its main paradigm (Wittgenstein's language games). Of course, Wittgenstein does not believe in the first epistemology, but he needs to use its shows to justify his own thesis; and, in fact, he does that recurrently from the beginning. For example: he does not believe in "mental processes" as something occurring and developing independently of our behaviour and its language games, namely, as if something as the Kantian "subject" and its "conscience" and respective representations would exist; but he needs to use, therapeutically, such analogical reasoning.

Example 6: Wittgenstein's fly, as an explanatory and argumentative analogy
308 How does the philosophical problem about mental processes and states and about behaviourism arise? The first step is the one that altogether escapes notice. We talk of processes and states and leave their nature undecided. Sometime perhaps we shall know more about them—we think. But that is just what commits us to a particular way of looking at the matter. For we have a definite concept of what it means to learn to know a process better. (The decisive movement in the conjuring trick has been made, and it was the very one that we thought quite innocent.)
And now the analogy which was to make us understand our thoughts falls to pieces. So we have to deny the yet incomprehended process in the yet unexplored medium. And now it looks as if we had denied mental processes. And naturally we don't want to deny them.
309 What is your aim in philosophy?
To show the fly the way out of the fly-bottle. (Wittgenstein 2001, p. 103)

Now, not all philosophical analogy has argumentative purposes; what I mean, as I mentioned regarding Copi and Cohen's (1994) distinction between explanation and argumentation, is that not all analogical comparison is conducted with the purpose of being discussed and counter-argued. To discuss and counter-argue a comparison like this is like discussing and counter-arguing any thesis which was never intended in principle to be counter-argued. A large portion of metaphysics and, particularly, of ontology in the history of Western philosophy, is conceptual descriptive and explicative in the sense I have just mentioned. It may also sometimes be argumentative in nature. But in most cases, as I suggested before, the philosophical address of the subjects in question is not (nor intends to be) argumentative; and it is very close to the poetic and religious approach. The connection with poetry and religion is generally evoked by the philosophers in question. The philosopher introduces, describes and explains the essential metatheoretical concepts, and it is in the light of these concepts that human experience as a whole fits in and is organised, without having to take into account possible contestation and counter-arguments. He will say ultimately: "This is the setting (or the scope) in which I settle myself and speculate, and that which we are allowed to see or understand on this plane." M. Heidegger's illustrious comparison between the human being (Da-sein) and a "shepherd of being" is a good example of this:

Example 7: Heidegger's shepherd of being
Human beings do not decide whether and how beings appear, whether and how God and the gods or history and nature come forward into the clearing of being, come to presence and depart. The advent of being lies in the destiny of being. But for humans it is ever a question of finding what is fitting in their essence and corresponds to such destiny; for in accord with this destiny the human being as ek-sisting has to guard the truth of being. *The human being is the shepherd of being*. (Heidegger 1977, p. 221, author's emphasis)

This comparison has all of the characteristics of a real analogy: A (the human being) is for B (Being), as C (the shepherd) is for D (his herd), i.e. always alert, vigilant, careful, etc. However, as shown by Heidegger's comments and comments made by others about the analogy, the expression "the shepherd of being" is used essentially metaphorically. The objection to the interpretation that it is a real analogy and that it could therefore be discussed in argumentative terms is that the analogical expression "shepherd of being" is only one, among many others, that seems more relevant, considering the insurmountable constraints of language. The comparison (human being ⇔ "shepherd of being") is, ultimately, not arguable, because it takes us to a setting which cannot be entirely verbalised without inevitable and inextricable ambiguities (which I could call the plane of mysticism itself).

16.5 Conclusions

Throughout the history of Western philosophy, from Ancient Greece to our days, not always did philosophers have due conscience of the importance of argumentation as a fundamental tool for exercising critical thinking. In effect, such conscience-at least when understood historically—is, in the opinion of some commentators and historians of philosophy, rather recent (see Cohen 1986 about analytical philosophy). In most cases, their basic attitude consists of explaining and not necessarily arguing. This is reflected in the exaggerated use of processes of rejection of the role of argumentation, as is the case of intuition and the call for mysticism; in particular, it is reflected in the overuse of explanatory and metaphorical-type of analogies, at the expense of the argumentative ones *per se*. Anyhow, nowadays—as philosophers and lovers of arguing—we would like to be able to reconstruct all explanatory discourse as an argumentative one, but we are lacking the necessary concepts and tools to that end. This is not a problem of rhetoric, at least as it was addressed in Perelman and Toulmin, but of argument theory itself. These missing means mentioned earlier would otherwise, first and foremost, permit us to understand what is going on in a philosopher's discourse when he argues and, above all, to analyse and represent—in a diagram or otherwise—a philosophical argument. This occurs principally because philosophical discourse is substantially different from general discourse in ordinary language. It is a metatheoretical and/or metaconceptual discourse, wherefore, in most cases, philosophical arguments are meta-arguments. From this perspective, as argued herein, the distinction between the two kinds of analogies addressed can provide valuable support for understanding the argumentative nature of philosophical discourse.

References

Burrell, D. 1973. *Analogy and philosophical language*. New Haven: Yale University Press.

Cohen, L. J. 1986. *The dialogue of reason: An analysis of analytical philosophy*. Oxford: Clarendon Press.

Copi, I. M., and D. Cohen. 1994. *Introduction to logic*. 9th ed. New York: Macmillan Publishing Company. (First published 1953).

Descartes, R. 1996. *Meditations on first philosophy* (trans: Cottingham, J.). Cambridge: Cambridge University Press. (First published in French 1641).

Finocchiaro, M. 2005. *Arguments about arguments: Systematic, critical and historical essays in logical theory*. New York: Cambridge University Press.

Finocchiaro, M. 2010. *Defending Copernicus and Galileo: Critical reasoning in the two affairs*. Dordrecht: Springer.

Finocchiaro, M. 2013. *Meta-argumentation: An approach to logic and argumentation theory*. London: College Publications.

Heidegger, M. 1962. *Being and time* (trans: Macquarrie, J., and E.Robinson). New York: Harper & Row. (First published in German 1927).

Heidegger, M. 1977. *Basic writings: From 'Being and Time' (1927) to the 'Task of Thinking' (1964)* (Edited with general introduction and introduction to each selection by D. F. Krell). New York: Harper & Row.

Husserl, E. 1960. *Cartesian meditations* (trans: Cairns, D.). The Hague: Hijhoff. (First published in German 1931).

Johnstone, H. W. 1965a. A new theory of philosophical argumentation. In *Philosophy, rhetoric and argumentation,* eds. M. Natanson and H. W. Johnstone, 126–134. Pennsylvania: The Pensylvania State University.

Johnstone, H. W. 1965b. Persuasion and validity in philosophy. In *Philosophy, rhetoric and argumentation,* eds. M. Natanson and H. W. Johnstone, 138–148. Pennsylvania: The Pennsylvania State University.

Kant, I. 2010. *The critique of pure reason by Immanuel Kant* (trans: Meiklejohn, J. M. D.). Pennsylvanya: An Electronic Classics Series Publication and The Pennsylvania State University. http://www2.hn.psu.edu/faculty/jmanis/kant/critique-pure-reason6x9.pdf. Accessed 20 June 2013.

Kirk, G. S., and J. E. Raven. 1957. *The presocratic philosophers: A critical history with a selection of texts*. Cambridge: Cambridge University Press.
Locke, J. 1995. *An essay concerning human understanding*. Amherst: Prometheus Books. (First published 1690).
Moore, H. 2009. *Plato's analogical tought*. Theses and dissertations. Paper 7. http://via.library.depaul.edu/etd/7. Accessed 25 June 2013.
Nagel, E. 1974. *La estructura de la ciencia* (trans: Míguez, M.). Buenos Aires: Paidos.(Nagel, E. 1961. *The structure of science*. New York: Harcourt, Brace & World).
Perelman, C. 1989. Analogie et métaphore em science, poésie et philosophie. In *Rhétoriques,* ed. M. Meyer, 395–409. Bruxelles: Editions de l'Université de Bruxelles. (Paper first published 1969).
Perelman, C., and L. Olbrechts-Tyteca. 2008. *The new rhetoric: A treatise on argumentation* (trans: Wilkinson, J., and P. Weaver). Notre Dame: University of Notre Dame Press.(Perelman, C., and L. Olbrechts-Tyteca. 1958. *La nouvelle rhétorique: Traité de l'argumentation*. Paris: Presses Universitaires de France).
Plato. 1992. *The republic* (trans: Grube, G. M. A.). Indianapolis: Hackett Publishing Company.
Popper, K. 1959. *The logic of scientific discovery*. London: Hutchinson.
Popper, K. 1963. *Conjectures and refutations: The growth of scientific knowledge*. London: Routledge.
Quine, W. V. O. 1966. The scope and language of science. In *The ways of paradox and other essays,* ed. W. V. O. Quine, 228–245. Cambridge: Harvard University Press. (Paper first published in 1954).
Quine, W. V. O. 1969. *Ontological relativity and other essays*. New York: Columbia University Press.
Rescher, N. 1985. *The strife of systems: An essay on the grounds and implications of political diversity*. Pittsburgh: University of Pittsburgh Press.
Rescher, N. 1998. The role of rhetoric in rational argumentation. *Argumentation* 12:315–323.
Toulmin, S. 1958. *The uses of argument*. Cambridge: Cambridge University Press.
van Eemeren, F. H. 2010. *Strategic maneuvering in argumentative discourse*. Amsterdam: John Benjamins Publishing Company.
van Eemeren, F. H., and R. Grootendorst. 2004. *A systematic theory of argumentation: The pragma-dialectical approach*. Cambridge: Cambridge University Press.
Verene, D. P. 2007. Philosophical rhetoric. In *Philosophy and rhetoric in dialogue,* ed. G. A. Hauser, 27–35. Pennsylvania: The Pennsylvania State University.
Walton, D., C. Reed, and F. Macagno. 2008. *Argumentation schemes*. Cambridge: Cambridge University Press.
Whistler, D. (n.d.). Post-established harmony: Kant and analogy reconsidered. http://www.academia.edu/2500611/PostEstablished_Harmony_Kant_and_Analogy_Re-Considered. Accessed 26 June 2013.
Wittgenstein, L. 1933. *Tractatus logico-philosophicus, with an introduction by Bertrand Russell*. London: Kegan Paul. (First published 1921).
Wittgenstein, L. 2001. *Philosophical investigations* (trans: Ascombe, G. E.). Oxford: Blackwell. (First published 1953).

Index

H. J. Ribeiro (ed.), *Systematic Approaches to Argument by Analogy*,
Argumentation Library 25, DOI 10.1007/978-3-319-06334-8,

The manufacturer's authorised representative in the EU is Springer Nature Customer Service Centre GmbH, Europaplatz 3, 69115 Heidelberg, Germany. If you have any concerns regarding our products, please contact ProductSafety@springernature.com

Printed and bound by CPI Group (UK) Ltd, Croydon, CR0 4YY
05/10/2026
02228131-0007